The Other Emerson

THE
OTHER
EMERSON

BRANKA ARSIĆ AND CARY WOLFE Editors

Afterword by STANLEY CAVELL

University of Minnesota Press
Minneapolis
London

Chapter 1 was previously published in Sharon Cameron, *Impersonality: Seven Essays* (Chicago: University of Chicago Press, 2007). Chapter 3 was previously published as Branka Arsić, "Brain Walks: Thinking," in *On Leaving: A Reading in Emerson* (Cambridge, Mass.: Harvard University Press, 2010), 134–68; copyright 2010 by the President and Fellows of Harvard College; reprinted by permission of the publisher. Chapter 4 was published in *Cities without Citizens*, ed. Eduardo Cadava and Aaron Levy (Philadelphia: Slought Books, 2004); reprinted with permission of Slought Foundation. Chapter 5 was previously published as Donald E. Pease, " 'Experience,' Anti-Slavery, and the Crisis of Emersonianism," *boundary 2* 34, no. 2 (2007): 77–103; copyright 2007 Duke University Press; all rights reserved; reprinted by permission of Duke University Press. Chapter 10 was previously published in Cary Wolfe, *What Is Posthumanism?* (Minneapolis: University of Minnesota Press, 2009).

Published by the University of Minnesota Press
111 Third Avenue South, Suite 290
Minneapolis, MN 55401-2520
http://www.upress.umn.edu

PS 1642
.P5
086
2010

Library of Congress Cataloging-in-Publication Data

The other Emerson / Branka Arsić and Cary Wolfe, editors ; afterword by
   Stanley Cavell.
      p.   cm.
   Includes bibliographical references and index.   0 617508670
   ISBN 978-0-8166-6747-5 (hc : alk. paper) — ISBN 978-0-8166-6748-2
   (pb : alk. paper)
      1. Emerson, Ralph Waldo, 1803–1882—Criticism and interpretation.
   2. Emerson, Ralph Waldo, 1803–1882—Philosophy. 3. Emerson, Ralph Waldo,
   1803–1882—Political and social views. I. Arsić, Branka. II. Wolfe, Cary.
   PS1642.P5O86 2010
   814'.3—dc22

                                                                2010030717

Printed in the United States of America on acid-free paper

The University of Minnesota is an equal-opportunity educator and employer.

18 17 16 15 14 13 12 11 10   10 9 8 7 6 5 4 3 2 1

Contents

Acknowledgments

Cary Wolfe thanks the English department at Rice University for its support of this project in the form of research assistants and sabbatical. In particular, Sarah Graham and Kate Sullivan were immensely helpful in preparing the final manuscript.

The editors thank all of the contributors for their work and their patience, as well as the thoughtful readers and outstanding staff at the University of Minnesota Press.

BRANKA ARSIĆ AND CARY WOLFE

Introduction

"Where do we find ourselves?" That sentence, which famously opens Ralph Waldo Emerson's essay "Experience," will do quite well to announce the volume you have before you: not just because of its distinguished provenance ("Experience" is, perhaps, Emerson's most important single essay), but also, as Sharon Cameron and Stanley Cavell have noted, because of the multiple senses in which that question is to be understood, senses that conspire to produce a kind of "vertigo" sketched in Emerson's answer to his own question:[1] "In a series, of which we do not know the extremes, and believe that it has none. We wake and find ourselves on a stair: there are stairs below us, which we seem to have ascended; there are stairs above us, many a one, which go upward and out of sight" (3:27). We find the vertiginous sense of (dis)location invoked here by Emerson quite appropriate for our purposes, for our aim is to induce a similar kind of dislocation in our readers regarding the dominant understandings of Emerson's work since the inception of American studies. In our view, many of the assumptions that have underwritten our reading of Emerson's work and our estimation of its philosophical significance, its political character, and so on, are themselves subjected to rather patient and humbling scrutiny in Emerson's own work. For the sake of both breadth and focus, the essays collected here trace that process of scrutiny, and the reassessment of Emerson that it necessitates, on three primary terrains: Emerson and subjectivity, Emerson and the political, and Emerson and philosophy.

RETHINKING SUBJECTIVITY

From its initial claim that Emerson conceived of the self as an enclosed and willful individuality, to the subsequent view that he proposed a scarcely existing self with a fragile identity (or perhaps with no identity at all), Emersonian criticism had already made considerable progress. Though it is impossible to trace even the major interpretations of Emerson's theory of subjectivity within the space of a short introduction, several snapshots and flashbacks of this trajectory in Emersonian criticism should suffice to signal the significance of the essays devoted to this topic in this collection.

In 1898, John Jay Chapman published an important essay diagnosing Emerson as a thinker of immobility: "He is probably the last great writer to look at life from a stationary standpoint." In Chapman's account, nothing in Emerson's philosophy moves; the world is stable, nature is fixed, and persons don't grow and develop and are never in transition: "We miss in Emerson the underlying conception of growth, of development, so characteristic of the thought of our own day, and which, for instance, is found everywhere latent in Browning's poetry."[2]

Fifty years later, in his extraordinarily influential *Freedom and Fate* (1953)—and as if echoing Chapman by also referencing Browning—Stephen Whicher allowed that there are moments in "Self-Reliance" (such as, precisely: "Power . . . resides in the moment of transition" [2:40]) that point to flux and instability. But like Chapman, he concludes that transition—understood as "striving as an end in itself"—is in fact highly unusual for Emerson. In "Self-Reliance," Whicher writes, Emerson "comes for the moment to echo a strain of Romantic thought not generally characteristic of him, the ideal of striving as an end in itself, the Browningesque moral ideal of a *Strebung nach Unendliche*."[3] If there is transition and movement, it occurs only until a definitive—perfect—form is achieved. Emerson, from this point of view, appears as a thinker of fixity, completeness, and stability.

Similarly, Sherman Paul opens the chapter "The Arc of the Circle" of his *Emerson's Angle of Vision* (1952) by referring to the sentence from "Nominalist and Realist" in which Emerson claims completeness to be an optical illusion: "We have such exorbitant eyes, that on seeing the smallest arc, we complete the curve, and when the curtain is lifted from the diagram which it seemed to veil, we are vexed to find that no more was drawn, than just that fragment of an arc which we first beheld" (3:133). However, Paul decides to quote only the first part of the sentence, which then reads as follows: "We have such exorbitant eyes, that on seeing the smallest arc, we complete the curve."[4] Emerson's thesis that there is no completeness is thus turned into its opposite. Premised on the idea that completeness is not only possible but necessary, Paul's chapter then goes on to read Emerson's ontology of becoming as merely provisional. Only from the point of view of the intellect receptive, Paul claims, is "the full circle" "never fully realized" and the "progressive ascent into unity" remains "only aim." But the poetic or constructive intellect would know how to close the circle so that the genius of the poet would be a totalizing mind capable of complete vision and so of absolute truth: "The poet, then, represented the complete man and the complete mind" (107). Thus, in Paul's interpretation as well, Emerson's ideal is completeness and closure, hence stability and the fullness of the unchangeable.

These influential readers of Emerson seem reluctant to reconcile Emerson's idea of self-reliance—which they understand as the call for an individual to be powerful, active, firm, and stable—with the idea of a universal fluctuation and instability that includes the self, a self that would have therefore to be understood as fragmentary and fragile. Revision of their interpretations came in the late 1980s and 1990s. In 1987 Stanley Cavell gave his Frederick Ives Carpenter lectures, which included a talk on Emerson's "Experience" titled "Finding as Founding." There he read Emerson as a philosopher of transitions and the Emersonian self as exposed to disfiguration and powerful transformation. This is how he summed up the stakes of that lecture in 1990: "Emerson's 'Experience' as taken in my 'Finding as Founding' is essentially a working out of the violence of the image of change, of the taking of a spiritual step, as it were, as a series of remembering, say disfragmentings, reconstitutions of the members of, and of membership in, one's stranded state."[5] In 1987 Richard Poirier published *The Renewal of Literature: Emersonian Reflections,* in which he read Emerson's idea of experience as working toward dissolution of the self and Emerson's writing as the pragmatics of what he called "writing off the self." Emerson, he claimed, is interested in the loss of self-present identity. Emerson's writing mimes the experience of the transparency reported in *Nature* as the vanishing of the self: "Our reading-writing brings into existence a moment in which we are actively *there*, but it is also a moment in which self-present identity is reportedly lost."[6]

In 1998 Sharon Cameron published the groundbreaking essay—which we republish here to open the collection—on the question of the impersonal in Emerson, "The Way of Life by Abandonment: Emerson's Impersonal."[7] Unpacking Emerson's claims from "The American Scholar" that "the human mind cannot be enshrined in a person" (1:66), Cameron interprets the Emersonian self to be lacking in itself; its identity is ravished by the discrepancy between what we call persons and the mental states with which we falsely identify ourselves: "Emerson goes more than a step further, suggesting, it would seem, that there is *no* mental experience with which we are to be identified, for there is no permanence to any mood, perception, or belief." Reversing the inherited image of Emerson's self as willful, Cameron instead finds it willingless: "It is not a matter of willing to be better than we are or different than we are. It is a matter of not-willing." Emerson's "impersonal" thus results in an "erasure of identity."

Cameron finds three basic modes of the impersonal: One way of understanding the impersonal is as something that appears through *bodies* (as visible in the eyes) as a critique of the personal. A second way of understanding the impersonal is in terms of moods and *mental states*. In yet a third example the impersonal is associated not with the body and not with the affective life of the mind but rather with a law (alternately called "the moral sentiment") to which the "self" adheres, disregarding as it were the conditions of body and mind. The body and mental states are, in effect, channels through which the impersonal soul passes in order to manifest itself. Impersonality, then, is in Cameron's reading the activity of ravishment of persons, which she defines as a "process through which the person is annihilated by the impersonal."

While identifying the impersonal as the core of Emerson's understanding of subjectivity, the two other essays in Part I, "Rethinking Subjectivity," either try to make the distinction between personal and impersonal undecided (Russell B. Goodman, "Paths of Coherence through Emerson's Philosophy: The Case of 'Nominalist and Realist'") or offer a somewhat different understanding of the impersonal and what it does to persons (Branka Arsić, "Brain Walks: Emerson on Thinking"). Arsić's view of the impersonal somewhat contradicts Cameron's. While Cameron sees the relationship between personal and impersonal as disjunctive (there are either persons or the impersonal), Arsić sees it as in-clusive: the fact that the impersonal operates within persons does not annul their personalities. Since impersonal life traverses us and inhabits us, in Arsić's view the impersonal in Emerson does not cancel out the personal but instead contrives it. In the same way in which the fact that we all share one universal life doesn't prevent us from having and liv-ing our particular lives, we are, as persons, made of experiences to which our reflexive self can attend only in retrospect. In focusing specifically on the relation of the impersonal and thinking, Arsić argues that although it sounds counterintuitive, the thesis that thinking operates in us imper-sonally is, in fact, almost an analytical statement, since it is not possible for an "I" to think an object and to think itself thinking it at the same time. While thinking is going on, the "I" is absent in the sense that it does not, and cannot, think itself at the same time. Conceived in this way, the impersonal does not cancel persons nor does it contradict Emerson's call to self-reliance.

Even though Goodman doesn't explicitly mention the concept of the impersonal, his essay is also about the ways in which Emerson thinks subjectivity. Goodman sees Emerson's person as being in process, or in a type of flux that changes it. His thesis is that contradictions that appear within a stable identity through fluctuations can be accounted for without negating the idea of personal identity, through what he calls Emerson's "doctrine of moods." And he extends the argument to Emerson's writing practice as well, so that that the inconsistency of the mind that Emerson advocates is performed by his writing. An epistemology of moods, Goodman claims, "provides a way of understanding what might other-wise seem to be contradictory outlooks, viewpoints, or doctrines in his writings. If, as is supposed by such an epistemology, we never apprehend anything 'straight' or in-itself, but only under an aspect or mood, then the contrary viewpoints are perhaps as good as we can get." However, as Goodman shows, an identity contrived of moods and its corresponding epistemology can, in fact, be in perfect accordance with reality, which is itself always in process, following the theory Goodman terms the "meta-physics of aspects." Thus, Goodman proposes, even if obliquely, that any inconsistency may be seen as Emerson's way of saving personal continui-ties; paradoxically put, inconsistency is the way to be consistent if reality is made of aspects and is itself processual.

In opening this collection with a section on Emerson's rethinking of subjectivity, we were guided by the idea that what happens to persons and their identities is decisive for how one is going to address the question of the political in Emerson. In other words, whether Emerson's self is to be read as imperial, colonial, closed, corporate, aggressive, or, to the contrary, fragile, processual, fluctuating, open, affected, can determine, as it has so often in the past, the way one understands Emerson's politics. If Emerson's self is fragile to the point of lacking itself—and there is enough textual evidence in Emerson to support this reading—then, perhaps, such a self cannot be seen primarily as a bearer of American colonial politics in the mid-nineteenth century or as the embodiment of antebellum corporate society. With this immanent connection between subjectivity and the political in mind, we have dedicated Part II, "Rethinking the Political," to the question of the political.

RETHINKING THE POLITICAL

Emerson's work does to the idea of politics what it does to the idea of subjectivity: we can no longer simply take for granted that we know what it is and act upon that notion unproblematically. In the face of this realization, the question "how shall I live?" that opens Emerson's essay "Fate" suddenly becomes a dizzying one because (unlike the question "What is to be done?" that Lenin would later famously enunciate) it focuses our attention squarely on the nongeneric nature of the problem: not "how shall *one*, just anyone, live?" as if a one-size-fits-all answer were available, but "how shall *I* live?" (6:1). And since that "I," as we suggested a moment ago, is in Emerson "subjected" to the "predicate" of the new, the "arrival" (to use a favorite word of Emerson's) of the event, in which the subject may be transformed at any moment, the question of politics becomes an even more complex one. In fact, we might well suggest (as some of the essays collected here do) that one of Emerson's great themes—from essays such as "Self-Reliance" through the extraordinary meditations on the topic in *The Conduct of Life* and the address on the Fugitive Slave Law—is the complex conjugation of the relationship between politics and ethics, the irreducible antagonism between what Jacques Derrida will come to call "Law" (the question of the just that resists all "calculation," all formulaic solutions in advance) and "law" (the body of statutes and other institutional iterations through which, and only through which, Law is instantiated).[8] For if Emerson is typically (and understandably) viewed as subordinating questions of politics to questions of ethics, his "aversive" relationship to the former and to social institutions generally (as in his assertion that self-reliance is the aversion of conformity, as Cavell notes) suggests that the only place our freedom *can* be realized is in a transformative (rather than conformative) relationship to those very institutions and structures. We turn away from conformity, from the necessarily generic nature of politics, in aversion, only to return *to* it, in transformation, after *our* transformation.[9]

Understanding Emerson's contribution to philosophical thinking about politics, and its relation to ethics, is difficult for several reasons. One problem, as Eduardo Cadava points out in chapter 4, "The Guano of History," is that Emerson is often misread as promoting and endorsing the very discourses—of biological determinism, manifest destiny, and the like—that in fact he is "ventriloquizing" (to use Cadava's felicitous phrase), the better to expose them to scrutiny and then undo them in the services of a distinctly performative notion of philosophy and of justice. (Who has taught "Experience," for example, and not regularly had the experience of students thinking that Emerson is endorsing rather than staging the assertions of the "mid-world" section of the essay?) A second problem is that just as Emerson's thinking of philosophy as non-propositional is at odds with recent norms in professionalized academic philosophy in the United States, his thinking of politics is fundamentally at odds with the assumptions that have largely been taken for granted in the relatively recent professional norms of American studies.

Here, the opening pages of Donald Pease's detailed discussion of Emerson's "Experience" in chapter 5, "'Experience,' Antislavery, and the Crisis of Emersonianism," are instructive in their overview of how Emerson is typically viewed as either a protopragmatist reformer (but ultimately a failed one), whose political force is limited by his liberalism, or (worse) a Transcendentalist, who is at best "literary" and apolitical and at worst elitist, escapist, and racist. As Pease writes, "Whether Emerson's interpreters have analyzed the relationship between the Transcendentalist and the Reformer ... as enabling paradoxes or as disabling contradictions has depended on whether they assumed that Emerson's essays should exercise a political or a strictly literary efficacy." But what both sides have

taken for granted, Pease argues, is precisely the liberalism (both philosophical and political) that Emerson everywhere goes out of his way—
indeed, goes to *extremes*—to challenge. As Pease puts it, such readings
presuppose that "what Emerson called self-reliance was interchangeable
with the possessive individual who was the constituent subject of the discourse to which they made it conform. But what Emerson referred to as
'my genius [when it] calls me' achieved effects that were independent of
the processes of identification, interpellation, and internalization associated with liberal institutions."

The point we would emphasize is that the assumptions about politics that have shaped Emerson's contemporary reception aren't so much
wrong as they are beside the point of understanding Emerson's distinctive contribution to thinking about politics and its relationship to ethics
and to philosophy. Such is the implication, for example, of Pease's concluding suggestion that any sufficiently rich and responsible notion of
politics must take account of the psychoanalytic dimension—what he
calls a "crisis of witnessing"—that is not just on display in Emerson's
"Experience," but also plays havoc with any liberal notion of politics as
rationalist decision making carried out in a classical public sphere by a
subject more or less transparent to its own intentions.

As many of the essays in this collection argue, such assumptions
(however admirable their sentiments may be), in their rush to directly
link literary and cultural forms with political effectivity, take for granted
some very problematic notions about ethics, politics, subjectivity, and
identity—notions that Emerson himself submits to extraordinarily searching, indeed often torturous, investigation. With such approaches, Eric
Keenaghan shows, in chapter 6, "Reading Emerson, in Other Times: On
a Politics of Solitude and an Ethics of Risk," that we are often left with the
deadening generalization of the political subject—a becoming-generic,
you might say—that Emerson's philosophical understanding of the subject is everywhere calculated to short-circuit. But "rather than choose a
side by adopting a ready-made politics we blindly apply to our critical
endeavors," Keenaghan suggests, "we might use Emerson's lessons to reexamine our own investment in a liberalist ethos." Indeed, Keenaghan
argues, one of Emerson's fundamental lessons for liberalism is that "if
difference is indeed experiential, it is what occurs when we, alone, suddenly become so empowered (or run through by liberty) that we become

dispossessed. We lose our selves." Far from being escapist, isolationist, or "transcendental" in the worst possible sense, Emerson sees "this dissolution of self as anything but isolated or isolating." Keenaghan writes, "Rather, it is a shared experience, the common groundwork for our eventual production of a new narrative that allows us to lay to rest the old chronicles of identitarian design" that rear their ugly heads once more in our own era of "Homeland Security."

It is here, on the site of this empowering difference that is by turns intoxicating, vexing, and emboldening, that we need to pay attention, as Sandra Laugier points out in chapter 7, "Emerson, Skepticism, and Politics," to the specificity and texture of Emerson's writing, what she variously calls (following Cavell) his "tone," "voice," and "pitch." If we do pay attention to it, take our attention to it as "representative" of our duty to the democratic other, then we begin to understand that the "illegitimate demand" that "my subjective voice be a 'we' is at the heart of the political thinking" of Emerson. This transforms rather completely what the notion of political representation might mean, of course; it opens the question of *my* representativeness anew, as if for the first time—a theme, Laugier writes, that is "an obsession with Emerson"; indeed, it is "the central enigma of politics."

To begin to address these questions in ways that don't thoroughly take for granted and reproduce the structures and assumptions of our own sovereign identity (call it liberal humanism) and our own historical moment (call it baldly, with Richard Rorty, "the rich northern bourgeois democracies"), we must move to a deeper level of thought—a slower one, as it were—that will be able to articulate Emerson's contribution to political thinking only on the prior basis of understanding the contours and systematicity of Emerson's philosophy. If we do take time for this understanding, we will be led by Emerson, Cadava suggests, to an examination of the conditions of possibility for political discourses themselves—not just an examination of the "gestures and the language without which they would never take place," but also the concepts of justice and of freedom about which Cadava rightly notes that "we might even say that Emerson's works are nothing but the very trial of these two concepts."

A similar point is made in Stanley Cavell's brilliant analysis in the mid-1990s of the transvaluation of the terms "public" and "private" in Emerson's essay "Fate" and how in staging the relationship between philosophy and the question of slavery it demonstrates what a properly philosophical response to that question might look like.[10] As Emerson writes in that essay, "A man must ride alternately on the horses of his private and his public nature.... Leaving the dæmon who suffers, he is to take sides with the Deity who secures universal benefit by his pain" (6:25–26). And earlier in the essay, famously—even, apparently, scandalously (given the date of the essay's composition, just months after the passage of the Fugitive Slave Law)—Emerson announces, "Intellect annuls Fate. So far as a man thinks, he is free. And though nothing is more disgusting than the crowing about liberty by slaves, as most men are, and the flippant mistaking for freedom of some paper preamble like a 'Declaration of Independence,' or the statute right to vote, by those who have never dared to think or to act, yet it is wholesome to man to look not at Fate, but the other way: the practical view is the other" (6:13).

As Cavell puts it, "If 'taking sides with the Deity' does not, for Emerson, (just) mean taking the right side in the crowing about slavery, the side Daniel Webster failed to take as the armies were closing on the issue, how might it be taken?" From Cavell's point of view, this is clearly, for Emerson, a matter of principle, one that goes to the very heart of philosophy's role in democracy. For as Cavell writes, "taking sides with the Deity" here means "a refusal to take sides in the human *crowing* over slavery," for or against, and "leaving the dæmon who suffers" means "leaving one's private, limited passions on the subject of slavery, for or against," and taking on instead the public duty—the *representative* duty—of thinking: not because it is easy, but precisely because it is hard, because philosophy's image (and performance) of freedom is that each of us must speak, and think, for ourselves and not hand ourselves over to be "the parrot of other men's thinking" (as Emerson puts it in "The American Scholar" [1:53]), whether left *or* right, for *or* against.[11] What is at stake here is an ethics of thought, one that subtends any subsequent question of what political action might be *for*, what the just political act might look like, at this moment. As Cavell reasons, "If slavery is the negation of thought, then thinking cannot affirm itself without affirming the end of slavery.... Philosophy cannot abolish slavery, and it can only call for abolition to the extent, or in the way, that it can call for thinking." From this vantage, to take for granted the validity of our contemporary political agendas and the efficacy of our counterhegemonic identifications is actually, as Keenaghan suggests, a "private" indulgence that, in the name of "public" political utility, serves as an "an evasion, or renunciation," as Cavell phrases it, of our responsibility to democracy in the very character, the "representativeness," of our thinking.

This suggests a very different understanding of politics, of political "representativeness" and responsibility, one that is for Emerson inseparable from questions of freedom and democracy. We can perhaps gain some perspective on Emerson's unique contribution by revisiting how we understand, or misunderstand, the rather unexpected political implications of a figure we have already mentioned glancingly: Nietzsche. As Gianni Vattimo has recently written, "Whoever today does not become superman (one able to interpret for himself) is destined to perish, as a free individual at any rate."[12] Far from being elitist or escapist, however, the idea of the *Übermensch* points, for Vattimo, toward the fact that "to live in the world of plurality, that is, in the postmodern Babel of cultures irreducible to a common core," requires "a superhuman effort" of interpretation, a continuation of thinking after all the dependable road signs by which it had traditionally been carried out have been removed—hence the demanding nature of what Emerson, anticipating a core theme of existential philosophy, calls our fatedness to freedom, the freedom to which we are in this sense (to borrow Sartre's well-known formulation) condemned. Against the grain of a similar (and similarly common) misreading of Emerson's notion of self-reliance, Vattimo argues that, for Nietzsche, "in a situation in which all were aware that there was no objective truth to give us guidance, it would not be the violent who would prevail but more moderate individuals, ones with a certain capacity for irony toward themselves," or, to put it otherwise, "one who is able to look at many cultures with a gaze more esthetic than 'objective' and truth seeking."[13]

This crucial transposition or transvaluation of "public" and "private," "objective" and "subjective" (to blend now the characterizations by Cavell and Vattimo), grows out of Emerson's rendering of the self's relationship to itself, which is in turn fundamental for understanding how the self can relate to others—that is to say, for the question of political representation, "representativeness," and democratic difference. As Cavell puts it, emphasizing the difference between Emerson's early and late work, Emerson's "praise of 'the infinitude of the private man' is not a praise of any existing man or men but an announcement of a process of individuation . . . before which there are no individuals, hence no humanity, hence no society."[14]

This theme is central to Sandra Laugier's emphasis on what Cavell has called the crucial role of "moral perfectionism" in Emerson's thought to the concept of democracy (which she, like Cavell, counterposes squarely against John Rawls's liberal theory of democracy, which sees such a project as elitist and antidemocratic): namely, that perfectionism consists of an ongoing difference from *myself*—what Emerson variously calls my "onwardness" or "abandonment"—the necessity to surpass the self that I was yesterday, the self that has already settled into conformity (whose opposite, as we have noted, is self-reliance).

As Cavell characterizes the project of Emersonian perfectionism in *Conditions Handsome and Unhandsome,* in Emerson, "'having' 'a' self is [a] process of moving to, and from, nexts. It is, using a romantic term, the 'work' of (Emerson's) writing to present nextness. . . . That the self is always attained, as well as to be attained, creates the problem in Emerson's concept of self-reliance—he insists on it, though not in the following terms exactly—that unless you manage the reliance of the attained on the unattained/attainable . . . you are left in precisely the negation of the position he calls for, left in conformity."[15] With Rawls obviously in mind—and focusing squarely on the Emerson themes that most concern Laugier—Cavell writes:

> Since the task for each is his or her own self-transformation, the representativeness implied in that life may seem not to establish a recognition of others in different positions, so to be disqualified as a moral position altogether. "Representativeness" invokes one of Emerson's "master-tones," both as characterized in his writing and as exemplified by his writing. And I think we can say: Emerson's writing works out the conditions for my recognizing my difference from others as a function of my recognizing my difference from myself. (53)

Thus, my openness to the democratic other—to all others—is based not in my confidence in myself, my self-assurance that I already am what I need to be, already know what I need to know—which I then just freely (imperially) extend to others—but rather in my impatience with myself, my constitutive uncertainty to which I have to be paradoxically, absolutely faithful in a total openness to the moment when my genius calls me. And while another face of that impatience, as Sharon Cameron suggests, has often created consternation for Emerson's readers—namely, consternation about his impatience with others—we are in a better position to appreciate its significance when we realize that it is rooted not in hubris but in what the essays collected here variously characterize as the reception, passivity, vulnerability, and impersonality of the Emersonian self—a self that, in its openness to what these essays call "the event," to what Emerson calls "the casual," drives its project of democratic differentiation as a kind of ongoing negative capability: not as the supposedly benevolent imaginings of otherness issued from a fully fortified citadel of subjectivity, but rather as a self finding others (only) by already leaving itself behind, so that my strangeness to myself forms the basis of my affinity with you. And in that sense, then, the title of this volume—"The Other Emerson"—marks first of all the otherness of Emerson to himself, an otherness that, as we have been suggesting, is not just philosophically but also politically representative.

RETHINKING PHILOSOPHY

Whether Emerson is a philosopher or not is a question with a long history. It is a question, one should remember, posed several times by Emerson himself before being inherited by various philosophers and literary critics. For some, however, the question may sound dated. Already in the 1940s Perry Miller argued that Jonathan Edwards was the first American philosopher of modernity, and he claimed that Emerson thus inherited an already hundred-year-long tradition of New England philosophy. Thus (however obliquely), Miller identified Emerson as a philosopher and placed him squarely within an existing philosophical tradition. Some forty years later, the point was argued in a more complex way. Stanley Cavell's 1979 essay "Thinking of Emerson" read Emerson's epistemology as an epistemology of moods, relating it to Kant in order to suggest that Emerson demands to be read as carefully as any German speculative idealist. That Emerson's writings are philosophical was reaffirmed a few years later when, in 1992, Richard Poirier's *Poetry and Pragmatism* turned him into the father of process philosophy, locating him at the imaginary source of that quintessentially American philosophical project called pragmatism.

However, Poirier, like Cavell, was not convinced that Emerson had been properly acknowledged as a philosopher by even his most serious readers. In the introduction to his book, Poirier wrote: "The many exceptionally able interpretations of Emerson produced over the past few decades have consisted for the most part of explications of his essays and poems and have tended to shy away from the effort to show how powerful Emerson's impingement could be on the larger cultural, social, and critical issues."[16] Poirier thus seems to be saying that no matter how competent a reading of an isolated Emerson essay may be, such a reading may still be the effect of a presumption that there is nothing—no systematicity, thematic or conceptual rigor—that connects Emerson's essays and gives us the right to read them from a philosophical (or what he termed "larger cultural") point of view. Even though there are exceptions to Poirier's diagnosis—he doesn't mention, for example, David Van Leer's powerful argument in favor of Emerson as philosopher in his book *Emerson's Epistemology* (1986)—his main point is still very pertinent: in spite of efforts by some to see Emerson as a philosopher, he is still not, for the most part, taken to be one.

Critics who disavow that Emerson is a philosopher point to the fact that he was more of a libertine, a free thinker, hence a poet. Or else, they define him as an essayist, and since essays depict things in flux—by Montaigne's definition—they never end up claiming the truth. In celebrating truth's instability rather than making an effort to stabilize it and grasp it, essays (so the story goes) work against the main interest of philosophy. In contrast to philosophers, Emerson avoids the stability of a given position, disclaiming everything he claimed, unlearning everything he knew. Because philosophers define the position about which and from which they then go on to philosophize, analytically speaking, Emerson would have to be considered, more or less automatically, a non-philosopher. To the list of reasons that work against seeing Emerson as a philosopher, one can add that certain critics insist on the fact that he thinks in paradoxes, that his essays are often self-contradictory, and that he avoids giving clear definitions, whereas the first interest of philosophy is to identify, name, define, and so apprehend. Emerson, the charge continues, habitually uses different terms to refer to the same concept (for example his "ocean," "soul," "over-soul," "becoming," and "love" all refer to what ontology calls "being"), and he thus behaves antiphilosophically since philosophy's first task is to gather differences under one concept. Or again, in advocating self-abandonment, receptivity, and ecstatic experiences as models of subjectivity, Emerson opposes—at least to a certain degree—the absolute privilege philosophy gives to rational discourse. And by incorporating biographical material into his essays, he makes them private, personal, and literary—that is to say, less philosophical.

The problem with such reasoning is not that it is false but rather that it presupposes a particular understanding of what philosophy is, and hence privileges a certain idea of rationality. In other words, it presupposes as settled the very thing that requires questioning: What is thinking? What is philosophy? Can it be said to have a "proper" shape and protocol? If so, on whose authority? Without exploring in any detail the question of philosophy's multiplicity and the quite different forms of rationality that have appeared throughout its history, we will nevertheless refer briefly to several points that can help us situate Emerson's writing within a history of philosophy, and at the same time provide a rationale for the type of criticism and revaluation of Emerson that this volume will offer.

To say that Emerson is not a philosopher because he expresses his thinking in the form of essays is to forget that modern philosophy begins with Descartes' *Discourse on the Method,* which is an autobiography, includes many personal references, and certainly contains elements that we would these days classify as literary. What is more, in a letter addressed to Arnault, Descartes explains that he decided to call his book a "discourse" rather than a "treatise" because "discourse" means *excursion,* whereas "treatise" is more systematic and presumes to offer the truth, which he doesn't possess or want to offer. Other examples in the history of philosophy abound: John Locke formulates his massive statement as an essay; Leibniz's main ideas are developed in private correspondence; Rousseau's and Diderot's philosophies are given in the novelistic genre; Bishop Berkeley writes his main philosophical statement in the form of a dialogue, reviving an ancient literary genre. And yet, surely, personal letters, autobiography, and novels cannot possess more philosophical rigor than the essay.

Similarly, to say that Emerson is not a philosopher because he privileges intuition over philosophical ratiocination is to forget that such is the case throughout the history of modern Western rationalism. Descartes claims that intuition *(lumen naturale)* is the highest form of knowledge and that the *cogito* itself is only a moment, a glance luminously enlightened by its own intuiting. Spinoza famously wrote his *Ethics* in geometrical form in order to show that intuition is the highest form of any cognitive procedure. And Kant saw in "pure intuition" the condition of possibility for pure reason. The history of modern rationalism is the history of intuition, and at least when it comes to his description of epistemological practices, Emerson's work should be seen as a constitutive moment of that history.

It is true that Emerson's thought does not produce an overarching philosophical system, but in fact neither do most of the major figures in Western philosophy. If producing a philosophical system were a criterion for determining who is a philosopher, then the history of philosophy would be reduced to several names at the most. What is more, there are long periods in the history of philosophy (Hellenism, the Renaissance, the post-Hegelian nineteenth century, twentieth-century Continental philosophy) where philosophers—to risk a paradoxical expression—systematically oppose systematic thinking. Against this background, it is easier to see that while Emerson doesn't produce a philosophical system per se, his thinking does have an identifiable systematicity, since certain concepts—such as soul or over-soul, becoming, power, transformation, intuition, abandonment, circularity, compensation, the now, impersonality, intellect—keep recurring in his writings. They appear in almost all of his essays, and it is safe to call them philosophical concepts as they serve the purpose of redefining subjectivity, formulating an ontology of becoming, and developing an ethics of self-renewal.

Emerson always insisted that the truth cannot be obtained by purely cognitive procedures but rather occurs only if the subject who accesses those procedures changes in the process of coming to know them. This means that truth has to work a "revolution" in a person, converting him by triggering the process of self-reformation. To those who don't see philosophy as a pragmatics of self-transformation but instead as a cognition that does not have to transform the subject of knowing, Emerson's thesis may sound unphilosophical. However, in proposing philosophy to be the practice of self-reformation, he follows the trend of nineteenth-century philosophy as a whole in its concerted effort to include pragmatics into philosophical thinking. As Michel Foucault puts it:

> All of nineteenth century philosophy—well, almost all: Hegel any-
> way, Schelling, Schopenhauer, Nietzsche, the Husserl of the *Krisis*,
> and Heidegger as well . . . In all these philosophies, a certain structure
> of spirituality tries to link knowledge, the activity of knowing, and the
> conditions and effects of this activity, to a transformation in the sub-
> ject's being. . . . The entire history of nineteenth century philosophy
> can, I think, be thought of as a kind of pressure to try to rethink the
> structures of spirituality within a philosophy.[17]

Hence, to deny Emerson the status of philosopher because his criterion of truth is the transformation of subjectivity rather than the refinement of strategies of cognition is to exclude him from the broader context of nineteenth-century Continental philosophy.

According to Cornel West, such an exclusion, or as he calls it, "eva-sion," has a long history. Many insightful readings of Emerson, West ex-plains in *The American Evasion of Philosophy*, "hide" the extent to which "Emerson's perspective is infused with historical consciousness," and the extent to which—in a cosmopolitical way—he transcends the bound-aries of the New England, or even American, cultural context. The ef-fort to root Emerson in a specifically American cultural climate—and to evade his belonging to the context of nineteenth-century philosophy—leads West to conclude that some insightful readings of Emerson were, at the same time, an effect of a kind of blindness:

> These interpretive blindnesses result, in part, from situating Emerson in
> the age of the American literary renaissance (along with Hawthorne,
> Melville, Thoreau, and Whitman) rather than relating him to the
> European explosions (both intellectual and social) that produced Karl
> Marx, John Stuart Mill, Thomas Carlyle, and Friedrich Nietzsche. We
> can no longer afford or justify confining Emerson to the American ter-
> rain. He belongs to that highbrow cast of North Atlantic cultural crit-
> ics who set the agenda and the terms for understanding the modern
> world.[18]

West proposes that we release Emerson from his "confinement"—eman-cipate him from his "Americanness," presumably in the way Nietzsche is emancipated from his Germanness—in order to start treating him as a great intellectual and philosophical figure who responded to the exigencies of the modern world. Such emancipation would then require our seeing him not as a person deeply rooted in, say, the Unitarian context of New England and at odds with cosmopolitan modernity, but rather as a philosopher who, like Marx, understood modernity at the moment of its occurring and set a conceptual agenda for thinking it that is still with us.

Without referring explicitly to West's call, the three essays gathered in Part III, "Rethinking Philosophy," do just what West proposes: they release Emerson from the American Renaissance context in order to relocate him within the tradition of Western philosophy. To be precise, they don't ask if Emerson is a philosopher but instead proceed to unpack his philosophy and its strategies. Significantly, both Cary Wolfe and Gregg Lambert see the importance of Emerson's philosophical intervention in his redefinition of the question of subjectivity, and both argue that Emerson proposed a way out of representational thinking. For both writers, Emerson (rather than, say, Nietzsche or Heidegger) thus becomes the thinker of the end of metaphysics, since modern metaphysics proposed the subject to be a representational force and the world to be what has been produced or pictured by it.

In chapter 10, "'The Eye Is the First Circle,'" Wolfe explicitly frames his analysis of Emerson as an effort to minimalize the question of whether Emerson was a Transcendentalist or a pragmatist, the better to read his thinking as an engagement with modernity. Emerson's response to the challenges of modernity is most clearly visible in his effort to invent a thinking that would do away with the image and with representation. And it is along those lines—imageless thinking—that even the question of skepticism in Emerson, as it is formulated by Cavell, should be rephrased. Because skepticism is enabled by a certain experience of representation—that is, since it occurs as the response to our "loss of the world," in which the world cannot be seen and thus felt—the recovery from such a loss (as Wolfe reads Cavell) would be in a certain recovery of representation itself: not of any *specific* representation, but of the idea (or desire) of representation itself. But as long as the question of skepticism remains related to the question of representation, Wolfe argues— that is, to the question of modern subjectivity—it remains insoluble, since it is based on the very nature of that subjectivity that Emerson is intent on undoing. To make it soluble, then, would mean to think about the subject and about language in a thoroughly different way. As Wolfe puts it, "To take the unsolvability of skepticism to heart is not just, at the same stroke, to abandon the representationalist philosophical project; it is also to change our view of the relationship of thinking and language." Emerson abandons the modernist representationalist project precisely because he abandons the idea of subjectivity it takes for granted. Instead of siding with the Cartesian subject as the power of appropriating the represented, Emerson, Wolfe proposes, outlines a subjectivity in motion. Such a motion, however, is predicated on the following paradox: the self recovers itself only as a self-about-to-be. Such a self, by definition, escapes our power of representation. All of Emerson's talk—and it is a considerable amount—of "self-recovery" both early and late in his work (*Nature*, "Experience") directs us toward not an originary substance but a *power* and a *process*, not toward the past but rather toward the future, or rather futurity itself, conceived as a horizon where, paradoxically, the only "self" to "recover" is a self always (about) to be. This motion constitutes its world as it moves, but because the pace of its constitution is faster than the slowness needed to fix the image of it, the world thus recovered is experienced beyond the possibility of its being represented. In fact, the very question "Has the world vanished or has it returned?" loses its sense.

The idea of a self recovering itself in motion owes much to Stanley Cavell's discussion of Emerson's "moral perfectionism." Yet, Wolfe argues, the question of skepticism in Cavell remains tethered to the possibility of representing the world: "skepticism remains tied . . . to the representationalism he would otherwise seem to disown, because skepticism holds onto the desire for a representational adequation between concepts and objects even as it knows that desire to be unappeasable ([hence] Cavell's insistence on taking seriously the 'mourning' of the loss of the world . . . in Emerson's 'Experience')." Instead, Wolfe proposes that Niklas Luhmann's systems theory can offer a way out of the representationalist project and help us explain the seeming paradoxes of Emerson's thinking (such as, for example, the relationship between a self-enclosed individuality and a moving, changeable, affective person). Such apparent paradoxes may now be viewed as instead quite rigorously systematic—philosophical, if you like—for we can now see, as Wolfe explains, that "the autopoietic closure of a system—whether social or psychic—is precisely what *connects* it to its environment." Hence, we can begin to understand how the "closed," reliant self can at the same time be receptive and open.

Like Wolfe, Lambert finds that Emerson works towards a-representational thinking, and for that reason he is, like Nietzsche, an "untimely," antimetaphysical thinker. In chapter 8, "Emerson, or *Man Thinking*," Lambert argues the point by analyzing Emerson's ideas of silence, which he parses into three major forms—formal, topological, and moral—and suggests that because it is imageless, silence must also be thought as a pure act, which Lambert identifies as an act of thinking: "Silence must be understood to be without image, which to say that it is equal to an action that determines . . . the act of thinking itself." Such an imageless thinking, Lambert proposes, is in fact profoundly anti-Cartesian: "Things are not revealed through representation (via Ideas, nor even clear and distinct perception), but rather may appear only in what Emerson defines as a 'conversation with things' that is said to take place outside words and knowledge." However, to claim that thinking reveals things through channels different from ideas or even distinct perceptions is to redefine not only the concept of modern subjectivity but, equally radically, the epistemological premises of Cartesian philosophy, with its clear and distinct ideas as the criteria of truth.

Because it occurs outside of ideas or perceptions, Lambert terms Emerson's theory of thinking the "outside thought." However—and here lies the importance of Lambert's intervention—"outside thought" is far removed from the mystical experience of "freshness." Lambert defines the outside as a strategy meant to restructure our understanding of thinking both formally and topologically. As he puts it: "Formally, the thematic of outside thought concerns the question of style, the manner of writing. . . . Topologically, the outside has to do with the position from which the philosophy speaks to us, with the 'untimely' character of the philosopher's stance."

Lambert proposes that the "outside thought" sought by Emerson and Nietzsche be further analyzed through the philosophy of Gilles Deleuze, which is not just accidentally related to Emerson (on the basis, for instance, of external similarities). The relationship between Deleuze and Emerson is established via Nietzsche, since, as Lambert proposes, several major concepts in Deleuze—the nomadic, the outside and the imageless—are developed through his interpretation of Nietzsche's philosophy, which was itself influenced by Emerson. Like Emerson, Deleuze proposes a thought of the outside and formulates it as a paradox: "As Deleuze chooses to pose this problem, how does one speak of an outside thought without already giving it an image? How does one imagine thought without image?" The paradox can be solved only through experiences that escape representation, such as difference, repetition, intensity, and force.

Emerson, Lambert argues, formulated his own version of the same question in "The American Scholar," where he "poses the question of thought without image in the figure of Man Thinking. In a very definite sense, this question runs parallel to the one posed by Deleuze: how to begin? How does one truly begin to think without already proposing a prephilosophical image of thought, or a common sense?" Thinking without an image—a proposal that makes Emerson one of the most prominent thinkers of the nineteenth century—is summed up in the word "nature," which designates the "being of the sensible," what one senses when representation and images collapse. Nature is, in other words, a sensorium, a transcendental experience of nomadic intensities that overwhelm a personal identity predicated on representational thought. As Lambert puts it: "It seems that I am hypothesizing that what Deleuze calls the 'being of the sensible' is identical with Emerson's 'nature.'" In claiming that "sensing" is the core of Emerson's epistemological maneuvers, Lambert, in fact, overturns a longstanding tradition by which Emerson is interpreted as an idealist. However, sensing as the infinite production of intensities does not affect only our epistemological habits; because it both traverses and transcends the boundaries of the person—because, therefore, it is an impersonal sensing—the new, outside thought becomes, for Lambert, a form of impersonal thinking. Thus, as if echoing some of the theses proposed in the first part of our book and so closing its circle, Lambert proposes that Emerson's major contribution to the history of philosophy is the invention of the impersonal, as the outside thought: "And yet, rather than understanding the kind of action this would require as a power to intervene directly into the state of things . . . Emerson again alludes to a certain state of silence and to the impersonal power of nature itself as the only agency of such action. Here, nature . . . is thus presented as a moment of passive synthesis, in which one finds a limit of the sensible in what is sensed."

Like Lambert and Wolfe, in chapter 9, "Emerson's Adjacencies: Radical Empiricism in *Nature*," Paul Grimstad sees Emerson as working toward a thought of the external and relational, and like Lambert, he also sees Deleuze's thought as intrinsically related to Emerson's. For Grimstad, however, the link between Emerson and Deleuze is William James, who was profoundly influenced by Emerson and, in turn, fundamentally influenced Deleuze. Grimstad argues that Emerson not only formulates a theory of external thinking—a thinking of adjacencies, as he calls it—but that he also practices what he formulates. Emerson's writings execute their own theory, in other words, which is, according to Grimstad, a sort of radical empiricism. Following William James, Grimstad understands radical empiricism, in which "the relations that connect experiences must themselves be experienced relations," to be the organizing principle of Emerson's thought, and for that reason, he too sees it as a thought of the outside: "If radical empiricism argues that even such organizing principles are part of experience (and not the other way around), then this sort of empiricism amounts to an exact reversal of the Kantian transcendental critique. Radical empiricism finds its 'faculties' within a transcendentally *empirical* field of pure experience, where the relations that connect the terms of experience are as real as the terms themselves." Emerson, then, reverses Kant precisely by establishing an experiential field made of relations that evade representation, and he does so doubly, as it were: first, through his openness to experimentation with the ecstatic (which negates the phenomenological per se); and second, by trying to experience the relation between the ecstatic and reason, which Grimstad identifies in Emerson's abiding interest in the continuity between reason and revelation.

Grimstad's major interest, however, is less the analysis of subjectivity than the linguistic effects of its destabilization: once we presume there is an external thought, then what kind of logic, grammar, and rhetoric would sustain it? It is in that network of questions that he finds collusion between Emerson and Deleuze: "What I want to focus on in Deleuze's linkage of the concept to 'logical possibility' is the alignment of this relation with an a priori deduction that would move from universals to particulars (logical demonstration from general axiom to particular case), and, conversely, a 'hidden art' that would be external to this operation." Grimstad finds that Emerson practices such a dynamism in what he calls an "extra-logical" way of writing: "This extra-logical writing, this 'ecstasy' of side-stepping discrete instantiations of the concept, occurs when words begin to function independently of the subject-predicate grooves of deductive reasoning." It is important to note that Grimstad is not simply reviving an old thesis that we have already aired—that Emerson's writing is nonlogical—but instead is insisting that Emerson's writing obeys another *kind* of logic, one that does what it says, thus performatively instantiating the materialism, rather than the idealism, of exteriority.

Anne Carson once said that a "scholar is someone who takes a position. From which position, certain lines become visible."[19] Scholarship is thus, in our view, about lighting; its lamp is directed toward lines that not many of us have underscored. Thanks to it, the text—that which is old and well interpreted—becomes new again. The book that follows hopes to offer such illumination and such newness. From proposing that Emerson's self is fragile, impersonal, or involuntary rather than willful, powerful, and personal, to signaling its passivity rather than its activity; from redefining power in Emerson as strength and endurance of receptivity rather than as willful self assertion, to proposing that his thinking is on the "outside," imageless, and a-representational; from claiming that Emerson is materialist or sensualist rather than idealist, empiricist rather than rationalist, to pointing out that his political philosophy was about de-appropriation, decolonization, and to arguing that he tried to formulate certain possibilities for the ethics of testifying and mourning—the voices heard in this book endeavor to light certain lines in Emerson's texts that might help us reshape the image of his philosophy, even if, as we have been suggesting, that image is finally of *no* image, as befits a nonrepresentationalist philosophy. The "otherness" we thus have in mind in titling the book *The Other Emerson* is not oppositional in that it does not primarily oppose this or that particular interpretation of Emerson. Rather, it is an otherness that emerges from the weaving of various philosophical traditions and the forms of understanding they make available that need not finally converge into an image or icon. Such an "Emerson," one only now beginning to come into focus, provides, we believe, a singular key (as Cornel West rightly suggests) to our ability to understand our own modernity.

NOTES

1. Ralph Waldo Emerson, *The Collected Works of Ralph Waldo Emerson*, ed. Alfred R. Ferguson, Robert E. Spiller, et al., 8 vols. to date (Cambridge, Mass.: Harvard University Press, Belknap Press, 1971–2010), 3:35. Subsequent quotations from Emerson's writing are from this source and are cited parenthetically in text by volume and page numbers. Citations may include essay title if the essay from which a quotation is taken is not clear from the text. Wherever possible in this collection, we have standardized references to Emerson's writings using the *Collected Works* cited above. In cases where the quoted material does not appear in the *Works*, we have used the best available scholarly edition (for example, *Emerson's Antislavery Writings*, ed. Len Gougeon and Joel Myerson [New Haven, Conn.: Yale University Press, 1995]). The reader will notice in some of the essays a difference between the punctuation, spelling, and so on that appears in the quoted passage and the version of the text that appears in the cited *Works*. This is so because most of the contributing authors originally drew upon texts other than the *Works*, and in some cases the particular spelling and punctuation that appears in those other editions of Emerson's work are important to their interpretation. We trust that the reader will thus appreciate our intention to locate the passages from Emerson's work in the authoritative text, while at the same time providing leeway for the variations in spelling, punctuation, and the like that obtain across the various collections of Emerson's work in active circulation among scholars and students.

2. John Jay Chapman, *Emerson and Other Essays* (New York: Moffat, Yard, 1898; rpt. 1909), 43.

3. Stephen E. Whicher, *Freedom and Fate: An Inner Life of Ralph Waldo Emerson* (New York: A. S. Barnes, 1961), 96.

4. Sherman Paul, *Emerson's Angle of Vision: Man and Nature in American Experience* (Cambridge, Mass.: Harvard University Press, 1952), 103–4.

5. Emphasis in original. Stanley Cavell, *Conditions Handsome and Unhandsome: The Constitution of Emersonian Perfectionism* (Chicago: University of Chicago Press, 1990), xxx.

6. Richard Poirier, *The Renewal of Literature: Emersonian Reflections* (New York: Random House, 1987), 201.

7. The essay was published in *Critical Inquiry*, Autumn 1998, and reprinted in Cameron's book *Impersonality: Seven Essays* (Chicago: University of Chicago Press, 2007).

8. See, for example, Derrida's essay "Force of Law," in *Deconstruction and the Possibility of Justice*, ed. Drucilla Cornell (London: Routledge, 1992).

9. See Cavell's chapter "Aversive Thinking" in *Conditions Handsome and*

Unhandsome: The Constitution of Emersonian Perfectionism (Chicago: University of Chicago Press, 1990), 33–63.

10. Stanley Cavell, "Emerson's Constitutional Amending: Reading 'Fate,'" in *Emerson's Transcendental Etudes* (Stanford, Calif.: Stanford University Press, 2003), 192–214.

11. Ibid., 198.

12. Gianni Vattimo, *Nihilism and Emancipation: Ethics, Politics, and Law,* trans. William McCuaig, ed. Santiago Zabala, foreword by Richard Rorty (New York: Columbia University Press, 2004), 45.

13. Ibid., 53–54, 55. Vattimo points out, "Naturally this . . . is too brief to serve as the basis for a Nietzschean 'politics' that would clear him of the suspicion aroused by his repeated declarations about the necessity for the weak to perish so that the *Ubermensch* might live" (54). But "it is not a question," he points out, "of trying to save Nietzsche at all costs but only of reading him, without any pretence to historical 'objectivity' (something he would certainly have rejected), in relation to a defensible project, precisely through an act of quite self-aware interpretation" (53).

14. Cavell, *Conditions Handsome and Unhandsome,* 11.

15. Ibid., 12.

16. Richard Poirier, *Poetry and Pragmatism* (Cambridge, Mass.: Harvard University Press, 1992), 6.

17. Michel Foucault, *The Hermeneutics of the Subject: Lectures at the Collège de France, 1981–1982,* ed. Frédéric Gros, trans. Graham Burchell (New York: Picador, 2005), 28.

18. Cornel West, *The American Evasion of Philosophy: A Genealogy of Pragmatism* (Madison: University of Wisconsin Press, 1989), 11.

19. Anne Carson, *Plain Water* (New York: Vintage Books, 1995), 93.

I.
RETHINKING SUBJECTIVITY

SHARON CAMERON

1. The Way of Life by Abandonment

Emerson's Impersonal

"**M**ost of us have false beliefs about our own nature, and about our own identity, over time," Derek Parfit writes in *Reasons and Persons,* a book that challenges commonsense ideas about personal identity, and whose conclusions, I shall suggest, pertain directly to the writings of Ralph Waldo Emerson.[1] The false view, according to Parfit, centers on the idea that we are separately existing entities. We hold such a view because we mistake the psychological continuity of consciousness for the continued existence of a separately existing self in whom that consciousness inheres. But since experience gives no proof of this premise, we ought, Parfit writes, to reject it. We ought to accept the Reductionist claim that "the existence of a person just consists in the existence of his brain and body, and the doing of his deeds, and the occurrence of various other physical and mental events" (225). In other words, we ought to see there is no identificatory extra essence, distinct from our brains or bodies, on which a discrete or personal identity could be founded. I shall return to this characterization, described by Parfit as "impersonal," at the end of my discussion, but before leaving it, I want to underline Parfit's understanding of the radical implications of his theory. Granting that personal identity does not matter, is equivalent to, or has the consequence of, supposing that "if tomorrow someone will be in agony [it is] an empty question whether this agony will be felt by *me*," of seeing that "if I am about to lose consciousness, there may be no answer to the question 'Am I about to die?'" (280, emphasis in original), what would it mean

3

not to care if pain were *your* pain, to find the question empty? To find unanswerable the question of whether the loss of consciousness would mean *your* death? These are the central questions raised, I shall argue, obliquely, one might even say unconsciously, by the centrally recurring idea of the impersonal in Emerson's essays, to which I now turn.[2]

In the middle of "Nominalist and Realist" Emerson articulates *his* disillusion with the conventional idea that persons are separate and integral entities: "I wish to speak with all respect of persons, but sometimes I must pinch myself to keep awake, and preserve the due decorum. They melt so fast into each other, that they are like grass and trees, and it needs an effort to treat them as individuals."[3] The essay equivocates between belief in individuals and disbelief in them ("Though the uninspired man certainly finds persons a conveniency in household matters, the divine man does not respect them" [3:139]), seeing this equivocation as a matter of shifting moods. But in the end Emerson's point of view is unambiguous, in favor of acknowledging what in "Montaigne" he names the "catholic sense," the "larger generalizations" (4:104), in effect the impersonal, called by him "the Over-Soul" in the most famous example: "In youth we are mad for persons. Childhood and youth see all the world in them. But the larger experience of man discovers the identical nature appearing through them all. Persons themselves acquaint us with the impersonal" (2:164).[4] Impersonality is the antidote for the egotistical, the subjective, the solipsistic. It is so specifically because it refutes the idea that the mind is one's "property," that one's relation to being is that of ownership on the one hand, and separate identity on the other ("The Over-Soul," 2:164–65). From the perspective of the truth Emerson advocates in "The Over-Soul," subjectivity and egotism are delusions about personal identity. From the vantage of the truth Emerson advocates in "The Over-Soul," what defines "thoughts" as well as "events" is "alien energy" not "the will I call mine" (2:159–60). Thus the private will is overpowered by a force—variously named in this essay a "common heart" (2:160) and in others a "universal mind" ("History," 2:3–4), an "identical nature" ("Spiritual Laws," 2:95)—that inhabits all. By light of this identical nature, ownership is nonsensical; it is a mistake to call a talent, an idea, an achievement, or even a heart (and therefore body) one's own, as it is a mistake to entertain the more abstract idea that persons have discrete identities. When Emerson in "The Over-Soul" writes "we do not yet possess ourselves" (2:165), he means that we live out of synch with the truth of this impersonality. Yet to live *in* synch with it is to become indifferent to any fate one might conceivably call "mine" (the point ultimately made by the essay "Fate").

In section I of the following I examine formulations that elaborate the mechanics of impersonality, an examination necessary to specify how persons come in contact with the impersonal; in the second half of section I, I examine Emerson's analysis of the way in which body and mind counterintuitively exemplify attributes of impersonality, as well as the way in which that "divine law," outside of body and mind, is equally said to epitomize it ("Montaigne," 4:100).

In section II, I consider the features of the person who is expounding impersonality. I argue there is a connection between the anonymous voice of the speaker, the essays' stylistic singularity, and the compensating features of the erasure of personality. Throughout this and the following section I consider a series of concerns that threaten to produce a devastating critique of Emerson in any serious reading of him. Someone might reasonably feel that Emerson's idea of the impersonal is ethically illegitimate if not indeed simply delusional. If it is neither of these, what keeps it from being so? I understand such a question to mean from what vantage *could* one relinquish the personal perspective one inevitably has as a delimited self? At the heart of the question is the issue of what licenses the abdication of a perspective one can't in some sense abdicate— what licenses it for oneself and what sanctions such a claim when it is made on another's behalf. For instance, Emerson makes the following astonishing assertion:

> If in the hours of clear reason we should speak the severest truth, we should say, that we had never made a sacrifice. In these hours the mind seems so great, that nothing can be taken from us that seems much. All loss, all pain is particular: the universe remains to the heart unhurt. . . . It is only the finite that has wrought and suffered; the infinite lies stretched in smiling repose," this seems the sort of claim that cannot be made by one person for another. ("Spiritual Laws," 2:77)

In section III, I turn to "The Poet," the practitioner of impersonality— the poet being he who relinquishes the "jail-yard of individual relations," who lays aside his private self so as to "draw" on "great public power . . . by unlocking, at all risks, his human doors" (3:16). Although public power appears to require an indifference to persons, specifically to the distinction among persons, and especially to the particular status of the person who is writing, I argue that it does so at the peril of calling its own authority into question. Thus I claim that the deficiency in Emerson's representation of the impersonal lies peculiarly in the missing sense of a person.

I

How one gains access to the impersonal is a question that precedes all others in Emerson's essays. In "The Divinity School Address" the question receives an explanation that initially differentiates between what "the true preacher" is to do from what others are to do (1:86). The preacher is to decline any secondary relation to God: "to go alone; to refuse the good models . . . and dare to love God without mediator or veil" (1:90). Disavowing custom and authority, the preacher is "to live with the privilege of the immeasurable mind" (ibid.). He is to become visible to himself. The ocular image is Emerson's in that the "immeasurable mind" is what the preacher will see when "fashion, custom, authority, pleasure, and money . . . are not bandages over [his] eyes" (ibid.). When the preacher is visible to himself, he is enjoined to make himself visible to others, so that they will have a model. ("Let their doubts know that you have doubted, and their wonder feel that you have wondered" [ibid.].) What they will have a model *for* is precisely autonomy, which leads, in turn, to their ability to look within themselves, to do what the preacher does: like the preacher, "to go alone." From the preacher's point of view, what is advocated is a theory of interpenetration: the self with "the immeasurable mind" and consequently with others. In this formulation inspiration turns inward and outward at once: to be visible to yourself is to make yourself visible to others, which will make visible the fact that what is in you is also in them. Such visibility will bequeath to them the autonomy that Emerson in his sermon is arguably bequeathing to the young student.

The paradigm for access is somewhat different in "The American Scholar," where the self "going down into the secrets of his own mind . . . has descended into the secrets of all minds" (1:63). The American Scholar has access to others *by* having access to himself, unlike the "Divinity

School" preacher who, having access to himself, consequently (as opposed to identically) has access to others, and who therefore can show others how to have access to themselves. But the difference is without ultimate significance since (disappointingly from a pedagogic vantage) the lesson in both cases is that "the man has never lived that can feed us ever. The human mind cannot be enshrined in a person" (1:66).

In context this is an astonishing statement. It does not mean that no man is an exemplary, in the sense of adequate, incarnation because each is partial (what it would mean in *Representative Men* or "Nominalist and Realist"). Nor does it precisely suggest that you should look to yourself rather than to others, though, like "The Divinity School Address," it also counsels autonomy, but for slightly different reasons. The American Scholar become autonomous will discover that no person (not even his own person) is adequate to enshrine the human mind. Thus while other persons produce a barrier to what "The Divinity School Address" calls "the immeasurable mind," so does one's own self understood in any conventional way. In effect, then, what self-reliance turns out to mean for Emerson is a strong recognitional understanding of the inadequacy of any person: other persons *or* this person.[5] And what the preacher and the American Scholar know how to do is to break out of the tyranny of egotistical self-enclosure.

But what is meant by a person? And what is the alternative to supposing that the human mind can be "enshrined in a person"? "Compensation" provides one answer to the second of these questions. In the essay Emerson has been arguing the need for recompense ("each thing is a half, and suggests another thing to make it whole" [2:57]), on the one hand, and, on the other hand, the means *of* recompense ("We can no more halve things . . . than we can get an inside that shall have no outside" [2:61]; in this way a theory of dualism turns into a theory of ultimate totality). But the essay also wishes to illustrate some fact "deeper than" recompense that does not therefore require it: "The soul is not a compensation, but a life. The soul *is*. Under all this running sea of circumstance, whose waters ebb and flow with perfect balance, lies the aboriginal abyss of real Being. Essence, or God, is not a relation, or a part, but the whole" (2:70, Emerson's emphasis). Not part of the system of compensation (not necessitating it, not contributing to it), the soul is free of the drama of "More and Less" that is also the drama of "*His* and *Mine*" or, put differently still, free of the drama of the "inequalities of condition" and circumstance (2:71–72, Emerson's emphasis).

In "Compensation," then, the soul is free of particulars, good or bad; impersonality is a consequence of that liberation. The following paragraph from "Self-Reliance" elaborates the nature of this freedom. It does so by identifying the features of "real Being" (the name for it in "Compensation"), a state so stripped down that it is defined by negations. In such a state, characterized in the following passage as intuition without an object, one lives impersonally, that is, "in the present, above time" and "with God":

> And now at last the highest truth on this subject remains unsaid; probably, cannot be said; for all that we say is the far off remembering of the intuition. That thought, by what I can now nearest approach to say it, is this. When good is near you, when you have life in yourself, it is not by any known or accustomed way; you shall not discern the foot-prints of any other; you shall not see the face of man; you shall not hear any name;—the way, the thought, the good shall be wholly strange and new. It shall exclude example and experience. You take the way from man, not to man. All persons that ever existed are its forgotten ministers. Fear and hope are alike beneath it. There is somewhat low even in hope. In the hour of vision, there is nothing that can be called gratitude, nor properly joy. The soul raised over passion beholds identity and eternal causation, perceives the self-existence of Truth and Right, and calms itself with knowing that all things go well. Vast spaces of nature, the Atlantic Ocean, the South Sea,—long intervals of time, years, centuries,—are of no account. This which I think and feel underlay every former state of life and circumstances, as it does underlie my present, and what is called life, and what is called death. (2:39–40)

In the state Emerson describes, immediate experience is incomparable, not contingent on others' experience or on one's own experience. But what does it mean to get beyond others' and one's own experience? What is one *beyond*?

The answer offered by the passage has something to do with extrication from emotion, including all those emotions like hope, gratitude, joy, which one might suppose Emerson to wish to cultivate. Hope is understood to be "low" presumably because, by definition, it supposes the inadequacy of the present state; "gratitude" that is inspired by the sufficiency of the present presumes, albeit implicitly, some alternative state that *would not* be adequate. In effect it assumes a discrimination between the actual and an alternative to the actual. "Joy" especially implies the possibility of its opposite; moreover, the very meaning of joy, and the experiential sense of joy, presupposes an excess, a going beyond the bounds of bare awareness to which the soul has penetrated. Joy is a reaction, albeit a pleasant reaction. But the state Emerson describes is empty of reaction. That is its beneficence, its great gift. Vision undistracted by passion (by hope, gratitude, joy) is vision that is equanimous; Emerson calls it "calm." The passage asserts no reliable distinction between what underlies this present state of mind and what underlies either of those states supposed to be categorically other, between "what is called life, and what is called death."

If "this which I think and feel" is also foundational—is the *same* foundation—for "what is called life, and what is called death," then the all-substantial present, the present made substantial by the clairvoyance of one's seeing of it ("the hour of vision"), is the predicative ground for what we suppose to be different in both magnitude and category. That is what we see when we see the present as it is: without passion, and without comparison, as if it alone were real.

Though it might seem surprising, the impersonal, as instantiated in the passages I have touched on, *leads* to the social in its highest form. In Emerson's words, the "consciousness of . . . divine presence . . . makes society possible" ("The Over-Soul," 2:167). Thus in Emerson's account the impersonal enables the social world it appears to eradicate. "The Over-Soul" offers a rigorous analysis of how the impersonal is incarnated.

The Over-Soul makes itself manifest through particular properties within particular persons, who act as its conduit. This Over-Soul is not an entity, nor is it a property. Call it a manifestation, even always a particular manifestation, though not always the same particular manifestation:

> All goes to show that the soul in man is not an organ, but animates and
> exercises all the organs; is not a function, like the power of memory,
> of calculation, of comparison, but uses these as hands and feet; is not
> a faculty, but a light; is not the intellect or the will, but the master of
> the intellect and the will; is the background of our being, in which

they lie,—an immensity not possessed and that cannot be possessed. From within or from behind, a light shines through us upon things, and makes us aware that we are nothing, but the light is all. A man is the façade of a temple wherein all wisdom and all good abide. What we commonly call man, the eating, drinking, planting, counting man, does not, as we know him, represent himself, but misrepresents himself. Him we do not respect, but the soul, whose organ he is, would he let it appear through his action, would make our knees bend. When it breathes through his intellect, it is genius; when it breathes through his will, it is virtue; when it flows through his affection, it is love. And the blindness of the intellect begins, when it would be something of itself. (2:161)

The passage is precise in its analysis of how this power (not an organ, like Descartes' gland; not a function; not a faculty) becomes embodied *by* organs, by functions, by faculties. The Over-Soul inhabits, vivifies, or traverses the mind, the will, the heart, but it is *not* the mind, the will, the heart. The Over-Soul can be seen in those incarnations through which it "breathes": "genius," "will," "virtue," "love," and "action." Not separate from and also not equal to any particular trait, but also manifesting itself only through recognizable particularities—through actions, emotions, properties, only through what is actual and even at times visible (action would be visible, and genius, will, virtue, love might be so). In Emerson's essay "Nature," transparency cancels being. But the Over-Soul animates and makes being palpable. It is precisely this palpability that compels the personification of tribute: "would [a man] let it appear through his action, [it] would make our knees bend." In fact, it could be argued that it is the Over-Soul's visibility *in* action, function, property, and person that permits us to mistake action, function, property, person for the manifestational power that animates them.

The Over-Soul, then, *is* associated with the individual, though one can have no proprietary relation to it. ("The notions, '*I am*,' and '*This is mine*,' which influence mankind, are but delusions of the mother of the world" ["Illusions," 6:173, Emerson's emphasis].) The trouble begins when the mind falsely identifies with the powers that inhabit it. The mistake lies in associating the Over-Soul with the self and particularly with the voluntary self. It *is* associated with the person, but not as his property, and not through his will (therefore not through "eating," "drinking," "planting," "counting"). These activities misrepresent the person not because they are palpable and also not because they are functional or social but rather because they are limited.

In pointing to something other than the experiential world of the fragmentary (a world whose piecemeal nature he would describe most eloquently in "Experience"), Emerson is not mystically gesturing to an alien nature that he domesticates, converting the not-me into something with recognizable contour. The Over-Soul always remains other, while all the time being all-accessible ("Over-Soul," 2:160). In fact it is precisely the point that we cannot relinquish our difference from it. No procedure is performed that would cancel the egotistical person, the person with interests, needs, desires, will. It is not a matter of willing to be better than we are or different than we are. It is a matter of not-willing, of seeing what we are when the will stops executing its claims. When we give ourselves up to the involuntary, "the walls are taken away. We lie open on one side to the deeps of spiritual nature, to all the attributes of God" ("Over-Soul," 2:161). I take Emerson's spatial image as testifying to the necessarily divided nature of our allegiance to the egotistical and the impersonal. On one side there is access, on the other there is not.

In seeing that one's true alliance is not with will or desire, not with anything piecemeal, but rather with the totality, the personal becomes impersonal. But to put it like this still implies a conventional choice, and I take Emerson to be insisting that at such a moment there is no real choice, no other way to be in *proper* relation. If what's given up by the isolate self is a deluded sense of its power, what's given back is what Emerson, silently quoting Plotinus, calls innocence, that to which the "religious" cedes when it stops being an idea: "The soul gives itself alone, original, and pure, to the Lonely, Original and Pure, who, on that condition, gladly inhabits, leads, and speaks through it. Then is it glad, young, and nimble. It is not wise, but it sees through all things. It is not called religious, but it is innocent" ("The Over-Soul," 2:174–75). Thus in acceding to the impersonal, one is beyond emotions, beyond the idea that identity is fixed. But not beyond the social or the recognizable. We are continuously enjoined to see if we can recognize the impersonal (called "the Over-Soul" or, in "Spiritual Laws," the "homogeneous" [2:93]), though not in the familiar terms by which we customarily mistake it: not connected to sequence, not in relation to the voluntary, and not as an anomaly.

The interest of Emerson's essays lies in moments when the impersonal *emerges*. To put this in different terms: while it has frequently been noted that Emerson's essays dramatize contradiction, the *content* of the contradiction can repeatedly be specified by the process through which the personal becomes the impersonal, as in "Nominalist and Realist" where the science of universals alternates with the science of parts and where nature (one of Emerson's ways of denominating the whole) rises up against persons, specifically against "each person, inflamed to a fury of personality" (3:139). In the following examples, differently epitomized—by the eyes, by moods, by moral law—the impersonal is set against "the fury of personality." This contest takes the place of narrative or *is* the narrative of Emerson's essays.

In the essay "Behavior," allegiance to the universal is immediately articulated by a glance of the eyes. Interestingly, unlike in "Culture," where an adherence to the universal needs to be *learned,* the eyes confess the truth, from one perspective, and penetrate to it from another, immediately and involuntarily. ("The communication by the glance is in the greatest part not subject to the control of the will. It is the bodily symbol of identity of nature" [6:95].) What the eye reveals is the degree of discrepancy between the "generous and universal" and "the fury of personality":

> There are asking eyes, asserting eyes, prowling eyes; and eyes full of
> fate,—some of good, and some of sinister omen. The alleged power
> to charm down insanity, or ferocity in beasts, is a power behind the
> eye.... 'Tis very certain that each man carries in his eye the exact in-
> dication of his rank in the immense scale of men, and we are always
> learning to read it. A complete man should need no auxiliaries to his
> personal presence. Whoever looked on him would consent to his will,
> being certified that his aims were generous and universal. The reason
> why men do not obey us, is because they see the mud at the bottom of
> our eye. ("Behavior," 6:95–96)

Although the beholder reads the eye with respect to an index of behaviors (that pertain to action, to speech, to hospitality, to security), the standard for assessing each remains an alliance of the personal with the universal. The personal is the "mud at the bottom of the eye." The eyes give the lie first to what the person would *have* believed, indicating a discrepancy between what is asserted and what is true; second, they reveal when there is not in fact harmony between one person and another, hence not between the person and the universe, that the "bodily symbol of the identity of nature" (Emerson's presumptive ideal) stands degraded and betrayed. Thus the eyes reveal the personality and reveal *beyond* it. One way of understanding such a divided revelation is to see "the fury of personality" as a mere part of being that inherently also reflects something extrinsic to it. The eyes "are the bodily symbol of identity in nature" because they reveal an impersonal register of value identically legible to all (6:95).

Emerson's representation of the transience of moods further erodes the commonplace idea that mental states are personal and that we govern what occurs "within." "Circles" radically tells us that our moods determine *us*. Further, "our moods do not believe in each other.... I am God in nature; I am a weed by the wall" (2:182). In "Experience" life is described as a flux, "a succession of moods" (3:32). In "Nominalist and Realist" the very propensity to believe in universals over particulars or vice versa is a consequence of shifting moods. Thus so-called fixtures (like truth in "Circles," like perspective in "Nominalist and Realist," but also like temperament in "Experience") are subject to alteration. That there is no security against moods in effect calls into question the idea of any fixture legislating what is thought, believed in, felt, experienced. If every insight, like every mood, is, as Emerson implies, partial, fleeting, and mediate, then we are merely inhabited by these truly extrinsic (hence impersonal) mental states that we host without controlling. They are events in our history without being properly identified as ours. Harry Frankfurt writes: "A person is no more to be identified with everything that goes on in his mind ... than he is to be identified with everything that goes on in his body."[6] Emerson goes more than a step further, suggesting, it would seem, that there is *no* mental experience with which we are to be identified, for there is no permanence to any mood, perception, or belief ("Permanence is a word of degrees" ["Circles," 2:180]) and, further, no ability to determine when, affected by these moods, one experiences the self as "God in nature" or, oppositely, as a "weed by the wall."[7] This extrinsicality, even of those determinations that most apparently define us, is underscored and—from one point of view outrageously—extended in "Uses of Great Men" where Emerson asserts, "The power which [great men] communicate is not theirs. When we are exalted by ideas, we do not owe this to Plato, but to the idea, to which also Plato was debtor" (4:12). Such erasure of identity, such a consistent dramatization (in "Circles," "Experience," "Nominalist and Realist," "Uses of Great Men") of moods as constitutive of belief and even of personality and temperament suggests that moods exist "irrespective of persons," that "moods" like the forces described in "Uses of Great Men" become "power[s] so great, that the potentate is nothing." Moods, like those forces, "destro[y] individualism" (4:14).

Thus, to say, as I did earlier, that mental states are things we "host without controlling," are "events in our history," is still to suppose a personal identity inhabited by moods extrinsic to it, just as to imply an alien physical state (like "the broken sleep" described next) is to suppose an essence to which that physical state is contrastively other. But this sense of contrast is only rhetorical (it has no significant application). Nothing is "ours" except rhetorically, or positionally. In that rhetoric a person lays claims to some elusive property that he cannot really own.

One way of understanding the impersonal then is as something that appears through *bodies* (as visible in the eyes) as a critique of the personal (also visible there), that which shows up its limits, as in the passage I quoted from "Behavior." A second way of understanding the impersonal is in terms of moods and *mental states*—the very moods that we might suppose to define our individual persons, but when scrutinized in Emerson's representations rather contradict the idea of the personal (though not necessarily the idea of the individual, since one could be individuated by mental states that were not properly one's own). Thus if in "Behavior" the impersonal speaks *through* the self (is visible in the eyes), in an essay like "Nominalist and Realist" the impersonal calls into question the very idea of a self as a stable or predictable entity, for the moods that define our perceptions, beliefs, and thoughts are in effect only contingent on circumstance (in "Montaigne," even principles—opinions on right and wrong, on fate and causation—are "at the mercy of a broken sleep or an indigestion" [4:99]). In yet a third example, the impersonal is associated not with the body and not with the affective life of the mind but rather with a law (alternately called "the moral sentiment" [4:103]) to which the "self" adheres, disregarding as it were the conditions of body and mind: "All moods may be safely tried, and their weight allowed to all objections: the moral sentiment as easily outweighs them all.... This faith avails to the whole emergency of life and objects" (4:103). So much so does the ideal of law prevail against body and mind that the ideal survives the degradation of it, passionately represented in the penultimate passage from "Montaigne":

> Charles Fourier announced that "the attractions of man are proportioned to his destinies;" in other words, that every desire predicts its own satisfaction. Yet all experience exhibits the reverse of this; the incompetency of power is the universal grief of young and ardent minds. They accuse the divine Providence of a certain parsimony. It has shown the heaven and earth to every child, and filled him with a desire for the whole; a desire raging, infinite, a hunger as of space to be filled with planets; a cry of famine as of devils for souls. Then for the satisfaction;—to each man is administered a single drop, a bead of dew of vital power, *per day,*—a cup as large as space, and one drop of the water of life in it. Each man woke in the morning with an appetite that could eat the solar system like a cake; a spirit for action and passion without bounds.... but on the first motion to prove his strength,—hands, feet, senses, gave way.... In every house ... this chasm is found,—between the largest promise of ideal power, and the shabby experience. (4:103–4, Emerson's emphasis)

Despite the hyperbolically exampled discrepancies between the ideal and the experienced, the conclusion of the essay adheres to the ideal, though without Fourier's illusions. The personal (what is experienced by the hands, the feet, the senses, and epitomized by an "appetite that could eat the solar system like a cake") is cast aside, not afforded weight, in favor of "the moral sentiment." It is not cast aside because its presence is immaterial, because it does not affect the person. From one point of view it *constitutes* the person's desire, his aspiration, his endeavor, and his voraciousness and registers the thwarting of these. But if such frustration defines the *personal,* from another point of view it does not define the *person* who rather "resist[s] the usurpation of particulars" so as to "penetrate to their catholic sense" (4:104). Here body and mind are subordinated to a manifestation of the impersonal that cannot be assigned to a will or a desiring self. And this impersonal force (called in "Montaigne," as in

"The Divinity School Address," "the law") also becomes the object of our affirmation against the evidence of the personal and, even more to the point, against the interests of the person.

II

In Emerson's writing, style functions as a validation of propositions in lieu of logic or as a supplement to logic, as I shall explain. This distrust of formal argument originates in Emerson's critique of the commonplaces of prayers and sermons. In "The Divinity School Address," against the deadliness of the formalist preacher who substitutes "doctrine" for life, Emerson posits what is impossible to formulate:

> The child amidst his baubles, is learning the action of light, motion, gravity, muscular force; and in the game of human life, love, fear, justice, appetite, man and God, interact. These [divine] laws refuse to be adequately stated. They will not by us or for us be written out on paper, or spoken by the tongue. They elude, evade our persevering thought, yet we read them hourly in each other's faces, in each other's actions, in our own remorse. . . . This sentiment [the perception of lawfulness] is the essence of all religion. (1:77)

In the passage Emerson gets his reader to accede to an important experience that only subsequently is characterized as *religious,* as "the essence of all religion." Religious experience is *integral* to ordinary experience, but because it is not separable from ordinary experience, it is not knowable in terms of easily detachable criteria. Nor can it be articulated, though it cannot help but be intuited. Moreover, arising out of concrete experience, such laws are nonetheless "out of time, out of space, and not subject to circumstance" or summary account (ibid.). They are within and without particular experiences; embodied by experience to which they are nonetheless not reducible. Such "laws," elsewhere cumulatively called "the religious sentiment," are by definition impersonal and in "The Divinity School Address" are repeatedly juxtaposed to the person of Jesus. Such law can be analogized to a natural phenomenon ("It is a mountain air. . . . The silent song of the stars is it" [1:79]); it is knowable *in* nature and often *as* nature. It is also knowable as *depth.* Thus Jesus' "name is not so much written as ploughed into the history of this world." That name is said to be an "infusion" (1:80).

In "Self-Reliance" the impersonal (which alone has depth and thus ultimate reality) is associated with "*Whim*," with the "involuntary," with "genius," and with "intuition" (2:30, 2:37, 2:39, 2:37). In "The Divinity School Address" the impersonal is associated with "the soul." My point here is that, unlike a systematic thinker, Emerson makes no attempt to confer consistency on his designations or even to establish connections among terms that occupy the same structural position in respective essays. Intuition has depth, as the soul has depth, as Jesus' name (in "The Divinity School Address"), which is "ploughed into the history of this world," has depth; but whether these are different terms for the same phenomenon remains, I believe, intentionally unaddressed. The consequence for a reader is to encounter phenomena that clearly overlap without being clearly identical. And this nonidenticality seems a purposeful block to the summarizing definition that could characterize the impersonal but cannot do so here because the experiences in which it is shown to be situated eschew logical "comparative" relations.

If in "The Divinity School Address" Emerson preaches the soul against the religion of the person, in "The Over-Soul" this entity is recognizable as what is "public and human" ("The Over-Soul," 2:175). Though incarnated in form, it always points inward to some identical "nature," some "centre of the world," some "influx of the Divine mind into our mind" (2:164, 2:166). That "influx" is characterized sequentially in one passage as coming on condition of an "entire possession," of coming as "insight," as "serenity," and conclusively (but always nondefinitively) of coming as "grandeur" (2:171). Thus again we note the asymmetry of terms by which manifestations of the impersonal defy systemization: they are connected in this discourse, but not logically. Their originality lies in their deliberately unexplained relations often perceptible as mere contiguity.

But if the designations for the soul keep us off balance through a non-alliance, and if we are commensurately enjoined to renounce description of the soul for habitation within it—that is, if we are enjoined to reside in "that influx of the Divine mind into our mind" (called at this moment "the religious sense")—Emerson does then characterize the experience of such an influx consistently as "enthusiasm," as "extasy," as "trance," or "inspiration," and, "in the case of . . . remarkable persons" like Socrates, Plotinus, George Fox, and Behmen, as what he calls "ravishment" ("The Over-Soul," 2:167). In fact "ravishment" (that proprioceptive sense of what occurs at that moment when the personal is annihilated by the influx of the impersonal) is what the essays attempt to dramatize.

What replaces philosophic logic is something like the representation of ravishment, a phenomenon all the more difficult to recognize because it occurs in relation to experiences that seem at last, as at first, categorically different from each other (the name of Jesus ploughed into the history of the world; the baubles of the child's play ingrained as law; innocence that results when the "soul gives itself, alone, original, and pure, to the Lonely, Original and Pure" [2:174]). There is, moreover, another reason that the representation of moments of ravishment is disorienting. In narrating such moments, Emerson assumes a stance and a voice above and beyond the personal, for his authority in these essays with respect to the "religious sentiment" (elsewhere "innocence," the "soul," "laws that refuse to be adequately stated" ["Divinity School Address," 1:77]) is the authority of one who has access to principles of organization that are conferred beyond individual experience.[8] Hence, for instance, the difficulty in attributing individuality to the voice that says "the soul gives itself, alone, original, and pure."

This is not Emerson's voice because it is Plotinus's.[9] *But* it is not Plotinus's either because *in* Emerson it is legible as no one's voice at all. And that this anonymous voice, which is not a recognizable voice because not legible as a single person's voice, should tell of "ravishment"— ravishment being the precise moment marked in extraordinary persons at "the influx of the Divine mind into our mind"—is remarkable, given the fact that if the imperative for someone voicing the impersonal is access to experience that transcends his own, the imperative for someone voicing ravishment is to inhabit the very experience whose particularity must be owned (and experienced as such) before it is annihilated, if the experience is to register as one of ravishment. Thus the experience being described ("the Divine mind into our mind," the obliteration of the personal, call it, as Emerson does, ravishment) reveals a weird absence, the opposite of which is stylistic mimesis, since nothing counts or registers as "personal" even prior to the epiphanic moment of its proclaimed disappearance.

The voice of no private person, Emerson's voice in his essays is public and is engaged in a performance. What is being performed is something like ravishment as a consequence of self-abandonment. In Emerson's essays the personal is most marked at the moment of its obliteration—or it would be so if it were initially iterated, as it rarely is, in instances like the following. In the most celebrated example, from *Nature,* the self that is lost is briefly first owned: "Standing on the bare ground,—my head bathed by the blithe air, and uplifted into infinite space,—all mean egotism vanishes. . . . I am part or particle of God" (1:10). In this example the person is forfeited for "Universal Being," whereas in "Experience" what is forfeited is something like personal affect: "In the death of my son, now more than two years ago, I seem to have lost a beautiful estate,—no more. I cannot get it nearer to me. . . . This calamity . . . does not touch me" (3:29). In "Circles," self-abandonment is theorized as that philosophically necessary position that makes ravishment possible: "The one thing which we seek with insatiable desire is to forget ourselves, to be surprised out of our propriety, to lose our sempiternal memory, and to do something without knowing how or why; in short, to draw a new circle. . . . The way of life is wonderful: it is by abandonment" (2:190). Typically, however, while the impersonal is ostensibly represented at the moment of its emergence in Emerson, and though this emergence is ostensibly performed, there is characteristically vacancy in the place where we might expect to find a person.

Thus although the essays perform the task of ravishment—that process through which the person is annihilated by the impersonal—no sacrifice is customarily really exacted because rarely is it the case that a discrete or particularized self initially occupies the subject-position. What is great about nature, Emerson argues in an early essay, "The Method of Nature," is "that there is . . . no private will, no rebel leaf or limb, but the whole is oppressed by one superincumbent tendency, obeys that redundancy or excess of life which in conscious beings we call *ecstasy*" (1:127, Emerson's emphasis). We could say that what occupies the subject-position of Emerson's essays—how the voice we call Emerson's implicitly comes to be defined—is as a rhetorical construction whose most enduring feature impedes or staves off any apparent individuality, any representation of a "private will." That is the sine qua non of the Emersonian "I," ostensibly styled without either point of view or idiosyncrasy. (Of course voices in writing are always rhetorically constructed, but the rhetorical construction of Emerson's "I" can be characterized by its fetishized universality, its obsessively constructed anonymity.) The platitudes that often seem stunning in an Emerson essay—stunning that a writer who displays so much expertise in crafting powerful sentences could also write so vapidly—well serve this goal of voicing words whose particular source is undiscoverable. It precisely serves Emerson's purpose to rehearse commonplace remarks that could be spoken by anyone. In "Intellect," we are told that "silence is a solvent that destroys personality, and gives us leave to be great and universal" (2:203). In Emerson's essays contradictory propositions (along with the abstracted "I," constructed at once, as if indiscriminately, out of original, vital images and empty, enervated ones) are the solvent that dissolves personality.

There is a hypnotic and vertiginous momentum to the (much discussed) contradictory drift of these essays that advocate, on the one hand, self-trust and, on the other, self-abolition. Precisely because of this self-contradiction, the essays implicitly promise an overall logic or an argumentative progression that would make sense of and therefore rectify the self-canceling propositions. In lieu of this context—one could say in defiance of it—the propositions, like the self who voices them, are constructed as momentary: good for the moment, but again and again cast off and re-created. The "endless seeker, with no Past at my back" ("Circles," 2:188)—one of Emerson's most wishful self-descriptions—staves off perspective, duration, and therefore questions about limit. The "person" that Emerson represents himself as being is one with no situational givens—one who, like the poet's language in "The Poet," is "fluxional," "vehicular," "transitive," and therefore a man indifferent to needs (3:20). This Emersonian self, the "I" of the essays, can invoke the impersonal, purporting to be embodied by or fed to it (and this without sacrifice, or with "nothing . . . that seems much"), the celebration of which process is said to produce excess, ecstasy, and, alternately, ravishment because his own being is so spectacularly unconstituted by anything *physical*. The Emersonian speaker who celebrates the impersonal is something like the "soul" he frequently catechizes. Or if not a soul, then "a method, a progressive arrangement; a selecting principle" (in "Spiritual Laws," these explicitly constitute the definition of "a man" [2:84]). Or he is an intellect ("intellect goes out of the individual, floats over its own personality"

["Intellect," 2:194]), or a force like love, which we are told "must become more impersonal every day" ("Love," 2:107).

In view of these peculiarities—speech that is unsituated, unreferenced to a body; constituted by contradiction and by nonsummatory arguments; conciliatory with respect to loss ("nothing that can be taken from us seems much" ["Spiritual Laws," 2:77]); and delegating away various properties like love, like intellect—I wish to ask: what is the appeal of the impersonal; what makes it attractive?

The context that might explain the enticement of the impersonal above what Henry Ware Jr., in 1838, writing against Emerson, called "the happiness of human life" is the heroic—a model, or an ideal that, it could be argued, Emerson shares with Kant.[10] Thus for example, when Emerson advocates dismissing "the eating, drinking, planting, counting man" for the Over-Soul, what is being distinguished is personal interest in an entity aspiring to be "something of itself" for the sake of interest in "an immensity not possessed and that cannot be possessed" ("The Over-Soul," 2:161).[11]

When Kant distinguishes the categorical from the hypothetical by saying that in the case of the former "all interest is renounced, which is the specific criterion of categorical as distinguished from hypothetical imperatives,"[12] this self-abnegation sounds peculiarly like Emerson, although Kant is talking about what constitutes the basis of proper (ethical) action and Emerson is talking about what constitutes the basis of proper identification (since the interested or partial man "does not . . . represent himself, but misrepresents himself" ["Over-Soul," 2:161]). For Kant—at least in regard to ethical action—the worth of rational beings lies in their capacity to adhere to "a mere idea" that serves as "an inflexible precept of the will" (in other words, dignity is the result of the autonomy of man's will from "the physical law of [the self's] wants").[13] I call this "heroic" because it presupposes a contact with the real that is not contingent on this or that condition. For Kant "personal worth" consists in adhering to the requirements of pure practical reason independently of inclination (81). Hence, what is involved is choice of nobility. According to the *Fundamental Principles of the Metaphysics of Morals,* only in the moral world "is [a person] his proper self (being as a man only the appearance of himself)" (91). For Emerson, as for Kant, a higher interest and identification with something higher presupposes a person's access to a real stripped of inessentials. Thus in "Worship," "we are never without a hint that these powers [of the senses and the understanding] are mediate and servile, and that we are one day to deal with real being,— essences with *essences*" (6:113–14, emphasis added). The promise of the essays is access to "real being," to being that is further irreducible (at the end of "Worship" called "the superpersonal Heart," the "nameless Power" [6:128]), to contact with the real—a sudden, often apocalyptic encounter with it ("I am nothing. I see all" [*Nature*, 1:10]). In comparison, contingent or personal identity not only misrepresents the self but is in effect trivial. Emerson dismisses the eucharist—the conventional trope for figuring such an encounter—in order to reinvent the necessity of some way of representing unmediated, face-to-face contact with this reality ("real being,—essences with essences") whose fundamental nature must each time be gleaned anew.

It is an unmediated "face to face" that the essays again and again retrieve. They can do this again and again precisely because there is no rite, no symbol or authorized entity—not Christ, not the moral sentiment, not the Over-Soul—nothing *repeatable* to be apprehended in these essays. It is exactly Emerson's point that an encounter with the real cannot be repeated. Hence there is no single name for it and often only negative attributes. Contact is mystified because it is irreducible to anything but style and the idiosyncrasies of style. What is performed is idiosyncrasy. At the emergence of the idiosyncratic formulation, conventional features of the prose—the sententious exhortation ("Trust thyself" ["Self-Reliance," 2:28]); the apostrophe ("O my brothers, God exists" ["Spiritual Laws," 2:81); the aphoristic and pedantic formulation ("The soul's emphasis is always right" ["Spiritual Laws," 2:84]); the propositional banality ("We must go alone" ["Self-Reliance," 2:41])—drop away. The point about the revelatory language that replaces such banal formulations is to dramatize the heuristic, often in arcane images that thwart *understanding* of the exact relation ostensibly being adduced.

One could argue that the ultimate prestige in an Emerson essay depends on the direct discrepancy between a straightforward claim and the eccentric, sometimes grotesque, and often mysteriously physical trope in which it is enveloped—as in the following passage where at one level the experience is recognizable, and at another level it cannot be recognized. The "surprise" part of the following passage, from the second essay "Nature," and the climactic finish in which it is couched, is key to the Emersonian formula. Such a moment cancels the person's servitude to particulars, in effect by illuminating that everything outside of the self is composed of the same elements:

> Man imprisoned, man crystallized, man vegetative, speaks to man impersonated. That power which does not respect quantity, which makes the whole and the particle its equal channel, delegates its smile to the morning, and distils its essence into every drop of rain. Every moment instructs, and every object: for wisdom is infused into every form. It has been poured into us as blood; it convulsed us as pain; it slid into us as pleasure; it enveloped us in dull, melancholy days, or in days of cheerful labor; we did not guess its essence, until after a long time. ("Nature," 3:113–14)

This is a signature Emersonian paragraph. It has all the recognizable components I have been considering: at issue is "essence," in the Emersonian world not only startling when ascertained but also violent, as the verbs imply; a power that affects physical being through pain (as the word "convulsed" reiterates), but also through pleasure (as the word "slid" reiterates), raising an irrelevant question about a potentially confused relation between pleasure and pain and about conferred physicality in general ("is infused . . . has been poured"). It is easy to forget the *subject* of such a passage. (What is difficult about the passage is the constant drifting of reference and a syntax that can't be sustained because this would keep persons in their place.) Most immediately, that subject is "wisdom," the antecedent of "it." But it is wisdom about "Power" ("Nature," 3:113), and if we read back further still, it is wisdom about the power of the *general*—the ability to see that what is said to "exist in the mind as [an] ide[a]" in nature is forever embodied (3:113). The ultimate discovery, then, concerns a perceived *identity* among animal, vegetable, mineral, between mind and nature. And the specific gesture accomplished by style here (as well as by the asymmetry of terms such as "moments" and "objects," which are given syntactical equality, both being subjects of "instructs") is to make such identity unmistakable. There would be a discrepancy between container (the human body) and thing contained (the blood) because of the latter's source in the world, which we could assume to be substantial, were it not the case that all aspects of the passage are at work to critique a term like "discrepancy" to refer to a phenomenon the confrontation of which—the seeing it face to face—cancels any distinction between "the whole and the particle." Therefore essence can be spoken of in terms of drops of rain *and* in terms of human blood. Nature is not outside of us. If we can't oversee nature, that is not because it is alien but rather because it is internal. These half-implicit propositions are enacted by style. They could never be made in logical form because such terms would subvert the "originary" impulse of these essays, which generate endless text in order to dramatize the essayist's encounter with the "catholic sense" of things, a sense that is best discoverable again and again at the core of one's own being.[14] Being in all cases what the essays have worked toward (often in explicit and trite formulation), the tenor of such a passage and its denotative meaning is all but unmistakable—it is never in doubt—while the vehicle, as well as the statement's residue, characteristically prohibits easy, or even intelligible, formulation (as in the indecipherable relation between "man impersonated" and "man imprisoned").

Thus oddly enough, although the goal of these essays *is* generality (however it is called) and although the style is often inimitably general—Emerson writing in no man's voice—the point of the essays' climactic figures is the representation of an encounter whose truth is somehow tied to its stylistic or rhetorical singularity. The untransmissible trope, irreducible to symbol or rite and buried in unmistakable, often clichéd figuration, counts as evidence in lieu of evidence that the author of the essay—in distinction to the reader whose tutelage the author implicitly takes on—has knowledge of an encounter with ultimate reality. In this way Emerson's banal assertions combine with his solecisms to produce a style whose inimitability serves a logical function.

I have argued that in Emerson's essays what is dramatized is the fact that the impersonal speaks despite us, though *through* us (it is visible in the eyes), even as it perpetually (in the transformation of moods) calls the idea of a fixed self into question or is otherwise seen as an alternative to moods (in the fixture of the "moral sentiment"), something having a stability no experienced self could have. But this impersonality is not, for Emerson, abstractly dissociated from the idea of self. It is viscerally represented as what must be "own[ed]" by the very self with which it is understood not to be identical.[15]

When Emerson recommends "own[ing]" what is other, this endorses a logic equivalent to Hegel's idea that the single individual is incomplete Spirit. But, readers commonly object, while Emerson has the right to sacrifice his personal interest—the interest of *his* person—to that universal spirit, he does not have the right to sacrifice another's personal interest to it or for something higher. He can neither ethically approve such a sacrifice for others nor ethically recommend it to them. Nor can he define interest (whether higher or lower) for another. Moreover, he cannot define *his* interest as equivalent to another's. He cannot assume that *his* higher interest is precisely *theirs*. He has no authority to do so. Although this complaint is posed by readers who object to Emerson's social conservatism (as discussed in the next section), such a question about authority is in my view also raised by a more theoretical question about what kind of alliance to, and difference from, other persons a speaker must acknowledge or prove in order to speak on their behalf. The subject of authority and legitimacy with respect to another's interest raises the odd question of whether Emerson speaks on his own behalf.

III

The subject of authority might be usefully examined in relation to William Ellery Channing. When Channing writes "We conceive that the true love of God is a moral sentiment" and "We see God around us because he dwells within us," such sentences sound like Emerson's. But they are not in fact comparable, for what authorizes Channing's assertions is his position as a minister—specifically, it is as a minister that he has authority to create analogies between the human and the divine and to show they are *only* analogies. For Channing the source of divinity is not the impersonal but is rather the *person* of "God the Father and quickener of the human mind."[16]

To make statements about the divinity of the soul without authority is to make them *casually,* to construct or imagine them. No tradition is being explained in such statements; rather, something is being composed and invented against tradition. But why trust this invention about a universal that demands the same sacrifice as conventional religion without any of its compensations? Moreover, although Emerson proclaims a nonsectarian universal, we have only to look at Emerson's distinctions—and his dismissal of those distinctions—to see that persons are not always the undifferentiated beings constructed by the prose. The great shame of Emerson, as his detractors observe, is his callous indifference to the very social distinctions he occasionally recognizes.

"Compensation" of course *denies* social distinction by immediately trivializing it: "In the nature of the soul is the compensation for the inequalities of condition. . . . The heart and soul of all men being one, this bitterness of *His* and *Mine* ceases. His is mine" (2:72, Emerson's emphasis). But except in the verbal world of the essay there is no impersonality of ownership. *His* is not *mine.* Nor do "we all take turns at the top" as "Nominalist and Realist" would have it (3:140). This barbarous idealism infects all of the writing. Emerson's capitalist economic theory, his proprietary individualism, sanctions the drama of social injustice by denying its existence (as in the citations above) or by *justifying* its existence as in the following from his early book *Nature:*[17] "Debt, grinding debt, whose iron face the widow, the orphan, and the sons of genius fear and hate;—debt, which consumes so much time, which so cripples and disheartens a great spirit with cares that seem so base, is a preceptor whose lessons cannot be foregone, and is needed most by those who suffer from it most" (1:24). In writing that *denies* the differences of persons, that *justifies* those differences, or that *deprecates* the acknowledgment of difference as petulant, finally, in writing that, as above, sees "grinding debt" as moral and as imposing a moral that some require and others, differently, do not—how, but as barbarous, shall we read "All loss, all pain is particular: the universe remains to the heart unhurt" ("Spiritual Laws," 2:77)? For it looks suspiciously as if what is being made light of is someone else's pain. What one wants, given the dissonance in Emerson's writing between an impersonality that enables by providing access beyond one's own limited self-interest and an impersonality that imperiously dismisses others' interest, is something like the Kantian acknowledgment of happiness. Kant does not deny the legitimacy of either happiness or interest; he merely specifies that neither may be consulted as motivations for moral action. And while the categorical imperative is the same for all—unlike things, all beings have unconditional value and must be treated as ends in themselves—one function of that imperative is to prescribe certain duties, among them beneficence. But if one has a duty to promote another's happiness, this involves the recognition that there are different specifications of that general end. In other words, the Kantian universal or categorical imperative does not preclude the idea of individuals at variance with each other; in fact it presupposes that difference. The Kantian universal does not presuppose impersonality. What one wants in Emerson is the acknowledgment of the legitimacy of material self-interest. In addition, one wants something to separate those statements that enlarge the idea of (one's own) interest from those that annihilate the idea of (another's) interest.

It is in the context of Emerson's failed acknowledgment of material difference in a social world that I return to the subject of the heroic, for the acknowledgment of singularity, and so of difference, is conceptually central to the idea of the heroic and therefore to the Emersonian impersonal, from which it may seem so dissociated. I refer here to something like a reinvented American heroic (reinvented in the sense that its emphasis on the face-to-face confrontation with the divine is originally Homeric as well as Old Testament), a heroic as it is reimagined by Whitman, Dickinson, Melville, and Thoreau. When Whitman, in "Crossing Brooklyn Ferry," says, "Floodtide below me, I see you face to face! . . . you furnish your parts toward the soul";[18] when Dickinson's speaker is stopped dead in "Our Journey had advanced" by "Eternity's White Flag—Before— / And God—at every Gate—";[19] finally when Melville in *Moby-Dick* constructs tragedy and in *Pierre* and *The Confidence Man* the parody of tragedy upon the *masking* of a face, these pivotal moments recall exactly the logic of Emerson's impersonal. In so doing, they also, indirectly by counterexample, reveal the source of its deficiency.

What deprives Emerson of the authority to speak of the soul's manifestations of divinity is not after all—or, precisely, not *at* all—that his pronouncements are personal rather than ministerial. Conversely, what deprives Emerson's voice of authority is that his statements are *insufficiently* personal, except in the passages I have discussed, and there only by inference. That is, their authority is neither functional *nor* personal. The *content* of Emerson's impersonal implies a heroic *context*: an encounter with the real, however indecipherable its name, the "own[ing]" of that encounter, as well as an acknowledgment of the real or, in the language of "Character," the "*know[ing of] its face*" (3:67, emphasis added). But the heroic implies a *person's* contact with the real. This source and this source alone gives it authority, as Dickinson, Whitman, Melville, and, of course,

Thoreau knew. Emerson, strangely, *doesn't* know this. He invents a mode of discourse dissociated from the institutionally religious. He produces a discourse that has access to the real prior to the mediating symbol or rite whose necessity it obviates. The legitimacy of that discourse therefore depends on the visibility of the person speaking. It depends on the fact that an epiphanic encounter occurs to someone *in particular* who, by virtue of that particularity, is in a position to describe it. But except in the essay's climactic moments—moments that, as I've argued, are typified by their idiosyncrasy—Emerson then erodes the representation of any self-articulated distinction that would make his discourse legible and meaningful. Not able to countenance or represent what differences himself, he similarly betrays the differences of others, which he either denies or denigrates. Thus Emerson is unable to represent the encounter for the sake of which his discourse exists—for there is ultimately no one to whom that encounter happens. The deficiency in Emerson's representation of the impersonal lies peculiarly in the missing sense of the person. The power of such an encounter could therefore only be rhetorical. The "person" of Emerson—by which I mean something like the invented persona, Foucault's author-function—is not visible, except through style, and except perhaps in "The Poet," one essay where a person comes frontally into view.

In "The Poet," we are offered serial descriptions of what imprisons us ("the custody of that body in which [we are] pent up" [3:16]); of "the inaccessibleness of every thought but that we are in" (3:19); of our phlegmatic nature and of how the poet—"a beholder of ideas, and an utterer of the necessary and causal" (3:6)—can liberate us. Among his many skills, he "invite[s]" us "into the science of the real" (3:8). In other words, the poet makes our birthright discoverable to us. Significantly, he can do this because "beside his privacy of power as an individual man, there is a great public power, on which he can draw, by unlocking, at all risks, his human doors" (3:15–16). ("Public" here means something like "universal.") The poet is, therefore, a transformer: he is free and he makes us free. The mechanism for escape, called here "true nectar," is "the ravishment of the intellect by coming nearer to the fact" (3:16). (Such immanence is marked by a talismanic naming precisely coincident with the poet's liberation "from the custody of that body," and from "that jail-yard of individual relations in which he is enclosed" [ibid.].) "Ravishment" is a word we encountered before, in the context of "the influx of the Divine mind into our mind." In "The Poet" the "fact" occasioning ravishment is a man's "passage out into free space" (ibid.). As elsewhere, ravishment signals the transformation whereby the person vanishes into what is "own[ed]" as other. But one difference between this and the other essays is the fixture of "The Poet" at the nexus of transformation, the act and iteration of which is, as it were, diffused throughout the essay. There is no climactic moment at which the transformation could be said to be performed.

Power, a "*dream*-power . . . transcending all limit and privacy" "intoxicates" the poet ("Power," 3:23, Emerson's emphasis; 3:17). But it does not intoxicate thoroughly enough. For though the essay tirelessly dramatizes the poet in relation to his liberating task, this very repetition produces a felt sense of *what* is being transformed, specifically of the person prior to his emergence from the private and the individual, therefore of a person locked in his thought, limited by self-identification and excluded from full expressiveness. In "The Poet" the transformation from the personal to the impersonal does not occur. The essay ends by resorting to a promissory note on what will be performed but is *not yet* performed ("I look in vain for the poet whom I describe" [3:21]). While the poet is not visible, the one who calls him into being is precisely visible as a presence whose rhetoric fails. If we ask, with Foucault, "What are the modes of existence of this discourse?" and "Who can assume these various subject functions?" then a response would gesture toward the crossed viewpoints that the essay inevitably expresses. On the one hand the reference for the speaking voice is the *un*emancipated person who anticipates the poet, but on the other, the poet being evoked also seems referenced to the subject-position we call "Emerson." The one who calls for the poet, who calls the poet forth, is the one who knows enough of bondage not to be wholly or even mainly defined by freedom. Thus the essay charts two positions and has a double voice. The all-consuming frenzy ("ravishment") epitomized at the essay's end by the figure of "transparent boundaries" ("The Poet," 3:24) is repeatedly contested by the essay's enumerated impediments (caves, cellars, prisons, drifts, chains, pans and barrows, stuttering and stammering, jail-yards) that the frenzy can't vanquish. These movements, or subject-positions, are inseparable in Emerson's "The Poet." In the space of their negotiation a person is almost legible, making credible, as well as meaningful, an idea of the impersonal incompletely realized again and again in the space of this essay.

Modern criticism shows the point at which the idea of the impersonal is completely detached from religion, which initially gave it life (either traditionally defined as sourced by a God or Law, or alternatively defined—as Whitman, Dickinson, Melville define it—as sourced by a spectacle of the real apprehended by a person). Emerson proleptically marks the moment when the idea of the person is evacuated from the scene of the impersonal. The discourse that remains exhibits an apparently unrecognized nostalgia for the idea of the person on whom the impersonal is imagined to register. This is how I understand the odd pathos of the summary accounts that make a gesture of dramatizing the impersonal even as they retreat from actualizing such a confrontation in the climactic or figural moments whose style I discussed in the passage about "man impersonated."[20] Yet as I have suggested, something is deficient in Emerson's representations, and this deficiency directly pertains to the understood relation between impersonality and individuation. I conclude by elaborating the contours of this relation as it is made visible by two sets of reflections upon it.

In *Time and the Other*, Levinas posits a state of impersonality that *precedes* individuation; in *Reasons and Persons* Parfit posits a state of impersonality that *constitutes* individuation. I want briefly to consider these two notions for the light that, albeit differently, they shed on Emerson's relation to his central construct of impersonality. Levinas distinguishes between existing and an existent, between an anonymous and impersonal "there is" and a state of consciousness "where an existent is put in touch with his existing," hence with his materiality and solitude. In Levinas's account the anonymous, impersonal state precedes the formation of a material "I" for whom suffering is a direct consequence of being imprisoned in the experience of personal identity. Thus, "solitude is not tragic because it is the privation of the other, but because [the self] is shut up within the captivity of its identity, because it is matter." The experience of the "I am" is, therefore, what Levinas calls "enchainment."[21] Parfit also argues that the idea of personal identity enchains. But for Parfit, in a passage I cited earlier, that idea is understood to be *false*:

> We are not separately existing entities, apart from our brains and bodies, and various interrelated physical and mental events. Our existence just involves the existence of our brains and bodies, and the doing of our deeds, and the thinking of our thoughts, and the occurrence of certain other physical and mental events. Our identity over time just involves . . . psychological connectedness and/or psychological continuity.[22]

In this Reductionist view there is no deeper fact—no spiritual substance (or soul), no purely mental construct (a Cartesian pure ego), no separate physical entity "of a kind that is not yet recognized in the theories of contemporary physics," nor any other ineffable essence—to which we can ascribe identity (210). (The consequence of this, Parfit argues, is that there is no distinct entity that constitutes identity, that the unity of consciousness and the unity over time need not be accounted for by the claim that "the experiences in this person's life are had by this person" who is a separately existing entity [210]. Such unities can rather be explained by the relations of psychological connection and continuity; we can therefore understand our life in an impersonal way, and the Reductionist view has radical moral consequences.)[23]

What strikes me, it might seem randomly, is the subject of resistance, even "suffering" (Levinas's term), which attends both discussions of impersonality. For Levinas personal identity is the *cause* of suffering, while for Parfit, at least initially, the absence of personal identity has central afflictive power. (Ultimately Parfit will claim that the impersonal view is not only the more beneficial but is also personally consoling: "It makes me less concerned about my own future, and my death" [347].)

There is, however, a compelling moment in a chapter titled "Is the True View Believable?" in which Parfit, who has been arguing against the absence of some deep fact beyond physical and psychological continuity—no soul, no pure ego, no extrapolated physical presence that would testify to a person's unique, unreplicable identity—exemplifies, shockingly, the practical implications of his austere theory. In relation to a science-fiction fable that Parfit invents to preface his analysis of the *absence* of any extra identificatory essence on which discrete personhood could be founded, he asks whether the idea of being replicated (physically and psychologically) and teletransported to Mars produces someone who *"would* be *me"* or "someone else who has been made to be exactly *like* me" (200, 201; emphasis added). The question here is whether if the Replica is qualitatively identical with me, but not numerically identical with me, the Replica is the same person as I am (see 201). Parfit concludes his discussion by arguing that there is nothing extra that would define me (like a soul or a cogito) that could make such a question intelligible:

> When I fear that, in Teletransportation, *I* shall not get to Mars, my fear is that the abnormal cause may fail to produce this further fact. As I have argued, there is no such fact. What I fear will not happen, *never* happens. I want the person on Mars to be me in a specially intimate way in which no future person will ever be me. My continued existence never involves this deep further fact. What I fear will be missing is *always* missing. Even a space-ship journey would not produce the further fact in which I am inclined to believe.
>
> When I come to see that my continued existence does not involve this further fact, I lose my reason for preferring a space-ship journey. But, judged from the standpoint of my earlier belief, this is not because Teletransportation is *about as good as* ordinary survival. It is because ordinary survival is *about as bad as,* or little better than, Teletransportation. *Ordinary survival is about as bad as being destroyed and having a Replica.* (279–80, emphasis in orginal)

Ordinary survival is as bad as being destroyed and replicated because ordinary survival does not presuppose anything that would distinguish a self as a discrete separate entity whose personal identity matters. What the truth about ordinary survival destroys is the idea of the person and the personal.

I mark these moments in Levinas and Parfit because, albeit to different ends, they represent a *person's* resistance to the idea of impersonality nonetheless being expounded.[24] Suffering is occasioned by the friction of *feeling* oneself a person (Levinas's "I am") where such a feeling is shown to be unfounded. There cannot help but be resistance to the idea of the impersonal since the consequences of the impersonal destroy being the only way we think we know it.

But Emerson's accounts of the impersonal exist without such acknowledgment, uncontaminated by resistance and free of any hint of the registration of suffering whose expression might taint them. It is as if the perspective from which Emerson's words are voiced is an imaginary perspective, purified of unideal motivation. Emerson's perspective does not take into account what thwarts the ideal or how it might affect the voice that is propounding it. The plea for impersonality has been evacuated of religious content. Yet there is something evasive, incomplete, and empty about the fact that Emerson does not acknowledge what replaces the idea of a God, as if the idea of God had not actually been dismissed but had rather been transferred to the omniscient speaking voice (hence Nietzsche's valorization of Emerson). That is, Emerson does not take the responsibility a person should take for his words and therefore betrays the complexity of a person's response to their desirability. But can there be real knowledge of the impersonal if its consequences, and even its constitutive terms, remain unintelligible? If one tries to answer the question "What is a person?" no answer with any coherent substance can be produced with reference to Emerson's writing.

One of the reasons Emerson fails to acknowledge others' suffering, which is never very real to him, is that he fails to acknowledge his own suffering, which is never very real to him. I don't mean to suggest that suffering, or any other displayed affect, is a criterion for successful theorization. But I do mean to repeat one last time that Emerson's words are iterated in a register unmarked by the ambivalence that, one might suppose, would challenge a wholehearted endorsement of a machine as undiscriminated as a superpersonal Heart, an immeasurable mind, or an Over-Soul. Ambivalence to the impersonal is the one contradiction Emerson successfully resists. Yet, as Parfit makes clear, if we assume the truth of the impersonal, "ordinary survival is about as bad as being destroyed and having a Replica." Thus Emerson does not become accountable to the implication of his words, which are voiced without penetrating. It is as if, in his sentences, his life failed to be experienced as his own. If this is a supreme fulfillment of the imperative of impersonality—to speak without the registration of any affect that would contest the *construct* of impersonality—it nonetheless leaves undisclosed the *experience* of impersonality (ravishment), to which the essays, from first to last, seductively promise access.

NOTES

1. Derek Parfit, *Reasons and Persons* (Oxford: Oxford University Press, 1984), ix.

2. Parfit's argument contains two strands that I find productive for thinking about Emerson's "impersonal." The first strand involves Parfit's claim that there is no substantial entity in virtue of which it is true to say of a person that he is the "same" person over time. (Selfhood, or what Parfit calls "the unity of our lives" [*Reasons and Persons,* 446] is a complex relation among psychological states capable of degrees we can affect.) The second strand is more specifically ethical and pertains to the relation between self-interest and concern for other persons. Parfit links these two strands through the suggestion that a change in our view of the conditions of personal identity can rationally lead us to a more impersonal concern for the quality of human experiences, regardless of *whose* experiences they are.

3. Ralph Waldo Emerson, *The Collected Works of Ralph Waldo Emerson,* ed. Alfred R. Ferguson, Robert E. Spiller, et al., 8 vols. to date (Cambridge, Mass.: Harvard University Press, Belknap Press, 1971–2010), 3:138–39. Subsequent quotations from Emerson's writing are from this source and are cited parenthetically in text by volume and page numbers. Citations may include essay title if the essay from which a quotation is taken is not clear from the text.

4. Emerson's primary understanding of the meaning of *person* and of *personality* (hence of impersonality) originated with the sense of the three-personed God. Despite the fact that Webster, following Johnson, in 1828 never mentions that there's a millennial idea of person bound up with the idea of Christ, Emerson certainly would have known this from Patristic sources. Thus although Emerson uses the idea of the impersonal as if its divinity is part of his intuitive sense of the word, rather than part of its etymology, when he brings in the idea of God, what he is bringing in is the long history of "person" associated with the theology of the Trinity.

In fact what Emerson inherits is a misunderstanding. For the word *person* when it pertains to God was not originally meant to indicate an individual but rather to denote a way of subsisting, a way of being, a hypostasis. Not pertaining to aspects of God, nor to mythological intermediaries for God, and certainly not to any modern sense of individual, the Trinity originally implied a sameness of divine essence through three modes that belied the idea of "person as individual" that Emerson found so abhorrent. See the entry by M. J. Dorenkemper, "Person (In Theology)," in *New Catholic Encyclopedia,* ed. Catholic University of America, 18 vols. (New York: McGraw Hill, 1967), 11:168–70, for the sense of *person* as Emerson would have inherited it. For the more modern, philosophical sense of person as self, as in *personality,* see J. Ellis McTaggert on "Personality," in *Encyclopedia of Religion and Ethics,* ed. James Hastings, 13 vols. (New York, 1908; reprint, Kessinger Publishing, 2003), 11:773–81.

For a historically nuanced account of Emerson's complex relation to "individuality," see Sacvan Bercovitch's clarifying discussion of the understanding of *individualism* Emerson inherited from the socialists, of his reconception of this idea in the 1840s as a "vision of cosmic subjectivity" (opposed to socialism), and of his ultimate understanding in the 1850s of individuality as allied with industrial-capitalist "Wealth" and "Power" (Sacvan Bercovitch, "Emerson, Individualism, and Liberal Dissent," in *The Rites of Assent: Transformations in the Symbolic Construction of America* [New York: Routledge, 1993], 310, 323, 330, 340). Bercovitch charts the shifts in Emerson's understanding of individualism as it moves from the utopian to the ideological, but in doing so he fascinatingly demonstrates the dynamic relation between these impulses throughout Emerson's thought and writing.

5. All major critics of Emerson have understood that if one threat to self-reliance is conformity, the other is petty self-interest or self-cherishing. See, for instance, Barbara Packer's discussion of self-reliance and self-abandonment (self-reliance, in Packer's account, rests not on "persons but powers") (B. L. Packer, *Emerson's Fall: A New Interpretation of the Major Essays* [New York: Continuum International, 1982], 137–47); Harold Bloom's analysis of the dialectical relation between an "Apollonian Self-Reliance" and a "Dionysian influx," the latter often perceptible as ecstatic energy that transforms mere individualism (Harold Bloom, "Emerson and Influence," in *A Map of Misreading* [New York: Oxford University Press, 1975], 166); Richard Poirier's discussion of "genius," as countering the self as a conventionally defined entity, genius being what is not psychological, not moral or political, not stable, indeed not recognizable— rather, to be seen as something "vehicular, transitive, mobile," something performed in writing (Richard Poirer, "The Question of Genius," in *The Renewal of Literature: Emersonian Reflections* [New York: Random House, 1987], 89–90). I understand Emerson's "impersonality" to be *related* to, but not identical with, Poirier's "genius," Bloom's "energy," Packer's "powers"; impersonality is his corrective to the deformation of personal identity. These terms rely on a neoplatonic, upward, sublimatory movement away from material particularity, whereas Emerson's impersonal moves in the opposite direction. For in impersonality Emerson is elaborating a paradox that truth to the self involves the discovery of its radical commonness.

An important contribution to this debate is George Kateb's *Emerson and Self-Reliance* (Thousand Oaks, Calif.: Sage, 1995), a book notable on a number of counts. First, he presents an excellent discussion of how antagonism and contrast lie at the heart of Emerson's notion of identity. Specifically, Kateb claims that Emerson's self-reliance depends on an acknowledgment of the otherness and impersonality one might suppose antithetical to it (17). "Impersonality registers an individual's universality or infinitude" (31). In this registration what is reduced is the "'biographical ego'" and one acts "at the behest of 'the grand spiritual Ego,' at the behest, that is, of one's impersonal reception of the world" (33). Second, Kateb correctly associates Emerson's impersonality with the religious: "Emerson is ravenously religious. Anything in the world . . . matters and is beautiful or sublime only if seen and thought of as part of a designed, intentionally coherent totality; indeed as an emanation of divinity" (65). But, third, Kateb tries to divorce the idea of the impersonal from the religious (because its piety embarrasses him and because it appears to him that the driving thrust for unity, at the heart of the religious, betrays Emerson's commitment to antagonism). Kateb approves of Emerson's sense of the "interconnectedness" of things; he likes the idea of affinity, but not the idea of an "all" or a "one" with which "interconnectedness" is integral in Emerson's thought. But the very impersonality so crucial to Kateb's explanation of self-reliance is also, I will argue, inseparable from the religiousness from which Kateb would sever it. The radicalness Kateb admires depends on the "religiousness" that he fears trivializes it. Also central in this context is Stanley Cavell's "Aversive Thinking: Emersonian Representations in Heidegger and Nietzsche," in *Conditions Handsome and Unhandsome: The Constitution of American Perfectionism* (Chicago: University of Chicago Press, 1990), 33–63, an earlier, important reading of "Self-Reliance," antagonism, and transfiguration. Cavell understands Emerson's "moral perfectionism" as specifying a structure within the self that requires constant "martyrdom" (56). In other words, in Cavell's analysis of Emerson, as in his reading of Nietzsche, the "higher" self is not elsewhere or other, but is located "within." In this idea of perfectionism the self is not fixed, but neither is it absent. Perfectionism, so defined, supposes a structure essentially more conservative than that of impersonality.

6. Harry Frankfurt, "Identification and Externality," in *The Identities of Persons,* ed. Amélie Oksenberg Rorty (Berkeley: University of California Press, 1976), 242. Frankfurt's preliminary distinction between desires that are external to a self and those that are identified with it revolves around a decision made with respect to these desires (a decision rather than an attitude, for a decision, unlike an attitude, cannot be disowned). See 243–50 for what kind of decision qualifies a desire for being situated outside the person.

7. In this connection, see also this passage in "Montaigne": "There is the power of moods, each setting at naught all but its own tissue of facts and beliefs" (4:99). This passage, and the essay as a whole, are brilliant for the way in which

they ventriloquize the absoluteness of point of view conferred by a mood that another mood undermines. Understood in terms of the "machinery" of moods registered in the essay, there is only "rotation" of all "the states of mind" (ibid.).

8. In Emerson's "Experience," such moments of impersonal authority are dispersed across that essay after its initial pages. "Experience" dramatizes the slide of the personal to the impersonal, when the dissociation of a particular, personal experience (grief at the death of Emerson's five-year-old child) is discovered to be the spectacularly undifferentiated common denominator of *all* experience—the mirror in which the features of all experience can be read. "Experience" therefore atypically makes visible a person's relation to impersonality. See "Representing Grief: Emerson's 'Experience,'" in Sharon Cameron, *Impersonality: Seven Essays* (Chicago: University of Chicago Press, 2006), 53–78.

9. Emerson echoes a line from *The Enneads* (1.6.7) but not an idea, in the sense that for Plotinus impersonality is the result of an ontological change: in Plotinus the self or personality is there to be relinquished. In distinction, Emerson's text is more radical since, however oddly, as I will argue, impersonality characterizes both sides of the conversion marked by the passages discussed. See Pierre Hadot's discussion of the "levels" of self in *Plotinus, or The Simplicity of Vision*, trans. Michael Chase (Chicago: University of Chicago Press, 1993), 23–24, as well as Arnold I. Davidson's introduction to that volume, "Reading Hadot Reading Plotinus," 1–15.

Emerson's Plotinus was most likely from Thomas Taylor's 1817 *Selected Works*. See Walter Harding's *Emerson's Library* (Charlottesville: University of Virginia Press, 1967), 217.

10. Henry Ware Jr., *Personality of the Deity* (Boston, 1838), 12. In Ware's reply to Emerson's "Divinity School Address," this happiness is directly attributable to "the interest the soul takes in persons." For Ware, to destroy personality is effectively to annihilate everything recognizable, including divinity.

11. In using the word "heroic" here I have in mind what Gregory Nagy identifies as that nobility or honor that in Homer and the Bible are a direct consequence of a face-to-face encounter with God or with another heroic human. See Gregory Nagy, *The Best of the Achaeans: Concepts of the Hero in Archaic Greek Poetry* (Baltimore, Md.: Johns Hopkins University Press, 1979). Emerson reimagines something like the idea of the heroic in the presumption of a direct confrontation with the Over-Soul, the superpersonal Heart, the immeasurable mind, while in Kant this direct access to something ultimate is epitomized by moral law, possible to realize if all empirical interest is subordinated to it. It is the direct apprehension of something supreme or ultimate that in both cases suggests what might appear a bizarre analogy to the heroic. For an analogous contemporary reimagining of the heroic as defined by the immediacy of encounter

with the divine or with an ultimate reality in the human, see Thomas Carlyle, *On Heroes, Hero-Worship, and the Heroic in History,* ed. Carl Niemeyer (1841; Lincoln: University of Nebraska Press, 1966).

12. Immanuel Kant, *Fundamental Principles of the Metaphysics of Morals,* trans. T. K. Abbott (Amherst, N.Y.: Prometheus, 1988), 60.

13. Ibid., 68.

14. Such an erasure of distinction between container and thing contained, between self and universe, is repeatedly enacted in Emerson's off-scale representations of the human, as in this formulation from "Character": "a man should be so large and columnar in the landscape, that it should deserve to be recorded, that he arose, and girded up his loins, and departed to such a place" (3:63). Or as in this one from "Montaigne": The universe "has shown the heaven and earth to every child, and filled him with a desire for the whole; a desire raging, infinite; a hunger, as of space to be filled with planets" (4:103–4). In the first example, what is human and personal is matched to the landscape, is given its dimensions, as in the second example desire is matched to the stratosphere. These reconstructed propositions of the human, the human made gargantuan, are a reciprocal gesture, an accommodation in scale to the "catholic sense" of things (4:104).

15. See, for instance, the last paragraph of "Character" where the language of ownership for what is alien is explicit. Here *identifying* (in the sense of detecting) "the holy sentiment we cherish" quickly turns into *identification with* it ("only the pure and aspiring can know its face, and the only compliment they can pay it, is to own it") (3:67). Such ownership is understood in terms of a religious discovery.

16. William Ellery Channing, *Unitarian Christianity and Other Essays,* ed. Irving H. Bartlett (New York, 1957), 31, 92, 108.

17. Examples of both types of statement appear frequently in the essays. Of the first type, see, for instance, all of "Compensation" and the philosophy of "Gifts," which presumes that all have enough; for the second kind of statement, see *Nature* for an implicit critique of "the private poor man" (1:12); "Intellect," which critiques "he who is immersed in what concerns person or place" (2:194); and "Prudence" for a dismissal of that class that needs to be concerned with health and wealth. Finally there is a third category of statement that deserves mention in this context—those statements that dismiss the idea of social reform because you can't reform society if you don't first reform the self (the argument of "New England Reformers"). If suffering is one's own fault, or the fault of one's too limited identification (the argument of "Spiritual Laws"), one can, according to "Fate," rectify it accordingly: "So far as a man thinks, he is free" (6:13).

18. Walt Whitman, "Crossing Brooklyn Ferry," in *Leaves of Grass* (New York: New York University Press, 1980), 144, 149, secs. 1, 9.

19. Emily Dickinson, "Our Journey had advanced" (no. 453), in *The Poems of Emily Dickinson: Reading Edition,* ed. R. W. Franklin (Cambridge, Mass.: Harvard University Press, Belknap Press, 1998), 209.

20. Both nostalgia and rhetorically heightened summary equally testify to an eviscerated religious sense and, I have argued, to a deficient sense of the individual. They testify to a religious sense that is dismissed incompletely, that is absent but not forgotten. In the space of that absence autobiography will ultimately link up with philosophy as a newly constructed subject. This is epitomized by Nietzsche's *Ecce Homo* (trans. Walter Kaufmann [New York: Vintage, 1969]) and differently attested to by Derrida's *The Ear of the Other: Otobiography, Transference, Translation* (trans. Peggy Kamuf and Avital Ronell, ed. Christie McDonald [Lincoln: University of Nebraska Press, 1988]) on the one hand, and Cavell's *A Pitch of Philosophy: Autobiographical Exercises* (Cambridge, Mass.: Harvard University Press, 1994), on the other.

Nietzsche presumes a separation of autobiography and philosophy that *Ecce Homo* will rectify. The exceptionalism of his position is continuously reiterated there. For instance: "I only attack causes against which I would not find allies, so that I stand alone—so that I compromise myself alone" (232). Derrida, writing about *Ecce Homo,* asserts, "Let it be said that I shall not read Nietzsche as a philosopher (of being, of life, or of death) or as a scholar or scientist if these three types can be said to share the abstraction of the bio-graphical and the claim to leave their lives and names out of their writing" (*The Ear of the Other,* 7). Cavell argues that "philosophy's arrogance is linked to its ambivalence toward the autobiographical" and that, following Austin and Wittgenstein whose methods demand an engagement of the philosophical with the autobiographical, he will "think about an autobiographical dimension of philosophy, together with a philosophical dimension of the autobiographical" (*A Pitch of Philosophy,* 3, 6). My point is that the attempt to fashion anew a connection between autobiography and philosophy occurs in just that space where, as in Augustine's *Confessions,* impersonality once *assumed* the centrality of a personal existence to a discourse of the impersonal.

These three endeavors to join the autobiographical with the philosophical raise a question about a related conjunction, the personal and the impersonal—namely, the question of how the two were ever separated.

21. Emmanuel Levinas, *Time and the Other,* trans. Richard A. Cohen (Pittsburgh: Duquesne University Press, 1987), 51, 57. The project in this book is to show the trajectory from "anonymous" existing to subjectivity, to the alterity of the other person, an alterity with which time is associated. What interests me about this early work of Levinas is where he locates suffering (as produced by the experience of personal identity) as opposed to where Parfit locates suffering (as produced by relinquishing the idea of personal identity).

22. Parfit, *Reasons and Persons,* 216.

23. Of course it could be argued that to say there is no entity that would distinguish what makes persons separate is to invent an absence. For if Parfit's point is that we can't make sense of the thought that there is such an entity, why should we expect the negation of this thought—expressed in the assertion that there is no such entity—to be any more intelligible? That is to say, someone might feel that Parfit's discussion does not adequately distinguish between what is true and false and what makes sense.

24. Such resistance is not the point of Parfit's argument; on the contrary, Parfit's "point" is the moral and personal freedom of the impersonal view he espouses. But his resistance surfaces despite the point: "I would never completely lose my intuitive belief in the Non-Reductionist View [of identity]. It is hard to be serenely confident in my Reductionist conclusions. It is hard to believe that personal identity is not what matters" (*Reasons and Persons,* 280). This perseverative intuitive view enables Parfit to speak of a "person's" response to the nonexistence of personal identity.

For a fascinating discussion of how "personality" and "persons" are differently constructed by Bloom, Lévi-Strauss, and Bentham, see Frances Ferguson, "Canons, Poetics, and Social Value: Jeremy Bentham and How to Do Things with People," *MLN* 110 (December 1995), 1149–64. I am particularly interested in Ferguson's discussion of how for Bentham persons are "reciprocal" constructions, "produced" by groups (1161). No sense of this reciprocity characterizes Emerson's essays; what is missing from Emerson's account of impersonality is any sense of the persons who constitute it.

2. Paths of Coherence through Emerson's Philosophy

The Case of "Nominalist and Realist"

This essay begins with a short introduction to Emerson's thought by means of some *paths of coherence* running through it. For although one must acknowledge opposing tendencies in his thinking, and even Emerson's own advertisements of his inconsistency, his thought does hang together. After following a few of these paths, I will turn to Emerson's "Nominalist and Realist," which brings the *Essays: Second Series* to a close precisely by raising and answering questions about the coherence of Emerson's thought.

Consider the idea of process, which for Emerson is at once a metaphysical character and a mark of moral and artistic elevation. In "Circles," for example, he holds that "permanence is but a word of degrees,"[1] that around every circle of our being another can be drawn. He opens "The Over-Soul" not with an account of a stable unity but with the claim that "there is a difference between one and another hour of life, in their authority and subsequent effect." And he follows this with the claim that "there is a depth in [certain] brief moments, which constrains us to ascribe more reality to them than to all other experiences" (2:159), thereby emphasizing the instability as well as the authority of these hours of life. Even when Emerson talks of "Being," as in "Experience," he represents it not as a stable "wall" but as a series of "interminable oceans" (3:42).

Emerson's metaphysics of process has epistemological consequences, for example, that there is no final explanation of any fact, that each law will be incorporated in "some more general law presently to disclose

41

itself" ("Circles," 2:181). Again, if all is in flux, we at best have glimpses, not a steady vision of things. A child in "Experience" asks, "'Mamma, why don't I like the story as well as when you told it me yesterday?'" "Alas, child," the Emersonian epistemologist answers, "it is even so with the oldest cherubim of knowledge" (3:33).

Process is essential for our moral development, construed not as a path to a given or original set of rules or virtues, but as the transition to new and better virtues. This transition is rooted in what Emerson calls "the active soul," which he asserts is "the one thing in the world of value" ("The American Scholar," 1:56). Of course this is not to say what such activity is. It is not mere busyness or habit, not what Emerson will call the "uniform tune which the revolving barrel of the music-box must play" ("Experience," 3:31). It is a process that gets somewhere, that ascends or expands.

If one starts from the idea of the active soul as the one thing of value, one comes to many of Emerson's most striking moral, aesthetic, and religious statements, for example, the place in "Self-Reliance" where he writes that he would risk striking out on his own impulses and being "the Devil's child" rather than remain in a state of conformity. It is precisely the original activity of such a striking-out that will be of value. Again, in "The Divinity School Address," the active soul takes the form of the person experiencing the "religious sentiment" or "imparadising of the soul"; the contrasting, inactive soul inhabits the routinized rituals that have no expansion or transition in them, and is displayed in the prose of a minister who does not give his hearers the slightest reason to believe that he has actually lived. Emerson's poet understands that "the quality of the imagination is to flow, and not to freeze," and therefore finds no "rest in . . . meaning." In contrast, what Emerson calls "the mystic" "nails a symbol to one sense, which was a true sense for a moment, but soon becomes old and false" ("The Poet," 3:20). The mystic, with no sense of the living flow, murders meaning. The poet lives in and helps direct meaning's flow.

Many paths run through these sentences about the poet and the mystic—paths of language and meaning, for example. Here I shall follow another path, that of the "new." Emerson's valorization of process and the active soul is often expressed as a dedication to "'the newness'" (3:40) of the present moment, to the surprises, creations, and unexpected expansions of life. In *Nature,* he tries to see the world anew by looking at it upside down between his legs, but he also recognizes less mechanical encounters with the new in what he calls "untaught sallies of the spirit" (1:39). In "Self-Reliance," he finds that the power that resides in each person is "new in nature" (2:28), and in one of the ecstatic moods of "Experience," he writes of his proximity to a "new yet unapproachable America" (3:41). In "Circles," the new by its nature is said to give an impulse, a form of expansion, to the world, but the expansion does not last, piles up, solidifies, and defends its way of configuring things. "The new statement," Emerson writes, "is always hated by the old, and to those dwelling in the old, comes like an abyss of skepticism. But the eye soon gets wonted to it, for the eye and it are effects of one cause; then its innocency and benefit appear, and, presently, all its energy spent, it pales and dwindles before the revelation of the new hour" (2:181). Even history, which seems obviously about the dead past, has its true use, Emerson holds, as the servant of the living present: "The student is to read history actively and not passively; to esteem his own life the text, and books the commentary." ("History," 2:5).

We have been following the path of process from the epistemology of the momentary and the morality of the active soul, to the self-reliant individual and the poet, and finally to the new and the present. Using the terms of the essay that I will soon consider, we have been following the path of *nominalism*, of particularity. However, "Nominalist and Realist" discusses two aspects of the world; particularity or process is one, and universality or stability is the other. At the end of my discussion I raise the question whether process does not win out after all, since the essay moves—and depicts us as moving—from realist vision to nominalist vision and back again.

One of my guiding thoughts is that Emerson's "epistemology of moods" (so named by Stanley Cavell in "Thinking of Emerson")[2] provides a way of understanding what might otherwise seem to be contradictory outlooks, viewpoints, or doctrines in his writings. If, as is supposed by such an epistemology, we never apprehend anything "straight" or in-itself, but only under an aspect or mood, then the contrary viewpoints are perhaps as good as we can get. I do not say this is an unproblematic idea either in itself or as an interpretation of Emerson (or of Kant, who is in the background here), but I do think it takes us deeply into his thought. The epistemology of moods leads to a corresponding idea: a metaphysics of aspects. This idea is present in many of Emerson's essays, but is developed most explicitly in "Nominalist and Realist," where Emerson speaks of the universe as an "old Two-face . . . of which any proposition may be affirmed or denied" (3:144). Emerson knows quite well that "contradiction" is the word for an affirmation and denial of the same proposition, so this is an extreme formulation.

As we work toward "Nominalist and Realist," I begin with two passages about "consistency" and "contradict[ion]" in "Self-Reliance," where Emerson may appear to, but does not really, take the extreme position he embraces in that later essay. Here is the first passage:

> The other terror that scares us from self-trust is our consistency; a reverence for our past act or word, because the eyes of others have no other data for computing our orbit than our past acts, and we are loath to disappoint them.
>
> But why should you keep your head over your shoulder? Why drag about this corpse of your memory, lest you contradict somewhat you have stated in this or that public place? Suppose you should contradict yourself; what then? It seems to be a rule of wisdom never to rely on your memory alone, scarcely even in acts of pure memory, but to bring the past for judgment into the thousand-eyed present, and live ever in a new day. (2:33)

Consistency emerges here as something to be avoided, and contradiction as something sometimes to be tolerated. Consistency is to be avoided because it is bound to be inadequate to the flux of the world, and contradiction is to be embraced if it issues from the "judgment" of "a new day." But Emerson doesn't really embrace contradictions here. His position is in some respects that of the fallibilist, or simply the reasonable person, who finds, sometimes, that a belief firmly held ("the levee will hold") is not true, or that a true proposition ("there is a grocery store at the corner of Fifth and Main") may become false. Emerson is talking not just about individual propositions but rather about a whole texture of life, which helps explain the tone of exhilaration about his discovery that he can abandon the old without quite knowing what the new will be. The exhilaration here is of a piece with his commitment to "Whim" (to be written on the lintels of his doorpost) earlier in the essay and his self-reliant, irresponsible statement, "'If I am the Devil's child, I will live then from the Devil'" (2:30).

Emerson's nonresponsibility to the mores of the past is at the same time a responsibility to the present, to the thousand opportunities and events of the ever-new day. It is not a forgetting of the past but rather "bring[s] the past for judgment" in the new day. In his talk of the ever-new present as the site of knowledge and virtue, Emerson shows himself here to be a Heraclitean, or process philosopher. In the terms of "Nominalist and Realist," he is a *nominalist*.

The second passage about consistency from "Self-Reliance" will be familiar:

> A foolish consistency is the hobgoblin of little minds, adored by little statesmen and philosophers and divines. With consistency a great soul has simply nothing to do. He may as well concern himself with his shadow on the wall. Speak what you think now in hard words, and to-morrow speak what to-morrow thinks in hard words again, though it contradict every thing you said to-day.—"Ah, so you shall be sure to be misunderstood."—Is it so bad, then, to be misunderstood? Pythagoras was misunderstood, and Socrates, and Jesus, and Luther, and Copernicus, and Galileo, and Newton, and every pure and wise spirit that ever took flesh. To be great is to be misunderstood. (2:33–34)

As in the first passage, Emerson opposes consistency and embraces contradiction, and again it is temporal progression that elicits contradictions. Whereas in the first passage, Emerson speaks in the first and second person plural ("we" and "you"), here he speaks also in the third person about "great soul[s]" such as Pythagoras, Socrates, Luther, and Galileo, who are guided by what they think, or perceive at any time, rather than by allegiance to past action or thought.

It is important, however, to notice two qualifications built into this paragraph in its first and last lines. The first sentence opposes "foolish consistency," leaving open—indeed inviting us to consider—the possibility of what we might call a wise consistency. And at the end of the paragraph, Emerson states that "to be great is to be misunderstood." He does not say that to be misunderstood is to be great, nor does he say that the misunderstanding of what is great is necessary or permanent. Indeed, he sets out a theory of genius in the first paragraph of "Self-Reliance" according to which the genius in each person finds "that what is true for you in your private heart, is true for all men" (2:27). If greatness can be *mis*understood, then it can also be understood. "Self-reliance" does not contain the assertion that the genius's thoughts are ultimately contradictory. Rather Emerson speaks of the genius as making "universal sense" (2:27).

Emerson's doctrine of moods, a touchstone for our still anticipated journey through "Nominalist and Realist," shows up in "Circles," where Emerson writes that "Our moods do not believe in each other" (2:182). In "Experience," the dominant essay in *Essays: Second Series*, he states that "life is a train of moods like a string of beads, and, as we pass through them, they prove to be many-colored lenses which paint the world their own hue, and each shows only what lies in its focus" (3:30). Notice that Emerson is concerned with moods as holding or incorporating "belie[fs]" in the first quotation, and with moods as "show[ing]" us things, as ways we see the world, in the second. It is because he sees moods as ways of understanding or knowing the world that Cavell speaks of Emerson as offering an "epistemology of moods."

Emerson's moods, then, are said to believe, but not in each other. They are also said to condition what we know. Because these are conditions of what we know and what we say, they are akin to Kantian categories. (Conditions are literally what we say together, our together-diction, not our contra-diction.) But unlike Kant's categories, these mood-conditions fluctuate, like much else in Emerson's universe. Life is a succession rather than an unchanging structure of such belief/moods, and each offers only a partial view, "only what lies in its focus." Sometimes Emerson complains of the instability of these partial views and of our inability to grasp a world of "slippery sliding surfaces" ("Experience," 3:28). At other times—in other moods I may now say—the transition from one mood to another is exhilarating. "We do not guess to-day," Emerson states in "Circles," "the mood, the pleasure, the power of to-morrow, when we are building up our being" (2:189).

A final touchstone before I turn to "Nominalist and Realist." For convenience we can call it "the One," a term Emerson uses, though he also uses a series of related terms, such as "Unity," "Soul," and "Divine mind." As I have said, Emerson is in many respects a *process* philosopher. But there is also strong pull in his thought toward that which does not change, toward the Ideal, as he puts it in "Experience," "journeying always with us" (3:41). "If I have described life as a flux of moods," Emerson states, "I must now add, that there is that in us which changes not, and which ranks all sensations and states of mind" (3:42). In the terms of "Nominalist and Realist," this is the claim of the realist.

Even in "Self-Reliance," not a particularly metaphysical essay, there is a moment when Emerson gives stability and Oneness its due:

> In the hour of vision, there is nothing that can be called gratitude, nor properly joy. The soul raised over passion beholds identity and eternal causation, perceives the self-existence of Truth and Right, and calms itself with knowing that all things go well. Vast spaces of nature, the Atlantic Ocean, the South Sea,—long intervals of time, years, centuries,—are of no account. This which I think and feel underlay every former state of life and circumstances, as it does underlie my present, and what is called life, and what is called death....
>
> This is the ultimate fact which we so quickly reach on this, as on every topic, the resolution of all into the ever-blessed ONE. (2:39–40)

This passage has obvious affinities with Neoplatonism in its idea of a supreme cause that "enters into all lower forms," in its sense that "long intervals of time" become "of no account," and in its depiction of a "calm" "hour of vision." The fleetingness and rarity of these hours recalls Emerson's statement at the beginning of "The Over-Soul" that "our faith comes in moments; our vice is habitual" (2:159). These statements all assert the reality or supreme authority of these moments, minutes, and hours, while at the same time emphasizing their temporary nature. Time becomes "of no account"—but in the *hours* of vision. In this way the universe presents two faces to us, neither of which believes in or can see the other, neither of which has the final word. With this idea, and this example, we are now ready for "Nominalist and Realist."

Like all the essays in the *Second Series*, "Nominalist and Realist" has its moods, not so much corresponding to its two parts as occurring within them. Reversing the order of his title, Emerson begins the essay by considering Realism, and he starts not with a celebration of the "Real," but with a lament that we do not find it:

> I cannot often enough say, that a man is only a relative and representative nature. Each is a hint of the truth, but far enough from being

that truth, which yet he quite newly and inevitably suggests to us. If I seek it in him, I shall not find it.... The man momentarily stands for the thought, but will not bear examination; and a society of men will cursorily represent well enough a certain quality and culture, for example, chivalry or beauty of manners, but separate them, and there is no gentleman and no lady in the group.... We have such exorbitant eyes, that on seeing the smallest arc, we complete the curve, and when the curtain is lifted from the diagram which it seemed to veil, we are vexed to find that no more was drawn, than just that fragment of an arc which we first beheld. We are greatly too liberal in our construction of each other's faculty and promise. (3:133)

This is the voice of the essay "Experience," a voice that has had some experience—for example with promising young men who then "die young" or "lose themselves in the crowd" (3:30–31). Here in "Nominalist and Realist," Emerson traces our disappointment to two sources: our "exorbitant eyes," which seem to see more than is there, and a world where we find only fragments of arcs or momentarily representative persons. The world is not without form, but it is incomplete, partial, broken, fallen, in shards.

The disappointment Emerson expresses is slightly tempered by his remark that societies, unlike individuals, may "cursorily represent well enough a certain quality and culture." But in another mood and another paragraph—the essay's third—the reality of nations, cultures, and artistic traditions is celebrated:

There is a genius of a nation, which is not to be found in the numerical citizens, but which characterizes the society. England, strong, punctual, practical, well-spoken England, I should not find, if I should go to the island to seek it. In the parliament, in the playhouse, at dinner-tables, I might see a great number of rich, ignorant, book-read, conventional, proud men,—many old women,—and not anywhere the Englishman who made the good speeches, combined the accurate engines, and did the bold and nervous deeds. It is even worse in America, where, from the intellectual quickness of the race, the genius of the country is more splendid in its promise, and more slight in its performance. (3:135–36)

Despite the failure of the individual to live up to the ideal, Emerson draws the metaphysical conclusion that national characters are "real":

"We conceive distinctly enough the French, the Spanish, the German genius, and it is not the less real, that perhaps we should not meet in either
of those nations, a single individual who corresponded with the type"
(3:136). These types, characters, and patterns are parts of our experience
and guide our lives and understanding.

Emerson's argument for the reality of universals, essences, general
ideas, and patterns culminates in the essay's fourth paragraph, which
opens in an explicitly philosophical register:

> In the famous dispute with the Nominalists, the Realists had a good
> deal of reason. General ideas are essences. They are our gods: they
> round and ennoble the most partial and sordid way of living. Our pro-
> clivity to details cannot quite degrade our life, and divest it of poetry.
> The day-laborer is reckoned as standing at the foot of the social scale,
> yet he is saturated with the laws of the world. (3:136)

The mood here is upbeat and confident in reporting on our ennobling
tendencies and in concluding that there is "a good deal of reason" on the
side of the realists. Emerson is not denying what he had begun by observing, that most individuals do not fit the pattern but are only fragments.
But he now looks at these facts differently, and his positive spin sends us
off in the direction of a grand design—"the laws of the world," available
even to a "day-laborer."

The celebration of these "real" "laws of the world" continues in the
essay's fifth paragraph, where Emerson moves into the first person to describe his own experiences with music and literature. He recounts a performance of Handel's *Messiah* in which the imperfections of the players
were "overpowered" by the "genius" of the composer. And he describes
literature as seeming to have been written by "one person,"

> as if the editor of a journal planted his body of reporters in different
> parts of the field of action, and relieved some by others from time to
> time; but there is such equality and identity both of judgment and
> point of view in the narrative, that it is plainly the work of one all-
> seeing, all-hearing gentleman. (3:137)

Emerson's invocation of the "one all-seeing, all-hearing gentleman"
chimes with the opening of "The American Scholar," where he writes
of the "old fable . . . that there is One Man,—present to all particular

men only partially, or through one faculty." Instead of the whole man, Emerson finds only parts or "members" that have "suffered amputation from the trunk, and strut about so many walking monsters,—a good finger, a neck, a stomach, an elbow, but never a man" (1:53). But Emerson's mood is different in "Nominalist and Realist." No longer complaining about our incompleteness, he feels the power of the one man who writes all the good books:

> The modernness of all good books seems to give me an existence as wide as man. What is well done, I feel as if I did; what is ill done, I reck not of. Shakspeare's passages of passion (for example, in Lear and Hamlet) are in the very dialect of the present year. I am faithful again to the whole over the members in my use of books. (3:137)

Emerson identifies with the author of the great work of art. Does he therefore depart from the "Self-Reliance" doctrine that "in every work of genius we recognize our own rejected thoughts: they come back to us with a certain alienated majesty" (2:27)? The two statements are in fact sides of the same coin, as we can see by remembering that in "The American Scholar," Emerson maintains that books may be well or ill used: ill used when they warp us out of our own orbits, well used when they inspire us. In "Nominalist and Realist," Emerson reports moments of inspiration and authority, moments of the good use of books; whereas in the passage in "Self-Reliance," he reports a moment of "shame," in which the consciousness of one's own power in the presence of a work of genius shows one the opportunities one has foregone (2:27).

Emerson recaptures the brash and confident tone of "Self-Reliance" when he writes, later in the fifth paragraph of "Nominalist and Realist":

> I read Proclus, and sometimes Plato, as I might read a dictionary, for a mechanical help to the fancy and the imagination. I read for the lustres, as if one should use a fine picture in a chromatic experiment, for its rich colors. 'Tis not Proclus, but a piece of nature and fate that I explore. It is a greater joy to see the author's author, than himself." (3:137)

Emerson brags for humanity—at least in his own person—as much as Thoreau does at the beginning of *Walden*. The reference to the Neoplatonist Proclus recalls "The Over-Soul" and *Nature*, where Emerson's Neoplatonic realism of the One is prominent. It is no accident that these references to

Neoplatonic metaphysics are found in the first half of "Nominalist and Realist," that part devoted to Realism. From the perspective of this fifth paragraph there is a commanding reality that we can apprehend and participate in—in our best moments. And so Emerson is able to come to the end of the first half of "Nominalist and Realist" in a mood of calm confidence, speaking as from a higher place: "All things show us, that on every side we are very near to the best. It seems not worth while to execute with too much pains some one intellectual, or æsthetical, or civil feat, when presently the dream will scatter, and we shall burst into universal power" (3:138).

The second part of "Nominalist and Realist" begins with a response to the assertion in the last paragraph of the first part that it is not worth our while to engage in the world of action because it is a dream whose episodes will eventually "shatter." "Thus we settle it in our cool libraries," Emerson's nominalist now begins, "that all the agents with which we deal are subalterns, which we can well afford to let pass, and life will be simpler when we live at the centre, and flout the surfaces" (3:138). The word "surface" repeats a main term of "Experience," where it names one of the "Lords of Life." The message now is that we cannot flout the surfaces, that they are necessary or inextricable. Nature will not allow us to live only the simple life of the center.

Emerson admits that the nominalist, who sees separate persons rather than the Whole or One, is uninspired: "though the uninspired man certainly finds persons a conveniency in household matters, the divine man does not respect them: he sees them as a rack of clouds, or a fleet of ripples which the wind drives over the surface of the water" (3:139). However, as Emerson puts it in one of his strange and memorable sentences: "Nature will not be Buddhist" (3:139). By this he means that nature resists our generalizing and calming propensities. It "insults the philosopher in every moment with a million of fresh particulars" (3:139). Of course, it is the realist philosopher who is insulted and disappointed, for the nominalist has learned to expect and expand with them.

At this point, it is worth saying that the term "realist" as opposed to "nominalist" is something of a misnomer because it implies that the realist believes in reality and the nominalist does not. But both have a metaphysics: the realist believes in the reality of "the One" and of types like the English or French; and the nominalist holds that reality is as much particular or fragmentary as it is general or universal. In this way, the nominalist position is broader and less discriminating. From the nominalist perspective, the realist misses the reality of the particular, whereas the nominalist accepts the reality of the universal. Discussing realist and nominalist versions of the self, Emerson puts the point this way: "as much as a man is a whole, so is he also a part; and it were partial not to see it" (3:138–39). From the nominalist perspective the realist is partial.

The nominalist does not so much see a different reality as report the other face of things seen by the realist. The realist had not missed seeing that mostly we live amid details and only rarely achieve visionary moments. Rather than lamenting the situation, the nominalist accepts it with good humor:

> It is not the intention of nature that we should live by general views. We fetch fire and water, run about all day among the shops and markets, and get our clothes and shoes made and mended, and are the victims of these details, and once in a fortnight we arrive perhaps at a rational moment. (3:139)

And there are benefits to the whirl of particulars. For one thing, they help us resist the tyranny of any strong personality, genius, party, or culture. When we come out of our solitude into "the public assembly," we meet men and women with manners different from our own, and we find that some of these manners are as admirable as our own (3:140). We learn a certain modesty and skepticism about ourselves and come to realize that even the greatest styles are a kind of "trick" that is endlessly repeated rather than continually created (3:140). Nature's succession of particulars serves to break up these tricks:

> Each man, too, is a tyrant in tendency, because he would impose his idea on others; and their trick is their natural defence. Jesus would absorb the race; but Tom Paine or the coarsest blasphemer helps humanity by resisting this exuberance of power. Hence the immense benefit of party in politics, as it reveals faults of character in a chief, which the intellectual force of the persons, with ordinary opportunity, and not hurled into aphelion by hatred, could not have seen. Since we are all so stupid, what benefit that there should be two stupidities! (3:140–41)

The argument builds, in the third nominalist paragraph, to an enthusiastic celebration of particularity. The millions of particulars appear now not as disappointing fragments of a great whole, but as instances of the ecstatic "newness" Emerson celebrates in "Experience." Indeed, the word "new" occurs seven times in this paragraph. Emerson's joyful nominalist finds divinity in the perfectly developed moment, in something that never existed before, not simply in a return to something already complete. In this way he breaks with the Neoplatonic tradition, of which he is also a part:

> If John was perfect, why are you and I alive? ... Why not a new man? Here is a new enterprise of Brook Farm, of Skeneateles, of Northampton: why so impatient to baptize them Essenes, or Port-Royalists, or Shakers, or by any known and effete name? Let it be a new way of living. Why have only two or three ways of life, and not thousands? (3:141)

Emerson celebrates the thousand new ways of living—as he had the "thousand-eyed present" in "Self-Reliance"—for their creative, elevated profusion, but his focus is, as always, on his own new life. "We want the great genius," he continues,

> only for joy; for one star more in our constellation, for one tree more in our grove. But he thinks we wish to belong to him, as he wishes to occupy us. He greatly mistakes us. I think I have done well, if I have acquired a new word from a good author; and my business with him is to find my own, though it were only to melt him down into an epithet or an image for daily use. (3:141)

There is a lot of "my" and "I" in these sentences, expressions of a strong self who melts down the genius and reforms him or her in the fire of his inspiration. This is the self for which Emerson calls in "The American Scholar" when he writes that one "must be an inventor to read well," that there is "creative reading, as well as creative writing" (1:58). Emerson's own practice of reading was to take what he could make use of or live with, and to leave the rest behind. He once "owed a magnificent day" to an eagerly awaited translation of the *Bhagavad Gita,* when he heard "the voice of an old intelligence which in another age and climate had pondered and thus disposed of the same questions which exercise us." But he writes in his journal that he sees no need to read it again: books are "like rainbows to be thankfully received in their first impression & not examined & surveyed."[3]

Emerson's nominalist discusses surfaces and succession—two of the "Lords of Life" that Emerson names in "Experience." These "Lords," or inescapable forms of our lives, also include Temperament, Surprise, Dream, and Use. "Succession" means that we find ourselves in a temporal world, where nothing lasts. "Surface" means that we live far from the center of things, that we slide from one thing to another without grasping or absorbing them. Yet the "true art of life," Emerson states in "Experience," is to "skate well" on its surfaces (3:35). In "Nominalist and Realist," he writes, "If we were not kept among surfaces, every thing would be large and universal." Still, the succession of surfaces allows for a kind of universality, spread out in time: "'Your turn now, my turn next,' is the rule of the game. The universality being hindered in its primary form, comes in the secondary form of *all sides:* the points come in succession to the meridian, and by the speed of rotation, a new whole is formed" (3:142, Emerson's emphasis).

Emerson retains his confident, pragmatic, assessing tone in the next, short paragraph, where he advises that we learn to "see the parts wisely, and infer the genius of nature from the best particulars with a becoming charity" (3:143). This notion of inference recalls the opening paragraphs of the essay, where he had complained of the inferences we make on the basis of what is only a fragmentary world. The world is certainly no more complete from the nominalist perspective here than it is from the realist perspective of the essay's opening. But whereas the realist complains that our inferences falsify what lies before us, by completing the arc of which we see only a section, Emerson now finds that such inference may be handsome, if conducted "with a becoming charity." He names love as the agent of that handsomeness: it "shows me the opulence of nature, by disclosing to me in my friend a hidden wealth, and I infer an equal depth of good in every other direction" (3:143).

The last four paragraphs of Emerson's essay move from the case for the nominalist to a summarizing view of both nominalism and realism. The first of these sets out the theme that gives the essay its title: that there are two powers in nature, and we must learn to live with both of them. Emerson acknowledges the confusion brought by the conflicting claims of these powers. Although we sometimes step back and see them both, when we are in a realist moment or mood, we cannot credit the nominalist, and vice versa. We have no "security against moods" (3:144).

Emerson wrote in "Circles" that "our moods do not believe in each other" (2:182), and here at the end of "Nominalist and Realist" he observes "two amicable powers," each of which "denies and tends to abolish the other" (3:143). Standing back from their battle, he counsels us to

> reconcile the contradictions as we can, but their discord and their concord introduce wild absurdities into our thinking and speech. No sentence will hold the whole truth, and the only way in which we can be just, is by giving ourselves the lie; Speech is better than silence; silence is better than speech;—All things are in contact; every atom has a sphere of repulsion;—Things are, and are not, at the same time;—and the like. All the universe over, there is but one thing, this old Two-Face, creator-creature, mind-matter, right-wrong, of which any proposition may be affirmed or denied. (3:143–44)

Here we reach the metaphysical figure that corresponds to Emerson's epistemology of moods. For if the world is known only through moods, we live in a world of shifting aspects, a world that is an "old Two-Face." Emerson presents yet another example of these changing aspects in the figure of "a fair girl" who appears amid the world's predominant ignorance and sensuality. She shows us another face of things by "making the commonest offices beautiful, by the energy and heart with which she does them" (3:144).

Emerson does not hope for a final reconciliation of the "contradictions" or multiple faces of life. Indeed the strategy of his essay is to present and acknowledge them. In this respect, not only in his allegiance to process, he resembles the ancient Greek philosopher Heraclitus, known as "the dark one." About Heraclitus, Philip Wheelwright has written:

> To him nothing is exclusively this or that; in various ways he affirms something to be *both* of two disparates or two contraries, leaving the reader to contemplate the paradox, the full semantic possibilities of which can never be exhausted. . . . To be sure, the logicizing intellect will undertake to analyze each of these paradoxes into its elements, explaining in just what pair of respects, or in what pair of circumstances, or from what opposite points of view, something is at once such and

non-such. But Heraclitus regards the paradox itself, and not its logical transformation, as more truly representing the real state of affairs.[4]

Some such position is suggested at the end of "Nominalist and Realist" when Emerson writes that "the only way in which we can be just is by giving ourselves the lie" (3:144). This statement affirms the truth of paradox, even the truth of contradiction. Emerson is not merely saying that we contradict a statement *p* when we find that *not-p* is in fact the case, nor that *p* may be the case at one time and *not-p* at another. Rather he embraces contradictions in the moment: "Things are, and are not, at the same time" (3:143–44).

However, unlike Heraclitus, Emerson is unhappy about these contradictions, no matter how truthful they may be, for he returns to a tone of complaint as the penultimate paragraph ends:

> If we were not of all opinions! if we did not in any moment shift the platform on which we stand, and look and speak from another! if there could be any regulation, any "one-hour-rule," that a man should never leave his point of view, without sound of trumpet. I am always insincere, as always knowing there are other moods. (3:145)

The writer's equanimity is disturbed, and he has no clear way of handling the "wild absurdities" in his thought, other than to acknowledge them while also giving their due to the moments of ideal clarity, particular intensity, and expansion that he also records in all his essays.

A tone of irony and mild, accepting skepticism prevails in the last paragraph of "Nominalist and Realist," which ends with a stunning withdrawal on the part of the author. Emerson begins by again considering the deceptions of what is called sincerity: "How sincere and confidential we can be, saying all that lies in the mind, and yet go away feeling that all is yet unsaid, from the incapacity of the parties to know each other, although they use the same words!" (3:145). Sounding the theme of the essay once more, Emerson asks: "Is it that every man believes every other to be an incurable partialist, and himself an universalist?" (3:145). He follows this rhetorical question not with an intellectual reconciliation nor with a statement of despair, but by an action of withdrawal. Emerson ends the paragraph by pulling his privacy up about him, separating himself from his readers, his society, and from "a pair of philosophers"— could they be Mr. Nominalist and Mr. Realist? (3:145):

I talked yesterday with a pair of philosophers: I endeavored to show my good men that I love everything by turns, and nothing long; that I loved the centre, but doated on the superficies; that I loved man, if men seemed to me mice and rats; that I revered saints, but woke up glad that the old pagan world stood its ground, and died hard; that I was glad of men of every gift and nobility, but would not live in their arms. Could they but once understand, that I loved to know that they existed, and heartily wished them Godspeed, yet, out of my poverty of life and thought, had no word or welcome for them when they came to see me, and could well consent to their living in Oregon, for any claim I felt on them, it would be a great satisfaction. (3:145)

This ending is quite different from the drama at the end of "Experience," where a somewhat battered writer urges himself up again, and in a spirit of resolve foretells "the transformation of genius into practical power" (3:49). It is certainly not the stirring and aggressive end of *Nature,* where Emerson writes of entering the "'kingdom of man over nature . . . without more wonder than the blind man feels who is gradually restored to perfect sight'" (1:45). It is rather more like the end of "Circles," where Emerson speaks of a "wonderful" way of life "by abandonment" (2:190) and advises his readers not "to set the least value on what I do, or the least discredit on what I do not, as if I pretended to settle anything as true or false" (2:188). Here at the end of "Nominalist and Realist" Emerson has no patience for the partiality and bias of either of his two philosophers. He wishes them well but has nothing to say to them, not even a pregnant paradox.

Although he withdraws from the dispute after presenting it, Emerson may be said to side with the nominalist in his emphasis on a universe of aspects that does not permit a final or stable account of itself, and in his depiction of himself as liking "everything by turns and nothing long." Yet the acknowledgment of moods that don't believe in each other means that Emerson knows there will be moods—as good as any—from which the flux is only apparent or beside the main point. Emerson's final position, if stated, is thus unstable. Having revealed and enacted these instabilities, Emerson turns away at the end of his essay and at the end of the *Second Series* toward his own-self cultivation, or perhaps that of his beloved fruit trees, leaving his readers, like the two philosophers, on their own. Yet if he had no words for the philosophers yesterday, he has written an essay of words for them and for us, today.

NOTES

1. "Circles," in Ralph Waldo Emerson, *The Collected Works of Ralph Waldo Emerson,* ed. Alfred R. Ferguson, Robert E. Spiller, et al., 8 vols. to date (Cambridge, Mass.: Harvard University Press, Belknap Press, 1971–2010), 2:179. Subsequent quotations from Emerson's writing are from this source and are cited parenthetically in text by volume and page numbers. Citations may include essay title if the essay from which a quotation is taken is not clear from the text.

2. Stanley Cavell, "Thinking of Emerson," in *Emerson's Transcendental Etudes* (Stanford, Calif.: Stanford University Press, 2003), 10–19.

3. *The Journals and Miscellaneous Notebooks of Ralph Waldo Emerson,* ed. William H. Gilman et al., 16 vols. (Cambridge, Mass.: Harvard University Press, 1960–1982), 10:360. Cf. Russell B. Goodman, "East-West Philosophy in Nineteenth-Century America: Emerson and Hinduism," *Journal of the History of Ideas* 51, no. 4 (1990): 625–45.

4. Philip Wheelwright, *Heraclitus* (Princeton, N.J.: Princeton University Press, 1959), 91–92.

3. Brain Walks

Emerson on Thinking

Emerson's essay "Intellect" voices a somewhat bizarre idea about thinking by claiming—counterintuitively—that it is the most difficult thing in the world: "What is the hardest task in the world? To think." By calling thinking "the hardest task" Emerson is saying—in contrast to a whole tradition of philosophy—that thinking is not simply available to us, that we are not simply thinking beings, but rather that thinking is a "task" or goal to which we must respond in order, precisely, to be responsible beings. However, as it turns out, this highest duty is the most difficult to respond to: "I would put myself in the attitude to look in the eye an abstract truth, and I cannot."[1] The thinker is saying that in spite of his will to think he cannot, and that therefore a fundamental incapacity accompanies our effort to think. But what kind of thinking is it that, on the one hand, maintains that the capacity to think is not given to us and, on the other, insists that we have to be able to do what we cannot do? How does one do what one cannot? How do we think? What is called thinking, according to Emerson?

Answering this question will require analyzing a whole network of concepts that traverse Emerson's essays, and that, once connected, display something that perhaps may be called Emerson's image of thought. Such an image—from which the role of the "I" is radically omitted—is made of notions such as moods, involuntary perceptions, passivity, intellect receptive, and intellect constructive. I will suggest by way of interpreting those concepts that Emerson advances an idea of impersonal thinking and that such a thinking constitutes the interiority of the "I" rather than being constituted by it. Because of that, the external, the outside, and the communal assume fundamental importance in his image of thought. Moods, for instance, being both the modes of thoughts and the tonality of life (since life is said to be "a train of moods" ["Experience," 3:30]), emerge from impersonal (or unintended) influences conceived of as a communal life we share with others. This understanding of moods— as a communal force constituting the self—not only puts in question the inherited image of the Emersonian individual as self-enclosed and willful, but also marks his radically novel way of thinking about personal identity. Because moods are crucial to the destabilization of the identity that we tend to call personal, where only a very fragile borderline separates it from others, my analysis of thinking in Emerson will have to start from them.

MOODS

To say that Emerson understands moods as the communal forces that constitute a self is to suggest that his thinking about moods has departed from a whole tradition of logic as well as from common linguistic usage. In insisting on the subject as the ground of its moods, the grammatical understanding of a mood reflects a primacy of *topoi* (of the Aristotelian logic of terms) and by extension of word-based linguistics. According to the latter a mood is an aspect of a verb, hence of a motion that represents the subject's attitude toward its action. A mood is thus an indicator of the subject's point of view. It tells us whether it regards something as a fact, a possibility, or a command, which then translates into the indicative, subjunctive, or imperative mood. Linguistics thinks of moods as variable expressions of the self-same person.

Calling the grammarian "wearisome"—in the essay on "Intellect" where he outlines his philosophy of thinking (2:200)—Emerson reverses this understanding. Moods are not representations of the relation the subject establishes with an object. Such an understanding presumes moods to be outcomes of a person's will, whereas for Emerson they are something that the person suffers; the person is "floated" into a mood by other persons or events. In "Intellect," the "I" so floats: "I have been floated into this thought, this hour, this connection of events, by secret currents of might and mind, and my ingenuity and *willfulness* have not thwarted, have not aided to an appreciable degree" (2:195, emphasis mine). The connection of events into which the "I" is floated becomes what affects and thus makes it. The consequences of this are tremendous, for if "we lie open to the mercy of coming events" (2:194), and if for that reason it is always possible that something "incalculable" will "balk the very next moment," thus becoming an "hour" that has "authority" over us (2:159), then we are made of what masters us. This already signals the importance Emerson gives to exteriority (the world, community, others) in constituting who we are.

Deliverance to more or less merciful events—which is one of the ways Emerson describes fate—does not, however, refer to anything rare, supernatural, or mystical. Rather, it says something about how it is with us in "common and happy hours." The connection of events into which we are floated is a network of circumstances that make our daily life: "All that mass of mental and moral phenomena, *which we do not make objects of voluntary thought,* come within the power of fortune; they constitute the circumstance of daily life; they are subject to change, to fear, and hope" (2:194, emphasis mine). When Emerson talks about events, he seems to have in mind more ordinary (it is a question of a mass of phenomena) and almost imperceptible things, rather than happenings that have an extreme, mystical, or spiritual character. We wake up in a good mood, but the person we share life with is sad, and without even realizing it, we are floated into a different mood closer to his sadness, like a glove, being folded inside out, becoming a mode of the outside. Whereas in the "Over-Soul" the formulation of this exposure as a fundamental mode of our existential situation—"we lie open on one side" (2:161)—suggested a doubleness of our self, "Experience" implies a more radical formulation according to which our "persons" are only changeable manners of the outside.[2] For if "the new molecular philosophy shows astronomical interspaces betwixt atom and atom, shows that the world is all outside: it has no inside" ("Surface," 3:37), then the self cannot be such an interiority of the world either. In "Experience" and elsewhere, Emerson radically suggests that what we call the self is made not only of other people's thoughts, emotions, or words, but also of the influences of meteorological conditions, food, or indigestion. A number of commentators have recognized this. Eduardo Cadava, for example, argues that Emerson's recourse to climatic and meteorological imagery is always more than a mere motif or theme in his writing: "If his writing can never avoid its meteorological figures . . . it is because this has been his way of telling us what it is. Emerson's writings are themselves a kind of weather," which for Cadava embodies the rapid transitions of Emerson's thinking.[3] Commenting on the influence of digestion on the formation of the self, Sharon Cameron suggests that "in 'Montaigne,' even principles—opinions on right and wrong, on fate and causation—are 'at the mercy of a broken sleep or an indigestion.'" The "I" is thus the effect of the "winds" of outsideness, the mood of otherness. It is never close to itself in the sense of being able to quite decide what it is or what it will be. Even "in the most worn, pedantic, introverted self-tormenter's life, the greatest part is incalculable by him, unforeseen, unimaginable" ("The Conservative," 1:194).

Our response to the other is thus a mood we are tuned into without knowing it: "That mood into which a friend can bring us is his dominion over us. . . . All the secrets of that state of mind, he can compel" ("Spiritual Laws," 2:84–85). That the other masters us does not mean that we are at the disposal of its will. This mastering is not a question of manipulative subjection, for not only are we attuned without our realizing it (impersonally), but the process of attuning is not willed by another and is never referred to explicitly. Our "moods are never quite transferable by means of words" but instead by the gestures of others, the tone of their voice, which independently of their own will—almost secretly—attunes us to their mood: "Men feel and act the consequences of your doctrine, without being able to show how they follow" (2:85). Beyond or underneath the meaning willfully conveyed by words there is a flow of subterranean meanings into which another unwillingly puts us. We are floated into a mood without realizing it by another who has brought us there without knowing it.

Moods are thus relational;[4] man, being made of those relations, resembles a cobweb or a network of some sort, metaphors supported by an analogy from Emerson's later lectures where he compares persons to the lines of a leaf, each line being a relation, each person being multirelational: "man is rich as he is much-related" ("Introductory Lecture," 1:170), or, as "History" puts it: "man is a bundle of relations" (2:20). Relations escape representation and imperceptibly grab hold of us, which is why in "Illusions" Emerson compares them to atmospheric conditions that cannot be stabilized into a written trace: "We cannot write the order of the variable winds. How can we penetrate the law of our shifting moods and susceptibility?" (6:172). Persons are always translational or transitional. What we call the "I" is a provisional knot or, as Emerson also calls it, a "bud" that will unfold into a different form-mood. Our "self" is always *medial*.

So it is that when in "Spiritual Laws" Emerson compares us to photometers—"We are the photometers, we the irritable goldleaf and tinfoil that measure the accumulations of the subtle element. We know the authentic effects of the true fire through every one of its million disguises" (2:96)—he is saying that instead of being a stable sign like a photograph we are the sheer sensitivity to light, the goldleaf medium, which makes the encounter between the photographed and photographer possible. Our persons are something like a photogenic mood brought about by the radiance of another, hence a pure sensitivity to its radiations. (It is therefore not accidental that Emerson substituted goldleaf for the silver that was actually used in photography, making reference to the alchemical metal of life and its transformations.) We are exposed to the "fire" of others that passes through us and turns us to fire (we are thus partial and passionate) in myriad subtle ways. Our faces are sensitive leaves (unstable signs) that will mirror a million faces ("million disguises") of others. It is this registering of otherness on our faces that Emerson calls "authentic effects," suggesting both that "our" face is made of traces whose inscription we cannot control and that there is rupture or discontinuity between those inscriptions.

Even though "Experience" opens up the possibility that temperament would be something like a more stable ground of changeable moods ("Life is a train of moods like a string of beads.... Temperament is the iron wire on which the beads are strung" [3:30]), many other essays contradict it, almost systematically: "Take pains to observe the variety of actions to which he is equally inclined in certain moods of mind and those to which he is averse" ("History," 2:10). "How can we penetrate the law of our shifting moods and susceptibility? Yet they differ as all or nothing" ("Illusions," 6:172). "I believe not in two classes of men but in man in two moods" ("New England Reformers," 3:159). The idea that man in two moods can differ from himself as two classes of men or as "all or nothing" does not quite mean that there is no self, that "I" is only a rhetorical contrivance, nor does it suggest that moods don't have their duration and cannot hold us for a long time. But it does signal a discontinuity of personal identity, for moods are said to be shifting. The emancipating aspect of Emerson's thesis is his opening a possibility for each of us to become somebody else, renewed and better (what Stanley Cavell termed Emerson's "moral perfectionism"), since it promises auspicious beginnings for each of us and affirms—in spite of all suffering—the value of life: life is what floats us into new personalities. But this emancipation from the old (self or life) comes in the form of a necessary, because involuntary, response to the other (person or event). Freedom thus becomes a form of new confinement (which is only another way of saying that our persons are medial).

The self-liberating aspect of shifting personalities has its troublesome ethical side also, which sometimes causes Emerson to despair over the fact of their mobility. By establishing impersonal relations between persons, moods constitute a peculiar type of responsiveness to another, which, because it occurs involuntarily and imperceptibly, cannot be repeated or controlled. Responsibility becomes something like an irresponsible response. As we usually understand it, the "re" in "responsibility" refers to the iterability of the past (responses), hence to a certain continuity of our selves, whereas moods operate by causing discontinuity. The ethical dilemma caused by moods can be formulated as follows: if man in two moods differs from himself as two classes of men differ, can we be held completely responsible for our words and acts performed in certain moods?

It is this aspect of moods that worries Emerson the most. "Nominalist and Realist" ends with his lamenting over the fact that the whole impersonal journey of persons does not give us any ontological stability or ethical certainty: "If we could have any security against the moods! If the profoundest prophet could be holden to his words, and the hearer who is ready to sell and join the crusade, could have any certificate that tomorrow his prophet shall not unsay his testimony!" (3:144–45). That no one can be held to their words—that the testimony of prophets cannot be trusted and that we perhaps live in a world abandoned by Gods—does not necessarily mean for Emerson that nobody is sincere. Rather, it means that we change more quickly than the time needed for words to be uttered. Our change is more rapid than the speed of tropes: "My companion assumes to know my mood and habit of thought, and we go on from explanation to explanation, until all is said which words can, and we leave matters just as they were at first" (3:145). If we are never known to the other, it is not because we are not sincere but because the truest self-explanation misses its referent, since the self it refers to has already been transformed. Because words cannot convey the present mood, they are left explaining the past one, no longer in us. Thus, the current state of our thoughts undermines the truth value of our frank explanations, which are incapable of affirming the changeable thing uttered, as George Kateb puts it by means of this paradox: "Knowing that the full power of a mood is discernible only after the mood passes, we must be wary of thinking that we can ever rest in a present certainty. Mobility is the check on mood."[5] It is perhaps for that reason that, as "Spiritual Laws" has it, "The sentence must also contain its own apology for being spoken" (2:89).

A sincerity that consists of short habits necessarily changes our understanding of truth. The speed of its transformation, however, does not mean that there is no truth. Rather, to be truthful now means to be faithful to change. The truth would thus have the features of a weather report; instead of reaffirming the content of what has been said—thus confirming the value of consistency, which Emerson believes is foolish—it would require loyalty to the variable. As Emerson writes in a journal entry: "Truth is such a flyaway, such a slyboots, so untransportable & unbarrelable a commodity that it is as bad to catch as light."[6]

INVOLUNTARY PERCEPTIONS

But how does it happen that we are floated into a different mood? Perhaps we can be so floated because we are open on one side, but what does that mean? The ruse of Emerson's formulation from "Over-Soul,"—"We lie open on one side" (2:161)—lies, I am proposing, in its literalness: moods insinuate themselves into us on the side on which we are open literally, through senses and sense perception. And they can intrude because we don't have power over perception. Our perceptual field is, thus, made not only of what we want to see or hear but—and for Emerson this is more important—of minute perceptions also, which not only have we not chosen to perceive but which we are not aware of at the moment of perception. In "Love," Emerson gives an example of a "soul" that without realizing it "detects incongruities" in another while consciously or will-fully paying attention only to its good sides, to its virtues and beauty, explaining how in spite of the fact that we love another we involuntarily perceive things we dislike, without at first attaching great importance to them. It is the perception of those imperceptibly registered "defects"—a kind of miscellaneous perception, which Emerson calls "involuntary"—that settles and works in us. Once they have accumulated those percep-tions can become a "clear thought" that will radically change our image of the other person, as when we ask ourselves, "How was it that I didn't see that in him, was I blind?" Perception is faster than our choice of the object of perception.

For that reason Emerson insisted that perception was fatal. Only "thoughtless people," he says in "Self-Reliance," "contradict as readily the statement of perceptions as of opinions, or rather much more read-ily.... They fancy that I choose to see this or that thing. But perception is not whimsical, but fatal" (2:38). The fatality of perception lies in the fact that I am chosen by it, exposed to it, and forced into it. Hence our willful actions count little, says Emerson, in "Self-Reliance" of all places. Such actions are the effect of our already existing feelings, opinions, or con-cepts (of what we want to see), and they therefore have nothing much to do with real changes affecting our perception, contradicting our notions. Because the materialism of this affecting is what shapes us, rather than what he called our abstract notions (because they contradict perception), the involuntary, in Emerson, is given primacy over the voluntary: "My willful action and acquisitions are but roving;—the idlest reverie, the faintest native emotion, command my curiosity and respect" (2:37–38). If the idlest reverie is more fatal than a willful action, it is because the will is at the mercy of whatever involuntarily falls upon it.

This is not to say that there is no will at all, for Emerson does talk about willful acquisitions even if they are but roving; rather, it means redefining the idea of the willful capacity, for that ability will now be formed by involuntary perceptions and by their control over its prefer-ences and actions. It is on such a will—which cannot rely on itself—that a self-reliant person is invited to rely. This invitation, then, marks the most profound tension in Emerson's concept of self-reliance, since it ad-mits that the basis of our reliance, the will, is not adequate to itself. Or, as Sharon Cameron puts it in her analysis of the impersonal in Emerson: "In effect, then, what self-reliance turns out to mean for Emerson is a strong recognitional understanding of the inadequacy of any person: other persons *or* this person."

This involuntary perceiving marks us universally: "Every man discriminates between the voluntary acts of his mind, and his involuntary perceptions, and knows that to his involuntary perceptions a perfect faith is due" ("Self-Reliance," 2:37). However—and in this insight lies perhaps the most radical intervention of Emerson's philosophy of thinking—not only our will but our understanding too is predicated on involuntary perceptions. New perceptions that force us to change the way we see reality have to affect our notions and concepts, thus destabilizing our understanding. Our understanding—like our will—is not able to stand firm on its own position but is at the mercy of ex-position or interruption: "My will," as Emerson writes in "Spiritual Laws," "never gave the images in my mind the rank they now take" (2:78). That certain images will assume a high rank in our mind without either the will or the mind assigning it to them has to entail a reorganization or overturning of the values we ascribe to already existing ideas and beliefs: images or concepts we valued highly will be withdrawn in favor of new ones. This rearranging entails a crisis of our understanding, since we have to question what we thought we knew. It marks the moment in which the capacity of understanding performs the action its name derives from: its firm standing goes under, is crushed—profoundly affected—by the currents of involuntary perceptions. This falling under of the understanding is not a sinking into some sort of unconsciousness; rather, it is the breakdown that thinking suffers whenever it faces what Emerson calls the wholly new or completely nonrecognizable. Only out of the night of this nonunderstanding will a new understanding appear.

To say that our capacity to think in a new way emerges out of a profound crisis is also to propose that the new understanding exposes the person to irreparable loss. A few years after "Self-Reliance," in the lecture on the "Relation of Intellect to Natural Science" delivered on June 8, 1848, in London, Emerson refers to a "new perception" as exposure to "absolute" loss: "Besides, he found that really and truly there were no short cuts, that every perception costs houses and lands.... Every image, every truth, cost him a great neglect; the loss of an estate; the loss of a brilliant career opened to him; the loss of friend; wife; child; the flat negation of a duty."[7] And even though these formulations are indices of Waldo's death, they nevertheless draw on what in "Self-Reliance" was already called the "new perception." It becomes clear why Emerson found that what he privileged—thinking as the process of changing and growing—is perhaps the most difficult thing there is. For the effects of a new perception are not exclusively cognitive. No new perception or truth can be turned into knowledge unless it transforms the one who acquires it. To know or to grow is thus to suffer self-transformation, which, each time it happens, can turn us into different persons who no longer recognize their previous duties as worth satisfying or their friends as worthy of the name. To the extent that it adjusts us to the new, thinking acts on us, confronting us with a risk of personal crisis such as Emerson equates with the loss of a child or lover. Our growth is therefore elegiac.

On the other hand, to willfully resist such a crisis or loss is to adhere to our already existing thoughts or notions and thus to face yet a greater danger of being a simpleton: only "thoughtless people, contradict as readily the statement of perceptions . . . for, they do not distinguish between perception and notion." Stupidity, then, resides in the effort to corroborate notions even when they oppose the mobility of moods and perceptions.

When Emerson, in "Self-Reliance," says that a "foolish consistency" is "adored by little statesmen and philosophers and divines" (2:33), he is identifying in doctrinaire personages—the priest, the politician, the philosopher—the image of willful thoughtlessness. It belongs to their office to weaken our self-trust so as to force us to entrust ourselves to the power of their idea. Their idea of consistent truth, opposed to the fluctuation of perceptions, turns out to be an ideological version of truth, and aversion to it becomes for Emerson the only ethical gesture we have at our disposal, the only way to reach the other truth of the elusive world. The ideologically induced illusion is based on insisting on an adequate relation of our notions with the world. But it is this insistence that imposes the ideology of a stable reality, not vice versa. Our theory of truth is illusion: "The secret of the illusoriness is in the necessity of a succession of moods or objects. Gladly we would anchor but the anchorage is quicksand" ("Succession," 3:32).

MEDIAL PERSONALITIES

Thoughts stripped bare of notions and without anchorage represent a thinking of the unnameable and involve facing the unrecognizable, what Emerson sometimes calls the "wholly strange and new." He seems to be claiming that thinking thinks only when it risks taking on the unthought—the nonconceptual—which devastates the thinking facing it, opening the abyss in which nothing can be said (as there is no longer any notion that "works"). What comes from such an abyss— the new perception, the strange—is thus the only "real" entity, what Emerson also calls "event." And even though the occurrence of an event changes everything—to the point, as I was suggesting, of causing radical loss—an event in Emerson is not an event in the sense that German Romanticism gave to it, that of *parekbasis*. The poetic *parekbasis* of German Romanticism, as Werner Hamacher puts it, "constitutes an un-controllable, dramatic-grammatical trope whose exorbitant movement displaces the framework for every epistemological paradigm of reflective representation."[8]

An Emersonian event—the way we are floated into a mood or faced with a new perception—may be considered similar to the "romantic" *parekbasis* insofar as it too "displaces the framework for every epistemo-logical paradigm of reflective representation." But it differs radically in the way it performs its transformative effects, for it never "makes" drama. Paradoxically, the violence of the Emersonian event changes everything by being gentle, imperceptible, or "atmospheric," a word that in Emerson points to "the reality of relation" ("Manners," 3:78). For example, "Self-Reliance" refers to the event that is radically foreign to everything we have ever experienced but that, nevertheless, approaches us mildly, silently, invisibly, in ways we cannot discern: "you shall not discern the foot-prints of any other; you shall not see the face of man; you shall not hear any name; the way, the thought, the good, shall be wholly strange and new. It shall exclude example and experience" (2:39); "Over-Soul" mentions the old proverb "God comes to see us without bell" only because it signals the fact that the arrival of the new is "too subtle. It is un-definable, unmeasurable" (2:161); "Experience" claims that "we thrive by casualties" only because our "chief experiences have been casual" (3:39); "Nature" proposes that the "quick cause" arrives at consummate results without a shock or a leap," which is why "All changes pass without violence" (3:104); and finally, "History" reads events that belong to the realms of nature, civil history, and the "trivial experience of every day" as so many "mutable clouds" (2:8), "broad clouds," "the rising moon break[ing] out of the clouds" (2:11), and historical events are said to move "silently," like clouds, forming "the chain of affinity" (2:10).

"Manners" even goes as far as to claim that we carry ourselves like so many atmospheres ("A man should not go where he cannot carry his whole sphere or society with him,—not bodily, the whole circle of his friends, but atmospherically" [3:78]). The atmosphere that is a whole "circle of friends" is a discreet population of many selves, which conveys what is in a man or something about him to others—floating them into a different atmosphere or mood. Carrying oneself atmospherically is like turning oneself into an atmosphere (into a style or a manner). Such persons are like those delicate events Emerson talks about in "Manners." They enter the dance ball like an atmospheric change. We don't even have to see them, but we sense their presence and everything is henceforth different. And, vice versa, we inhabit the atmosphere of a "fine" person who has left: "The best effect of fine persons is felt after we have left their presence, as the greatest chemical energy of the prismic spectrum is a little out of the spectrum."[9] Fine or atmospheric persons move into us, imperceptibly, so that once they leave, they are still within us. Atmosphere does precisely that: it negates the difference between inhabiting and being inhabited.

The ball can become a street walk; the event is then like seeing girls on the street, an encounter that will change everything: "We keep a running fire of sarcasm at ignorance and the life of the senses; then goes by, perchance, a fair girl, a piece of life, gay and happy, and making the commonest offices beautiful" ("Manners," 3:144). In "Nominalist and Realist" it is the realist—the one who readily believes in concepts rather than in singularities or events—who is brought to his "senses" by the feeling of life that is perchance floated into him; when girls pass him by all his skepticism is gone, the feeling of life becoming the undeniable truth. The atmosphere is altogether different. That is why only the truly experienced man can say: "I never know, in addressing myself to a new individual, what may befall me" (3:32).

Not only do moods and perceptions inhabit us as so many atmospheric events, but our thoughts perform in a similar manner, as if coming from the outside, registering changes in the weather. Mild and peaceful days are good for thought because they turn it into such an atmosphere; even more generally, all atmospheric changes are good for a thinker as they signal to him the meteorological and atmospheric character of thinking: "Yesterday (Sunday) was a beautiful day, mild, calm, & though the earth is covered with snow, somewheres two feet deep, yet the day & the night moonlit were as good for thought, if the man were rested & peaceful, as any in the year. The meteorology of thought I like to note."[10]

Atmosphere, mist, clouds, fog thus in Emerson come to represent a series of terms raised almost to the level of a technical terminology, referring both to the delicacy of events and the mediality of persons. From "Over-Soul," where incalculable events overwhelm us like a river that "streams into me" (2:160) to "Fate," where the impressionable thinker is open for "delicate events" (6:21, 22) there is a persistence of this dialectics of events that modify persons who will in turn unknowingly trigger events. In "Fate," what is more, the fatality of events and the way they enter into a mutual relation of modification with persons is called "the secret of the world." It is this mutual mediation that constitutes persons as medial: "The secret of the world is, the tie between person and event. Person makes event, and event person. . . . Thus events grow on the same stem with persons; are sub-persons. . . . Life is an ecstasy" (6:21–22).

What Emerson here calls ecstasy is a general condition of life as such—referred to by a universal affirmative claim: "Life is an ecstasy"— and not an exceptional subjective state. It points to the way life is and not to a series of meditative practices a mystic undertakes in order to reach self-negation. Life as such (of animals, plants, and humans) lives by leaving its posts, by being restless (being out of stasis). That life per se is ecstatic also says something about how our persons function, for they are made of that life, of delicate events that come into us like so many "sub-persons"—what "Self-Reliance" also calls "aboriginal selves"—and they shape us without our will in order to make us leave what we are, arranging our leaving when we think we are settled in and ready to stay. The good posture of "Self-Reliance"—far from being standing or sitting, or staying in place[11]—thus means walking away, leaving, and moving toward: "Leave your theory, as Joseph his coat in the hand of the harlot, and flee" (2:33). Enforcing this claim, "Experience" suggests that the only experienced ones are those who know how to leave and therefore how to live: "We need change of objects. Dedication to one thought is quickly odious." Whatever we have seen well, "we must take our leave of it; we shall never see it again" (3:33). Life becomes ecstasy in the sense that living functions as a process of leaving.

The self is not the agent of this overcoming but rather its patient, for it leaves itself thanks to the overwhelming power of life. It is thus not only different from Hegel's speculative transcendence through self-mediation ("Life is not dialectics," writes Emerson in "Experience" [3:34]), but also from Kant's transcendental apperception, since no self-same "I" persists to accompany and connect our diverse representations, moods, or perceptions. On the other hand, that does not necessarily mean that Emerson fell back on the naïve position of psychological empiricism proposed by Burke and criticized by Kant. The main problem with Burke's empiricism, according to Kant, was that by grounding our thinking in the "empirical exposition of the sublime,"[12] he ended up in the sheer fluctuation of the empirical. Thinking was seen only as a succession of gratifications or pains, which is to say of moods, that precluded the possibility of establishing a firm judgment, subjectivity, or stable personality. A simple listing of moods, Kant objects, fails to ensure the conditions for a judgment that would give itself as "universally valid and therefore assert a claim to necessity." Without "necessity, which rests either on concepts of the object a priori or on the subjective conditions for concepts, which grant them a priori"—without "I"—there will be nothing universally and necessarily valid (39). There will be nothing more than a flux of impersonal moods, which for Kant raises not only aesthetic but also ethical concerns.

Kant's objection to Burke is a version of Cavell's interpretation of "Self-Reliance." Cavell reads the argument of "Self-Reliance" as seeking to ensure the stability of the "I." The privilege, which, as he reads it, Emerson gives to postures of sitting and standing, signals such stability. The one who is immobile in his firm standing represents the apperceptive "I," self-identical in spite of the changes in perceptions and thoughts: "What is good in these postures [standing and sitting] is whatever makes them necessary to the acknowledgment, or the assumption, of individual existence, to the capacity to say 'I.'"[13] Moodiness and consistent leaving

would thus suggest the person's inability to exist, the radical impover-
ishment of the "I," to the point of its negation. That is precisely how, in
contrast to Cavell and closer to my reading, Richard Poirier understands
the outcome of the essay when he says, "Necessarily, then, self-reliance
in Emerson, insofar as it is insufficiently understood to refer to the assertion of one's unique personality, gives way recurrently to its opposite,
to self-dissolution, to the abandonment of any already defined Self."[14]
Following Poirier one may then argue that the stake of "Self-Reliance"
resides in accepting the paradox of a self that relies on itself to leave itself.
For if it is good to stay, then the ethical imperative the essay insists on—
leave your theory and fly—would be of a diabolical kind, as it would ask
us to negate what the essay proposes as good.

Rather than opt for an interpretation whereby Emerson comes from
a devil, I want to propose that holding life to be ecstatic or the impersonal
fluctuation of moods doesn't suggest that there are no persons—that is
not what Emerson says—nor is it to enact a contradiction. For Emerson
the question about persons and the impersonal is never disjunctive but
rather all-inclusive . When he talks about persons and the impersonal, I
suggest, Emerson is not proposing a radical choice: either persons or the
impersonal. Both of those concepts understood in their purity are futile
and differ from what he is saying. If we understand a person to be always
controlling its moods and thoughts, acting not under the influence of
others but remaining in possession of its own will, then we are like those
thoughtless ones who prefer concepts to reality, for persons are fragile
and open to others, exposed to encounters that affect them in incalculable ways. That may be of concern to theorists of human agency and self-
identical subjectivity, but that is beside the point. The point is rather that
Emerson is offering a diagnosis with the precision of a phenomenologist,
a diagnosis that, in fact, may affect him too; he is trying to describe persons as they are (not as they should be), and he sees them as affected and
shaped by forces they cannot control. Persons are made of many impersonal influences that transform them, making them different persons. As
Lawrence Buell succinctly puts it in explaining the relation between the
impersonal and persons in Emerson: "Do I think my thoughts, or does
thought think me? Why should it make sense for the answer to this question to be 'both'?"[15] Because, as Buell suggests, it does make sense for the
answer to this question to be "both," Emerson can claim that simply to

state "I am" is to state an abstraction: "In strict speech it seems fittest to say, I Become rather than I am. I am a Becoming."[16] "I am" functions as a loose metaphor that does not translate the situation of the "I," since the "I," rather than a stable being (something that merely is), is a Becoming. Far from suggesting that there is no "I," "I am a Becoming" points to its ontological paradox: in becoming, the person is always abandoning itself while at the same time becoming another self. Such a paradox embodies what I call the Emersonian medial personality.

This idea can be argued from the opposite point of view, namely, from the vantage of what Emerson says about the impersonal. For instance, nature (identified with universal life) and called the only properly impersonal force since only "nature is transcendental" ("Transcendentalist," 1:206), nevertheless needs and so creates persons in order to sense or express itself. The properly impersonal requires persons in the same way that persons suffer the influence of the impersonal, for nothing is ever pure and proper in Emerson but always mixed and bipolar (thus, to imagine a personless impersonal would be to offer yet another abstraction). Emerson points to nature's need for persons on many occasions. Nature "will not remain orbed in a thought, but rushed into persons; and when each person, inflamed to a fury of personality would conquer all things to his poor crotchet she raises up against him another person" ("Nominalist and Realist, 3:139); or "All persons that ever existed are [nature's] forgotten ministers" ("Self-Reliance," 2:39). Persons may be "supplementary" to the impersonal ("Over-Soul," 2:164), but this supplement is absolutely necessary inasmuch as "one mode of the divine teaching is the incarnation of the spirit in a form—in a form like my own" (ibid.). Persons themselves, therefore, "acquaint us with the impersonal" (ibid.). In this theory of expressionism, which is not specific to Emerson, persons are modes of expression of the impersonal, its moods: "What is a man but nature's finer success in self-explication? What is a man but a finer and compacter landscape, than the horizon figures?" ("Art," 2:209).[17]

It is here that one encounters a bizarre consequence of Emerson's thinking about persons: if everything individualized or formed is the expression of the impersonal, then everything individualized is a person. Emerson's thesis that a man is only a finer expression of nature than a landscape ("what is a man but a finer ... landscape") signals such an interpretation. And conversely, what passes commonsensically for impersonal—a landscape, for instance—becomes, since it is formed, a type of a person. However, for man to be a more compact landscape (or form) than figures on the horizon suggests that some "persons" will necessarily be more and less personified than others. Trees are thus said in the essay "Nature" to be somewhat less personified than man: "If we look at [nature's] work we seem to catch a glance of a system in transition. Plants are the young of the world . . . but they grope ever upward towards consciousness, the trees are imperfect men . . . rooted in the ground" (3:105–6). Trees are thus men in the process of becoming human; their disadvantage in comparison to men seems to derive from their reduced mobility, their rootedness. In contrast to trees, a rose, which in "Self-Reliance" is the embodiment of perfection because it doesn't refer to anything other than itself, may be more personalized than Plato, for Plato needs Socrates to scar him and personalize him ("Socrates and Plato are the double star" ["Plato," 4:39]). On the other hand, Plato is perhaps more personalized than Swedenborg, whose internal organs are not "united" but made of "so many little organs," and whose stomach is made "of so many little stomachs" ("Swedenborg," 4:65), like a compound of some sort that can fall apart any time. Personality, too, becomes a question of degrees.

So far I have been referring mostly to perceptions and moods, which destabilize the "I," turning its being into a becoming. But is there nothing more stable in us, something that would prevent this erasure of distinctions among species such that we become like so many roses or trees? One has to wonder how thinking figures in Emerson's schema; couldn't such a stability be found in our thinking, which differs from perceptions and moods?

Emerson answers this question in degrees also. From "Intellect" to "Experience" such a stability is redefined to become an instability of a different order. Whereas in "Intellect" the suggestion was that despite the proliferation of moods ("subject to change, to fear, and hope") there might be something stable, "Experience" defines stability as the sliding motion of instability: "If I have described life as a flux of moods, I must now add, that there is that in us which changes not. . . . The consciousness in each man is a sliding scale, which identifies him now with the First Cause, and now with the flesh of his body; life above life, in infinite degrees" (3:42). The flux of moods may be differentiated from consciousness, but consciousness, first said to be unchangeable, now comes to be identified with the "sliding scale," with "life above life" or, simply, with instability.

I suggest that Emerson's thesis that both moods and consciousness are sliding is not tautological, that moods are not thoughts. However, if thoughts too are said to be sliding, rather than being anchored—since they are both fluctuating and incalculable—one may still suppose them to be events of some sort, although different from events of moods. In "Fate" Emerson explicitly identifies thoughts with events: "He thinks his fate alien, because the copula is hidden. But the soul contains the event that shall befall it, for the event is only the actualization of its thoughts. . . . The event is the print of your form" (6:21). The questions he raises here (What kind of events are thoughts? If they befall us where do they come from? Who are "we" who suffer them?) all point to the hidden copula, and hence to the being of our thinking and to the way that relates to personal identity. The epistemology of moods thus turns out to be an ontology of thinking.

INTUITING, OR THINKING AS REMEMBERING

In "Powers of the Mind" Emerson offers this fascinating description of human thinking:

> For my thoughts, I seem to stand on the bank of a river, and watch the endless flow of the stream before me floating objects of all shapes, colors, and natures, nor can I much detain them as they pass, except by running beside them a little way along the bank. But whence they come, or whither they go, is not told me. Only I have a suspicion that, as geologists say, "Every river makes its own valley"; so does this mystic stream; it makes its valley, makes its banks, and makes perhaps the observer too.[18]

To understand what kind of events that thoughts represent and how the mind works according to Emerson is to unpack this passage.

Such an interpretation should begin, I propose, with the essay "Intellect." At first sight, this may seem too obvious, for where else would one begin looking for Emerson's philosophy of thinking but in the only essay whose title explicitly refers to the faculty of thought? And yet, most commentators interested in the question of thinking in Emerson pay scant attention to it. Stephen Whicher, for example, refers to it but always in passing, without ever offering a sustained reading of it; David Van Leer's *Emerson's Epistemology* mentions "Intellect" only once, as the essay in which Emerson resists the idea of completion of knowledge.[19] Cavell doesn't mention it at all.[20]

One of the reasons for this neglect within the Emersonian canon may be that many interpreters prefer to focus on Emerson's early usage of concepts, such as reason and understanding, with which the concept of the intellect doesn't quite fit. Or, it may be—but I am, of course, only guessing here—that the image of thought he offers in that essay contradicts the predominant understanding of the Emersonian self as a self-absorbed, active, and reliant individual, since Emerson is there suggesting the intellect to be a faculty that precedes all action and thus proposing thinking as fundamentally passive. It may also be that because Emerson there offers something like a systematic image of thought, it remains unclear to interpreters whether such a systematicity should be treated as a failed attempt or as a more pervasive orientation of Emerson's philosophy. Nevertheless, following the publication of Emerson's *Later Lectures* there is no doubt that he continued unfolding the arguments from "Intellect" at least until 1858 and therefore that the ideas he proposed in that essay represent perhaps the most enduring interest of his thinking. Both the series of lectures called "Mind and Manners of the Nineteenth Century" (1848–49), which includes lectures such as "The Power and Laws of Thought" and "The Relation of Intellect to Natural Science"; and the series of six lectures called "Natural Method of Mental Philosophy" (1858) are further elaborations of "Intellect." If we take into account the facts that Emerson began to entertain the idea of "the First Philosophy, . . . the original laws of the mind" in the journal notebook now designated as *RO Mind* (1835),[21] that the lecture "The Head" (1837) contains many of the ideas later to be found in "Intellect," and that as early as 1838 he is thinking about writing a natural history of the mind—which found its first formulation precisely in "Intellect"—it becomes clear that his reflections on what he called "intellect" span a period of at least twenty of the most productive years of his thinking. For that reason the essay should be read attentively.

Even though after his Jardin des Plantes revelation Emerson gradually toned down his excitement about becoming a naturalist, his interest in natural history persisted. However, and importantly, what Emerson began to envision was not a natural history of nature but of the mind. His first idea was to write a natural history of Reason, rather than of the Intellect. Such a history would have to account for "everything that is alive ... in thought": "Could not the natural history of the Reason or Universal Sentiment be written? One trait would be that all that is alive & genial in thought must come out of that."[22] What was raised by this rudimentary form of the biology of thinking was the possibility of isolating the motion (life) of thought independently from its connections to other capacities of the mind, from the will, for example: "Write the Natural History of Reason. . . . Show that Will is absurd in the matter."[23] What Emerson wants then, is to understand thinking per se, not as related to intention, volition, or determination; to examine it outside of its own contextual or temporal entanglement with other faculties. He wants something like thought taken out of its own temporality or historicity, as though it were not conditioned by anything.

The idea may seem naïve but it explains why he needs a natural history. As Michel Foucault interpreted the question, "For natural history to appear, it was not necessary for nature to become denser and more obscure . . . it was necessary—and this is entirely the opposite—for History to become Natural."[24] History become natural is divorced from the desires, motives, or actions of persons. In it everything happens naturally, that is to say, without the responsibility of a human agent; such a history is then like nature—impersonal. That is precisely how Emerson understands it: "Natural History is elegant, astronomy sublime for this reason, their impersonality."[25]

Because it is impersonal, natural history gives privilege to space over time, to taxonomy over narrative, which then explains the possibility of Linnaeus's classifications, for example. Things that would follow one another temporally can now be displayed simultaneously, in the same space and at the same time. Such continuities are spatial rather then temporal. As Foucault put it, natural history knows of continuities but "it is not . . . that time or duration ensures the continuity. . . . For continuity precedes time. It is its condition."[26] The processes of a natural history are thus the effect of spatial serialization rather than of temporal succession.

I suggest that in order to reflect this privilege given to space over time Emerson opts for the term "intellect" rather than "reason," even though, following Coleridge, he also tried to use the latter term. Reason, as Emerson recognized, involved a temporal and dialectical relation to understanding, to persons, and to nature. On the other hand, he understood intellect as answering precisely to spatial organization rather then temporal conditioning. He describes it as a space with walls ("Intellect," 2:196), as a cave lit with lanterns (2:196, 2:197), or as a dark chamber (2:198). And it is conceived of as an impersonal force: "the intellect goes out of the individual, floats over its own personality, and regards it as a fact, and not as *I* and *mine*" (2:194, Emerson's emphasis). This impersonal intellect has, as Emerson specifies, two major strata, which he calls intellect receptive and intellect constructive. In accordance with his ontological credo that everything is bipolar, both of those intellects will be twofold. Intellect receptive therefore comprises intuition and reflection.

By now it has became customary to refer to Emerson as a philosopher of intuition, to such an extent that Cavell, for example, is annoyed by it:

> The path I am not taking at this point leads from Emerson's speaking of "primary wisdom as Intuition," to which he adds, "All later teachings are Tuitions." I note this path to commemorate my annoyance at having to stand the repeated, conforming description of Emerson as a philosopher of intuition, a description that uniformly fails to add that he is simultaneously the teacher of tuition, as though his speaking of all later teachings as tuitions were a devaluing of the teachings rather than a direction for deriving their necessary value.[27]

It seems that Cavell sees intuition as a kind of irrational knowing to which more rational (tuition) is opposed. But Emerson is in fact in accord with the Western rationalist tradition since all modern rationalists—Descartes, Spinoza, Leibniz, Pascal, Kant—saw intuition as the highest form of rational knowing. Western rationalism sees in it its highest capacity.

In his book on *Kant and the Problem of Metaphysics* Heidegger offers a most economical summary of the ways in which the West has thought of intuition. I will introduce it here for no other reason than for its precision. Intuition was conceived of in two major forms, Heidegger explains: in the first place as divine knowledge *(intuitus originarius)*. This "divine knowing is representing which, in intuiting, first creates the intuitable being as such."[28] Since nothing exists before God, his thinking of something is at the same time his creating it. But rationalist philosophers were less interested in this type of intuition precisely because it concerned only God. The second type of intuition, the only one that concerns humans, is noncreative: "Finite intuition sees that it is dependent upon the intuitable as a being which exists in its own right. The intuited is derived from such beings; thus, this intuition is also called *intuitus derivativus*" (18). Far from being an inspiration that comes to the genius from his superior visionary interiority—as some interpreters have in fact understood intuition in Emerson—what is intuited is here derived from the outside and is received through the senses. Heidegger explains: "Because human intuition as finite 'takes-in-stride' and because the possibility of a 'receiving' which takes-in-stride requires affection, therefore organs of affection, 'the senses,' are in fact necessary" (18–19). Intuition is thus receptive knowledge and can be used synonymously with the term "reception." It takes in stride what is out there, and since that type of knowing happens all the time and to everybody, Heidegger can say that "knowledge is primarily intuition" (19).

Emerson understood that correctly; intuition for him too is both receptive and primary knowing: "The mind is first only receptive."[29] Or, as he states in "Intellect," using Pascal's terminology: "we shall perceive the superiority of the spontaneous or intuitive principle over the arithmetical or logical" (2:195). As receptive knowing, intuiting is in Emerson also a way of being attuned to the outside, not an irrational attitude toward objects; it is receiving, hence, taking in stride. But Emerson, I suggest, does more than just repeat the inherited understanding of intuition. He modifies it in such a fascinating way that if for no other reason than that alone, he deserves a prominent place in the history of philosophy. In Emerson—and I am now summarizing what I will develop in the rest of this section—intuition has a complex temporality since in his version of it the mind does not immediately intuit what it has taken in stride. His idea of intuition—and hence its strangeness—is counterintuitive. It works as follows.

Through involuntary perception something is at first imperceptibly taken in or, as Emerson puts it in "Intellect," "inscribed" on the walls of the intellect. The experience is in fact common, as we often perceptually register something subliminally, as it were, without being aware of the fact that we have done so, without thinking of it. The intellect thus resembles an open cave where perceptions fall down and inscribe themselves: "The walls of rude minds are scrawled all over with facts, with thoughts. They shall one day bring a lantern and read the inscriptions" (2:196).[30] It is this inscription (perception) that will at some point be enlightened by the lantern and so intuited. Because perceptions affect one another in the intellect without the mind knowing anything about it, Emerson can claim that there is thinking prior to reflection, that is, before we become aware of it. And the moment of our becoming aware of the perception long active within the mind is what might be called intuition: "Long prior to the age of reflection is the thinking of the mind. Out of darkness, it came insensibly into the marvelous light of to-day" (2:194). Or, perhaps even more explicitly: "There lie the impressions on the retentive organ, though you knew it not. So lies the whole series of natural images with which your life has made you acquainted in your memory, though you know it not, and a thrill of passion flashes light on their dark chamber, and the active power seizes instantly the fit image, as the word of its momentary thought" (2:198). This momentary thought, which the mind seizes as though it were a new one, without realizing that it had been stored there for some time, is what is intuited and intuited as truth: "Then, in a moment, and unannounced, the truth appears. A certain, wandering light appears, and is the distinction, the principle, we wanted" (2:197).

Intuition thus "befalls" us as something new, as an event, which is the meaning of Emerson's thesis, in "Fate," that "the soul contains the event that shall befall it" (6:21). But this newness is somewhat paradoxical, for the mind intuits as new what had been in it for some time, affecting it without its knowing. On the one hand, since it occurs within what has already been inscribed in the intellect, the newness of the intuition is only a mode of recollection. On the other hand, since the mind does not remember its own past, the intuited is for it properly new. The paradox of Emersonian intuition consists in encountering for the first time something that has already been encountered impersonally. It is the encountering of an *impersonal remembrance*.

To say that intuition befalls the "I" is a rather radical claim: that the "I" is not intuition's agent but its patient, that it doesn't create the thought but is given the thought in order to be able to think it. For the "I" is something that arrives at intuition: "But every insight from this realm of thought is felt as initial, and promises a sequel. I do not make it; I arrive there and behold what was there already. I make! O no! I clap my hands in infantine joy and amazement" ("Reality," 3:41). In occurring thus to the "I" it interrupts the latter's continuity, which is why it can be called an event in the first place. As Emerson puts it in "Intellect" (still in the passage that analyzes the question of intuition): "They [thoughts] catch us up for moments into their heaven and so fully engage us, that we take no thought for the morrow, gaze like children, *without an effort to make them our* own. By and by we fall out of that rupture, bethink us where we have been, what we have seen, and repeat, as truly as we can what we have beheld" (2:195, emphasis mine). Emerson's formulation is important: we do not fall out of ourselves into a rupture of thinking but rather the other way around; we fall out of the rupture into ourselves, as if the limitless outsideness of thinking were an interior out of which we fall into the position of a person.

That there is the thinking called intuition that occurs without the "I," or that the "I" does not have to accompany all our representations— whether because it happens as Emerson says before reflection or because it only "befalls" the "I"—suggests that the "I" is only one thought among others, not their condition. Already in the "Transcendentalist" Emerson had supposed that what we call "I" is only a name for a thought: "I— this thought which is called I,—" (1:204). Such an insight anticipates the similar idea from the lecture on the "Powers of the Mind:" "Thought constitutes personality"[31] and not vice versa; as well that from "Illusions:" "The notions '*I am,*' and '*This is mine,*' which influence mankind, are but delusions of the mother of the world" (6:173). Being non-posited by the "I," thinking posits that "I" as an involuntary thought. The "I" is a fragment of thinking; or else, it is only a part of ourselves, our self being the motion of involuntary thinking.

Only now can I return to the "bank of a river" passage with which I started this section, since it should be clear that it describes, on the basis of the imagery of natural history, the Emersonian profound thought I have just attempted to explain: the "I" is a part of us or simply one thought among others:

> For my thoughts, I seem to stand on the bank of a river, and watch the endless flow of the stream before me floating objects of all shapes . . . nor can I much detain them as they pass, except by running beside them a little way along the bank. But whence they come, or whither

they go, is not told me. Only I have a suspicion that, as geologists say, "Every river makes its own valley"; so does this mystic stream; it makes its valley, makes its banks, and makes perhaps the observer too.[32]

The "I" here runs after its thoughts, which are like floating objects escaping it, coming to it and leaving it, without its managing to apprehend them. The "I," thus, neither makes thoughts nor shapes them ("whence they come, or whither they go, is not told me"). But it is thoughts that make the mind also, since the stream of watery thoughts turns the flat globe of the brain into the earth, with its rivers, valleys, deserts, and mountains, and along the way creates the observer. In that sense, thoughts are neither the globe (the intellect) nor the observer but a kind of *geography,* impersonal (natural) writing inscribed on the surface of the brain-earth.

Such a geography of the brain would have a natural rather than a personal history. The history of thinking, in Emerson, in a rather bizarre way, corresponds to the history of water, rocks, or vegetation, to the extent that, like the motion of grass, it too is impersonal:

> Thus the idea of Vegetation is irresistible in considering mental activity. . . . What happens here in mankind, is matched by what happens out there in the history of grass and wheat. . . . This curious resemblance to the vegetable pervades human nature, and repeats, in the mental function, the germination, growth, state of melioration, crossings, blights, parasites, and, in short, all the accidents of the plant. The analogy is so thorough. . . . In the living mind, the thoughts live and grow; and what happens in the vegetable happens to them.[33]

These theses articulated in 1848 are, however, but an elaboration of the claim Emerson formulated in his first published philosophical statement, *Nature* (1836): "The greatest delight which the fields and woods minister, is the suggestion of an occult relation between man and vegetable" (1:10). They thus testify to Emerson's lifelong preoccupation with the possibility of passive and impersonal thinking.

ENTERING THE VALLEYS OF THE BRAIN: REFLECTION

Although the "I" is one thought among others, it differs from those other thoughts. It is at the same time a thought that can perceive other thoughts, the instance of intellectual perception. This capacity to perceive thoughts or things puts the "I" at a distance from them, "and the fact of intellectual perception severs, once for all, the man from the things with which he converses."[34] Severed from other thoughts the person can now enter into the valleys made by them. The "I" is like an imaginary first inhabitant of the earth suddenly allowed to take a solitary walk upon it.

The position of the "I" as a solitary walker on the tracks of the brain will become epistemologically troublesome for Emerson. For as long as it is in a position to perceive objects and thoughts, it remains distant from them. From that distance it cannot report the moment of unity of thought and object called intuition, for in order to do so, Emerson thinks, it would have to be within that unity. The most central epistemological question Emerson asks will be how to recall and report—exactly, truthfully—the irruptive moment of knowing as intuiting. How does one record intuition? How are we to testify to something that has happened in our absence?

"Intellect" formulates the problem by saying that "intuition" or the "logic of the heart" has now to become the object of the "long logic" of "arithmetical" reason or reflection.[35] At first sight it seems as if Emerson is not saying anything new about the relationship between intuition and reflection: intuition as fast forwarded, compressed thought now has to be rewound by the slow motion of reflection. The movement forward has to be accounted for by a reflective retreat: "If we consider what persons have stimulated and profited us, we shall perceive the superiority of the spontaneous or intuitive principle over the arithmetical or logical. The first contains the second, but virtual and latent. We want, in every man, a long logic. . . . Logic is the procession or proportionate unfolding of the intuition" (2:195). But to say that reflection depends on intuition (since it is its unfolding) is to change the inherited—Cartesian—understanding of reflective thinking as an active power independent not only of intuition but of sense perception too. Because in Emerson reflection unfolds what it has received from intuition, there are no pure ideas or thoughts; there is no a priori thinking. Reflection (what Emerson calls "long logic") receives its object from intuition and works with it. Thus reflection— and this is Emerson's great novelty—is also passive or receptive, which explains why, along with intuition, it too belongs to what Emerson terms "the intellect receptive." This doesn't, of course, mean that in thinking reflection is not active, but rather and only that it receives its thoughts from elsewhere, that it does not produce them from within itself. There is no thinking that does not receive itself from somewhere else; hence, all "our thinking is a pious reception" (2:195).

Another radical characteristic specific to Emerson's understanding of reflection follows from here. In receiving its object from elsewhere, reflection avoids being self-reflection. The already quoted sentence about our falling out of the rupture continues in the following way:

> By and by we fall out of that rupture, bethink us where we have been, what we have seen, and repeat as truly as we can, what we have beheld. As far as we can recall these ecstasies, we carry away in the ineffaceable memory the result, and all men and all the ages confirm it. It is called Truth. But the moment we cease to report, and attempt to correct and contrive, it is not truth. (2:195)

But if reflection has to be the exact report of intuition, then, in a paradoxical way, it has to become identical with that intuition. Any discrepancy between the two—being the interventionist's gesture of the "I"—is a contrivance, whereas reflection should be, as Emerson wants it, a faithful record of the intuited, the very thought of the rupture: "But, the moment we attempt to say those things in memory, Charlatanism begins. . . . But the thoughts which wander through our mind, we do not absorb and make flesh of, but we report them as thoughts; we retail them as news, to our lovers and to all Athenians. At a dreadful loss we play this game."[36] As was the case with intuition, Emerson here explains the "long logic" of our thinking by speaking again of the "I" that has nothing to do with thoughts wandering through its head. It does not absorb them, it does not make its own flesh out of them. Reflection reports intuition only on condition that it is not appropriated and modeled by the "I." Thus, not only intuitive but also reflective thinking remains true as long as it does not get mediated by the "I." The "I" is thus strangely marginalized in Emerson's idea of thinking. As Richard Poirier notes in commenting on perhaps Emerson's most famous intuitive moment, the transparent eyeball experience (but the comment is applicable, I suggest, to the process of reflection also): "He [Emerson] does not claim even to have originated anything; and being 'transparent' he cannot be turned or troped or traced in any direction. The represented event on that bare common is, indisputably, only something that *has* happened, something always prior to the reporting of it."[37] Because both intuition and reflection happen independently of the reporter, Poirier can say that a moment of such an event called thinking (Poirier compares it to reading and writing) "is also a moment in which self-present identity is reportedly lost" (121). For that reason, reflection is not a representation of intuition within the "I"— Emerson eliminated that as "Charlatanism"—but a selfless multiplying of thoughts, as if in a mirror. It is a mirroring without self-mirroring.[38] Thoughts, not only intuited ones, but also elaborated, long or reflected ones, come to the "I" rather than being thought by it: "But a thought has its own proper motion which it communicates to me not borrows of me, & on its Pegasus back I override & overlook the world."[39] Thinking thus requires the removal of the "I."

"Intellect" claims the practice of self-removal to be the common and universal characteristic of thinking. What is more, the intellect receptive is possible only on condition that the "I" is denied: "We do not determine what we will think. We only open our senses, clear away, as we can all obstruction from the fact, and suffer the intellect to see" (2:195). Suffering an aversion to itself, personalized understanding always leaves itself, which is the only way it can think. But as we shall see, such a suffering requires a power of endurance.

The understanding of power as suffering is most clearly formulated in "Experience," where power is said to be the resignation of the will, the exposure to the involuntary: "Power keeps quite another road than the turnpikes of choice and will, namely, the subterranean and invisible tunnels and channels of life" (3:39). Power would be the capacity to expose form or the person to the very force of its deformation: "Human life is made up of the two elements, power and form, and the proportion must be invariably kept" (3:38). Very simply put, power would reside not only in the capacity to deform who we are but also in our ability to suffer that deformation in order to change. This restlessness that deforms us in order to form us differently is identified in "Nature" as the secret of life: "Motion and change, and identity or rest, are the first and second secrets of nature" (3:105). But, as "Intellect" makes clear, only change is identified with truth:

> God offers to every mind its choice between truth and repose. Take which you please you can never have both. He in whom the love of repose predominates . . . gets rest . . . but he shuts the door of truth. He

in whom the love of truth predominates will keep himself aloof from all moorings, and afloat. He will abstain from dogmatism, and recognize all the opposite negations, between which, as walls, his being is swung. He submits to the inconvenience of suspense but he is a candidate for truth. (2:202)

What Emerson has in mind when he talks about power is this submission to the "inconvenience of suspense," the capacity to let oneself be swung (passively) among positions or identities, to suffer restlessness, the unsettling of personal identity, in order to receive the truth and to do so patiently (Emerson repeats his call for patience time and again).

Cavell's detection of the pervasiveness of passivity within Emerson's thinking is, thus, perhaps the most accurate diagnosis of what that thinking is predicated on: "Emerson's emphatic call to patience should threaten a familiar idea of Emersonian power, for Emerson makes power look awfully like (from a certain platform, look exactly like) passiveness."[40] One can win at last on condition one is patient because through passive reception one receives the truth. Or, as Cavell puts it: "'The *last*,' at which we shall win, if we are patient, is an instruction about philosophical patience or suffering or reception or passion or power. It speaks of lasting as enduring, and specifically of enduring as on a track, of following on, as a succession of steps" (138; emphasis in original). Negating the rest (the safe or the personal) truth becomes the impersonal flight between resting points (walls, doctrines, identities). It is the restlessness of the impersonal, and transcendental inasmuch as the transcendentalist, as the 1842 Masonic Temple lecture specifies, is he who removes anything "dogmatic or personal" in order to "suffer" the impersonal influx of "light and power" ("Transcendentalist," 1:204). The thesis identifying the unspiritual or thoughtless with the personal is in fact from a year before, in the "Lecture of the Times," where Emerson also explicitly determines "inaction" and "patience" to be "the paramount duties of self-reliance" (1:177): "the spiritualist wishes this only, that the spiritual principle should be suffered to demonstrate itself to the end, in all possible applications to the state of man, without the admission of anything unspiritual, that is, anything positive, dogmatic, or personal" (1:181).

A power understood as the suffering restlessness of the impersonal is the major argument not only of "Experience" and "The Transcendentalist" but, paradoxically enough, of "Self-Reliance." There, in a similar way to

"Experience," the self's reliance on power is based on Emerson's understanding that "power ceases in the instant of repose; it resides in the moment of transition from a past to a new state" ("Self-Reliance," 2:40).
Thus, Emerson's main problem in that essay is to identify the "Trustee"
of such a reliance, to determine what kind of a "Self" is in question in
self-reliance. The answer to that question is what Emerson there termed
the "aboriginal Self," the essence of life, the incalculable or, at one point,
simply intuition, an impersonally contracted insight and therefore, according to commonsense logic, precisely what one cannot rely on:

> Who is the Trustee? What is the aboriginal Self, on which a univer-
> sal reliance may be grounded? What is the nature and power of that
> science-baffling star, without parallax, without calculable elements. . . .
> The inquiry leads us to that source, at once the essence of genius, of
> virtue, and of life, which we call Spontaneity or Instinct. We denote
> this primary wisdom as Intuition. (2:37)

Far from a personalized self, what reliance relies on here is the impersonal, nonpositioned life, *a life* "by which things exist" (2:37). It is to
that involuntary life—which alone is in the process of becoming—that
power belongs. Because this power is an involuntary capacity, the power
of depersonalization, Emerson will say: "To talk of reliance is a poor external way of speaking. Speak rather of that which relies, *because it works
and is.* Who has more obedience than me masters me" (2:40, emphasis
mine). Power, then, belongs to the "it." *It* is, *it* works, *it* thinks.

To return to our point of departure, if the hardest task in the world
is to think, it is because that task of "ours" is not something "we" can
perform since thinking is not ours, is not of our will: "What is the hardest task in the world? To think. I would put myself in the attitude to look
in the eye an abstract truth and I cannot" ("Intellect," 2:196). A fundamental incapacity to think accompanies the "I's" effort to do so, for the
power to think is the powerlessness of the "I." As if in a dramatic reversal of the Cartesian scenario, "I" is what cannot think, what is not en-
trusted with the power to think, for thinking is the power that crushes
the "I." Following a contrary path of argumentation (by claiming that
"Emerson goes the whole way with Descartes's insight—that I exist only
if I think"), Cavell nevertheless formulates a similar thesis by suggesting that Emerson "thereupon denies that I (mostly) do think, that the 'I'

mostly gets into my thinking, as it were."[41] Thinking is thus the hardest task in the world not only because it requires of the "I" what it is absolutely incapable of doing, but also because it announces the very catastrophe of the "I."

Furthermore, since the truth or reflection that was supposed to faithfully report the impersonal and silent intuition is impersonal, it too faces the problem it had to solve. There is truth, but nobody can say it or see it (as that would require its personalization, the interruption of reception, hence the negation of truth). The truth unfolds itself in and as impersonal silence. The intellect receptive (both intuition and reflection) is mute: "We want, in every man, a long logic; we cannot pardon the absence of it, but it must not be spoken. Logic is the procession or proportionate unfolding of the intuition; but its virtue is as silent method; the moment it would appear as propositions, and have a separate value, it is worthless" ("Intellect," 2:195). The real virtue of reflection, something like its morality, is its silence, a silence that is said to dissolve persons, since language, Emerson claims, betrays the truth of reflection. Intellect receptive thus receives the truth but is incapable of expressing it. To use the analogy from the "Natural History of the Intellect," it is as if the streams (of thinking) carve out their paths on the earth-brain so that its vegetation starts growing, as if leaves of grass appear on the desert sand, so that the beauty of the world is exposed to the eyes of the solitary walker on the Earth who cannot say or express in any other way what he sees. There is no one to testify to it. Is it really possible that no one will enter the valleys of the brain; is all that beauty of the truth for nothing and for nobody?

SILENT CONSTRUCTIONS

The force of expressing thought is called intellect constructive. What it constructs is precisely the expression. Like the intellect receptive, the intellect constructive is made of two layers: "In the intellect constructive, which we popularly designate by the word Genius, we observe the same balance of two elements as in the intellect receptive" ("Intellect," 2:198). The two elements are the intellect receptive plus something that might be called the "intellect expressive," that is, the force of communicating or publishing the received thought: "To genius must always go two gifts, the thought and the publication" (2:198). Thus, the intellect constructive has to construct "sentences, poems, plans, designs, systems" (2:198) by which it makes received thought—whether intuited or reflected on—public. In other words, in order to make thought communicable it has to turn it into something accessible to the senses of others so they can receive it: "To be communicable, it must become picture or sensible object" (2:198). Hence, what was received through the senses in order to be thought has now to be returned to the world of the senses. Expression is a moral imperative of Emerson's ethics of thinking; thoughts have to be publishable so that they can be shared.

Successful or truthful expression, however, seems to be a difficult task. In fact it almost seems to be more difficult than thinking, which is already the most difficult: "We are all wise. The difference between persons is not in wisdom but in art" ("Intellect," 2:197). Even though thinking, here called "wisdom," is difficult, it does, in the last instance, come to all of us as we are all receptive beings; to the extent that we all think and have good ideas, we can therefore be said to be wise. The difference among us resides in how well we construct our expressions. Good constructions are rare: "But if the constructive powers are rare, and it is given to few men to be poets, yet every man is a receiver of this descending holy ghost" (2:202). Because everyone has intellect receptive, we can all participate in and appreciate what is communicated and to a greater or lesser degree participate in art.

But if only some of us know how to communicate well—or how to express thoughts—it is because "construction" requires the right mixture of will and spontaneity, of personal and impersonal. The artist is so appreciated by Emerson precisely because by translating impersonal thoughts into personal expression he would finally know how to empower the "I;" his "I" would be able to exercise willful control over spontaneous thought. The function of the "I" thus seems to be found in its capacity to control and express the thought that it didn't think: "The thought of genius is spontaneous; but the power of picture or expression in the most enriched and flowing nature, implies a mixture of will, a certain control over the spontaneous states, without which no production is possible" ("Intellect," 2:199).

Yet, what seems necessary for artistic production—"the eye of judgment, with a strenuous exercise of choice"—is not what occurs: "Not by any conscious imitation of particular forms are the grand strokes of the painter executed. . . . Who is the first drawing-master? We may owe to dreams some light on the fountain of this skill; for as soon as we let our will go, and let the unconscious state ensue, see what cunning draughtsmen we are!" ("Intellect," 2:199–200). What holds for the painter holds for the writer who believes that "he can continue this communication at pleasure," whereas, as a matter of fact, "up, down, around, the kingdom of thought has no enclosures, but the Muse makes us free of her city" (2:200). Clichéd as it certainly is, the reference to the Muse taking the writer in and out of her city nevertheless suggests that writing involves the negation of the writer's will, referred to as the absence of thought's enclosures, that it is the inscription and the rhetoric of the impersonal. What appeared to be the exclusive domain of personal will—expression, art—thus becomes yet another manifestation of the impersonal.

Emerson here intensifies the argument. Not only is it impossible to willfully construct an artistic expression, but our common talk itself is beyond the reach of our power. Even the ordinary speaking necessary for expression seems to be incapable of publishing thought truthfully. Words, Emerson suggests, stabilize thoughts and so betray them; sentences position them and so modify them. Language, to the extent that it is positioning, forming, framing, personalizing, negates the very nature of thinking, which is never positioned, always mobile: "But if I speak I define, I confine, and am less" ("Intellect," 2:202). Emerson's argument about language failing our intentions differs, in fact, from the traditional claim that man is incapable of expressing himself, which led philosophers from Plato to Descartes to identify language as the source of error. What Emerson says is not simply that we fail in wanting to control language; rather, he is suggesting that—because of the power of the impersonal— it is language itself that constructs us and speaks us; that the only accurate expression occurs when the "I" is absent (for example in dreams). This is precisely a modern, twentieth-century idea, that language is the enormous power of impersonal speaking, a being outside the mind.

In the end impersonal language expresses itself in silence. Speaking never seems to say what it talks about. That is perhaps why, after insisting on the necessity of "publication," "Intellect" ends in a celebration of silence as if expression necessarily had to fail. After claiming the importance of the speaking method, Emerson introduces the "hearing man"

(2:202) who is greater than the speaking man because he still has the liberty to unfold the definitions made by the speaking man into manifold meanings, suggestions or allusions, thus turning the conveyed into a limitless possibility, the truth of the impersonal. As long as he listens he is not partial, his listening, too, is impersonal: "Happy is the hearing man; unhappy the speaking man. As long as I hear truth, I am bathed by a beautiful element, and am not conscious of any limits to my nature. The suggestions are thousandfold that I hear and see" (2:102). Listening is better than speaking because it is closer to silence, which is better still than listening since silence contains all possibilities at once; it is something like the absolute (godlike) affirmative: "The ancient sentence said, Let us be silent, for so are the gods. Silence is a solvent that destroys personality, and gives us leave to be great and universal" (2:203). With this leave given to us to leave ourselves, the intellect constructive turns into the receptive recording of the truth, a truth recorded in language, but which ends in silence. Expression remains an endless task, tragically always doomed to misunderstandings.

EMERSON'S BRAIN

In 1839, in a letter to Margaret Fuller, Emerson had written something to the effect that the truth remains withdrawn even from those who have withdrawn into solitude in order to practice an "art of living" as the art of thinking: "Even when we have extricated ourselves from all the embarrassments of the social problem it does not please the oracle to emit any light on the *mode* of individual life. A thousand negatives it utters clear & strong on all sides, but the sacred affirmative it hides in the deepest abyss."[42] Thinking that publishes itself through writing, conversing, or political speaking either remains personal (hence dogmatic and doctrinaire) or it attains impersonal truth, which then remains out of the reach of persons. The affirmative remains abyssal, something like a cave into which we can enter but from which our persons will not find an exit.

Perhaps echoing her friend's lament, in the review she wrote of the *Second Series* for the *New-York Daily Tribune,* December 7, 1844, Margaret Fuller compared Emerson's essays to the nervous system of the brain. The logic of her image, which relies on the impersonal functioning of the body, suggests that the sensations and fantasies from those nerves will be sent to the lungs, heart, and hands of the "body politic" that will gradually be affected, hence, infected by them:

> If New-England may be regarded as a chief mental focus to the New World, and many symptoms seem to give her this place, as to other centers the characteristics of heart and lungs to the body politic; if we may believe, as the writer does believe, that what is to be acted out in the country at large is, most frequently, first indicated there, as all the phenomena of the nervous system in the fantasies of the brain, we may hail as an auspicious omen the influence Mr. Emerson has there obtained.[43]

Emerson's essays would thus be the embodied recording of the impersonal truth that carves its way within the text-brain and so keeps sending involuntary perceptions, as if from an abyss, to affect other brains. As a result, the reader of the essays would know something about them in spite of or in contradiction to his voluntary understanding of them. And once that involuntary understanding became voluntary, then everything would depend on the ethics of reading them.

NOTES

1. Ralph Waldo Emerson, "Intellect," *The Collected Works of Ralph Waldo Emerson,* ed. Alfred R. Ferguson, Robert E. Spiller, et al., 8 vols. to date (Cambridge, Mass.: Harvard University Press, Belknap Press, 1971–2010), 2:196. Subsequent quotations from Emerson's writing are from this source and are cited parenthetically in text by volume and page numbers. Citations may include essay title if the essay from which a quotation is taken is not clear from the text.

2. In her crucial analysis of the relationship between moods and the impersonal in Emerson, Sharon Cameron suggests that the spatial image from "Over-Soul" points to the dividedness of the self: "'We lie open on one side to the deeps of spiritual nature, to all the attributes of God'" (2:161). I take Emerson's spatial image as testifying to the necessarily divided nature of our allegiance to the egotistical and the impersonal. "On one side there is access, on the other there is not." This and other quotations of Sharon Cameron are from chapter 1 of this volume, "The Way of Life by Abandonment: Emerson's Impersonal."

3. Eduardo Cadava, *Emerson and the Climates of History* (Stanford, Calif.: Stanford University Press, 1997), 2.

4. My reading of moods in Emerson thus differs from that of Russell Goodman for whom moods in Emerson—at least in the context of "Experience"—are subjective and "much like 'will.'" See Russell B. Goodman, *American Philosophy and the Romantic Tradition* (Cambridge: Cambridge University Press), 1990, 45–46.

5. George Kateb, *Emerson and Self-Reliance* (New York: Rowman & Littlefield, 2002), 13.

6. *The Journals and Miscellaneous Notebooks of Ralph Waldo Emerson,* ed. William H. Gilman et al., 16 vols. (Cambridge, Mass.: Harvard University Press, 1960–1982).

7. "The Relation of Intellect to Natural Science," in *The Later Lectures of Ralph Waldo Emerson, 1843–1871,* ed. Ronald A. Bosco and Joel Myerson, 2 vols. (Athens: University of Georgia Press, 2001), 1:166.

8. Werner Hamacher, *Premises, Essays on Philosophy and Literature from Kant to Celan,* trans. Peter Fenves (Stanford, Calif.: Stanford University Press, 1996), 249.

9. *Journals and Miscellaneous Notebooks,* 7:57.

10. Ibid., 5:457.

11. I have in mind here the way Cavell reads "Self-Reliance:" "Good posture has two principal names or modes in 'Self-Reliance': standing and sitting. The idea behind both modes is that of finding and taking and staying in a place." See Stanley Cavell, "Being Odd, Getting Even," in *Emerson's Transcendental Etudes* (Stanford, Calif.: Stanford University Press, 2003), 91. But it seems that Cavell offers the thesis about standing and sitting in specific relation to "Self-Reliance" only, for it is clear that elsewhere he sees Emerson as a philosopher of departure. Ever since his seminal essay "Thinking of Emerson," which ends in a long mediation on abandonment and leaving, Cavell has understood Emerson to be a philosopher of "the way" (see in particular "Thinking of Emerson," in *Emerson's Transcendental Etudes,* 18–19).

12. Immanuel Kant, *Critique of the Power of Judgment,* trans. Paul Guyer and Eric Matthews (Cambridge: Cambridge University Press, 2000), 158.

13. Cavell, "Thinking of Emerson," 91.

14. Richard Poirier, *Poetry and Pragmatism* (Cambridge, Mass.: Harvard University Press, 1992), 20.

15. Lawrence Buell, *Emerson* (Cambridge, Mass.: Harvard University Press, 2003), 228.

16. *Journals and Miscellaneous Notebooks,* 5:468.

17. It was Spinoza who worked out a "modern" expressionist ontology. Qualified infinite substance or nature (being unlimited) is also heteronomous and expresses itself in infinite parallel attributes that are then explicated through

an infinite series of finite modes, each of which is only a provisional site of impersonal expression, something like its expressive mobile focus, or what Spinoza calls modes of "affection" of the substance, a case of the infinite/impersonal affecting/enjoying itself. Baruch de Spinoza, *Ethics, Part One, Definitions,* ed. and trans. G. H. R. Parkinson (Oxford: Oxford University Press, 2000). In the essay "Nature," from *Second Series,* Emerson explicitly refers to this type of expressionist philosophy by using Spinoza's distinction between *natura naturans* (creating infinite nature) and *natura naturata* (created finite modes). In Emerson, *natura naturans* is the cause of forms, which are also deformed by it: "Let us no longer omit our homage to the Efficient Nature, *natura naturans,* the quick cause, before which all forms flee as the driven snows, itself secret. . . . It publishes itself in creatures" (3:104). The expressed is "nature passive," created form, or "*natura naturata*" (3:103).

18. *Later Lectures of Ralph Waldo Emerson,* 2:74.

19. David Van Leer, *Emerson's Epistemology: The Argument of the Essays* (Cambridge: Cambridge University Press, 1986), 190.

20. The exception to this is Lawrence Buell's recent engagement with the essay. For his fine reading of it, see Buell, *Emerson,* 229–36.

21. *Journals and Miscellaneous Notebooks,* 5:269–76.

22. Ibid., 5:481.

23. Ibid., 5:482.

24. Michel Foucault, *The Order of Things* (New York: Vintage Books, 1994), 128.

25. *Journals and Miscellaneous Notebooks,* 5:162.

26. Foucault, *The Order of Things,* 155.

27. Cavell, "Thinking of Emerson," 93.

28. Martin Heidegger, *Kant and the Problem of Metaphysics,* trans. Richard Taft (Bloomington: Indiana University Press, 1990), 17.

29. "The Relation of Intellect to Natural Science," 1:156.

30. It would be somewhat misleading to read Emerson's description of Mammoth Cave in Kentucky (visited in 1850), which opens "Illusions," as his version of Plato's cave. The cave is or could be an analogy of the mind (with its "niche" or "grotto," "domes," "bottomless pits," "echoes in these alarming galleries," each of them representing a "platform"), but Emerson is careful enough to distinguish that "structural" or "architectural" feature of the mind (open enclosure) from our erroneous cognition. The essay seems to say that the "illusions" of our thinking are, rather, due to the fact that we never think of our body, its senses, and its thoughts as something that interacts with the body of the earth and its caves. We give to natural objects names of "fine things" we value in our lives, but in so doing we become blind to the natural objects themselves, what

they have to teach us, and deaf to the names that call us. We miss the first lesson, the one that the Earth has to teach us: "The mysteries and scenery of the cave had the same dignity that belongs to all natural objects, and which shames the fine things to which we foppishly compare them." We think that Nature is "stupid" whereas it has a "mimetic habit," and its own "theatrical trick," providing a whole epistemology of the Earth. That is why "our conversation with Nature is not just what it seems. The cloud-rack, the sunrise and sunset glories, rainbows, and northern lights are not quite so spheral as our childhood thought them; and the part our organization plays in them is too large. The senses interfere everywhere, and mix their own structure with all they report of" (6:165–66). It does not follow from there, however, that we should not trust the senses, but rather that we should realize that we constitute a "mixed" organization, which, Emerson insists time and again, makes life "an ecstasy," in which "circumstance gives the joy which we give to the circumstance" (6:166), in a circular, vertiginous movement of mixing all our bodies together.

31. *Later Lectures of Ralph Waldo Emerson,* 2:78.

32. Ibid., 2:74.

33. Ibid., 1:156, 1:166.

34. Ibid., 1:166.

35. In "Circles," "Intellect," and "Worship," Emerson uses a version of Pascal's distinction between logic of the heart and logic of reason. In "Intellect" the logic of reason is called an "arithmetical" or "logical" principle, whereas in "Worship" Emerson actually quotes—or slightly misquotes—Pascal's sentence that "the heart has its arguments, with which the understanding is not acquainted" (6:115). In Pascal the logic of the heart is not only the source of religious knowledge but of mathematical axioms too, as often they can only be intuited and not articulated in the form of a proposition: "We know the truth not only by means of the reason but also by means of the heart. It is through the heart that we know the first principles, and reason which has no part in this knowledge vainly tries to contest them. The Pyrrhonists who have only reason as the object of their attack are working ineffectually." Blaise Pascal, *Pensées,* trans. Honor Levi (Oxford: Oxford University Press, 1995), 35, para. 142. Emerson's understanding of "heart" is thus very close to Pascal's: he conceives of intuition not only as a divinatory knowledge, but also as a way of knowing principles.

36. *Later Lectures of Ralph Waldo Emerson,* 1:183.

37. Emphasis in original. Richard Poirier, *The Renewal of Literature, Emersonian Reflections* (New York: Random House, 1987), 201.

38. In formulating his thesis about impersonal sites of reflection—the mirror that cannot reflect itself—Emerson may have been influenced by the Novalis represented in Carlyle's essay on the same (which, in fact, is less an essay than

a compilation of long quotes from Novalis that Carlyle translates in order to introduce English-speaking readers to German Romanticism). See *The Works of Thomas Carlyle, Critical and Miscellaneous Essays* (New York: Peter Fenelon Collier, 1897). For Novalis the world is an infinite series of mirrors reflecting each other—whatever we see sees us—and in which everything is reflected and so assimilated into something else: "here or nowhere lies the talisman. By the well of Freedom we sit and look; it is the grand magic Mirror, where the whole creation images itself, pure and clear" (523). The "intercourse" of two persons or objects (each of which is both gaze and object of the gaze) is the moment of assimilation: "Intercourse with the power of Nature, with animals, plants, rocks, storms and waves, must necessarily assimilate men to those objects" (522). The moment of assimilation, which Novalis also calls "metamorphosis," turns the two into one or makes of a couple an individual; it is this falling into one of the two that, for Novalis, becomes the moment of selfless "observation." Observation (the term that plays such an important role in Emerson's and Thoreau's thinking) is a gaze that is identical with its objects, a relation that Novalis wanted to call (as Tieck suggests and Carlyle reports [504]) a "Physical Romance." That is the title Novalis wanted to give his text, thereby suggesting how knowledge turns into a reflection without self-reflection (elsewhere Novalis will formulate it thus: "Perceptibility [is] an attentiveness" [quoted in Benjamin, "The Concept of Criticism in German Romanticism," *Selected Writings*, vol. 1, *1913–1926*, ed. Marcus Bullock and Michael W. Jennings, trans. David Lachterman, Howard Eiland, and Ian Balfour (Cambridge, Mass.: Harvard University Press, 1996), 145]). Carlyle himself allows that Novalis showed philosophical talent but, at the same time, claims that his philosophy of assimilation suffers the fault of passivity: "His chief fault, again, figures itself to us as a certain undue softness, a want of rapid energy, something which we might term *passiveness* extending both over his mind and his character" (emphasis in original; 542).

39. *Journals and Miscellaneous Notebooks*, 5:476.

40. Stanley Cavell, "Finding as Founding: Taking Steps in Emerson's 'Experience,'" in *Emerson's Transcendental Etudes*, 137.

41. Cavell, "Being Odd, Getting Even," 86.

42. Emphasis in original. Emerson, letter to M. Fuller, September 6, 1839. In *The Letters of Ralph Waldo Emerson*, ed. Ralph L. Rusk (New York: Columbia University Press, 1939), 2:220.

43. Margaret Fuller, "Emerson's Essays: Second Series," *New-York Daily Tribune*, December 7, 1844; reprinted in *The Portable Margaret Fuller*, ed. Mary Kelley (New York: Penguin Books, 1994), 365.

II.
RETHINKING THE POLITICAL

EDUARDO CADAVA

4. The Guano of History

> My recall is nearly perfect, time has faded nothing.
> I recall the very first kidnap. I've lived through the passage,
> died on the passage, lain in the unmarked, shallow graves of
> the millions who fertilized the Amerikan soil with their
> corpses; cotton and corn growing out of my chest, "unto the
> third and fourth generation," the tenth, the hundredth.
>
> —GEORGE JACKSON
> *Soledad Brother*

How is it that the dead speak? How is it that the dispossessed can tell their stories? How is it that the past survives in the present and informs the future, silently, but without pacifying or silencing a single torment or a single torture? What can memory be when it seeks to remember the trauma of captivity, loss, and displacement? What makes someone choose death over living? In what way does death leave behind a decomposing trace that, turning into earth at the time of death, gives meaning to the memory, the violence, the wounds, the protests, the cries of anger or suffering, the several death sentences on which a nation—America, for example—has been founded? How can an event that takes place only in its passage, only in its decomposition, leave something behind that, guarding a trace of itself, inaugurates, and even composes, a history—in this instance, a history of dispossession and diaspora, a history without which the history of America could never be written? The very moment there is death, the very moment slavery exists, the very moment populations are removed and exterminated, wealth and rights are distributed unequally, acts of discrimination are committed in the name of democracy and freedom, America finds itself in mourning, and what it mourns is America itself.

This mourning begins, Jackson suggests, with "the very first kidnap." Identifying himself with the millions lost in the passage and the fifteen million and more captured and enslaved in the Americas (we should not forget that he is in prison as he writes, that he is, as he puts it, living a kind of death, as if he were in the hold of a ship), Jackson transforms the space of his captivity into a space haunted by the ghosts of a broken and painful past. Remembering the wounds of history, the violent displacements effected by the transatlantic crossing of black captives and reinforced by the ensuing processes of exploitation and enslavement, he bears witness to a consciousness of dissociation that, acting as a mode of testimony and memory, registers the violence of the historical processes he describes.[1] The stakes of the past are experienced in terms of death and mourning. Jackson's act of memory endlessly reenacts this condition of loss and displacement—"'unto the third and fourth generation,' the tenth, the hundredth"—not in order to overcome captivity or facilitate survival, but to reenact the story of slavery, to embody the death and mourning that makes America America. Without the recognition of this loss, he seems to suggest, we could never respond to the historical caesura introduced by slavery. What is at stake here is a body that bears the traces of what it undergoes, the trace of its decomposition but also its loss of citizenship and rights, its transformation into commodities and capital, and its inscription within an exploitative economic system of international dimensions.

What is at stake is also a mode of language that would remain faithful to the traces and history of this body, that would give body to, make tangible, what it wishes us to understand. This strategy can be read in the way in which Jackson enacts his sense of dispossession and displacement by dispersing his voice across several voices, by sundering the singularity of the historical moment in which he is writing. The voice he stages—the voice of the "I" who has "nearly perfect" recall, but also the "I" who has "lived through the passage, died on the passage, lain in the unmarked, shallow graves of the millions who fertilized the Amerikan soil with their corpses"—belongs simultaneously to the past, the present, and the future. It is the voice of a living ghost, or, more precisely, the living voice of several ghosts. The movement of the passage reinforces this ghostly survival of the past in the present and future since, as is so often the case in black diasporic writing, everything in it proceeds by citation, not only when it cites a fragment of the biblical refrain—"unto the third and fourth generation"—that appears repeatedly in the five books of Moses. Nevertheless, by alluding to the story of Exodus, Jackson evokes the biblical story most central to the lives of his dispossessed and enslaved brethren. The appropriation of the Exodus story became a means for African Americans to articulate their sense of historical identity as a people. Identifying the story of the bondage and slavery of the Israelites with their own servitude, they drew from the story the hope that they, too, would be delivered to freedom.

This helps explain why, if Jackson evokes the centrality of the Exodus story within the history of enslavement and violence to which he refers, he does so not only to direct us to a significant, neuralgic point in the shared history and social memory of black religious discourse—a history and memory that belong to his inheritance—but also, in particular, to remind us that the refrain he cites belongs to the curse that God declares he will impose on *the guilty*—who will not be cleared of their transgressions and sins and who will have the "iniquity of the fathers" visited "upon the children and the children's children, unto the third and fourth generation." Jackson's use of the refrain therefore points, from his perspective, to the irony of God's curse: that the sins of *the guilty*—the sins of the slaveholders, for example, and not the sins for which he has been *declared* guilty—are visited on the damned of the earth. In other words, Jackson suggests that the suffering and death experienced by the violated bodies and minds of dispossessed populations is visited upon them by men and not God, by the greed and lust of men and not the jealousy or anger of God, by racist and capitalist policies and not heavenly dictates. If these oppressed minority populations are chosen, it is not by God but rather, as in this case, by an America that seeks to flourish over the fertilizer that these minorities will have become, over the death and mourning that defines their experience.

If we can take Jackson's passage as evidence of what would be required for us to speak in the name of freedom (there is little doubt that the passage belongs to his efforts throughout his prison letters to define the nature and conditions of freedom), what it tells us is that, in order to speak in the name of freedom, in the name of justice, we must speak of the past we inherit and for which we remain answerable; we must speak of ghosts, of generations of ghosts—of those who are not presently living, whether they are already dead or not yet born.[2] We must speak of the victims of political, nationalist, racist, colonialist, and capitalist violence, or of any of the other forms of oppression and extermination that we still today have not overcome. We must engage in a politics of memory that is also a politics of the future. This memory and this future, in order to be just, in order to be worthy of their names, would emerge from a respect for the dead, and perhaps especially for the living dead. Together, this memory and this future would name an obligation: remember the dead, keep the memory of the dead alive, think your relation to a past that, never behind you, haunts you, tells you for what you are answerable.

Why begin this way? For at least three reasons. First, because while these memories from a singular moment in our history may seem discrete, distant, even gnomic, many paths cross there among an entire network of motifs: slavery, destiny, fate, violence, racism, colonialism, subjectivity, memory, history, rights, language, death, mourning, and so forth—all of which raise fundamental questions about who we are in relation to what we call America. If this beginning imposes itself, it is not in order to begin an analysis of a singular political writer—here the Black Panther field marshal and founder of the People's Army, George Jackson—but rather to begin to expose something essential to our history that goes beyond his particularity, that gives us to our history. Jackson's assassination in San Quentin Prison on August 21, 1971, sealed the fame he already had achieved with the publication of *Soledad Brother* one year earlier and ensured that this hero of the movement against black oppression and American imperialism would become a canonical figure for various movements of resistance, for the often violent struggles for freedom and justice both inside and outside America—resistances and struggles that, as Jackson well knew, belong to the long history of efforts to actualize equality, to realize the promise of the right to representation for everyone, the promise of an America that to this day still does not exist, which is why it must always be mourned. It is toward this experience of mourning that Jackson's writings are oriented. If, as Jean Genet wrote in

1986, the Panthers were "haunted by the idea of death,"[3] Jackson argues that this hauntedness delineates the contours and conditions of ethical and political gestures that, organized around extended acts of mourning, can be joined to moments of affirmation, even if such affirmation is linked to a critical insistence on death and mourning.

Second, in this way I can begin to evoke and lay out the terms of what the work of Emerson compels us to think, especially as it engages the world of which his work is such an important articulation—a world that bore witness to vast capitalist development, to the rise of various secondary institutions (such as schools, asylums, factories, and plantations), rapid urbanization and industrialization, a growing inequality in the distribution of wealth, and several modes of displacement and extermination—a world in which debates over the nature of war, revolution, race, slavery, liberty, democracy, and representation were of crucial importance in America's effort to invent its national and cultural identity. Emerson's engagement with the changing historical and political relations of this world, wherein his language works to change further the shifting domains of history and politics and wherein the traces of the historical and the political are inscribed within the movement of his language, remains, I think, a model for us not only for thinking the relation between political gestures and the language without which they would never take place but also for responding to the demand that we become answerable for our future by, among so many other things, confronting the ways in which the past lives on in the present. Emerson's turn toward the past, his turn toward the loss, death, and mourning that characterize our experience, becomes the condition for his conviction (a conviction I believe he shares with Jackson) that, in transforming the language he inherits, he can perhaps change much more than language—he can perhaps work to transform the relations within which we live and perhaps, in spite of the impossibility of ever securing freedom and justice, delineate the experience of freedom and justice as a praxis of thought that begins from the presupposition that we are always, in advance, related to others. I emphasize this last point because, as we will see, a call to rethink the concepts of freedom and justice traverses his work. We might even say that Emerson's works are nothing but the very trial of these two concepts.

Third, I wish to respond to the dictates of a passage that is haunted both by the memory of the dispossessed over whose deaths America grows and expands and by its relation to the entirety of the history that is encrypted within the passage from Jackson with which I began. The passage can be found in Emerson's essay, "Fate," an essay that, although not published until 1860, had its beginnings in the months immediately following the passing of the Fugitive Slave Law in 1850 and in the context of heated debates over the question of slavery and the slave trade, the admission of territories into the union with or without slaves, the unfolding of the ideas of manifest destiny and racial difference, the removal and extermination of the native population, the expansion of the American empire into the Pacific and the Caribbean, and emancipation and secession. As such, "Fate" is perhaps Emerson's most profound and searching engagement of the idea of manifest destiny in terms of questions of race, his most moving effort to provide a kind of secret genealogy of what makes racism and slavery possible. Perhaps Emerson's principal statement about the conditions and possibilities of human freedom and justice, the essay seeks to convey to us the reasons why, already in antebellum America, three or four generations before Jackson's publication of his prison letters in 1970, everything is haunted by death, oriented around death and especially around the death encrypted within the American landscape. Indeed, in the closing lines of the passage to which I refer, Emerson tells us that "the German and Irish millions, like the Negro, have a great deal of guano in their destiny. They are ferried over the Atlantic, and carted over America, to ditch and to drudge, to make corn cheap, and then to lie down prematurely to make a spot of green grass on the prairie."[4] Once these few lines are contextualized within the historical moment in which they were written and within the essay to which they belong—both of which refer to the violent history of American colonization and imperialism—they put before us the violence, the inequality, the economic oppression, and colonialist and racist exclusions that affected, and continue to affect, so many human beings in the history not only of America but of the earth. Emerson here reminds us that, instead of celebrating the ideals of liberal democracy and of the capitalist market in an affirmation of America's expansionist desires, we should never neglect this manifest fact, composed of innumerable instances of suffering and death, a fact that was true in Emerson's time but is even more true today: never before have so many men, women, and children been subjugated or exterminated on earth; never have so many human beings been transformed into guano. It is here that Emerson and Jackson join forces as they suggest that any meditation on freedom and justice, any action taken in the name of these two experiences, should take its point of departure from this mournful and deadly fact.

If I have begun this way, it is because I have wanted to suggest that there is a way in which, before us, in advance of us, Jackson already will have read Emerson's essay "Fate" even if his eyes never once cast their glance on any of its pages. He will have taught us how to read Emerson, how to understand the reasons why, like him, Emerson is perhaps one of America's greatest mourners, which is to say one of its most significant and aggressive defenders. In asking us to remember the dead, to engage an inheritance that, even today, belongs to what we still call our future, Jackson and Emerson demonstrate that there can be no thought of the future, no experience of hope that is not at the same time an engagement with the question "How shall we conduct our life?" We can only begin to answer this question, they suggest, by learning to read historically, by learning to mourn, by exposing ourselves to the vicissitudes of a history in which we are inscribed and to which we remain urgently and danger-ously responsible because it is we who are at stake.

I begin again, this time with Emerson, although, as Jackson reminds us, time has perhaps faded nothing.

Emerson opens his essay "Fate" by noting the chances, the coinci-dences, that have led to several discussions in Boston, New York, London, and elsewhere on the theory of the age or the spirit of the times. For him, however,

> the question of the times resolved itself into a practical question of the conduct of life. How shall I live? We are incompetent to solve the times. Our geometry cannot span the huge orbits of the prevailing ideas, be-hold their return, and reconcile their opposition. We can only obey our own polarity. 'Tis fine for us to speculate and elect our course, if we must accept an irresistible dictation. (6:1–2)

As Stanley Cavell has rightly suggested, the question of the times is here the question of slavery.[5] What has yet to be noted, however, is the extent to which Emerson's essay is really less a challenge of the institu-tion of slavery—although it is this, too—than an attempt to engage and make manifest the "huge orbits of prevailing ideas" without which this institution could never exist. In particular, it is an essay about the idea of fate that prevailed in mid-nineteenth-century America—American manifest destiny—and all the discursive and material means whereby this concept was supported, maintained, and mobilized in order to sustain slavery. Emerson explicitly points to the role of the idea of fate in the justification of slavery in a journal entry from 1852 titled "Abolition." There, he writes: "*Abolition*. The argument of the slaveholder is one & simple: he pleads Fate. Here is an inferior race requiring wardship,—it is sentimentality to deny it. The argument of the abolitionist is, It is inhuman to treat a man thus."[6] What Emerson seeks to alert us to, in this passage but also within his essay, is the way in which fate (whether it appears as "manifest destiny," "providence," "natural law," or "predestination," to name only a few of the terms under which this ideologeme was circulated) served to inform and shape a racial ideology that could be used to describe and hierarchize the world's peoples. "Fate" therefore seeks to delineate the conditions under which (given the uncertainty with which we must struggle with the past in order to give the future a chance, with prevailing ideas, for example, that irresistibly move us, as if by a kind of dictation, in the direction of slavery) we may experience freedom—a freedom from fate, perhaps, but even so, a freedom that, taking its point of departure from the transit between the past and the future within which something new is produced, passes through what it inherits in order to invent its future.

Viewing "fate," in a first sense, as another name for limitation, for what limits us, Emerson directs his writing against not only the rhetoric of unlimited privilege and expansion that informs the idea of manifest destiny but also the blindness of such rhetoric to the death, the violence, and the injury it precipitates. "Let us honestly state the facts," Emerson writes. "Our America has a bad name for superficialness. Great men, great nations have not been boasters and buffoons, but perceivers of the terror of life" ("Fate," 6:2). Providing us with a list of the disasters and catastrophes—diseases, the elements, earthquakes, and all manner of accidents—that so often remind us of our finitude and mortality, he then proceeds to hint at the disasters and catastrophes that are of our own violent making. "The way of Providence is a little rude," he tells us:

> The habit of snake and spider, the snap of the tiger and other leapers and bloody jumpers, the crackle of the bones of his prey in the coil of the anaconda,—these are in the system, and our habits are like theirs.

> You have just dined, and, however scrupulously the slaughter-house
> is concealed in the graceful distance of miles, there is complicity,—
> expensive races,—race living at the expense of race. (6:4)

This passage about human carnivorousness, and the gracefulness with
which its conditions are concealed from itself, is, in Cavell's words, "a
parable about the cannibalism, as it were, in living gracefully off other
human races."[7] Emerson already had made this point in his 1844 address
on the tenth anniversary of the emancipation of the British West Indies.
Anticipating the figure of the slaughterhouse he will later use in "Fate,"
he writes, "From the earliest monuments, it appears, that one race was
victim, and served the other races." He continues:

> From the earliest time, the negro has been an article of luxury to
> the commercial nations. So has it been, down to the day that has
> just dawned on the world. Language must be raked, the secrets of
> slaughter-houses and infamous holes that cannot front the day, must
> be ransacked, to tell what negro-slavery has been.[8]

This is why so much of Emerson's effort in "Fate" is directed at evoking
and analyzing this language. As is so often the case, however, this work
of analysis can be read more easily in the *practice* of Emerson's writing,
in its staging and treatment of the rhetoric of manifest destiny, race, and
slavery, than in any explicit and straightforward arguments. This perhaps
is also why, in an essay that is throughout concerned with all the violence
committed in the name of America's manifest destiny, Emerson takes
the remarkable risk of never once using the term "manifest destiny."
Suggesting in this way that there is nothing manifest about "manifest
destiny"—nothing natural or obvious about it—he instead seeks to exhibit what are for him its as yet unpenetrated causes, the various arguments that, made in its name, make it possible.

The term "manifest destiny" was first coined by the editor of the
Democratic Review, John O'Sullivan, in an 1845 essay arguing for the annexation of Texas. Simply titled "Annexation," the essay predicted "the
fulfillment of our manifest destiny to overspread the continent allotted
by Providence for the free development of our yearly multiplying millions."[9] But the idea of the providential character of America's expan-
sionism was scarcely new. Not only did it rely on arguments drawn from
both Puritan claims for the preordained, divine purpose of their mission

and Calvinist conceptions of predestination, but O'Sullivan himself already had written of America's "boundless futures" in his 1839 essay "The Great Nation of Futurity."[10] The extension of American boundaries, he suggested, would secure the extension of democracy, or, as Andrew Jackson had put it in his justification for Indian removal, the extension of the "area of freedom."

As Emerson reminds us, however, these arguments—motivated by what he once referred to as the Anglo-Saxon's "Earth-hunger," his "love of possessing land"—only ensured the deadly fact that the territorial and economic expansion of the United States would be achieved at the expense of Native Americans and other minority communities.[11] In his 1856 speech on the Kansas-Nebraska Act, describing the way in which proponents of American "manifest destiny" disguise cruelty with euphemism, he writes:

> Language has lost its meaning in the universal cant. *Representative Government* is really misrespresentative; ... *the adding of Cuba and Central America* to the slave marts *is enlarging the area of Freedom. Manifest Destiny, Democracy, Freedom,* fine names for an ugly thing. They call it otto of rose and lavender,—I call it bilge water. It is called Chivalry and Freedom; I call it the taking of all the earnings of a poor man and the earnings of his little girl and boy, and the earnings of all that shall come from his, his children's children forever.[12]

The resulting cruelty and violence of such language was naturalized, however, by arguments that, gaining their strength from closely related Enlightenment ideas of progress, suggested, in the wording of Eric Sundquist, "that the exploration of foreign lands and the conversion of alien peoples through political and economic expansion took place according to organic laws of growth." Within the context of such arguments, the narrative of "a relentless conquest in which the march of one civilization destroyed or utterly changed many others through dispossession and absorption" was supported by what Sundquist goes on to call a "political and cultural medium in which conquest could be naturalized, or set within a panoramic elaboration of predestined history."[13]

In many respects, Emerson's discussions of race and manifest destiny during the 1840s and 1850s should be understood as his analysis of this medium—a medium that, including all the discourses of scientific racism, physiognomy, geology, ethnology, and evolution that worked together to consolidate the racial privilege and hegemony of white America, belongs to Emerson's inheritance. Emerson's analysis here follows not only the political implications of his antislavery discourse but also his attempt to measure and limit determinist explanations for human achievement. Emerson's essay "Fate" is in fact a kind of anthology of all the various determinisms at work in mid-nineteenth-century debates over the relations among the races. Arguing in the essay that "a good deal of our politics is physiological" (6:7), Emerson ventriloquizes nearly every scientific explanation for racial difference available to him. The entire essay can be read as an evocation and analysis of the various kinds of discourses that throughout history—especially throughout the eighteenth and nineteenth centuries—have worked to enable one race to live, as Emerson tells us, "at the expense of other races," of what he elsewhere calls "the guano-races of mankind."[14]

The emergence of ethnology by the late 1840s as a recognized science of racial differences presumably offered scientific validation of black inferiority and thereby reinforced the claims of southern slavery. "The mission of Ethnology," one southern writer declared, "is to vindicate the great truths on which the institutions of the South are founded."[15] Following the scientific ethnology of Samuel Morton's *Crania Americana* (1839) and *Crania Aegyptiaca* (1844)—works that sought to define mental capacity in terms of skull size and shape—the Alabama physician Josiah Nott notoriously defended and promoted polygenesis. Basing his claims on a wide range of biblical and ethnographic materials, he argued that, because the races had different origins and different degrees of development, they could be classified and hierarchized according to their general capacities. "Dr. S. G. Morton," he wrote in 1849, "by a long series of well-conceived experiments, has established the fact, that the capacity of the crania of the Mongol, Indian, and Negro, and all dark-skinned races, is smaller than that of the pure white man."[16] As he explained five years later in the *Types of Mankind*—a book he cowrote with the Egyptologist George R. Gliddon and that sought to justify the enslavement and eventual extinction of nonwhite peoples—the Caucasian races were fulfilling a law of nature. They were as "destined eventually to conquer and hold every foot of the globe," he argued, as the inferior races were destined to extinction: "Nations and races, like individuals, have each a special destiny: some are born to rule, and others to be ruled.... No two distinctly marked races can dwell together on equal terms. Some races, moreover, appear destined to live and prosper for a time, until the destroying race comes, which is to exterminate and supplant them."[17] Or, as he put it in his introduction to the book, "Human progress has arisen mainly from the war of the races. All the great impulses which have been given to it from time to time have been the results of conquests and colonizations" (53). Considered natural or organic, expansion and enslavement were justified by claims that they guaranteed freedom and independence, encouraged the development and regeneration of resources and land, and confirmed a fated and future-oriented historical process that could be supported by scientific models of racial difference.

Emerson's most remarkable passage in "Fate" about the deterministic languages with which slavery was justified—a passage that encrypts the entire history of the rhetoric of American colonization and imperialism and seeks to provide a genealogy of the rhetoric that served to justify the living of one race at the expense of another—occurs soon after he refers to the role of physiology in American politics and history. I cite the passage in its entirety:

> The book of Nature is the book of Fate. She turns the gigantic pages,— leaf after leaf,—never re-turning one. One leaf she lays down, a floor of granite; then a thousand ages, and a bed of slate; a thousand ages, and a measure of coal; a thousand ages, and a layer of marl and mud: vegetable forms appear; her first misshapen animals, zoophyte, trilobium, fish; then, saurians,—rude forms, in which she has only blocked her future statue, concealing under these unwieldy monsters the fine type of her coming king. The face of the planet cools and dries, the races meliorate, and man is born. But when a race has lived its term, it comes no more again.
>
> The population of the world is a conditional population; not the best, but the best that could live now; and the scale of tribes, and the steadiness with which victory adheres to one tribe and defeat to another is as uniform as the superposition of strata. We know in history what weight belongs to race. We see the English, French, and Germans planting themselves on every shore and market of America and Australia and monopolizing the commerce of these countries. We like the nervous and victorious habit of our own branch of the family. We follow the step of the Jew, of the Indian, of the Negro. We see how

much will has been expended to extinguish the Jew, in vain. Look at the unpalatable conclusions of Knox, in his "Fragment of Races,"—a rash and unsatisfactory writer, but charged with pungent and unforgettable truths. "Nature respects race, and not hybrids." "Every race has its own *habitat*." "Detach a colony from the race, and it deteriorates to the crab." See the shades of the picture. The German and Irish millions, like the Negro, have a great deal of guano in their destiny. They are ferried over the Atlantic, and carted over America, to ditch and to drudge, to make corn cheap, and then to lie down prematurely to make a spot of green grass on the prairie." (6:8–9, Emerson's emphasis)

There would be much to say about this passage, but here I only wish to signal four indices of the contexts in which it should be read, and to which I believe it responds.

First, Emerson's passage, with its innumerable layers and strata, comes to us in the form of the very geological strata of which he is writing. Like the earth that bears the traces of the entirety of its history, Emerson's language inscribes, within its very movement, the traces of all the texts that have informed his own. As such, it demands that we rake his language and reckon with it in order to see how it often ventriloquizes language that has been used to justify what, for him, goes in the direction of the worst, in the direction, that is, of the sentences that close this passage. The link between geology and language was pervasive during Emerson's day and we need only recall his claims in "The Poet" that "language is fossil poetry" or that "as the limestone of the continent consists of infinite masses of the shells of animalcules, so language is made up of images, or tropes, which now, in their secondary use, have long ceased to remind us of their poetic origin" (3:13) or Whitman's claim that "the science of language has large and close analogies in geological science, with its ceaseless evolution, its fossils, and its numberless submerged layers and hidden strata, the infinite go-before of the present."[18]

Second, Emerson's effort to relate the history of natural, geological processes to the theory of the evolution of man borrows its terms and figures from his readings in the geological sciences—readings that included the writings of, among others, Georges Buffon, Georges Cuvier, Charles Lyell, and Robert Chambers.[19] For Emerson, in bringing together time and space, geology seeks to make the past legible to the observer. Borrowing a figure from Chambers's *Vestiges of the Natural History of Creation*,[20] Emerson goes on to suggest that geological layers are "leaves of the *Stone Book*." He extends the metaphor even further when he describes Cuvier studying before a broken mountainside: "in the rough ledges, the different shades and superposition of the strata, his eye is reading as in a book the history of the globe."[21] If the book of Nature is the book of Fate, then it is because the history of the processes of nature is also a study of the irresistible processes that have led to the emergence of man.

But if present geological formations can be explained by studying the history of geological transformations, the study of previous changes in the earth also predicts the succession of deaths that, for Emerson, composes the movement of history itself. "Every science is the record or account of the dissolution of the objects it considers," he writes, "All history is an epitaph. All life is a progress toward death. The [sun] world but a large Urn. The sun in his bright path thro' Ecliptic but a funereal triumph . . . for it lights men & animals & plants to their graves."[22] To say that human history belongs to the history of nature is to say that human history is a history of death, or, more precisely, a history of the life and death of innumerable generations, all of whom have left their traces in the earth's strata. The lessons of geology are the lessons of one species or race succeeding or surviving another. As John Harris writes in his 1850 *The Pre-Adamite Earth*, referring to the time required to produce the earth's sedimentations and strata: "How countless the ages necessary for their accumulation, when the formation of only a few inches of the strata required the life and death of many generations. Here the mind is not merely carried back, through innumerable periods, but, while studying amidst the petrified remains of this succession of primeval forests and extinct races of animals, piled up into sepulchral mountains, we seem to be encompassed by the thickest shadow of the valley of death." Referring to geological strata as "monuments" or "platforms of death," he confirms Lyell's sense of the endless mutations and fluctuations that, characterizing both the organic and inorganic worlds, help account for the sudden extinction of whole organic creations, and the introduction of others.[23] These "catacombs" or "charnel-houses," "crowded with organic structures which lived and died where they are now seen; and which, consequently, must have perished by some destructive agency, too sudden to allow of their dispersion," bear the traces of "the thousands, not of generations, but of species, of races . . . which have all run through their ages of existence and ceased" (68, 71).[24] This is why, as Thoreau would put it, the world is to be considered a vast compost heap. The hieroglyphic of nature, he writes, "is somewhat excrementitious in its character, and there is no end to the heaps of liver, lights and bowels, as if the globe were turned wrong side outward; but this suggests at least that Nature has some bowels, and there again is mother of humanity."[25]

Third, in linking the rhetoric of a natural development that gives birth to man to the related processes of colonization and capitalism, Emerson alerts us to the rhetoric with which, as I already have suggested, the violent colonization and appropriation of land and peoples for political and economic reasons often was justified. This history of conquest and colonization, it was argued—in which "victory adheres to one tribe, and defeat to another," in which "the English, French, and Germans" could plant themselves "on every shore and market of America and Australia" and monopolize their commerce—was as natural as the successive superposition of one geological stratum upon another. Lyell himself notes, in a passage from *The Principles of Geology*, what Emerson may very well have had in mind here:

> When a powerful European colony lands on the shores of Australia, and introduces at once those arts which it has required many centuries to mature; when it imports a multitude of plants and large animals from the opposite extremity of the earth, and begins rapidly to extirpate many of the indigenous species, a mightier revolution is effected in a brief period, than the first entrance of a savage horde, or their continued occupation of the country for many centuries, can possible be imagined to have produced. (1:157)

Having pointed to this process of dispossession, however, Lyell goes on to emphasize that it belongs to the economy of nature:

> The successive destruction of species must now be part of the regular and constant order of Nature. . . . We have only to reflect, that in thus obtaining possession of the earth by conquest, and defending our acquisitions by force, we exercise no exclusive prerogative. Every species which has spread itself from a small point over a wide area, must, in like manner, have marked its progress by the diminution, or the entire extirpation, of some other, and must maintain its ground by a successful

struggle against the encroachments of other plants and animals. . . .
The most insignificant and diminutive species, whether in the animal
or vegetable kingdom, have each slaughtered their thousands, as they
disseminated themselves over the globe. (2:141, 156)

Associating the violence of colonization, possession, and extermination
with the progress of nature, Lyell's rhetoric here resonates with the justi-
fications that so often gave voice to American manifest destiny. Emerson
reinforces this point by describing the processes of colonization and possession as a kind of "planting."

As Patricia Seed argues, "The action of the colonists in the New
World was planting; the colonists were metaphorically plants in relation
to the soil, and hence their colonial settlements were referred to as plantations. Thus, when the English most commonly referred to their colonies
in the New World as plantations, they were referring to themselves metaphorically as taking possession."[26] This metaphor often was literalized by
one of the rituals whereby new lands were claimed: in addition to building houses and fences, settlers would assert their occupation and possession by cultivating and, in particular, fertilizing the land. Indeed, as Seed
reminds us, the verb *to manure* in sixteenth-century England meant,
among other things, "to own" (32). What is at stake for Emerson, then, is
an understanding of the ways in which violence and dispossession—and
the death that comes from them—are disguised by acts of naturaliza-
tion. If he identifies America with these processes of dispossession (he
tells us that America belongs to the same family of colonizers), the ner-
vousness of its "victorious habit" lies in its recognition—acknowledged
or not—that its drive for territorial acquisition, along with the enslavement and death this drive produces, betrays the promises of freedom and
independence on which it was founded.

Fourth, Emerson's final lines should be read in relation to the context of the importation of guano into America in the 1840s and 1850s—
both as a fertilizing resource and as a metaphor—a context that Emerson
understood to belong to the history of American colonization and imperialism. As James Skaggs notes, "Declining agricultural productivity in
the United States prior to the Civil War led to an ever-increasing demand
for fertilizers." "In middle and southern states such as Maryland and
Virginia," he goes on to explain, "farmers (growing crops such as tobacco
and cotton, both of which are especially hard on the land) faced bleak fu-

tures as soil exhaustion became increasingly pronounced."[27] In response to this exhaustion—the result of several factors, including climate, erosion, the removal of organic matter and nutrients, soil toxicity, destructive methods of cultivation, and a market that focused almost entirely on tobacco and cotton[28]—agricultural journals such as the *American Farmer*, the *New England Farmer*, *De Bow's Review*, *Southern Planter*, and *Southern Agriculturalist* urged crop diversification and rotation along with the application of fertilizers. The demand for fertilizer was partially filled by various artificial manures but especially by Peruvian guano. The best guano came from the Chincha Islands, just twelve miles from the coast of Peru, in the bay of Pisco. Since the islands received very little rainfall, the naturally high nitrogen content of the guano remained undiluted in a pungent, brownish-yellow concretion that was also very rich in phosphate. In some of the ravines of the islands, it was said to be nearly three hundred feet deep, and some speculated that it must have begun to accumulate there soon after the biblical flood.

At war with Bolivia in the late 1830s and experiencing several civil wars in the early 1840s, Peru found its economy shattered, and in order to reduce its enormous war debt, it began to negotiate with foreign companies for the selling of its guano. In 1841, Peru's president, Manuel Menéndez, formally nationalized the country's guano resources and, for the next thirty-five years, the Peruvian government would earn most of its foreign revenues from selling guano to other countries. In 1842, the London firm Anthony Gibbs & Sons shared a monopoly on exports for five years and, in 1847, gained sole control of British and North American markets. By 1846, Peru had received more than $1.3 million in guano advances and by the 1860s seabirds supplied more than 75 percent of the government's revenues. Exact figures for the first few years of what Lewis Gray has called the "guano mania" in the United States are not available because the Department of Treasury did not begin gathering import data on the commodity until 1847.[29] However, estimates suggest that between 1844 and 1851 approximately 66,000 tons per year (valued at $2.6 million, an average price of $49 a ton) entered the United States, mostly through Baltimore and New York. In 1851, the importation of guano into North America was consigned to the Peruvian firm Felipe Barreda and Brother, and by the late 1850s over 400,000 tons per year were coming in at $55 a ton. The first commercial fertilizer used to any significant extent in the United States, guano was advertised as a fertilizer that would help regenerate the American landscape. Horticultural journals of the period were filled with testimonials, chemical analyses, directions for its use, state-by-state statistics on its success with crops from tobacco and cotton to wheat, corn, oats, peas, potatoes, melons, asparagus, and so forth. It was repeatedly said to be more valuable than all the gold mines in California, and it was regarded, in the wording of one southern farmer, as "a blessing to the nation." In the mid-1850s, presumably citing a minister about to pray for the fertility of a Massachusetts farm, Emerson suggests that America's land "does not want a prayer, [it] wants manure."[30]

High prices, however, encouraged searches for substitutes and even encouraged fraud. By 1854, several varieties of guano had been imported from Africa, Central America, the Caribbean, and assorted Pacific islands, but, according to one contemporary U.S. government study, "they were either found to be worthless or far inferior in quality" to those of Peru. Dishonest businessmen also labeled several different products as pure Peruvian guano in order to defraud farmers and prospective clients. There was even a thriving underground market for used Peruvian guano bags— bags with the Peruvian government stamp—that some unscrupulous dealers refilled with spurious guano and sold as genuine guano. As Skaggs notes, "Such practices were so prevalent by 1846 that [the] Maryland legislature mandated oversight of all guano sold in its jurisdiction, a charge of forty cents per ton being tacked onto the retail price by the state's 'guano inspector,' William S. Reese, who officially inspected every sack at the port of Baltimore and issued grade stamps."[31] A test was soon devised to determine whether or not the guano was genuine or not, "genuine" meaning that it came from Peru. The buyer would place a small sample of the guano on a hot iron shovel. If the guano was genuine, it would leave behind a pearly white ash and, if it was fraudulent, a colored ash.[32]

Many farmers and legislators soon argued, however, that the only way to overcome these difficulties, to make sure that Peruvian guano was available to everyone, was to challenge the Gibbs monopoly. The United States made several efforts to persuade the Peruvian government to loosen its monopoly and to lower its prices, but without success. On December 2, 1850, in his first state of the union address, President Fillmore made special reference to guano. Amid remarks about such pressing matters as slavery, the increasing significance of foreign trade and commerce to the national economy, and the growing significance of the United States in the international arena, he declared: "Peruvian guano has become so desirable an article to the agricultural interests in the United States that it is the duty of the Government to employ all the means properly in its power for the purpose of causing that article to be imported into the country at a reasonable price. Nothing will be omitted on my part toward accomplishing this desirable end."[33]

After several episodes in which American businessmen tried to steal guano from Peruvian islands with the help of American officials (including then secretary of state, Daniel Webster), Senator William Seward presented a petition to Congress in March 1856 on behalf of the American Guano Company (a company formed in 1855 at a reported capitalization of $10 million and wishing to claim and mine the Baker and Jarvis islands in the mid-Pacific, which it believed to be rich in guano deposits). Seward hoped to make it easier for American entrepreneurs to claim global guano deposits under U.S. government jurisdiction. The resulting Guano Islands Act (1856) furthered Seward's drive for American commercial supremacy and resulted in America's first overseas territorial acquisitions. In the wording of the act, whenever the government "should have received satisfactory information that any citizen or citizens of the United States have discovered a deposit of guano on any island, or other territory not within the lawful jurisdiction of any other Government," then, at the discretion of the president, it shall "be considered as appertaining to the United States for the use and behoof of the discoverer or discoverers, and his and their assigns, and may, at like discretion, be taken possession of in the name of the United States, with all necessary formalities."[34] Within the ten years following the passage of the Guano Islands Act, American entrepreneurs sought to claim every island, rock, or key that might possess deposits of guano. They were soon followed by the French and the English, who hoped to share in the plunder that often included the enormous resources of native peoples whose cultures were violently altered or destroyed. As Skaggs tells us, "Between August 1856 and January 1863 (when the Lincoln administration suspended the law by declining to process additional requests for title during the duration of the Civil War), the U.S. Department of State accepted ten separate bonds on fifty-nine islands, rocks, and keys in the Pacific and Caribbean."[35]

When Emerson evokes the figure of guano in his essay "Fate," he recalls a commodity that bears the traces of the history of American imperialism and colonization, of the consequences, that is, of America's conviction in its so-called manifest destiny. But he also wants to suggest the ways in which political liberty and economic prosperity in antebellum America are entangled with the oppression, and often the death, of millions of slaves and ethnic immigrants. As he puts it elsewhere, "In each change of industry, whole classes & populations are sacrificed."[36] This point is confirmed with great force when we note that the workers involved in supporting and maintaining the guano trade included not only the German, Irish, and African Americans to which Emerson refers but also, among so many others, the Peruvian convicts, natives, and Chinese "coolies" that worked the Peruvian guano fields. According to Evelyn Hu-Dehart, from 1849 to 1874 as many as 100,000 contract laborers (coolies) were transported, under deception or coercion, across the Pacific to help meet the demand for cheap labor on the coastal guano fields.[37] There would in fact have been no guano trade without these laborers. Amid the ravages of war and the labor shortages resulting from the end of African slavery, Peru—hoping to encourage foreign investment and unable to find enough cheap labor among the small coastal peasantry, freed slaves, or the highlanders to meet the growing demand—decided to seek it overseas.

When it was clear that European immigrants were not drawn to the lack of available land and low wages in Peru, the Peruvian government—following the example of the British planters in the West Indies and Cuba—resorted to the importation of Chinese laborers. In south China, Westerners used Chinese "runners"—just as their counterparts in Africa were called—to "recruit" poor young men, often by force but also by persuading them that they were to work the gold mines in California. Some boarded ships in Amory or other Chinese ports, but the greater number probably passed through the Portuguese colony of Macao. As Hu-Dehart points out, many of the same ships and captains used in the African slave trade "transported Chinese coolies, packing them on board in the same way as slaves, across a 'middle passage' that was even longer in distance and more arduous."[38] Mortality rates on these ships—often referred to as "floating coffins"—were as high as 30 percent or more, due to overcrowding, insufficient food, lack of proper ventilation, and poor hygienic conditions.

Once the Chinese laborers arrived in Peru, they were auctioned and then housed in long, rectangular slave quarters. The working conditions on the islands were unbearable, not only because of their inhospitable nature—the climatic conditions on the islands made any work there a matter of privation and hardship, since the heat and lack of rainfall made water and food supplies very scarce—but also because of the viciousness with which the laborers were driven to dig and load the guano. In response to these harsh conditions, the coolies often chose to commit suicide in order to escape their enslavement. One contemporary account published in the *Southern Planter* in 1855 tells of mass suicides, sometimes involving up to fifty coolies at a time. These suicides were so frequent that the Peruvian government was forced to station guards around the cliffs and shores of the islands to prevent them. Stories about the atrocious work conditions in the guano fields, often similar to abolitionist accounts of the abuse and mistreatment of southern slaves, were published in several southern agricultural journals in the two decades before the Civil War. Eventually, the gross abuses in the recruitment and transportation of the coolies generated such fierce international and national criticism that the Peruvian government suspended the trade between 1856 and 1861 and only reopened it later under the more relaxed supervision of the Portuguese. But the pressure experienced by the Peruvian government to stop what often was referred to as "another African slave trade" did not prevent the deaths of tens of thousand of coolies and Peruvian laborers—many of whom, buried in the guano fields in which they died working, became, like the flesh and carcasses of birds and sea lions, part of the guano that soon would be exported to the United States to fertilize its lands and crops. To recall this history is to begin to delineate the world that made Emerson's figure possible.

If Emerson takes the risk of ventriloquizing the language of proslavery propaganda—we can find in "Fate" echoes of most of the important proslavery arguments: biological determinism, pre-Adamitism, the black's arrested evolution, and the eventual extinction of the black race, and his citations from Knox often have been understood as signs of his own latent racism—he seeks to recontextualize this language not only within an antislavery argument but also within a more general reflection on the nature of race and the violence that takes place in its name. In regard to the citations from Knox, for example, we need only register the adjectives he uses to introduce and describe the English anatomist's language. Far from endorsing Knox's evolutionary theories, Emerson states that the book's conclusions are "unpalatable," that its writer is "rash and unsatisfactory," and that its truths are "pungent and unforgetable" (6:9). With this last phrase, in particular—referring as he does to the one adjective that always is associated with guano, "pungent"—he suggests that Knox's book is a piece of guano, a book to be condemned, but a book that, fertilizing racist soil, enables the transformation of minorities into guano. The strength of Emerson's criticism becomes clearer if we recall that Knox's claims for the racial superiority of the Anglo-Saxon are made in the name of its racial purity. What kind of purity can there be, Emerson suggests, if America's prairies and crops are composed largely of foreign bodies: the seeds that are imported from England, the fertilizer imported from Peru and elsewhere, the bodies and blood of peoples from Africa, Germany, Ireland, Peru, China, and so forth—all of which will become part of the "American" body? What his extraordinary figure tells us is that the American body should be understood as neither "American" nor even entirely human.

If Emerson's identification between ethnic minorities and guano encourages us to rethink our relation to the violent enterprise of slavery, however, this identification does not belong to him alone. From Melville's allegorical assault on American imperialism, "The Encantadas," in which the white imperialist's desire to occupy the enchanted isles is associated with the whitish remains of the various seabirds that nest on them, the guano that covers and dominates the island's rocks and earth; to Thoreau's *Walden*, which tells us in its first pages that "men labor under a mistake" and that "by a seeming fate" or "necessity" their "better part . . . is soon ploughed into the soil for compost"; to Douglass's famous 1852 "Fourth of July" speech, which depicts a group of slavers headed for the slave market and mourns for those "wretched people" who "are to be sold singly, or in lots, to suit purchasers" and who will soon become "food for the cotton-field, and the deadly sugar-mill"; to Faulkner's *Absalom, Absalom!*, which, in an extraordinary passage that describes the spot of earth on which Charles Bon was born, refers to "a soil manured with black blood from two hundred years of oppression and exploitation until it sprang with an incredible paradox of peaceful greenery and crimson flowers and sugar cane sapling size and three times the height of a man," the figurative association between laborers and manure works to exhibit the violence of oppression and of colonialist and imperialist expropriation, the injuries and scars, the deaths, murders, and sometimes collective assassinations that have supported capitalist expansion.[39]

If such rhetoric offers a graphic rendering of the familiar trope of the black blood and tears that nourish the land (implicitly in the context of agriculture) that appears so often in abolitionist writing, it does so in order to work against proslavery arguments that, asserting a similar identification between slaves and the material bases of America's growth and development, argued for the necessity of slavery. Perhaps the most celebrated example of this proslavery position—a position that takes its point of departure from the tension between the twin imperatives of democracy and capitalism—is offered by James Hammond's famous "Mud-Sill" speech, delivered to the U.S. Senate in March 1858. There, aligning himself with the earlier proslavery rhetoric of Henry Clay, John Calhoun, and others, he claims that "the greatest strength of the South arises from the harmony of her political and social institutions,"[40] and he goes on to explain that "in all social systems there must be a class to do the menial duties, to perform the drudgery of life. That is, a class requiring but a low order of intellect and but little skill. Its requisites are vigor, docility, fidelity. Such a class you must have, or you would not have that other class which leads progress, civilization, and refinement. It constitutes the very mud-sill of society and of political government.... Fortunately for the South, she found a race adapted to that purpose to her hand. A race inferior to her own, but eminently qualified in temper, in vigor, in docility, in capacity to stand the climate, to answer all her purposes. We use them for our purpose, and call them slaves" (318–19). The relation between Hammond's metaphor and that of the "guano-races of mankind" that are fertilizing the land is reinforced when we remember that the mud-sill of a structure—the lowest part of the structure—is generally embedded in the soil. As Sundquist notes, "The spread of the Cotton Kingdom into the Deep South from the 1820s to 1850s (resulting in a tenfold increase in production, to a peak of nearly five million bales per year, three-fourths of the world's cotton, by the outbreak of the Civil War) guaranteed the survival and expansion of slavery."[41] Marx already had confirmed the South's dependence on slavery in 1847. "Without slavery you have no cotton," he tells us, "without cotton you have no modern industry. It is slavery that gave the colonies their value; it is the colonies that created world-trade that is the pre-condition of large-scale industry. Slavery is an economic category of the greatest importance."[42]

But what is the status of the principles of freedom and autonomy to which Hammond has recourse here? If Anglo-Saxon freedom and equality are achieved through slave labor, then what possibilities exist for this conduit of Saxon identity? In what way do emancipatory discourses of rights, equality, and citizenship depend on forms of racialization and on the invisibility of the practices of domination and discipline? As Marx explains—and here he points both to the history of racial subjugation and enslavement, and to the entanglement of slavery and freedom—despite the presumed universalism of such principles, the democratic rights to self-determination that Hammond proclaims depend on the success of a violent politics of oppression, of economical and ideological enslavement, and thus of the destruction of autonomy. In Werner Hamacher's words, "The process of the practical universalization of individual and social liberties"—the dream articulated by the rhetoric of manifest destiny—"often has gone hand in hand with a process of oppression, disenfranchisement, and the massacre of countless persons and peoples. And this process—one hesitates to call it a process of civilization—has to this day continued to thrive on the massive, capitalist exploitation of individuals and peoples."[43] The process of civilization and refinement to which Hammond refers has always been a process of capitalization. As Hamacher goes on to explain,

> The formation of cultural ideals, which is supposed to culminate in the *autonomy* of the self, is at the same time a process of the *automation* of the mechanism of capital. It is a process of the obliteration of labor, the obliteration of a violent history and of the particularity of the socio-economic and politico-cultural forces that sustain this autonomy, a process of the erasure of those who are always insufficiently paid and of that which cannot be counted. Whoever invokes the universalism of *this* freedom and *this* equality always invokes, whether or not he acknowledges it, *this* history of automatization, colonialization, and exploitation. (301, emphasis in original)

Whoever appeals to equality, Emerson would say, does so within a history of inequality, within a history in which the America that was to be the realization of the promise of the right to representation for everyone perhaps can never exist, perhaps can only exist in the form of a promise, but a promise that must be enacted and performed with every breath we take.

This is why, according to Hamacher, we "must call to mind the history of the universalization of the principle of autonomy . . . not in order to discredit the universalist ethics of the claim to freedom—this claim can never be simply fulfilled and never completely discredited—but rather to see the paradoxes of its principles clearly whenever they become political realities in history, that is, where they make history."[44] As Emerson reminds us in his essay "Man the Reformer," in a passage that again seeks to tell us why we must learn to mourn in order to be the Americans that we are, in order to be the Americans we are still not:

> We are all implicated . . . in this charge; it is only necessary to ask a few questions as to the progress of the articles of commerce from the fields where they grew, to our houses, to become aware that we eat and drink and wear perjury and fraud in a hundred commodities. How many articles of daily consumption are furnished us from the West Indies. . . . The abolitionist has shown us our dreadful debt to the southern negro. In the island of Cuba, in addition to the ordinary abominations of slavery, it appears, only men are bought for the plantations, and one dies in ten every year, of these miserable bachelors, to yield us sugar. (1:147)

Learn to mourn, then, remember the dead, keep the memory of the dead alive, think your relation to a past that, never behind you, haunts you, tells you for what you are answerable. As Walter Benjamin would have it: "To articulate the past historically does not mean to recognize it 'as it really was.' It means to seize hold of a memory as it flashes up in a moment of danger. . . . Only that historian will have the gift of fanning the spark of hope in the past who is firmly convinced that *even the dead* will not be safe if the enemy wins. And the enemy has not ceased to be victorious."[45]

NOTES

The epigraph is taken from one of George Jackson's prison letters. Dated April 4, 1970, the letter can be found in *Soledad Brother: The Prison Letters of George Jackson* (Chicago: Lawrence Hill Books, 1994), 233–34.

1. I am indebted here, and in the rest of this paragraph, to Saidiya Hartman's discussion of a memory born from violence and loss in *Scenes of Subjection: Terror, Slavery, and Self-Making in Nineteenth-Century America* (New York: Oxford University Press, 1997), 72–74.

2. I am indebted here to Jacques Derrida's discussion of the relations among capital, ghosts, and mourning in his *Specters of Marx: The State of the Debt, the Work of Mourning, and the New International*, trans. Peggy Kamuf (New York: Routledge, 1994), especially chapters 1 and 2.

3. Jean Genet, *The Prisoner of Love*, trans. Barbara Bray (Middletown, Conn.: Wesleyan University Press, 1992 [1986]), 259.

4. "Fate," in *The Collected Works of Ralph Waldo Emerson*, ed. Alfred R. Ferguson, Robert E. Spiller, et al., 8 vols. to date (Cambridge, Mass.: Harvard University Press, Belknap Press, 1971–2010), 6:9. Subsequent quotations from Emerson's writing are from this source and are cited parenthetically in text by volume and page numbers. Citations may include essay title if the essay from which a quotation is taken is not clear from the text.

5. Stanley Cavell, "Emerson's Constitutional Amending: Reading 'Fate,'" in *Philosophical Passages: Wittgenstein, Emerson, Austin, Derrida* (Cambridge, England: Blackwell Publishers, 1995), 14.

6. *The Journals and Miscellaneous Notebooks of Ralph Waldo Emerson*, ed. William H. Gilman et al., 16 vols. (Cambridge, Mass.: Harvard University Press, 1960–), 8:114.

7. Cavell, "Emerson's Constitutional Amending," 18.

8. *Emerson's Antislavery Writings*, ed. Len Gougeon and Joel Myerson (New Haven, Conn.: Yale University Press, 1995), 9.

9. John O'Sullivan, "Annexation," *Democratic Review* 17 (July and August 1845): 5.

10. John O'Sullivan, "The Great Nation of Futurity," *Democratic Review* 16 (November 1839): 426–30.

11. *The Complete Works of Ralph Waldo Emerson*, Centenary Edition, 12 vols., ed. J. E. Cabot (Boston and New York: Houghton Mifflin, 1903–1904), 12:135.

12. "Kansas Relief Meeting," in *Emerson's Antislavery Writings*, 13–14, Emerson's emphasis.

13. Eric Sundquist, "The Literature of Expansion and Race," in *The Cambridge History of American Literature*, vol. 2, *1820–1865*, ed. Sacvan Bercovitch (Cambridge: Cambridge University Press, 1995), 128, 182.

14. Cited in Phillip L. Nicoloff, *Emerson on Race and History* (New York: Columbia University Press, 1961), 134.

15. This passage is from a letter of Samuel A. Cartwright to William S. Forwood. Dated February 13, 1861, it is cited in *The Ideology of Slavery: Proslavery Thought in the Antebellum South, 1830–1860*, ed. Drew Gilpin Faust (Baton Rouge: Louisiana State University Press, 1981), 15.

16. Josiah Clark Nott, *Two Lectures on the Connection between the Biblical and Physical History of Man* (Mobile, Ala.: Bartlett and Welford, 1849), 36.

17. Josiah Clark Nott and George Robbins Gliddon, *Types of Mankind, or Ethnological Researches Based upon the Ancient Monuments, Paintings, Sculptures, and Crania of Races, and upon their Natural, Geographical, Philological, and Biblical History: Illustrated by Selections from the Inedited Papers of Samuel George Morton, M.D., (Late President of the Academy of Natural Sciences at Philadelphia) and by Additional Contributions from Prof. L. Agassiz, LL.D.; W. Usher, M.D.; and Prof. H. S. Patterson, M.D.* (Philadelphia: Lippincott, Grambo & Co., 1854), 79.

18. Walt Whitman, *Walt Whitman: Complete Poetry and Collected Prose*, ed. Justin Kaplan (New York: Library of America, 1982), 1170.

19. I am indebted in this discussion of Emerson's relation to geology to Joseph G. Kronick's *American Poetics of History: From Emerson to the Moderns* (Baton Rouge: Louisiana State University Press, 1984), especially chapter 2.

20. Robert Chambers, *Vestiges of the Natural History of Creation,* 3rd ed. (London: John Churchill, 1845), 58.

21. *The Early Lectures of Ralph Waldo Emerson*, ed. Stephen Whicher, Robert E. Spiller, and Wallace E. Williams, 3 vols. (Cambridge, Mass.: Harvard University Press, 1961), 1:18.

22. *Journals and Miscellaneous Notebooks of Ralph Waldo Emerson*, 3:220.

23. John Harris, *The Pre-Adamite Earth: Contributions to Theological Science* (Boston: Gould, Kendall & Lincoln, 1850), 69.

24. In Lyell's words, geology teaches us that "the successive destruction of species must now be part of the regular and constant order of Nature." See Charles Lyell, *Principles of Geology,* 2 vols. (Chicago: University of Chicago Press, 1990), 2:141. This edition is a reprint of *Principles of Geology, being an attempt to explain the former changes of the earth's surface, by reference to causes now in operation* (London: John Murray, 1830).

25. Henry David Thoreau, *Walden and Civil Disobedience,* ed. Owen Thomas (New York: W. W. Norton, 1966), 203.

26. Patricia Seed, *Ceremonies of Possession in Europe's Conquest of the New World, 1492–1640* (Cambridge: Cambridge University Press, 1995), especially 16–40. I am grateful to Al Raboteau for directing me to this text.

27. Jimmy M. Skaggs, *The Great Guano Rush: Entrepreneurs and American Overseas Expansion* (New York: St. Martins, 1994), 1–2.

28. On this point, see Avery Odell Craven's excellent *Soil Exhaustion as a Factor in the Agricultural History of Virginia and Maryland, 1606–1860* (Urbana: University of Illinois, 1925), especially 9–53.

29. Lewis Cecil Gray uses this phrase in a discussion of the importance of guano to the Cotton Belt in particular. See his *History of Agriculture in the Southern United States to 1860,* 2 vols. (New York: Peter Smith, 1941), 2:701.

30. *Journals and Miscellaneous Notebooks of Ralph Waldo Emerson,* 14:171.

31. Skaggs, *The Great Guano Rush,* 10. See also "Inspection Laws," *Southern Planter* 16 (March 1856): 80–90.

32. For a detailed account of this "test by burning," see Solon Robinson's *Guano: A Treatise of Practical Information for Farmers; Containing Plain Directions How to Apply Peruvian Guano to the Various Crops and Soils of America, with a brief synopsis of its history, locality, quantity, method of procuring, prospect of continued supply, and price; analysis of its composition, and value as a fertilizer, over all other manures* (New York: Theodore W. Riley, 1853), 69–70.

33. Millard Fillmore, "First Annual Message," in *State of the Union Messages of the Presidents, 1790–1966,* ed. Fred L. Israel, vol. 1, *1790–1860* (New York: Chelsea House, 1966), 797.

34. *U. S. Congressional Globe,* 34th Cong., 1st sess., July 22, 1856, 1296.

35. Skaggs, *The Great Guano Rush,* 71.

36. *Journals and Miscellaneous Notebooks of Ralph Waldo Emerson,* 14:16.

37. Evelyn Hu-Dehart, "Coolies, Shopkeepers, Pioneers: The Chinese of Mexico and Peru (1849–930)," *Amerasia* 15, no. 2 (1989): 92.

38. Ibid., 108.

39. Herman Melville, "The Encantadas, or Enchanted Isles," in *The Piazza Tales and Other Prose Pieces, 1839–1860* (Evanston, Ill.: Northwestern University Press, 1987), especially 134–37; Thoreau, *Walden and Civil Disobedience,* 3; Frederick Douglass, "What to the Slave is the Fourth of July?: An Address Delivered in Rochester, New York, on 5 July 1852," in *The Frederick Douglass Papers, Series One: Speeches, Debates, and Interviews,* vol. 2, *1847–54,* ed. John W. Blassingame (New Haven, Conn.: Yale University Press, 1982), 373; and William Faulkner, *Absalom, Absalom!* (New York: Vintage International Edition, Random House, 1990), 201–2.

40. James Hammond, *Selections from the Letters and Speeches of the Hon. James H. Hammond, of South Carolina* (New York: John F. Trow & Co., 1866), 317–18.

41. Sundquist, "The Literature of Expansion and Race," 2:245.

42. Karl Marx, *Poverty of Philosophy* (Moscow: Foreign Languages Publishing House, 1955 [1847]), 112.

43. Werner Hamacher, "One 2 Many Multiculturalisms," trans. Dana Hollander, in *Violence, Identity, and Self-Determination,* ed. Hent de Vries and Samuel Weber (Stanford, Calif.: Stanford University Press, 1997), 301.

44. Ibid., 304.

45. Walter Benjamin, "Theses on the Philosophy of History," in *Illuminations: Essays and Reflections,* trans. Harry Zohn, ed. Hannah Arendt (New York: Schocken Books, 1969), 255, emphasis in original.

5. "Experience," Antislavery, and the Crisis of Emersonianism

Two of the key terms in the title of this essay, "antislavery" and "crisis of Emersonianism," refer to familiar themes within the Emerson canon. Readings of Emerson have normatively assumed the form of variations on the theme of the crisis precipitated by conflicting interpretations of Emerson's ambivalence toward questions of social reform. Emerson's vexing relationship to the campaign to abolish slavery is the most recent object that his interpreters have invoked to represent this contention.

But the crisis with which I shall be concerned took place within the speaker of Emerson's "Experience." Although this speaker articulated it in an idiom that was implicated in the slavery question, the crisis he underwent was irreducible to that issue. Insofar as it could not be integrated within the preexisting antagonisms that have governed the reception of Emerson's work, the crisis in which the speaker of "Experience" was embroiled brought the Emerson tradition regulated by this conflict to its limits. I intend to describe the nature of that crisis and to explain why it cannot be incorporated within the Emerson legacy. However, I first need to distinguish the crisis to which I refer from the ideological conflict through which the Emerson tradition has been regulatively transmitted.

The interpretations through which Emerson has been institutionalized within the U.S. literary canon have isolated a depoliticizing transcendentalism and a politicizing social reformism as perennial yet antagonistic predispositions within his writings. The divisive antagonisms that are perceptibly at work within most of Emerson's collected essays have also precipitated an ongoing contestation among his critics and interpreters over whether Emerson the Transcendentalist or Emerson the Social Reformer should predominate. Ironically, the conflict among Emerson's interpreters over the relative importance to be ascribed to these personae has supplied the metanorm through which what Sacvan Bercovitch has called the "Emersonian legacy" has been normatively inherited.

Emerson encouraged contradictory readings of his work when he refused to consolidate the heterogeneous personifications of his project into a coherent identity. Rather than making them cohere, Emerson placed the persona of the Reformer, through whom he advanced powerful demands for social change, in a relationship of antagonistic cooperation with the persona of the Transcendentalist, who was averse to limit his thinking to questions of social reform.

Emerson called the structural performative that was the source and the outcome of the unending tension between these two figurations of address "self-reliance": "The virtue in most request is conformity. Self-reliance is its aversion."[1] In the following passage from the essay "Self-Reliance," Emerson set this structure of aversion to the work of disassociating him from the moral imperatives of two of the most powerful institutions of social reform—philanthropy and abolition—of his day:

> Every decent and well-spoken individual affects and sways me more than is right. I ought to go upright and vital, and speak the rude truth in all ways. If malice and vanity wear the coat of philanthropy, shall that pass? If an angry bigot assume this bountiful cause of Abolition, and comes to me with his last news from Barbadoes, why should I not say to him, "Go love thy infant; love thy wood-chopper: be good-natured and modest: have that grace; and never varnish your hard, uncharitable ambition with this incredible tenderness for black folk a thousand miles off. Thy love afar is spite at home." Rough and graceless would be such a greeting, but truth is handsomer than the affectation of love. Your goodness must have some edge to it—else it is none. The doctrine of hatred must be preached as the counteraction of the doctrine of love when that pules and whines. I shun father and mother and wife and brother, when my genius calls me. I would write on the lintels of the door-post, *Whim*. I hope it is somewhat better than whim at last, but we cannot spend the day in explanation. Expect me not to show cause why I seek or why I exclude company. Then, again, do

not tell me, as a good man did to-day, of my obligation to put all poor
men in good situations. Are they *my* poor? I tell thee, thou foolish philanthropist, that I grudge the dollar, the dime, the cent I give to such
men as do not belong to me and to whom I do not belong. (2:30–31,
Emerson's emphasis)

In the course of this essay I shall have occasion to return to different
phrases within this passage by way of disparate points of entrance and
exit. This passage does not merely represent Emerson's ad hoc response
to random demands on his purse and conscience. The protocols laid
out in this scene comprise the technology of the self whereby Emerson
gained access to his primal scene of writing. I turn to it now for its co-
gent exemplification of the speaker's relationship to the antagonisms that
have preoccupied Emerson's readers.

"Self-reliance" was the outcome of the speaker's expressions of resistance to the economic and moral causes with which he otherwise might
have felt inclined to affiliate himself. It is also the source of his capacity to disassociate from both the abolitionist's and the philanthropist's
campaigns. But the Emersonian Transcendentalist who would appear to
have been engendered out of the speaker's expressed aversions to abolition and philanthropy alike might also be described as having dispensed
philanthropy from a higher plane. In turning away from these reform
movements, the speaker has turned toward the concerns that he shared
with these reformers. Indeed, the speaker's representation of his imaginary conversation with these representatives of social reform records the
ways in which Emerson the Transcendentalist's instructions produced
the persona of Emerson the Reformer.

But the series of moral imperatives that the speaker addresses to the
abolitionist and philanthropist point in contradictory directions and
take effect at different levels of discourse. When he counsels the abolitionist to love his infant and woodchopper, the speaker presupposed that
the anger and bigotry discernible in the abolitionist's resolve to eliminate slavery had been undertaken at the expense of his familial and communal responsibilities. In ordering the abolitionist to transform these
misanthropic dimensions of his personality through the expression of
love for his family ("Go love thy infant") and for community ("love thy
wood-chopper") the speaker has quite literally adopted the persona of a
philanthropist. After finding the philanthropical advice he doled out to

the abolitionist too sappy to take hold, however, the speaker decided to fashion a more bracing alternative.

The injunction from the "doctrine of hatred" that the speaker addressed to himself operated at a different register of discourse than did his prior directives. His recommendations to the abolitionist would have brought about reforms within the family and the community that left existing social arrangements unchanged. But when he pledged himself to dissolve all social and familial ties, the speaker has responded to a demand from a noumenal dimension of his subjectivity that would have utterly transformed the coordinates of the existing social order.

In this passage the speaker traveled from his imagined conversations with the abolitionist and the philanthropist to his own family dwelling. But along the way the speaker turned each of the institutions about which they had conversed—the poor, the cause of abolition, family, and philanthropy—toward his higher calling. In dissevering all of his social relations, the speaker became poor in spirit so as to become the recipient of the spiritual advice of the higher-order philanthropist he called "my genius." The temporality of the passage is governed by the future perfect tense. Although he did not arrive at this destination until the conclusion of this journey, it was ostensibly the call of genius that endowed the speaker with the spiritual wealth that he will have already philanthropically distributed through the instructions that turned the philanthropist and the abolitionist (and himself) in the direction of "my genius" as well.

Whether Emerson's interpreters have analyzed the relationship between the Transcendentalist and the Reformer that is represented within this passage (and throughout most of Emerson's collected essays) as enabling paradoxes or as disabling contradictions has depended on whether they assumed that Emerson's essays should exercise a political or a strictly literary efficacy. Readers of this passage who are inclined to identify with Emerson the Transcendentalist have foregrounded the speaker's transformation of questions of social reform into spiritual admonitions. Advocates of the alternative persuasion have diagnosed an intellectual schizophrenia at the heart of this passage that Emerson could have only overcome by abandoning the precepts of transcendentalism in favor of the principles of his political activism.[2]

Rather than taking the side of either antagonist, Sacvan Bercovitch has elevated the ceaseless strife underwriting the Emerson legacy into the representative self-definition of U.S. political culture. In the course of doing so, Bercovitch redescribes the dissension between Emerson the Transcendentalist and Emerson the Reformer as subservient to the imperatives of the discourse of liberal individualism that regulated it. According to Bercovitch, the divisions within the Emersonian legacy represent the paradoxes of a political order that elevated the discourse of liberal individualism above any of the specific changes within the social order that liberal individuals might advocate. No matter whether they opposed or affirmed one or another of these Emersons, as Bercovitch explained, all of the parties to the Emersonian legacy were required to agree to the discourse of liberal individualism through which their antagonisms were transmitted. More specifically, Bercovitch has interpreted the contentious disagreements underpinning Emerson's essays as examples of what Bercovitch calls the "ideology of dissent" underwriting U.S. liberal individualism. Even in dissenting from specific cultural arrangements, Emerson, under Bercovitch's description, was required to conform to the transindividual liberal order whose institutions he would reform:

> The appeal of Emersonian dissent lies in an extraordinary conjunction of forces: its capacity to absorb the radical communitarian vision it renounces, and its capacity to be nourished by the liberal structures it resisted. It demonstrates the capacity of the culture to shape the subversive in its own image, and thereby, *within limits,* to be shaped by the radicalism it seeks to contain.[3]

In Bercovitch's view, the Emersonian legacy afforded the discourse of U.S. liberal individualism with a transcendental guarantee. But in *The American Evasion of Philosophy: A Genealogy of Pragmatism,* the African American philosopher Cornel West has criticized the Emersonian legacy as well as the liberal individualism that Bercovitch said it legitimated.[4] Rather than agreeing with Bercovitch's claim that liberal individualism supplied the terms through which progressive social change could be advocated, West castigated this political discourse as structured upon racial exclusions that the Emersonian legacy had authorized.

In pursuing this claim, West pointedly recharacterizes what Emerson had described as his "aversion" to the conformities of the abolitionist movement as an "evasion" of the slavery question. West faults Emerson for his refusal directly to confront the issue of Negro slavery within his collected essays, and he charges that this evasion was motivated by a racist dimension within Emerson's reasoning that West refuses to write off as merely an echo of prevailing social attitudes. Insofar as race was inextricably linked with Emerson's notions of "fate, circumstances, and, ultimately, history," Emerson's thought included, and perhaps has continued to command, a racist outlook.[5]

The crisis in the reception of the Emersonian project that has ensued in the wake of such negative reassessments as Cornel West's has recently been turned into the rationale for the recommendation that the future of American literature should involve a turning away from the Emersonian legacy. In *At Emerson's Tomb: The Politics of Classic American Literature,* a reexamination of Emerson's work that he published in 1995, John Carlos Rowe exemplified this newfound aversion to Emerson when he placed Bercovitch's representations of the Emersonian legacy into the service of building on Cornel West's critique. But unlike West, Rowe accused Emerson of collaborating with an oppressive order even when he turned against the specific institutions of slavery and advocated for the rights of women:

> In sum, what Bercovitch calls the primary cultural value of liberal dissent in Emerson is for me our long-standing problem. The "critical imperative" that Bercovitch reminds us is also our inheritance from the "Emersonian legacy" has too often served false gods or made Americans appear tolerant of differences when they are in fact intent upon maintaining the same old powers.[6]

There is great merit to be found in Rowe's criticism of Emerson. But after he correlates it with Bercovitch's account of the ideology of dissent, Rowe inadvertently leaves the critique that he directs against Emerson— that in failing to supply an actually viable political alternative, Emerson has simply ratified the existing liberal order—answerable to the same accusation. In failing to propose an alternative to the discourse of liberalism, has not Rowe's powerful repudiation of Emerson resulted in an instance of the very ideology of dissent that Rowe has also denounced?

When they propose that the Emersonian legacy is to be understood as indistinguishable from the discourse of liberal individualism, both Bercovitch and Rowe also presuppose that what Emerson called self-reliance was interchangeable with the possessive individual who was the constituent subject of the discourse to which they made it conform. But what Emerson referred to as "my genius [when it] calls me" achieved effects that were independent of the processes of identification, interpellation, and internalization associated with liberal institutions.

Although "my genius" could not be said to exist without such an addressee, Emerson's speakers did not produce the call, nor did they represent their calling as a recognizable social identity. The speakers' provocatives instead bore witness to influxes of creative power that could neither be fully generated by nor wholly assimilated to subjective consciousness. Genius introduced a constitutive division into the speaker's subjectivity that disallowed the possibility of any unified identity. Insofar as this influx of creative power penetrated in depth without depending on the mediations of the speaker's own representations, it compromised the autonomy of the speaker's will. But in so doing, "my genius" also undermined liberalism's conception of the possessive individual as its subject.

Because there was no social identity that "my genius" could take up that was not dependent on an already instituted social role, the self-reliance that genius effected was inherently nonsubstantial and lacking in positive content. As a generalized aversion to all taken-for-granted paradigms of social subjectification, self-reliance resulted in a subtraction from the order of things rather than a development within them. Unlike the primary integer within the discourse into which Bercovitch and Rowe have interpolated him, the speaker of the lines that I have cited from "Self-Reliance" did not possess an identifiable social role, nor did he come into possession of a recognizable private identity.

I have already considered how the speaker's stirring injunctions in "Self-Reliance" opened up a pathway leading from the world of signification into the realm of Emersonian provocation. I have also discussed how they did so through instructions that recommended dispossession from established institutions rather than self-development within them. As an inflooding of power that could not be integrated within the existing order, "my genius [when it] calls me" deprived its addressees—no matter whether Emerson the Reformer or Emerson the Transcendentalist—of their social personhood.

The speaker's capacity to respond to the call was the effect and the retroactive source of the structural performative Emerson called "self-reliance." It is because they were produced through the self-reliance that their utterances reproduced that the speakers of Emerson's essays could not be integrated into a coherent authorial identity. Through their relaying of serial acts of bearing witness to the call of genius, the speakers of Emerson's essays might instead be described as constituting a transindividual structure of self-dispossession that produced subject effects that were independent of Emerson's individual agency. What holds the discontinuous speakers together within this transindividual structure is the structure of aversion to which the speaker of "Self-Reliance" committed the entire relay of Emersonian provocations. The pledge—to dissociate from all social relations and to write "Whim" when genius calls—constituted the governing performative that interconnected the speakers of Emerson's essays.

West criticized Emerson's structure of aversion as an evasion of the problem that slavery posed for the political order. John Carlos Rowe invokes this critique as warrant for his recommendation against inheriting the Emersonian legacy. I shall draw upon West's criticism for the contours of my argument, and at the conclusion I shall return to Rowe's concerns with how or whether Emersonian thinking should be inherited. But the crisis in Emersonianism with which I shall be centrally concerned does not refer to the recent negative revaluation of the Emersonian legacy. It instead designates an event that took place within the essay "Experience" that resulted in the retraction of the pledge to which the speaker of "Self-Reliance" had committed the Emersonian project.

"EXPERIENCE" AND THE LIMITS OF EMERSONIANISM

"Experience" occupies an exceptional position in the Emerson corpus. Published in 1844, the same year as Emerson's breakthrough essay "On Emancipation in the British West Indies," celebrating its anniversary, "Experience" has in the past been selected as an example of the tragic sensibility believed to be otherwise missing from the Emerson corpus. The essay has also served as the vehicle through which to relegate such tragic expressions to the dimensions of a single essay. But I return to that essay now with the intention of bringing into focus a crisis in Emersonianism understood as a breakdown that took place within the figure through whom the Emersonian project was accomplished.

I intend the ambiguity in the word *figure* to mark the space between the antagonistic personae mandating Emerson's place within the literary canon and the subject position that its speaker took up whenever he felt called on to write an Emersonian essay. The essay "Experience" provides an insight into the difference between these figures in that it records what happens when what Emerson names "my genius" has not called him. Indeed, the essay seems written by someone who had either not read Emerson's other essays or who had not yet been overtaken by their stirring provocatives. The essay's absence of uptake, its failure to achieve Emerson's signature imperatives, discloses as a limit internal to "Emerson" a persona who has not yet been inspired by the structural performative Emerson named "self-reliance."

In the essay "Circles," Emerson designated the split internal to his writing persona as the following incompatible predications: "I am God in nature; I am a weed by the wall" (2:182). These utterly asymmetrical statements belong to different registers of discourse. The first assertion, "I am God in nature," refers to what happens through the exhortative performatives whereby Emerson replaced the order of social signification with the order that Emersonian provocations would call forth; "I am a weed by the wall" refers to what happens when the Emersonian event is not happening. The latter statement cannot be subsumed by the first, but its very status as lacking in the quality of performative uplift is nevertheless the condition for bringing "I am a weed by the wall" into proximate relation with Emerson's Genius. Such resonant Emersonian imperatives as "Trust thyself" were endowed with the cultural authority to turn the individual away from the already established social order and toward the order of provocation that Emerson's essays evoked in (and as) compensation ("Self-Reliance," 2:28).

But the speaker in "Experience" who declares, "I grieve that grief can teach me nothing, nor carry me one step into real nature" encountered an event for which the order of provocation cannot compensate (3:29). Unable to perform the speech acts through which a loss of this magnitude might be transformed, this figure was positioned between the self-reliant individual normatively assigned responsibility for their enunciation and the alternative social order which these pronouncements mandate.

Unlike the speakers of Emerson's other essays, the speaker in "Experience" appears stuck at the site of the unsuccessful transformation of creative power into an accomplished figure of thought. Rather than achieving self-reliance, the speaker of the essay "Experience" underwent a passage through the unsettling otherness of differences and death. The distinction between the transindividual identified retroactively as the agency responsible for the relay of provocative utterances constituting the Emersonian legacy and the speaker in "Experience" who cannot reperform those speech acts discloses what I mean by the crisis in Emersonianism.

In my efforts to discern the stakes of the "experience" of the loss of relation between an Emersonian event and the speaker who undergoes it, I shall of course be concerned with what has happened to that speaker. But I shall also try to explain the relationship between this loss and the figures of thought through which Emerson's speakers obtained access to the vocative stuff with which they wrote. Because I shall analyze both of these figures in terms of what Shoshana Felman and Dori Laub have called "crises of witnessing," the remainder of this essay will be devoted to an analysis of the pertinence of this complex phenomenon to Emerson's writings in general and to "Experience" in particular. Following a brief account of what is entailed by the term *crisis of witnessing,* I shall discuss the crisis in Emersonianism as an example of what happens when witnessing is in crisis. And after a discussion of the place in which this crisis takes place, I shall attempt to distinguish Emerson's aversion to witnessing from what Stanley Cavell has described as Emerson's aversive thinking.

EMERSON AND THE CRISIS OF WITNESSING

In its ordinary usages, the word *witness* is capable of designating an action, its agent, or agency, as well as the entirety of the event witnessed. The range of the word's possible meanings achieves relative stability only when situated within the legal model of the trial. The trial both derives from and proceeds by way of a crisis of truth that requires an assessment of conflicting testimony for its verdictive resolution. If the infinitive "to testify" represents the undertaking of a speech act whereby the speaker vows "to tell, to promise and produce one's own speech as material evidence for truth," the testimony produced through this speech act involves the recounting of a story that, like an oath, cannot be carried out by anyone else.[7] In giving testimony, a witness does not merely recount a preexisting truth; a witness begets truth by bearing its witness. The various acts of testimony provided within the precincts of a trial bear witness to facts on which justice must pronounce its verdicts.

But if a trial regulates the crises of truth that it also institutionalizes, a much more profound crisis proceeds from historical traumas—for example, cholera epidemics, the Middle Passage, slavery, the Nazi Holocaust, the AIDS epidemic—that explode any conceptual framework through which they can be adequately represented. What Felman and Laub refer to as "crises of witnessing" take place in relation to traumatizing historical events that remain unreferenced within the order of things and that cannot be articulated to that order by juridical norms. Activated within events that cannot be assimilated by a subject whose identity is predicated on its continuity throughout disparate experiences, such crises occur when an experience is undergone whose radical alterity to the limits of human comprehension "created the address for the specificity of a historical experience which annihilated any possibility for address."[8] Restoration of traumatic events that cannot be articulated to the socio-symbolic order requires a retroactive encounter between the survivor, who underwent the experience, and a belated listener, whose bearing the witness of the survivor constitutes the only materiality upon which the survivor's testimony can be inscribed. As substitute for the absent historical witness, the addressee must become the bearer of responsibility for an event that can be assimilated neither to the socio-symbolic order nor to the subjectivities that order legitimates.

Felman and Laub's accounts of such crises emerged from their work with survivors of the Nazi Holocaust. The composite of "event without witness" to which the survivors testified was comprised of the following factors: the world's refusal to acknowledge the historical fact of genocide *as it was happening,* the inability of the victims consciously to undergo the experience and maintain a recognizable self-identity, and the lack of any addressees willing to respond. Because the crisis of witnessing necessarily removed the survivor as well as the belated addressee from the preexisting symbolic order, the crisis could not be resolved by verdictive judgments legitimating that order. It bore witness instead against the order itself for its failure to witness the enormity of this injustice.

While Felman and Laub associated this crisis primarily with the victims of the Nazi Holocaust, Zygmunt Bauman, in his book *Modernity and the Holocaust,* has argued, without losing sight of either the singularity or the historical specificity of the Nazi Holocaust, that the crisis of witnessing can also be understood as a structure of cultural relations inherent to the dialectic of the Enlightenment. As a rationale for this extension of the crisis, Bauman redescribes the legacy of the Enlightenment as a symbolic order's systematic disavowal of mortality. Because Death threatened the conceptual order founded in a belief in Reason, the anxieties associated with Death were projected onto persons relegated to what Edith Wyschogrod calls death worlds: social regimes whose inhabitants were compelled to undergo experiences that were structured in the imagined conditions of Death.[9] The Enlightenment posited its symbolic immortality as the difference between the enduring value of its institutions and the sheer transience of events undergone in these death worlds.

According to Bauman, a generalized crisis of witnessing was the outcome of a symbolic order's deployment of figures—slaves, prisoners of war, the homeless—designated as socially dead to bear *false* witness to the immortality as against the mortality of the socio-symbolic order. Through its inclusion of this order of mortality, the Enlightenment imagined itself as having overcome the mortality that it included in the restricted form of one or another of institutions contained within its immortality structure. The Enlightenment's negation of witness to the order that would negate *it* thereby produced for the symbolic order an illusion of immortality. The Enlightenment's structure of false witness was thereafter generalized through the active negation of historical witness to persons the Enlightenment assigned the responsibility of undergoing the social trauma associated with death. By including the negation of witness to the mortality structures that the symbolic order had produced yet excluded, that order was permitted to imagine itself as having surpassed the social death that it had also constructed.

I have chosen "crisis in witnessing" as the concept-metaphor with which to discuss Emerson's "Experience" because this term enables me to designate the witness as an Emersonian speaker who differs from the Emerson who holds one or another of the subject positions organizing the conflict of interpretations through which the Emersonian legacy has been inherited. More specifically, I will propose that in "Experience" the death of Emerson's son effected a crisis in the transindividual structure through which Emerson had averted witness to the historical trauma of slavery. "Experience" effected a crisis in the structure of aversion in that it confronted its speaker with an event to which he was compelled to respond but to which he could not respond according to the protocols of response laid out in "Self-Reliance." By titling this chapter "'Experience,' Antislavery, and the Crisis of Emersonianism" I intend to disclose "crisis of witnessing" as an unacknowledged figure of address in Emerson's experience and to bring that figure to bear upon Emerson's essay of that title, as well as on the protocols of reading by means of which that essay (and by extension Emerson) remains experienceable.

"EXPERIENCE": BEARING WITNESS TO THE CRISIS OF EMERSONIANISM

As if their phantom syntax, witnessing figures assume the burden of remaining in relation to traumatizing experiences, such as the death of the child Emerson records in the third paragraph of the essay, that in surpassing the limits of what can be experienced threaten to displace the experienceable world with a different order of eventuation, such as the one into which the essay opens:

> Where do we find ourselves? In a series, of which we do not know the extremes, and believe that it has none. We wake and find ourselves on a stair: there are stairs below us, which we seem to have ascended; there are stairs above us, many a one, which go upward and out of sight. But the Genius, which according to the old belief, stands at the door by which we enter, and gives us the lethe to drink, that we may tell no tales, mixed the cup too strongly, and we cannot shake off the lethargy now at noonday. Sleep lingers all our lifetime about our eyes, as night hovers all day in the boughs of the fir-tree. All things swim and glitter. Our life is not so much threatened as our perception. Ghostlike we guide through nature, and should not know our place again. (3:27)

These first lines of "Experience" open onto an essayistic ordeal in which their speaker has received a demand to respond but without the benefit of the self-reliance through which to undertake it. The respondent experiences the scarcity in his powers of response as a disorienting interruption. Rather than responding, the speaker appeared stuck at the site of an unlocatable transition. Enacting a delay at the site where Emerson would elsewhere transfigure events into the aphorisms through which his readers might take visionary possession of them, the passage renders the effort to accomplish this transition into an intransitive act. The figure who appears at the site of this interrupted transition bore witness to a crisis that was transmitted as a gap of consciousness.

In obstructing his awareness that it was knowable, the speaker of the opening lines of "Experience" did not bear witness to the death of Emerson's son so much as he underwent a crisis in the orientation of the figure who was obliged to bear witness to this trauma. What we have referred to as a crisis of witnessing occurs when Emerson as the historic witness to this event was displaced by this act of bearing secondary witness to the impossibility of experiencing the child's death. The traumatizing power of the event to be witnessed has brought the perceptions through which the witness would bear it into crisis.

Unable either to bear witness to the child's death as it was happening or to bear the irredeemable grief of the father who survived his son's death, the speaker of these opening lines was overtaken by a crisis of witnessing. The traumatic event that the speaker could not bear to witness resulted in a retroactive encounter between the survivor who underwent the experience of this trauma and this belated listener, who could not respond.

As if situated at an internal verge of consciousness recorded just after an event was undergone but immediately before the acknowledgment of its utter incommensurability, these lines are marked by the incapacity of their "we" to address a "you" able to accommodate their mode of eventuation. Rather than bearing witness to the trauma of the child's death, "we" bore witness instead to the gap between the son's death and the father's life.

In the generalized disorientation they convey, these opening lines seem written by someone other than Emerson, yet are in need of Emerson's other writings to find a way out of their generalized waywardness. A knot of intertwined questions underwrites this uneventuating event, questions that do not presume an answer: What comprises the limits of the experienceable? Can the limits of experience be experienced as such? Is it possible to experience what takes place without limits? What takes their place?

In displacing a specifiable experience with these questions concerning the preconditions for experiencing, the opening lines condense these questions into the wish to situate what is being undergone by way of *this* displacing. What exactly *is* being undergone? The "experience" these lines seemingly convey refers to an event wherein the *absence* of the preconditions for its taking place would render impossible what is ordinarily understood as experience.

Inscribed at the limit between sheer eventuation and the conditions whereby writing can transmit "event" as a legible experience, these lines, under this description, threaten to transgress the line separating the oblivion (into which happening vanishes) from what can be passed on as memorable. When represented under the alternative description of going through the motions of experience but voided of anything to experience, a description that these lines would also warrant, the opening lines turn us toward a personal trauma that the essay does not wish to claim as an experience: the death on January 27, 1842, of Emerson's firstborn child, Waldo Emerson Jr., of scarlet fever. "I grieve," Emerson wrote, in his displacement of the event with the impossibility of grieving for *it,* "that grief can teach me nothing, nor carry me one step into real nature" ("Experience," 3:29).

As if it provides warrant for removing the sutures binding it to the flow of experience, that death figures to be what cannot take place within Emerson's experience and be experienced as happening *there.* What cannot take place in the spacing continuous with other events in the stream of conscious experience is nevertheless witnessed in the alternative streams of figuration that these opening lines convey and that would grieve over the impossibility of assimilating grief to "Experience."

The injury to the speech acts through which an Emersonian speaker would have been delivered out of trauma gave the speaker access instead to the reality of the condition of woundedness that his experience obliged him to move through before he could move on. Rather than giving Emerson access to the realm of revealed Truth, as had his disseverance from his other family relations, his violent separation from his son led the speaker to the discovery that grieving could not take him there.

Upon discovering that the grieving that ensued after the death of his son had not enabled him to take one step into deeper nature, the speaker encountered a threshold space intervening between his grief and his Genius that was rendered insurpassable by an infinitude of steps that came from nowhere and led everywhere. As manifestations of grief's inability to enable him to exit the desolation in which he felt entrapped, these steps revealed the infinite layers of transference that separated these worlds.

In lacking access to the place through which he received them, the speaker quite literally lacked the words with which to come to terms with the death of his son. In turning his radical shelterlessness into a spatial practice, the survivor situated his avoidance of witness to the child's death at this juncture between the psychic and the material. Unable to find the words with which to let go of him, the speaker would appear to have entered what Bauman calls a death world—where he underwent a modality of nonbeing that was structured in the imagined condition of his son's death—"Ghostlike we glide through nature, and should not know our place again."

The opening lines of "Experience" record the voiding of what would have been percipient in the speaker's experience of the child's death. In his effort to recover the capacity to experience, the speaker oscillated between stipulating the preconditions (what the essay names "the Lords of Life": Mood, Temperament, Succession, Illusion) for experiencing and finding them inadequate to explain the most significant of his lived experiences. By way of this oscillation, the speaker proceeded to shift the burden of the remainder of the essay away from experiencing the child's death and toward "experiencing" the inability of these preconditions to lay claim to that experience.

THE UNENDING PASSOVER

But if the speaker of "Experience" did not bear witness to the death of his son, where, we might ask, does Waldo's death take place? An effort to answer that question leads me to acknowledge, as a proximate motive for this essay, the experience of reading on the same day Stanley Cavell's "Emerson's Constitutional Amending: Reading 'Fate'" (in which he directs Emerson's experience toward the slavery question) and Sharon Cameron's "Representing Grief: Emerson's 'Experience'" (in which she asks whether Emerson can store Waldo's death in a place of memory). The juxtaposition of these reading experiences reveals a tacit, yet deeply textual connection between the personal trauma Emerson suffered at

Waldo's death and the social trauma of slavery. While I shall require the rest of this essay to untie this intertextual knot, what is percipient in its witness can be stated quite directly: the location Sharon Cameron designated as the place of the dead child names as well the site where Cavell discovers that the precondition for Emerson's thinking was founded on the negation of slavery.

Cameron's reading of "Experience" is especially important for its insistence on the speaker's representation of his grief as a crucial dimension of Emerson's "Experience":

> "Experience" is an elegy, an essay whose primary task is its work of mourning, and in light of that poorly conceived fact, it is surprising that critics have consistently spoken of the child as only one of the several causes equal in their provocation of listlessness and despair. In those few discussions in which Waldo's death is acknowledged to have special status, it is still not seen as it crucially must be: the occasion that generates in a nontrivial way all the other losses that succeed it.[10]

Throughout "Representing Grief: Emerson's 'Experience,'" Cameron addresses, as if it were the question Emerson wrote the essay to answer, Where is the dead child's "place" in Emerson's essay? She thereafter restates the enigma at the core of "Experience" in terms of the ways in which the speaker attempted to represent the spatial dimension of an introjected object. Cameron is specifically interested in Nicholas Abraham's and Maria Torok's notion that "introjection is a process that takes place secretly—that the object introjected is kept in a secret place." This interest led Cameron to the following observations: "The essay introduces grief over the child's death only to usher it out of the text to some liminal place (for the essay's beginning suggests that grief is not only marginalized but will also frame what follows), some statutory nowhere else, where, undisturbed by the resolutions the essay records." Cameron concludes this quite literally cryptic line of reasoning, "Emerson preserves the loss he will not directly address" (37).

But the place I have found for this loss by way of reading Cavell's "Emerson's Constitutional Amending" is neither cryptic nor secret. The site to which I refer has emerged, in the numerous essays Cavell has published on Emerson over the last dozen years, as what might be described as the portal of entry through which he obtains access to the philosophical stakes of Emerson's thinking. Cavell broaches this site by way of quasi-ritualized, revisionary readings of the passage that I have already cited from "Self-Reliance": "I shun father and mother and wife and brother, when my genius calls me. I would write on the lintels of the door-post, *Whim*. I hope it is somewhat better than whim at last, but we cannot spend the day in explanation" (2:30).

In his expansive commentary on these lines, Cavell deployed them as an intertext that conjoined Emerson's philosophy with scriptural passages whose words they seemed to have reread by accentuating. "Shunning father and mother," Cavell explained, "is what Jesus required of who would belong to him." "To put writing on the lintels and the door-posts," Cavell proceeded with this biblical instruction, "is the Old Testament command specifically at the time of Passover, as a sign to the angel of death to pass the house and spare its first born."[11] "Accordingly" (Cavell now connects biblical with philosophical instruction), "it is in obedience to Emerson's Genius that he speaks of it wherever he is, showing that it speaks everywhere to him, not to acknowledge it would be not to keep faith with it."[12] I shall return to Cavell's important commentary on the scriptural and philosophical resonances of this passage shortly. For now I want to recall that the biblical referents condensed within these passages also allude to an actual event in Emerson's life that would propose a different reading of their significance. Cavell has described Emerson's writing "Whim" on the lintel of his doorpost as his re-enactment of the ceremony that resulted in the exemption of the Israelites from the slaughter of their firstborn in Egypt. But it was in fact Emerson's refusal to reenact the Passover ritual that led him to resign from his position as pastor of the Second Church of Boston on September 9, 1831. In proffering his resignation, Emerson preached a sermon titled "The Lord's Supper" in which he offered as his rationale the conviction that Jesus had not intended to institute a permanent ritual of commemoration when he celebrated the Passover. Rather than participating in the continuation of the tradition commemorating Jesus's transformation into Christ the Messiah, Emerson focused his attention on an internal event—what he described as the emancipation of the infinitude of the creative self—that the ceremony of the Lord's Supper merely memorialized.

After he resigned from the ministry, Emerson in effect subtracted himself from the social order so that he might inhabit a space that turned him toward the unending task of calling forth an alternative to that order. As an over-present site of transition, Emerson's scene of writing reinstalled the medium of Passover but voided the events. Emerson took up habitation here when he was taken up by the structural performative ("when my genius calls me") through which his essays were produced. In "Self-Reliance," Emerson described his pledge to dissever all institutional ties and his inscription of "Whim" on the lintel of the doorpost as co-constituting modes of obtaining access to this realm. The "Whim" that the speaker inscribed at the interspace between himself and the world of intersubjective communication was the signature that marked his pledging of himself to a writing practice that would sacrifice relations to things in the world in exchange for the provocative exercise in thinking called Emerson's Essays.

The "Whim" that Emerson inscribed at the threshold to his scene of writing was more specifically a sign that the speaker had become emancipated from figurative bondage to institutionalized conformities in general and to the commemoration of Christian Passover in particular. However, when it is resituated within the scriptural contexts from which, as Cavell reminds us, it was derived, "Whim" relays a series of metaphors in which the flesh and blood of his son had become signifying elements. Emerson left "son" off his list of the relatives he pledged to shun in "Self-Reliance." This omission may have been interpreted to indicate that his son was not one of the relations from whom the speaker pledged to dissever himself in exchange for the reception of genius. But rather than decoding "Whim" as a sign that he should spare the speaker's firstborn, the angel of death apparently found the son's name [W(aldo)him] encrypted within this enigmatic signifier and interpreted "Whim" as one of the family relations from whom the speaker had pledged to disaffiliate so as to secure his bond with genius.

Emerson's "Self-Reliance" was bound up with, and in a sense founded on, the relations from whom death had already separated him. In pledging to shun family members who were already dead, however, Emerson correlated admission to his scene of writing with the negation of witness to the dead. When he turned the negation of his witness to this mortality structure into the precondition for receiving the call of genius, did Emerson imagine his writing project as an immortality structure that had surpassed this death world?

If he did, death disabused him of this illusion in "Experience." When death appeared within the interspace where Emerson's genius otherwise came calling, death also broke down the transfer of the bodily entitlements that would have allowed the name "Waldo Emerson" to continue to assume a position as an authorized identity within the social order. And at the site of this breakdown, the speaker encountered limits to how far his annulment of social bonds could be taken.

Whereas in "Self-Reliance" Emerson pledged his willingness to sacrifice his bonds with his family in exchange for receiving the monstrations of genius, in "Experience" the speaker decided that there was no influx of genius that could compensate him for his son's death. "The only thing grief has taught me, is to know how shallow it is. That, like all the rest, plays about the surface, and never introduces me into the reality, for contact with which, we would even pay the costly price of sons and lovers" (3:29). Because there was no compensating the child's death, the speaker could only describe the flow from the cup that Genius offered him (What could Genius say in offering him this cup? "Drink of this for this is the blood of your first born Son"?) as drawn from the river of Lethe, which induced amnesia rather than awareness.

Waldo's death might be described as having occurred as an event through its disappearance as a historical actuality and its reappearance as a blockage of the speaker's taking the step from the realm of his personal trauma and into his scene of writing. After he discovered that his son's corpse was encrypted within the enigmatic signifier "Whim" inscribed at the border between the world he thinks and the world of intersubjective communication, Emerson addressed a demand to his Genius that transformed the conditions of his relationship to it: "Ah that our Genius were a little more of a genius" (3:27).

Through the expression of this desire, the speaker of "Experience" created a figure of address (a genius) that his Genius had denied to the speaker of "Self-Reliance." "Experience" thereby effected a turning point in the relationship between the Emersonian speaker and the world. The speakers of the essays that Emerson published prior to "Experience" turned away from the already constituted social order as the precondition for the reception of Genius. Each of these essays supplied the occasion wherein their speaker accomplished the transfiguration of the creaturely into the creative self. But the crisis the speaker underwent in "Experience" effected a change in Emerson's orientation:

I know that the world I converse with in the city and in the farms, is not the world I *think*. I observe that difference, and shall observe it. One day, I shall know the value and law of this discrepance. But I have not found that much was gained by manipular attempts to realize the world of thought. (3:48, Emerson's emphasis)

The speaker's recognition of the distinction between the world with which he converses and the world he thinks induced a desire to effect a reorientation in his relationship with the world. Since it resulted in his deciding to take up a position within conversations to which he had earlier expressed his aversion, this reorientation might be imagined as having transpired through the change of his position within the relay of conversations that established that structure of aversion in "Self-Reliance."

In "Self-Reliance," it was the speaker's imagined conversations with a philanthropist and an abolitionist that aroused the aversive reaction that resulted in his disaffiliating himself from a series of institutions— philanthropy, the family, abolitionism, and the community. The speaker of "Experience" forged a counterpath back into the world that reversed the itinerary of figurations through which "Self-Reliance" had called him out of it. In place of dissevering connections to family and society or treating the world as the repository of the metaphors reconnecting him to Genius, the speaker of "Experience" cultivated the desire to speak from within the world on the terms supplied by the world. "In the morning I awake, and find the old world, wife, babes, and mother, Concord and Boston, the dear old spiritual world, and even the dear old devil not far off" (3:36).

Before he could take up conversations within these institutions to which the speaker of "Self-Reliance" had formerly expressed his aversion, however, the speaker of "Experience" had to renounce the pledge—to dissever worldly ties in exchange for the call of Genius—to which "Self-Reliance" had committed him.

THE RETRACTED PLEDGE

Thus far, I have suggested, the speaker of "Experience" underwent an event in his life that was subject to what might be called the fate of the metaphors (dissolving family ties, writing "Whim") through which he had arrived at "Self-Reliance." "Experience" supplied the rationale for

the retraction of this pledge in the form of two complaints: the grief that
followed the death of his son had not taken him one step into deep nature, and that grief had not done so because the death of his son was a loss
that could not be compensated. Since the pledge that he took in "Self-
Reliance" had premeditated, as it were, his son's death, the speaker of
"Experience" undertook the retraction of the pledge through the change
of his position within the conversation in which he had formerly taken it.
In order to explain the form this retraction assumed, I need to recall the
conversation from the previously cited passage from "Self-Reliance" in
which he took the pledge:

> If an angry bigot assume this bountiful cause of Abolition, and comes
> to me with his last news from Barbadoes, why should I not say to him,
> "Go love thy infant; love thy wood-chopper; be good-natured and
> modest; have that grace; and never varnish your hard uncharitable
> ambition with this incredible tenderness for black folk a thousand
> miles off. Thy love afar is spite at home." Rough and graceless would be
> such a greeting; but Truth is handsomer than the affectation of love.
> Your goodness must have some edge to it else it is none. The doctrine
> of hatred must be preached as the counteraction of the doctrine of
> love, when that pules and whines. I shun father and mother and wife
> and brother, when my genius calls me, I would write on the lintels of
> the door-post, *Whim*. I hope it is somewhat better than whim at last,
> but we cannot spend the day in explanation. (2:30)

This passage is marked throughout by anxieties of address: how to address the truth to an abolitionist, how properly to respond to genius
when it calls. The hard truth that he addressed to the abolitionist characterized his antislavery commitments as an affectation derived from a
want of affection for his family and community. The slaves on Barbados
were made to solicit the representative status of strangers, which was
then defined against the representative status of kin. But in addition to
their geographical distance, the black folk of Barbados also represented
barriers to sympathetic identification that were the derivatives of the
social formation Orlando Patterson has described as natal alienation.
Members of slave communities were socially constructed as lacking in
the right to the guaranteed family bonds that the speaker repudiated the
abolitionist for abandoning. Natal alienation, or the social condition of
radical kinlessness, constituted, Patterson has explained, the communal

fiction through which slave societies rationalized slavery as a form of social death.[13]

In his transition from familial obligations to self-reliance, the speaker
retrieved images of the slave experience—in the occulted allusion to the
Passover blood on the lintel of the doorpost—but voided them of black
embodiment. Moreover, the space to which his genius called him tacitly
translated the kinlessness of slavery into the precondition for and the effect of that call of genius. A single trait distinguished the speaker's domestic disaffections from the abolitionist's. Whereas the speaker diagnosed
the abolitionist's solidarity with the kinless slave as an unconscious displacement of his lack of familial affection, the speaker's disaffection was
the outcome of a conscious decision. Indeed, the call of genius, insofar
as it has been acquired through the shunning of two generations of kin,
would appear to have turned the social death of radical kinlessness into a
prerequisite for the speaker's response.

The extraordinary emotional contradictions in this passage are evidenced in the speaker's juxtaposition of the utterly asymmetrical instructions concerning familial affection. When he enjoined the abolitionist to
substitute the love for his infant and his woodchopper in place of the affective structures underpinning the abolitionist movement, the speaker
diagnosed the abolitionist's "incredible tenderness" for the cause of antislavery as symptomatic of his alienation from domestic and communal
affiliations. But after he represented his dissolution of familial bonds as
the precondition for the reception of "my genius," Emerson correlated his
voluntary kinlessness with the involuntary kinlessness of persons forced
into slavery. Members of slave communities were socially constructed
as lacking in the right to the guaranteed family bonds that the speaker
chastises the abolitionist for having abandoned. But after the speaker
characterizes the abolitionist's affection for blacks as the displacement
of his want of affection for his family, what prevents his readers from diagnosing the speaker's expression of intimacy with genius (who inhabits
a space infinitely more distant than "black folk a thousand miles off") as
the result of a comparable displacement?

It was the call of genius that reversed the abolitionist's anger and
bigotry into the instructions to love his infant and woodchopper in the
name of reaffirming familial and communal ties, and it was the call of genius that sublated the abolitionist's bigotry into the willingness to give up

all ties in the name of becoming utterly absorbed in spiritual substance. The first instruction excluded the abolitionist from membership within a movement that would emancipate slaves, but the second instruction legitimated the condition of radical kinlessness that defined the social status of the slave community. In proffering these instructions, the speaker has exploited an unstated analogy between the slave master's absolute domination of the slave and the speaker's absolute subservience to genius.

Despite the fact that the realm in which the slave was subordinated to the slave master was utterly asymmetrical with the realm in which the speaker was wholly obedient to genius, however, the speaker of "Self-Reliance" never explicitly distinguished these worlds. In borrowing upon its structure of power to represent the nature of his relationship with genius, the speaker engaged in a symbolic transaction with the discourse of slavery that removed the actual institution of slavery from view. Because his aversion to abolitionism had become the primary focus of his instruction, the speaker never bore witness to the fact that slavery was an actually existing historical institution as well as the source of his metaphors.

Indeed, it was precisely because he never acknowledged the historical factuality of slavery that the speaker never felt obliged to express his solidarity with the abolitionist's renunciation of that institution. The speaker's instructions to the abolitionist achieved their most provocative effects when they were projected against the backdrop of slave power. But in failing to include his repudiation of the institution of slavery as an addendum to his expressed aversion to the institution of abolitionism, the speaker had rendered the provocative utterances that he enunciated within "Self-Reliance" open to the charge that they had compromised with slave power.

It may have been the speaker's foreclosure of his witness to slavery as a historical fact in "Self-Reliance" that led to its reappearance as the idiom through which the speaker of "Experience" expressed the loss of his affective bond with his son:

> I seem to have lost a beautiful estate,—no more. I cannot get it nearer to me. If tomorrow I should be informed of the bankruptcy of my principal debtors, the loss of my property would be a great inconvenience to me, perhaps, for many years; but it would leave me as it found me,— neither better nor worse. So is it with this calamity: it does not touch

me: something which I fancied was a part of me, which could not be
torn away without tearing me, nor enlarged without enriching me,
falls off from me, and leaves no scar. It was caducous. (3:29)

Figures of speech from the essay "Self-Reliance"—the infant, the
woodchopper, the abolitionist's "incredible tenderness" for "black folk a
thousand miles off"—have returned in this passage with hallucinatory
majesty. But the actions that had lain dormant in the speaker's juxtaposition of the figures of the woodchopper and the infant have awakened into
the specter of the violent separation of the parent from child that haunts
Emerson's "Experience" in its entirety.

In her splendid analysis of the relationship between grieving the loss
of a child and the political economy of slavery that is evidenced in this
passage, Karen Sanchez-Eppler has observed that "it seems to me that
Emerson's comparison of the death of his son to the loss of an estate and
the bankruptcy of its debtors is significant not only because it jars sentimental expectations (such losses are not comparable and to compare
them seems an affront to feeling, or a mark of disassociation), but also
because it insists upon a relation between grief and economic possession."[14] But, Jay Grosssman has noted, "These analogies between the loss
of an 'estate' and the loss of a child" become comparable only after their
readers restore the slave as the "vanishing mediator in between grief and
economic possession."[15]

In restoring the discourse of slavery as the unacknowledged backdrop for the affective economy underpinning this passage, both Sanchez-
Eppler and Grossman have discerned how the trauma of Emerson's son's
death has quite literally turned the speaker's prose in the direction of the
order of historical trauma that his aversion to abolitionism had formerly
removed from his view. But whereas they have presupposed a bankrupt
slaveholder as the figure Emerson has personified, the speaker of these
lines has in fact reanimated the affective structure of "incredible tenderness" that Emerson had formerly criticized in the abolitionist's relations
with the black folk of Barbados.

The speaker in "Self-Reliance" had informed the abolitionist that
the only love he could credibly express required that he withdraw his
declaration of love for blacks afar (on Barbados) so that he might re-
invest his affection at home. But in "Experience" the speaker discovered
that his pledge to estrange himself from his domestic ties turned the

"incredible tenderness" of the abolitionist's "love afar" into the spectral mediator for his love at home. The speaker in this passage encountered that specter when he discovered that his previous conviction concerning his son's death—that he could not undergo it without feeling bodily dismembered—was as "incredible" as the "tenderness" he had formerly repudiated in the abolitionist.

But the speaker now recognizes that it was his repudiation of the abolitionist's "love afar" that symptomatized what was defective in the expression of his domestic affections. In "Self-Reliance," the speaker had characterized the abolitionist's "love afar" as indicative of his "spite at home." After he pledged to disaffiliate himself from all family ties, however, the speaker turned his relationship with members of his own household into the affective equivalent of "love afar." Rather than maintaining the claim that it was impossible to have deep affective investments in their fate, the speaker now implies that he should have loved the black folk of Barbados as if they were members of his family, and that he should have loved the members of his family as the black folk of Barbados.

By this relay of transpositions, the passage has linked the impossibility of the speaker's bearing witness to the trauma of his dead son with his refusal to bear witness to the plight of black folk. Instead of reperforming that aversion, however, the speaker of this passage has developed an aversion to the attitude of emotional estrangement to which he had formerly pledged himself.

This change of stance toward the conversation (with the abolitionist) that had formerly justified his aversion to witnessing the condition of Negro slavery now obliged Emerson to bear witness to the plight of black folk. Emerson began to meet this obligation with the economic terms that he deployed in this passage to describe his reaction to the death of his son. The loss of a beautiful estate and the bankruptcy of debtors were the very same terms that Emerson used to describe the response of British plantation owners to the property and capital they had lost following the emancipation of the slaves in Barbados in the essay "An Address on the Emancipation of the Negroes in the British West Indies" that he published in the same year as "Experience."

But in taking stock of the death of his son as if it were the equivalent of the *emancipation* of an enslaved colony, Emerson has also changed the metaphor from "Self-Reliance"—inscribing "Whim" rather than apply-

ing the blood of the lamb on the lintel of his doorpost—that had preordained his son's death. In now representing it in terms of the relationship between an enslaved colony and a colonizing power, Emerson also
reconceptualized his son's death as his emancipation from the domination of the figures Emerson has named the "Lords of Life."

Emerson's revisionary relation to his imagined conversation with
the abolitionist also turned his readers' attention to the historical trauma
of slavery that Emerson had formerly averted witnessing. In the public
conversations that he composed after "Experience" ("On Emancipation
in the British West Indies" and the speeches that called for the repeal
of the Fugitive Slave Law), Emerson developed a figure of address who
inhabited the site of the distinction between the world within which he
conversed—which included actual slaves in actual death worlds—and
the alternative world in which he thought. In "On Emancipation in the
British West Indies," that figure of address articulated his obligation to
bear witness to this historical trauma in the following unforgettable sentence: "Language must be raked, the secrets of the slaughter-houses and
infamous holes that cannot front the day, must be ransacked, to tell what
negro-slavery has been."[16]

RETHINKING EMERSON'S AVERSION TO WITNESSING

Thus far I have argued that the "crisis of witnessing" that Emerson underwent in "Experience" produced a previously nonexistent distinction between the world he thought and the world with which he was obliged
to converse. And I have proposed that Emerson experienced this crisis
through a figure of address that correlated the historical trauma of slavery with the personal trauma of his son's death. Since this figure emerged
out of the structure of aversion that previously supplied the orientation
for his thinking, I shall attempt to distinguish this figure from the figuration of address that Stanley Cavell has indexed in the phrase "aversive
thinking."

"To think is to turn around, or turn back," as Cavell has explained
the relationship between thinking and averting, "the words of ordinary
life (hence the present forms of our lives) that now repel thought, disgust
it."[17] According to this definition, slavery, insofar as it is possessed of the
greatest power to disgust and repel thought, should also solicit the most

powerful turnings around. But when Cavell reflects on the relation between Emerson's thinking and the slavery question, he provided a standpoint on their correlation that insists on the untethering of that relation. "If slavery," Cavell begins this line of thought, "is the negation of thought then thinking cannot affirm itself without affirming the end of slavery" (205). If Emerson, now to associate his "experience" with Cavell's "constitutional amending," witnessed the death of the child from within the world of trauma, where thinking is also negated, that world, whose life structures simulate the imagined conditions of death, constituted the negative limits of what is thinkable.

It was the very waywardness of Emerson's thinking, its resistance to a strictly Americanist appropriation, that enables Cavell to address linkages between Emerson and Kant and the line of succession of continental philosophy—including Nietzsche and Wittgenstein and Heidegger—who, according to Cavell, inherited Kant's philosophical project by way of revisionist readings of Emerson. In "Constitutional Amending" Cavell takes up, as the most challenging legacy of the philosophical lineage, the topic of Heidegger's relation with Nazi tyranny. In turning to Heidegger and the Nazi question by way of Emerson and the slavery question, Cavell wonders whether the philosophical thinking he received and cares about has not been unredeemably compromised.

In response, Cavell argues that insofar as it proved crucial to an understanding of the philosophical stakes implicit in the nation's founding, Emerson's thinking provided him the power to revise (or amend) the nation's founding documents, to refound America on the ground that it lost when the Constitution did not itself call for the abolition of an institution that negated thinking. In gathering evidence that would verify his solution to the dilemma, Cavell depends on three of Emerson's uncollected essays related to this wish: an essay he published shortly after the anniversary of Waldo's death in 1844, commemorating the tenth anniversary of emancipation in the British West Indies, and two essays published four years apart, in 1850 and on March 7, 1854, condemning the Fugitive Slave Law and in particular the part Daniel Webster played in drafting that legislation.

What I find most compelling about Cavell's strategies of response bears upon the wish informing them, namely, the wish to amend Emerson's thinking by reconstituting its ground. But in drawing on Emerson's occasional (and uncollected) essays for the direction of his argument, Cavell indirectly acknowledges that he cannot quite describe Emerson's reaction to the slavery question as continuous with what Cavell otherwise finds characteristic of Emersonian thinking.[18] Moreover, in facing Emerson's essays toward the slavery question, Cavell puts his own thinking at risk of the mood of despair that he also found pervaded Emerson's attitude toward this matter. Unable to find the hope that would enable him to abandon the despair that is inseparable from the condition of enslavement, Cavell, in this essay, does not finally succeed either in working his way through to an explanation of Emerson's stance toward slavery or in finding a way back to his own thinking. Perhaps Cavell's essay might more appropriately be thought of, then, as an effort at amending, or rather as an effort at *amending thinking.*

In the final paragraph to this remarkable essay, Cavell, in his profound wish to render Emerson's aversion to thinking about slavery compatible with the unfulfilled philosophical conditions of the nation's founding document, *happens* upon a breach. That breach, in refusing to be mended, refinds the despair that returns when thinking is negated. I intend to address Emerson's thinking about slavery by way of a claim almost the reverse of Cavell in what follows. By way of a transition to that argument, and in anticipation of a return to the Emerson passage, I ask you to recall the opening lines of "Experience" as they resonate through Cavell's final paragraph:

> How do I guide myself? *Do* I guide myself by the thought that since Emerson is the philosopher of freedom I can, in his mediation through Nietzsche to Heidegger in principle trust to our eventual success in showing Heidegger's descent into allegiance with tyranny to be an aberration—hence redeemable of his philosophical genius. Or *must* I guide myself instead by the thought that since Heidegger is so radically unredeemably compromised, and since Emerson is mediated by philosophers of the powers of Nietzsche and of Heidegger, it is not even to be trusted that we will eventually succeed in showing Emerson's genius to be uncompromised by this mediation, so that the way of philosophy I care about most is as such compromised.[19]

The question by which Cavell finds his way to the conclusion, "How do I guide myself?" in its revisionary echo of Emerson's "Where do we find ourselves?" specifies the intertextual relation Cavell's essay animates as the site whereon witnessing is in crisis. Without being any longer able to rely on Emerson's or Heidegger's or Nietzsche's ways of thinking, Cavell, again like the speakers in "Experience," believes himself cut off from an addressee, as well as from the philosophical lineage whereby the experiences he underwent were recognized as thinking.

Cavell's efforts to reconstitute thinking by making amends for his precursor's breach of faith in the integrity of philosophical thinking led to these irredeemably opposed accounts under which that activity might be continued. At the splitting of decision with which this essay concludes, Cavell might be described as either having encountered the negation of thinking he had earlier identified as the consequence of slavery, or as having refound, in his very effort to find a recognizable self, a return in his own thoughts of the event without a witness Emerson had undergone in "Experience."

THE EMERGENCE OF THE ANTI-SLAVE

Rather than deciding between these alternatives, I want to conclude by redescribing the need to decide as a displacement of the ineluctable crisis of witnessing with which Cavell's essay concludes. In recalling the opening lines of "Experience," Cavell might be described as bearing witness to the crisis in the Emersonian witness as his means of inheriting his legacy. But in so doing, Cavell has also reanimated a figure of address through whom the crisis of witnessing can be borne. That figure is discernible in the transposition of Cavell's commentary on "Whim" from the context of "Self-Reliance" to Emerson's "Experience."

When Cavell comments on the significance of Emerson's writing "Whim" on the lintels of the doorpost to "Self-Reliance," he writes, "We may understand this marking to invoke the Passover blood and accordingly again see writing as creating division—between people we may call Egyptians and those we may call Jews—which is a matter of life and death, of the life and death of one's first born."[20] Cavell's interpretation has foregrounded protection against the loss of a firstborn child and emancipation from slavery as joint consequences of writing and averting. According to Cavell's reading of the event that writing "Whim" condenses, however, Emerson should never have been required to undergo what "Experience" records.

"Experience," after all, records the death of a firstborn child; its opening lines, moreover, could have been spoken by figures who are involved in an escape from slavery. They could have been expressed by figures who have escaped into a freedom that lacked safeguards for the conditions whereby that freedom could be experienced. They could have been enunciated, that is to say, by figures who could not locate a difference between absolute freedom (the act of escaping into freedom) and its absolute loss (the absence from the world of any order capable of constituting their freedom).

In the absence of any other space in which emancipation could be experienced, the repetition of the *act* of escaping from enslavement takes the place of any other species of experienceable freedom. Without any already constituted world wherein "becoming free" could be experienced as an event belonging to the fugitives' lives, the act of "becoming free" thus takes the place of what might otherwise assure freedom a place. The loss of the child and the experience of freedom as the absolute loss of a world became by this relay of associations equiprimordial Emersonian events.

Prior to "Experience," Emerson correlated freedom with the absolute loss of the already represented world. And he construed the relationship between the speaker called to enunciate an Emersonian provocation and "my genius" to be the inauguration of a wholly new world. Neither the speaker of the provocation nor "my genius" was part of the already created world. The speaker's lacking a part in the already instituted order empowered him to particularize a new order through his acts of provocation. In refusing to accommodate his thinking to the prevailing order of signification and in refusing to identify with a mandated social role, Emerson construed himself as included within the social order, but as what was extrinsic to its conditions of belonging. When Emerson resigned from the ministry, he imagined the place he opened up through his refusal to perform the Passover to have been subtracted from the given order.

As a part of the world that had no part in the order of things, the speaker called forth by "my genius" inhabited this extraneous space. But Emerson found an objective correlative for this place that lacked a place in the given order in the institution of slavery. His scene of writing and the institution of slavery were comparable insofar as both of these extraneous places described parts of the world that had no part in the order of things. As a modality of existence that was, like Emerson, unintegratable within the symbolic order, but, unlike Emerson, could not *turn* that lack of accommodation into the power of constituting an alternative, the slave materialized an exception to the given sociopolitical order.

Emerson did not, as Cavell claims, understand slavery as a negation of thinking that led to constitutional amending. Emerson understood slavery to be a precondition for his thinking. When I claim that Emerson's project presupposed the negative positioning of slavery, I mean that claim to be understood quite literally: as the materialization of an otherwise unrepresentable, nonsocial space dividing persons from nonpersons, citizens whose lives were understood as worthy of re-presentation from figures represented as lacking presence, persons whose deaths society officially mourned from those it constructed as already dead. Slavery demarcated a social limit for the negation of limitation.

Because slavery represented the completion of the negation to which, according to Emerson, all already instituted forms tended, slavery revealed the nothingness at the heart of the already constituted order. A slave, and for Emerson this term was not restricted to persons actually enslaved, named that category of person whose interests were identical with property. As what property had, by way of the activity Emerson assigned to "animal reason," totally appropriated, slavery, by this accounting, named the social estate of any person who lacked the "power to turn around" that Emerson believed a prerequisite to the exercise of freedom. As the limit to freedom internal to every person, slavery comprised the constitutive split dividing the transcendental "I am God in nature" from the empirical "I am a weed by the wall" aspects of the Emersonian enunciative doublet. Slavery, that is, named the condition of negation persons passed through in learning to desire the power to transfigure that condition (the desire of freedom). When transposed into Emerson's figures of thought, the disclosure of this interior absence aroused the negative capacity to turn away and initiate the Emersonian exercise Cavell has named *aversive thinking* (or what might also be called the power to return or re-trope).

Before "Experience," Emerson left out the figure of his thinking who inhabited the space between the desymbolization of the symbolic order and the emergence of the different social order to which genius called him. In the passage from "Self-Reliance" in which he obtained access to the figures of thought through which he called forth the alternative to the already constituted world, Emerson silently transfigured the death world of slavery into the signifier of the social order that would be wholly supplanted by the order of provocation. Following the death of his firstborn child, Waldo, however, Emerson's inability to transfigure Waldo's death into a figure who renewed his thinking led to his "experience" of the interspace between social death and the emergence of an alternative order.

When Waldo died at the site of the "Whim" that demarcated his scene of writing from the rest of the world, the difference between the subtracted space of his scene of writing and the nonspace of his son's death was evacuated into the dimensions of the dead child's corpse. Unable to metaphorize these losses, Emerson underwent a crisis of witnessing in the interspace between the death of the order of signification and the death of his son. The fact of Waldo's death displaced the order of provocation with an order of trauma that conflated the personal trauma of Waldo's death with the historical trauma of the death world of slavery that Emerson could no longer construe as a metaphor for his scene of writing.

When Waldo died at the site where the death of the order was transfigured into the order to come, Emerson witnessed the death of the child from within the imagined conditions of death that slavery materialized. And he called the figure of address through which he underwent this crisis the "anti-slave"[21] The anti-slave bore witness to the crisis of witnessing that took place here. As the figure whom the speaker desired to engender at the limit in between these two orders—the order of trauma and the order of Emersonian provocation—however, this figure did not belong either to the preexisting social order or to the Emersonian alternative. As the "experience" of the limit internal to the Emersonian provocation but external to its accomplishment, the anti-slave existed prior to as well as after the performative acts through which Emerson retroactively instituted his symbolic identity. The crisis that this figure effected in the speaker did not simply reanimate one or the other of the personifications (the Transcendentalist, the Reformer) of "Self-Reliance." The "anti-slave" borne of "Experience" instead effected a crisis within the transindividual discourse through which these antagonisms were regulatively opposed to one another.

In light of the metaphorical usage to which Emerson had formerly put slavery in his articulation of "Self-Reliance," it is perhaps appropriate that the racist logic informing this usage has been invoked by Rowe to call for the discontinuation of the Emersonian legacy. I wonder, however, whether this newfound aversion to Emerson will not also thereby effect an aversion to the crisis of witnessing that inhabits the heart of Emerson's "Experience" (and perhaps ours as well).

NOTES

1. Ralph Waldo Emerson, "Self-Reliance," in *The Collected Works of Ralph Waldo Emerson,* ed. Alfred R. Ferguson, Robert E. Spiller, et al., 8 vols. to date (Cambridge, Mass.: Harvard University Press, Belknap Press, 1971–2010), 2:29. Subsequent quotations from Emerson's writing are from this source and are cited parenthetically in text by volume and page numbers. Citations may include essay title if the essay from which a quotation is taken is not clear from the text.

2. Cary Wolfe has attempted to dampen, if not resolve, the contentious arguments among Emerson's legatees with the observation that the schism between Emerson the Transcendentalist, "trying to make his break and his peace with the religious tradition," and Emerson the Reformer, "who was intent on ameliorating conditions in Jacksonian America, was not to be healed simply by redirecting attention from one side of this antagonism to the other." Cary Wolfe, "Alone with America: Cavell, Emerson, and the Politics of Individualism," *New Literary History* 25 (1994): 137.

3. Sacvan Bercovitch, *The Rites of Assent: Transformations in the Symbolic Construction of America* (New York: Routledge, 1993), 304.

4. Cornel West, *The American Evasion of Philosophy: A Genealogy of Pragmatism* (Madison: University of Wisconsin Press, 1987), 9–41.

5. West, *The American Evasion of Philosophy,* 31. West alluded to Ralph (Waldo) Ellison's observation that blackface minstrelsy and Emersonian self-reliance were historically contemporaneous and socially interactive cultural agencies. According to Ellison, it was their assumption of a blackface mask that permitted Emerson's self-made men to construct an open future as the other to a socially immobilized Negro past. When they donned this mask, Emerson's self-reliant individuals dissociated from their previous identities—which they projected onto the nonidentity of the black mask.

6. John Carlos Rowe, *At Emerson's Tomb: The Politics of Classic American Literature* (New York: Columbia University Press, 1997), 41. Rowe argued that

whenever Emerson attempted to synthesize his transcendentalism with the practical demands of a new age, he subordinated his vision to the new demands of the urban capitalism in ways that contradict his earlier contempt for commercialism and material wealth.

7. Shoshana Felman and Dori Laub, *Testimony: Crises of Witnessing in Literature, Psychoanalysis, and History* (New York: Routledge, 1992), 5.

8. Ibid., 38.

9. Zygmunt Bauman, *Modernity and the Holocaust* (Ithaca, N.Y.: Cornell University Press, 1989), 69–78. Edith Wyschogrod describes death worlds in *Spirit in Ashes: Hegel, Heidegger, and Man-Made Mass Death* (New Haven, Conn.: Yale University Press, 1985), 15.

10. Sharon Cameron, "Representing Grief: Emerson's 'Experience,'" *Representations* 15 (Summer 1986): 25.

11. Stanley Cavell, "Hope against Hope," in *Emerson's Transcendental Etudes* (Stanford, Calif.: Stanford University Press, 2003), 179.

12. Cavell, "An Emerson Mood," in *Emerson's Transcendental Etudes,* 29. Cavell also offers the following alternative interpretation of writing "Whim" on the lintels and the doorposts: "Literal writing on the door-posts of one's house is more directly a description of the mezuzah (a small piece of parchment inscribed with two passages from Deuteronomy and marked with a name of God, which may be carried as an amulet but which is more commonly seen slanted on the door-post of a dwelling as a sign that a Jewish family lives within (the spiritual danger in putting 'Whim' in place of the name of God is mostly taken in the name of whim)" (29).

13. Orlando Patterson, *Slavery and Social Death: A Comparative Study* (Cambridge, Mass.: Harvard University Press, 1982).

14. Karen Sanchez-Eppler, "Then When We Clutch the Hardest: On the Death of a Child and the Replication of an Image," in *Sentimental Men: Masculinity and the Politics of Affect in American Culture,* ed. Glenn Hendler and Mary Chapman (Berkeley: University of California Press, 1999), 79.

15. Jay Grossman, *Reconstituting the American Renaissance: Emerson, Whitman, and the Politics of Representation* (Durham, N.C.: Duke University Press, 2003), 237.

16. Ralph Waldo Emerson, *Emerson's Antislavery Writings,* ed. Len Gougeon and Joel Myerson (New Haven, Conn.: Yale University Press, 1995), 9.

17. Cavell, "Emerson's Constitutional Amending: Reading 'Fate,'" in *Emerson's Transcendental Etudes,* 193.

18. In "Tears for Emerson: Essays Second Series," Julie Ellison has observed that Emerson's antislavery speeches were "destined by him for a planned 'Book

of Occasional Discourse' that set forth a pragmatic activist politics. The lectures that he revised for publication as 'essays,' by contrast, were suspicious of civic actions." *The Cambridge Companion to Ralph Waldo Emerson,* ed. Joel Porte and Saundra Morris (Cambridge: Cambridge University Press, 1999), 156.

19. Emphasis in original. Cavell, "Emerson's Constitutional Amending," 214.

20. Cavell, "An Emerson Mood," 29.

21. *Selections from Ralph Waldo Emerson,* ed. Stephen E. Whicher (Boston: Houghton Mifflin, 1955), 277.

ERIC KEENAGHAN

6. Reading Emerson, in Other Times

On a Politics of Solitude and an Ethics of Risk

In his early academic speeches, including "The American Scholar" address to Harvard's Phi Beta Kappa Society in 1837 and the following year's oration on "Literary Ethics" for the Literary Societies of Dartmouth College, Emerson goes to great lengths to define the intellectual enterprise with which he and many readers of the present volume identify. One's ability to realize this role, however, is obstructed by a constant obstacle, which he succinctly formulates in "Literary Ethics": "The condition of our incarnation in a private self, seems to be, a perpetual tendency to prefer the private law, to obey the private impulse, to the exclusion of the law of universal being."[1] If the human condition is just one of individuation, Emerson notes that, ironically, this very condition can lead to a form of dehumanization. When one is born into "the *divided* or social state," he complains in the earlier address, one is ascribed a particular social and economic role: priest, scholar, statesman, producer, soldier. "Man is thus metamorphosed into a thing, into many things" because of the ways in which the individual's socioeconomic status isolates one from the rest: "these functions are parcelled out to individuals, each of whom aims to do his stint of the joint work, whilst each other performs his" ("The American Scholar," 1:53). The academic's chief function, then, is to remediate this social division and to discover "the whole man," or that mythic entity Emerson designates as *Man Thinking* (1:53).

As is well known, his solution to the problem was the development of a philosophical and scholarly perspective termed Transcendentalism.

In the wake of deconstruction, historical materialism, or even American pragmatism, today we are likely to be suspicious of Emerson's apparently metaphysical rhetoric of humanistic universalism. Rather than risk a peremptory dismissal of his thought because of this metaphysics, I will dwell here on those ideas that lead Emerson to carefully consider the scholar's precarious position as both a social critic and an advocate of humanistic possibility. His early formulations of the travails the scholar must face in order to become Man Thinking attest to his own concerns about modern man's alienation. For Emerson, alienation is an ontological condition of separation that attends any experience or idealization of individualism. It is a material condition, reinforced by the antebellum United States' rudimentary divisions of labor, while the Industrial Revolution is still in its early throes and much of the national economy is regionally diversified and structured according to a model of cottage or plantation industries. His musings antedate Karl Marx's writing on capitalism's alienated labor as well as the emergence of Fordism and Taylorization in the early twentieth century. I am not claiming that Emerson is a materialist thinker (though he most certainly influenced pragmatism's rather materialist naturalistic empiricism), but his ontological concerns for his relatively new democratic nation are very much amplified by material conditions.[2] Despite its metaphysical and monistic overtones, Emerson's Transcendentalism and the course he plots for the American Scholar grow out of a career-long resistance to what I term a *liberalist ethos* in democratic relations. This ethos insists on privacy and its attendant material privations, as well as the individual's identification with an a priori social function and even an idea of personhood that blinds her to other forms of connection, collectivity, and historical being. If the contemporary American Scholar is to fulfill her charge—not only that charge levied by Emerson but also the one frequently cited in our own present-day adulations of the figure of the public intellectual—then we must entertain the possibility that an Emersonian-style ontological critique can pave the way for a political (or, at least, politicized) intervention in our conceptions of subjectivity, the citizen-subject, and democracy.

The privacy he saw as standing in the way of the American subject's overcoming of a liberalist individualism is an ontological constant, a formal and aporetic element with which we must always struggle in a truly functioning democracy. Liberalism has been historically inflected in different ways since Emerson's day. When "The American Scholar" was delivered during the last year of Andrew Jackson's presidency, liberalism was connected to the new rhetoric, democratic ideal, and policy of universal suffrage, a political right that was actually anything but universal yet still attempted to integrate the common man into the country's body of eligible voters. In the intervening 170 years, the term has experienced several resignifications. Liberalism has been understood as a progressive force bordering on democratic socialism with the rise of the welfare state during the Second World War, read as a politically reactionary and xenophobic response to the Red Scare during the late 1940s and through the 1950s, lauded as a desirable ideal for realizing equality on a personal basis with the rise of the New Left and the civil rights movement, and believed to be suspect by social critics and theorists with the rise of globalization and domestic inequities on account of an economic adoption of civil liberalist principles (in what is now called "neoliberalism"). For each of these manifestations, liberalism remains a celebration of individualism—often reinforced by socioeconomic divisions and encouraging individuals' identification with established identity groups. This usually occurs at the expense of another form of experience necessary to democratic life: collectivity. Collectivity need not be regarded as a metaphysical pipe dream. Indeed, even Emerson regarded it as rooted in our material existence, in the everyday. One could say that he struggled to articulate the collective promise of Jacksonian individualism by countering a fear of atomism through strengthening commonality's connection to the common man. In the present moment, liberalism is inflected differently. The individual's isolation from others reflects something in addition to an imperative that we fulfill our allotted socioeconomic function and to the decades-long insistence that we locate our selves among a prefabricated identity group. Now, liberalism also ensures an ideology of security and containment. The individual does her part to safeguard the Homeland by shoring up her own individual boundaries.

I will explore two interrelated themes that Emerson entertained in his thinking about the problem of liberalism in his day: reading and solitude. Treating these themes as theoretical concepts, I fashion a different understanding of Emerson out of several of his essays to help us rethink our own approaches to solving the problem of liberalism, as it is articulated at the time of this writing, in an age of Homeland Security. If we read

Emerson on his own terms, as he asks us and all American Scholars to read him, we are better poised to regard our present as "the merest appearance" wherein a different understanding of humanity and its commonality is drowned out by "some great decorum, some fetish of a government, some ephemeral trade, or war, or man, [that] is cried up by half mankind and cried down by the other half, as if all depended on this particular up and down" ("The American Scholar," 1:63). Rather than choose a side by adopting a ready-made politics we blindly apply to our critical endeavors, we might use Emerson's lessons to reexamine our own investment in a liberalist ethos. He can teach us of democracy's long-standing, even ontological, tendency to romanticize individualism and identity-specific distinctions that isolate us from others in our own time, as well as from our historical antecedents. Reading Emerson in an Emersonian way, yet against the grain of received critical narratives, we can learn the specific value of "bid[ing] [our] own time" (1:63). That is, we can learn what it takes to experience history differently, so as to live out of sync with our moment's grand narratives and those narratives' conditioning of our selves.

My other Emerson, then, has much to teach all of us who call ourselves American Scholars, those of us who share a commitment to two goals: (1) the activity of reading, which is, as Edward Said reminds us, the cornerstone of humanistic and democratic endeavors; and (2) our responsibility as critical citizens to ensure the preservation and evolution of democratic commonality.[3] Realizing the second objective by means of our love of reading will lead us to a new ethos, which we might oppose to the one expected of American citizens today. Rather than pursue an ethos of security, Emerson leads me to ask, Why not pursue an ethics based on risk? What is more, how is the humanities scholar especially equipped to realize this end?

READING TO RETHINK COMMONALITY AND
TO RESIGNIFY SOLITUDE

To reevaluate Emerson's charge for the American Scholar, we must begin with a more nuanced understanding of the principle of universalism embodied by his Man Thinking. His universalism should be closely associated with a term that he first uses in "The American Scholar" but that recurs in his later work: *the common*. "I ask not for the great, the remote, the romantic; what is doing in Italy or Arabia; what is Greek art, or Provençal minstrelsy; I embrace the common, I explore and sit at the feet of the familiar, the low" (1:67). He goes on to elaborate that "the near explains the far," that what is most banal, most particular, most familiar and closest to home—"the meal in the firkin; the milk in the pan; the ballad in the street; the news of the boat; the glance of the eye; the form and the gait of the body"—is what brings us into communion with the very spirit of humanity (1:67).

In other pieces, Emerson quite consciously establishes what we might call a conceptual rhyme between this banal or familiar version of "the common" and related terms that are not to be overlooked by the American Scholar or the country to which she belongs. For instance, in his 1844 address "The Young American," Emerson seems to go out of his way to suggestively link the common with a political futurity embedded in the very term used to distinguish some of his nation's states from others: *commonwealth*. Trade, he argues, supplanted the monarchical prerogatives of the Old Country with its "new and anti-feudal power of Commerce," which promises that "the legislation of this country should become more catholic and cosmopolitan than that of any other" (1:229, 1:230). Commerce, though, is but an imperfect rhyme with the commonality, for the "beneficent tendency" of the moneyed to improve the young nation's infrastructure and public works for future generations is often only a dubious altruism (1:232). Trade easily becomes despotic, a way "to make the governments insignificant, and to bring every kind of faculty of every individual that can in any manner serve any person, *on sale*" (1:233, emphasis in original). It can render men the literal or figurative slaves of a patriarchal investor. In the latter case, convention is concretized so that the supposed altruist's values are perpetuated in a manner of a perverse, fiscally driven reproduction. The pitfalls of Commerce are offset by "the Communism of France, Germany, and Switzerland" established by Fourier's experiment and, subsequently, "the spectacle of three Communities which have within a very short time sprung up within this Commonwealth [of Massachusetts]" (1:235).

Such political and economic Communism is not a perfect answer to Commerce's problems, but it does indicate, according to Emerson, a two-fold path that American democracy must pursue to realize its own promise: (1) a commitment to public education, which, in turn, will reflexively make apparent the need for (2) a site-specific, ecologically harmonious government that puts the individual into communion with the very land whereon her nation is founded. "Yes, Government must educate the poor man. Look across the country from any hill-side around us, and the landscape seems to crave Government. The actual differences of men must be acknowledged, and met with love and wisdom. These rising grounds which command the champaign below, seem to ask for lords, true lords, *land*-lords, who understand the land and its uses, and the applicabilities of men, and whose government would be what it should, namely, mediation between want and supply" (1:237, emphasis in original). An ennobling possibility for the commoner comes if the young American—and the government that supposedly represents her—simply listens, and responds, to the call of the land. Education begins as a response to the environment, to the necessities of life itself that will sustain a viable relationship between the individual and nature. This design is not a revival of the old feudalism, nor is it an abandonment of the possibilities of commerce. Rather, Emerson sees in this rethinking of educative possibility a resignification of the term *commonwealth,* an uncovering (or perhaps even a recovery) of a spirit of democratic socialism at the very heart of the founding of the North American colonies. Heeding the land's lesson that humanity must remain attuned to Nature, governmental public education and welfare programs would keep in check the all-too-human urge to use altruism to secure and reproduce one's own interests and values. Pursuant to realizing such a redefinition of the nation, the American citizen stands to claim her true inheritance: an authentic relationship to the land. Emerson does not aspire for autochthonous self-definition; instead, he makes a plea for a combinatory ontological, political, and economic ecological networking. From his nineteenth-century vantage, the United States' health depends on a multifaceted communion with one's immediate environment.

Such politically and economically inflected formulations of "the common" recast his famous Transcendentalist assertion in the opening sentences of "History": "There is one mind common to all individual men. Every man is an inlet to the same and to all of the same. He that is once admitted to the right of reason is made a freeman of the whole estate" (2:3). Commonality, figured here as the "one mind," is a conceptual vehicle for thinking democratic relations. It is a form of rationality through which the individual escapes an exclusive identification with a class-defined social sector and freely accedes to full inclusion in the republic, in the *whole* estate. If we recall his embrace of "the common" in "The American Scholar" and "The Young American," though, we must accede that even with this seemingly monistic and metaphysical idea of "the common" Emerson preserves a singularly individual distinction, a connection to the particulars of one's individual material existence, as well as to one's historical and geopolitical situation.

This move toward universality through the particular, this space where the common things of everyday life and a principle of commonality coincide, suggests an affinity between Emerson's ideas and recent concepts related to commonality, such as Jean-Luc Nancy's *being singular plural* or Michael Hardt and Antonio Negri's (as well as Paolo Virno's) *multitude*.[4] Working through the next several sentences of "History," though, it becomes clear that his version of "the common" is substantially different even from these more recent theorizations. Whereas they articulate a democratic possibility in which the individual's freedom is preserved but the liberal citizen-subject's sovereign condition is demystified or demythologized, Emerson regards commonality, much like the banally common items that transport him to that state, as a resource rather than as a goal. Commonality is principally a means of prioritizing and redefining the individual's present and future sovereign agencies. He remarks about his singular individual: "What Plato has thought, he may think; what a saint has felt, he may feel; what at any time has befallen any man, he can understand. Who hath access to this universal mind, is a party to all that is or can be done, for this is the only and sovereign agent" ("History," 2:3). His desired sovereign individual is the reader of history who accesses commonality because he is just another articulation of the authoring mind belatedly reading its own work. "This human mind wrote history, and this must read it" (2:3). If access to one's own history and the story of one's own past self is determined by literacy, commonality, as well as the civic agency and sense of humanization it supplies, is predicated only on the ability to read.

Since "The American Scholar," Emerson prioritized the importance of reading. Man Thinking could only re-present commonality and overcome estranging, individualizing socioeconomic divisions because this figure was the one who had mastered a particular sort of reading, "creative reading" (1:58). "When the mind is braced by labor and invention, the page of whatever book we read becomes luminous with manifold allusion. Each sentence is doubly significant, and the sense of our author is as broad as the world" (1:58). Reading is related to an inventive genius that is both forward-looking and hopeful ("Man hopes. Genius creates." [1:57]) and rooted in the material and the everyday at the very level of the labor one exerts with a book in hand. The possible political dimensions of the scholar's common practice are not to be overlooked, either. Speaking on behalf of abolition in 1854, Emerson overcomes his admitted reluctance to "speak to public questions" because he felt that his own liberty had been compromised by the Fugitive Slave Law, undesirably subjectivated as he was by the legislation (it "required me to hunt slaves").[5] The only hope he had to awaken the audience's consciousness of their shared condition was to remind them that "the ... class of scholars and students,—that is a class which comprises in some sort all mankind,—comprises every man in the best hours of his life:—and in these days not only virtually, but actually." He goes on to ask, point-blank: "For who are the readers and thinkers of 1854?" (74). Rather than an exclusive sensibility left to an elite few, then, commonality—or the principled pursuit of a shared condition of democracy and social justice—is a universal *potential,* even if the literacy enabling it is, in actuality, inequitably distributed.[6]

The antiliberalist Emerson, this thinker of commonality, is quite distinct from the one whom American lore valorizes, the father of a much-misunderstood principle of self-reliance. How can the man who comes close to praising communistic principles in "The Young American" be the same one who often is thought of as encouraging an individualistic spirit in line with meritocratic capitalism? Does it make any sense to align the name of Emerson—who directly, and quite famously, pronounced that "whoso would be a man must be a nonconformist"—with this interpretation of a celebrant of what is common, base, and shared ("Self-Reliance," 2:29)? Isn't his thought the very epitome of an American individualism? I would hazard a most unpopular assertion to the contrary. Even in "Self-Reliance," Emerson qualifies how we are to understand the very individual whom he praises. "Society everywhere is in conspiracy against the manhood of every one of its members. Society is a joint-stock company in which the members agree for the better securing of his bread to each shareholder, to surrender the liberty and culture of the eater. Self-reliance is its aversion. It loves not realities and creators, but names and customs" (2:29). Self-reliance is not a version of the social's individualistic imperative, which Emerson likens to a capitalistic principle of self-interest. Instead, it is adverse to society altogether, especially to those two features with which Emerson associates the social impediments to self-reliance: names and customs. The course of realizing the individual's potential is obstructed, then, by a faith in a fixed identity, which itself is linked to an entrenched, immutable sense of historical belonging. The proper—a proper self, customary propriety, and not least of all material property—are circumstances to be avoided so that the individual ("the eater") might come upon those other two, more highly esteemed elements in her consumption of experience: liberty and culture.

But how does reading bring us closer to these two more desirable elements? The answer may seem counterintuitive: reading necessitates that we be solitary. *Solitude is the only means of arriving at commonality.* The American Scholar is only able to perform her office when she cultivates a particular style of reading that challenges the seemingly unshakable foundations of a privatizing and depriving force of American liberalism, which cuts her off from any attempt to continue the never-ending struggle of trying to realize a common good. Such solitude actually resignifies understandings of privacy that obtain in a liberalist and capitalist understanding of democratic life, wherein individuals are actually separated from one another because of their own material and class interests. Take, for instance, how Emerson writes about reading in "History," that essay preceding "Self-Reliance" in the *First Series* and thus immediately frames the subsequent essay's advocacy of a sort of individualism: "Every revolution was first a thought in one man's mind, and when the same thought occurs to another man, it is the key to that era. Every reform was once a private opinion, and when it shall be a private opinion again, it will solve the problem of the age" (2:4). A circuit is opened whereby one returns to one's self and one's private experience via an encounter with an account that provides the revolutionary and public "key" to a past "era," as that period has been defined by the collective happening-upon of a single thought. As the reader, I cannot be part of that past era, but I pick up from my visit to it a key idea. It is not *my* opinion once I come upon it, though, no matter if I can share past figures' experiences. And since the idea moves with me, it is not even properly a property of that age where

I found it. When I return to my self, now attended by a private opinion belonging properly to no one in the past or in the present, *I am undone and so I become a truly sovereign agent.*

At this point, "the problem of the age" is solved. It is a moment of political resolution, but one in which there is only a private coming to terms about a particular problem. Emerson's phrasing leaves it ambiguous—the problem of which age is solved? The present of the reader? Or the past recounted in the history? Most likely, there is a third option: the age resolved is the one of the communal space and time opened between and joining the past and the present during the time of reading. This is the time of humanity itself, the time of Man Thinking. To solve the problem of this age, which amounts to furthering a process of realizing a universalistic and humanizing democratic ideal, I merely use the discovered "key" to be articulate, for the first time, about what drove me to read in the first place. That is, I learn to renarrate my relation to my own time, as well as the necessity of this relation to the past. Both are private experiences of my singularity, but in time we might imagine them to assume their own public functions because they inform my later attempts to reformulate shared crises and forge new alliances. In light of his thinking of reading's emancipatory potential, then, we might say that Emerson imagines a *politics of solitude,* which resignifies conventions of privacy and sovereignty and allows him to skirt what he believes are the opinion- and consensus-driven politics of democratic systems.

Is this really democratic or even political, though? Emerson states that it is imperative that we read (we *must* read). How free, how sovereign, is our cultivation of our selves if we are compelled to read? How does that compulsion resignify the terms *sovereign* and *commonality* and the relation between them? Can reading be political if it establishes a fictive form of community that remains irremediably private? Can it be political if it lures us into our private studies and out of our own time, rather than actualizing a politicized commonality in the present? Any reservations that we may have about the political potential of reading owe to how we have been governed by certain precepts about the democratic subject's agency. We need to discover the key to the age's problem, not so much to solve it in a definitive fashion but to change the terms we use to define it.

Rooted in its ability to allow us to "sympathize in the great moments of history, in the great discoveries, the great resistances, the great prosperities of men," the solitude of reading is not to be disdained, for it is a familiar—indeed, a rather common—experience through which we overcome loneliness, isolation, being stranded in the present ("History," 2:5). But the sort of sympathy Emerson imagines is different from that underlying today's liberal understandings of identity, collectivity, and even commonality. Indeed, if reading brings us to ideas that are alien to our selves and that are the only means of realizing a truly commonal vision of Man Thinking, it is because it overrides a normative and sentimental sympathy. We must move beyond "pity and respect" for our others in order to arrive at a new vision that "saves not by compassion, but by power." And, indeed, the only thing able to put us into contact with that power are ideas: "ideas only save races."[7] In short, Emerson's philosophy of reading and the humanistic enterprise pushes us beyond the position of the proverbial liberal sympathizer. Instead, it challenges liberalist premises altogether by seeking out solitude in order to forgo our humane inclination toward sympathy.

Because reading puts us into contact with "the universal mind," anyone can become like the figure of the past by sharing in the pinnacles and nadirs of human achievement. Such a relation seems to begin with, and preserve, an identity-based distinction of one's self from one's others (defined in terms of the distance between identity groups and even, conceivably, in historical location). What I maintain, though, is that Emerson can revolutionize how we think through difference. And the key to this shift owes to that curious element he calls "power." What is this power, and why is it grounded in ideas—the property of others and belonging to a future age oddly situated between past and present? To answer these questions, let us recall Emerson's caveat that history is written not for others but for the benefits of a future self that the author addresses. We write for our selves, the ones whom we don't know. Authors are like those "beneficent" investors about whom Emerson writes in "The Young American," those who build an infrastructure for the good of future generations or for a future of commonality. Embodied by historical texts, then, Emersonian commonality is the experience of hermeneutically working out the difference of one's self. What is more, unlike the altruism occurring in spheres of Commerce (only an abbreviated sort of commonality), practices of writing are less likely to be reinscribed in a liberalist ethos, to ensure the propagation of the interests of the beneficiary or of the donor, because they actually undermine identificatory premises. Reading is a strange and estranging experience. We come back from our solitary reading adventures with something else—a private opinion, a remainder—that is not properly ours or anyone else's. This does not automatically cause us to reproduce this past quantity. Rather, this opinion puts us into crisis with how we understand our selves today. By raising questions about our selves now, it mediates—rather than instantiates—our sympathies with past agents. It populates us, causes us to divide and multiply, and so catalyzes change. Emerson calls reading "our secret experience" ("History," 2:4). Perhaps we must keep it secret even from our selves. We cannot admit its political potency because it is our own tryst with otherness, a betrayal not just of a present order but also of our own integrity. Reading fractures us, splitting the atomistic self we took to be the basis of our democratic faith. When we return to the present, accompanied by a secret idea, the experience "remedies the defect of our too great nearness to ourselves" (2:4). The solitary journey, the full effects we may not even be conscious of, distances us from our selves. Multiplied, each of us discovers a new political language.

Thus, others' writings (which become recognized as really our own, yet not really ours to own, upon our belated discovery of them) instantiate our active resistance to, rather than escape from, the exigencies of the present. The reader "should see that he can live all history in his own person. He must sit solidly at home, and not suffer himself to be bullied by kings or empires, but know that he is greater than all the geography and all the government of the world. . . . He must attain and maintain that lofty sight where facts yield their secret sense, and poetry and annals are alike" ("History," 2:6). Alone and reading, we cannot regard our study of history any longer as simply unearthing the stuff of fact. Instead, it is living with the "secret sense," the occluded privacy of opinion from which all democratic action and resistance to authoritarian structures spring. When history is able to take a reader on such a journey, it is no longer a dry narrative that empirically keeps the past at a remove. No, it has become poetic, a lyric medium that closes distance between self and other, but, in the process, estranges self from self.

POETICALLY CULTIVATING A NEW POLITICS OF DIFFERENCE

We can further articulate Emerson's literary ethics and his politics of solitude—to get at how he uses power to move against the identificatory traps of liberalism and sympathy—by reading him against his contemporary Walt Whitman. Even the poet noticed a major difference between them. In one of his miscellaneous notes, Whitman complains that Emerson is hopelessly distanced from others. "And though the author has much to say of freedom and wildness and simplicity and spontaneity, no performance was ever more based on artificial scholarships and decorums at third or fourth removes, (he calls it culture,) and built up from them. It is always a *make,* never an unconscious *growth.* It is the porcelain figure or statuette of lion, or stag, or Indian hunter—and a very choice statuette too—appropriate for the rosewood or marble bracket of parlor or library; never the animal itself, or the hunter himself."[8] From the comfort of his study, surrounded by his beautiful things, Emerson refuses a creative spontaneity that would render him an active participant in a cultural process that grows, rather than makes. So removed, he assumes the role of diagnostician. "He is best as critic, or diagnoser. Not passion or imagination or warp or weakness, or any pronounced cause or specialty, dominates him. Cold and bloodless intellectuality dominates him" (ibid.).

Unlike Emerson, Whitman preferred a relational model of growth. This trope made his poetic conversant with a then relatively long-standing tradition of Jeffersonian republicanism. In this tradition, democracy and a nation's right to sovereign self-governance transparently and self-evidently grows from a common popular body, which is naturally free because the people are imbued by God with "certain inalienable rights." Whitman, though, translated the popular basis for sovereignty into an individual one, thus eradicating republicanism's representative premises while preserving its founding precepts of naturalness and free agency. In his poetic, it is the *individual poet's singular body*—rather than the people's common one—that is the seat of natural and inalienable rights. As extensions of his freedom and of his person, his poems metonymically come to stand in for his self. This form of representation aspires for a democratic transparency that will render the poet's body—as the seat of agency—visible and accessible, rather than using metaphorical devices that create linguistic distances and figuratively occlude his self. In reading any of his poems, then, we encounter "Walt Whitman, kosmos, of Manhattan the son, / Turbulent, fleshy, sensual, eating, drinking and breeding / No sentimentalist, no stander above men and women or apart from them."[9] But what are the consequences of such an ethic? By invoking his own physical presence he is able to stand with every reader, but that relation also renders us dependent on the poems and his self. Whitman can "make the songs of passion to give them their way"; but the poems' "way"—rooted as they are in his own body—is really just a means of securing his own interests.[10] D. H. Lawrence squarely criticized Whitman because such a passionate domination of others tends to dissolve subjective boundaries. *Leaves of Grass,* he argued, was written by a poet "with the private soul leaking out of him all the time."[11] This unstaunched self enables Whitman's "merging" with his subjects and his readers to produce "one identity" (ibid.). It is not the consolidation of a national or popular entity, though. No, poetry is the medium through which the poet absorbs alterity, thus erasing others' singularities while cosmically expanding his own liberal self.

Lawrence reminds us, too, that Whitman's project is driven by a need to look for sympathy. "Meeting all the other wayfarers along the road? And how? How meet them, and how pass? With sympathy, says Whitman. Sympathy. He does not say love. He says sympathy."[12] Community based on such sympathy necessitates a form of understanding that overlooks the differences and singularities that love preserves. It depends on a narration that fosters others' recognition of one's self as representative of a group or its interests. Paradoxically, Whitman could be said to draw on his audience's differences in order to domesticate alterity and permit identity to emerge. As Charles Taylor puts it, "Recognition forges identity."[13] Yet, it is only Whitman's own identity—not the collective's, not the readers', nor his *camerados'*—that emerges. We walk with Whitman so that he might speak *for* us: our difference from him is reduced to our relinquishing our own agency that allows the privilege of this body's voice to establish itself as *the* exemplar of American identity. Such is the foundation of a sympathetic liberal identity politics, a republican tempering of liberalist autonomy that originates in a narrative enunciated from one "representative" identity position.[14]

Out of his own body Whitman finds his freedom and his health, a "manly self-hood" and well-being that enable him not to meet persons but "to confront with [his] personality all the other personalities of the earth."[15] But, if we adopt Gilles Deleuze's formulation that "health as literature, a writing, consists in inventing a people who are missing," we can say that Whitman is inventing only a person, not a collective and certainly not a public, who is missing.[16] In the end, sympathy transforms his tropes of camaraderie and adhesion into egoistic attempts at confrontation and conquest, an incorporation and assimilation of others under the sign of his own name so that this person called Walt Whitman will no longer be missing. As a metonym for his body *and* the nation, *Leaves of Grass* embodies a democratic and poetic commonality whose liberalism paradoxically causes his populist ambitions of building a sympathetic public out of his private self to lapse into a totalitarian and demagogic imaginary.

In contrast, Emerson holds no truck with sympathy, and he makes no pretenses about the supposed naturalness of the individual or his rights. Rather, he prefers to imagine the individual as a cultivated monad. In his essay "Culture," he inveighs against "this goitre of egotism" and insists that "one of its annoying forms, is a craving for sympathy" (6:71, 6:70). He goes on to elaborate, "The sufferers parade their miseries, tear the lint from their bruises, reveal their indictable crimes, that you may pity them. They like sickness, because physical pain will extort some show of interest from the bystanders, as we have seen children, who, finding themselves of no account, when grown people come in, will cough till they choke, to draw attention" (6:70). Whitman's yawping may be intended to make a show of stalwart health rather than an infantile display of sickly hacking, but the effect is still very much that of an invalid's symptom. It plays on readers' sympathies, drawing them close so that he can merge with and make use of them. To treat the unsightly "goitre," Emerson prescribes a variety of "antidotes against this organic egotism ... the high resources of philosophy, art, and religion: books, travel, society, solitude" (6:73). Culture and its "high resources"—including something he calls "solitude"—are the private means of a public cure for the illnesses springing from an "organic egotism" like Whitman's.

One embarks on intellectual withdrawal in order to foreground ego boundaries that may permit that cure to take effect. In the late essay "Society and Solitude," Emerson remarks that an absolute solitude is not to be coveted for it is, in the end, "impracticable" (7:7). Yet, that impracticality is necessary because that other condition of experience—society where we discover sympathies and affinities with others—is "fatal": "We sink as easily as we rise, through sympathy" (7:7, 7:6). A balance between the two conditions must be struck. Only after embarking upon some solitary venture does alterity have some threshold to step over, to disrupt the self but not in the sense of utterly losing it to a sublime otherness. The self is split, and differences are preserved. In a counterintuitive fashion, withdrawal is a precondition for establishing a first contact with otherness. In the end, then, the "cold and bloodless intellectuality" that Whitman remarks upon in Emerson's writing is actually a form of seduction. It is not an act of seducing someone else; rather, it is allowing one's self to be seduced by something else. One remains set apart, yet one is not contained in a private sphere or in a safe, hermetic space. One embarks on a meditative leave-taking in order to find the other who will attract one away from one's identity and the historical boundaries of self. Thus, culture dissolves the very individualism that actually limits one's freedom if it is treated as a natural bulwark to be safeguarded or as an exceptional term to be expanded and imposed upon others. If one looks too much from one's own vantage, Emerson warns, one is prohibited from experiencing the desired "catholicity" of a "free and disengaged look [at] every object" ("Culture," 6:71). To freely appreciate the alterity culture presents, one must lose one's self.

Instead of offering a poetic picture of an individual exemplifying supposedly perfect health, Emerson invokes a healthy poiesis, a process of becoming healthier by articulating one's difference. Articulation should not be confused with narration: the former can occur outside linguistic formulas and codes. Feeling, affect, and gesture are emotive articulations of a nonnarrated or a nonnarratable difference. In contrast, narration can never occur outside codes, and it sets formidable, though necessary, limits to the work of communicating our experiences of healthy freedom. "Differences are what create individuals," Samuel Delany reminds us. "Identities are what create groups and categories. Identities are thus conditions of comparative simplicity that complex individuals might move toward, but (fortunately) never achieve—until society, tired of the complexity of so much individual difference, finally, one way or the other, imposes an identity on us. . . . Without identities, yes, language would be impossible (because categories would not be possible, and language requires categories)."[17] Emerson's value is not due to any support he might give to any argument for the wholesale rejection of identity and narration. On the contrary, he helps us tease out Delany's point that identities are the objectives of cultural becoming rather than the established ground or typed body out of which individuals later emerge. We do desire to narrate and thus share the experience of our selves. Even if we are not egoistically yawping about it, we want to hold a visible, even intelligible, health in common with others. The irony, though, is that if we "achieve"—or narrate—identity, we have stalled (not necessarily stopped) our individual experience of healthy difference in order to inhabit a plateau of solidarity. To mitigate that irony, we must see to it that identity does not surface in our selves or our bodies, as it does for Whitman. Instead, it surfaces only with the first act of social agency we can share, a form of cultural production that demands communicative rationality but can be repeated later, with a difference: narration.[18]

Identity is a social design, then, which reductively but necessarily limits our experiences of singular differences to narrations of liberal sovereignty. It is always an inevitable part of the individual's story and of our lives as social beings and citizens, but certainly it is not the whole story. And even though all forms of cultural production are implicated in producing something called "identity," insofar as all cultural products come to communicate something about an epoch, the individual who cultivates his self in solitude is not just engaging in a sovereign imposition of his will. When one decides to withdraw in order to read, one gives oneself over to a power that lies beyond one's self so as to elude, momentarily, the fateful social strictures of identitarian design. As Emerson conceives it, individuals experience a precarious balance of fate and power, design and liberty. "For, though Fate is immense, so is power, which is the other fact in the dual world, immense. If Fate follows and limits power, power attends and antagonizes Fate" ("Fate," 6:12). That antagonism cultivates a new commonality. Although it is experienced in solitude, power cannot belong to one individual. "It is not mine or thine, but the will of all mind," the commonal current in which all individuals are situated (6:15). Power is a means of finding one's autonomy through "a sharing of the nature of the world" ("Power," 6:30).

Individual subjects experience and articulate power and the commonality it produces differently: after all, the other element that Emerson values—liberty—is synonymous with this power that releases one from a deterministic Fate. Yet, if one confuses power with exclusionary socioeconomic success or leadership—as he occasionally does ("A man who knows men, can talk well on politics, trade, law, war, religion. For, everywhere, men are led in the same manners" ["Power," 6:30])—then one conflates articulation with narration, or uses preset social standards and values to identify who has a quantifiable degree of power. Reading Emerson against himself, though, I would argue that he primarily understands power as a commonality that cannot be identified or owned. It is improper. It may be the essence of those ideas that undo us in our reading, but it cannot be narrated because one does not own it. If one cannot possess power, one simply is powerful because one is possessed by, or articulates, power, and so exemplifies what it means to be alive and singular merely by living. Because it cannot be owned, because it differentiates each one who cultivates his life, it has the potential to be an utterly democratic resource. Let me clarify: wielding power over someone is the work of fateful narration; it is the consolidation of an identity through the assumption of a liberal voice that takes possession of power. In contrast, Emerson imagines a power that accounts for an ontological, rather than narrated, *experience* of democracy. Simply living is being so possessed that one is liberated from design, identity, narrative, the present. For a moment, one returns to a first condition of democracy and lives in, rather than talks about, freedom.

Difference, then, does play a significant role in our lives—indeed, it is our lives—but it is undervalued precisely because it escapes narration and so cannot be identified. We may talk about it a lot and think we are truly capturing it in our narratives, but we are merely paying our respects to it from the limited perspective of our own established identities. We actually kill off what makes this vitalist force different or powerful by respecting it as a multicultural or pluralist value. Difference is really the part of the story where story falters, that event when narrative simply ends so that it may recommence later, in a new way. If difference is indeed experiential, it is what occurs when we, alone, suddenly become so empowered (or run through by liberty) that we become dispossessed. We lose our selves. It is our awakening when the system that we use to guide our selves is thrown into question and our ability to narrate our selves through a story or a history founding and fixing our identities is unsettled.

To come into such an experience is to awaken outside our selves. Emerson famously begins his "Experience":

> Where we do find ourselves? In a series, of which we do not know the extremes, and believe that it has none. We wake and find ourselves on a stair: there are stairs below us, which we seem to have ascended; there are stairs above us, many a one, which go upward and out of sight. But the Genius which, according to the old belief, stands at the door by which we enter, and gives us the lethe to drink, that we may tell no tales, mixed the cup too strongly, and we cannot shake off the lethargy now at noonday. Sleep lingers all our lifetime about our eyes, as night hovers all day in the boughs of the fir-tree. All things swim and glitter. Our life is not so much threatened as our perception. Ghostlike we glide through nature, and should not know our place again. (3:27)

The moment when we are at our most powerful and most free, the moment when "we find ourselves," is precisely when we lose agency. We are unmoored, we lose our social bearings, and we are displaced from where we were in an order of things. We have forgotten and can "tell no tales." In this state of difference, we do not wake up in the middle of nowhere; we just don't know our coordinates or what it means to be *here,* on this particular stair. Our "perception"—not our life—is threatened.

Lacking coordinates from which we can orient our perspective, we are like an object in a general field of perception that suddenly discovers sentience. We are much like the child's toy called Harmony Clown through which poet Ann Lauterbach, thinking of Emerson's "Experience," narrates the travails of identification. This supposedly inanimate yet sentient object's plight is reminiscently like what we all come to suffer, according to Emerson. It awakens not on Emerson's stair, but on a shelf, only to discover a loss of voice: "I am missing / part of my throat." Its sentience, however, permits a rambling set of inquiries: "Am I lost or stolen? Did I belong to a thing? / Did I live in a tent or a stream? / Are these eyes borrowed? (they seem to be used)."[19] Story is improbable and history is impossible if we awaken to our selves as Harmony does. The precondition of such an awakening is that we must forget. As Emerson writes, experience is Lethe-al. It kills our selves because, once we drink from the river of forgetting, we are able to "tell no tales." Both our sense of self and our ability to give voice to the selves we have known have gone. Lauterbach's line break nicely emphasizes this Emersonian condition: "I am missing."

In difference, we are improper and unpropertied ghosts, haunting a place we cannot call our own. We are attached to it, but we cannot encompass it through narrative: "Life is a series of surprises, and would not be worth taking or keeping, if it were not.... All good conversation, manners, and action, come from a spontaneity which forgets usages, and makes the moment great. Nature hates calculators; her methods are saltatory and impulsive.... We thrive by casualties. Our chief experiences have been casual" ("Experience," 3:39). Rather than staving off death, the casual life always borders dangerously near death. Casual events are like "casualties," and life is not "worth taking or keeping"—murder would be inexplicable and suicide inevitable, life would be meaningless—if experience was not unexpected. This death hovers about our I's. From moment to moment, it blurs or even disintegrates our identities, just as the eyes of the half-awake are shadowed by an imminent sleep and so render reality uncertain. About our eyes there is a penumbra of "lethargy" because, as Lauterbach's poem suggests, our eyes/I have been subjected to abuse. They have been "borrowed" over and over again by others—by sympathizers like Whitman, who insist on using us as the other through whom they may narrate their selves. We are exhausted because we are always struggling to free our selves from others' sovereign designs. We try to lend our selves to more powerful, casual experiences that free us from the fated necessity that others speak through us to claim as their own a freedom really reserved for all. Our exhaustion and proximity to death are not symptoms to be treated, then, but are ill-seeming signs actually indicative of our good health. When boundaries dissolve as our eyes lose focus, when we forget who we are and so kill our selves, the goiter of egotism begins to be remedied.

Emerson's repeated use of the first person plural in "Experience" characterizes this dissolution of self as anything but isolated or isolating. Rather, it is a shared experience, the common groundwork for our eventual production of a new narrative that allows us to lay to rest the old chronicles of identitarian design. His metaphors of sleep and death allow him to stay as close as possible to the realm of the poetic or imagistic so as to elude philosophy's tendency to resort to narrative to identify and classify human conditions. Reading Emerson's convoluted parataxis, his mobile and ever-shifting metaphors, we are lulled into feeling as if we have also awakened with him on that stair. From our new, imaginative perspective we can visualize the stairs above and the ones below to which he is pointing. Here we find our selves brought into sympathy, but it is very different from that of Whitman's poetic. We find our selves with Emerson, and he with us, casually and by chance. The event of this unexpected occurrence mediates our sympathies, in which our recognition of difference is facilitated by a groggy lack of awareness of our exact boundaries, of where we are. Neither he nor we quite belong to our own "present" moments through which our respective identities might be told. Narratives are disrupted because we are brought out of time, and in that state direct agency is lacking. Emerson registers this very well when he remarks that, half-asleep, he keeps losing his grasp on natural objects, which slip through his fingers thanks to their "evanescence and lubricity" ("Experience," 3:29). From time to time, however, he finds that he does make some contact, albeit not an account of his own volition. "Direct strokes she [i.e., Nature] never gave us power to make; all our blows glance, all our hits are accidents. Our relations to one another are oblique and casual" ("Experience," 3:29–30). Rather than the chronicle of cause and effect narrating the atomistic individual as a historical agent, an experience of casualty and affect brings the individual into contact with others. Thus, he lives in a new relation to his own sovereignty. Emerson doesn't look for sympathy for his cause. He urges us to resist identifying who "we" are or looking for others' affirmation of who we think we are. Remaining open, "we" may exist out of time. That always partial awakening, that dreamy imagining, is the ethical basis for a different experience of commonality from which we can narrate our selves anew.

Emerson's commonality is meaningful only in those pedagogical moments when, while solitarily reading, one is brought outside one's own time into a new, mediated experience of difference, like that on the stair. To cultivate one's self, one must experience an epochally unbounded sort of collectivity. One must retreat to one's study so as to go abroad in a studied and careful form of self-education. "The world exists for the education of each man," Emerson writes in "History" (2:5). And in the course of that education, one finds a commonality that no longer requires one to speak of boundaries, historical or egoistic. "When a thought of Plato becomes a thought to me,—when a truth that fired the soul of Pindar fires mine, time is no more. When I feel that we two meet in a perception, that our two souls are tinged with the same hue, and do, as it were, run into one, why should I measure degrees of latitude, why should I count Egyptian years?" (2:15). Here, language mediates the boundary crossing, still maintaining differences but bridging the gulf of time. The phrasing "a thought of Plato" is not as properly possessive as "Plato's thought," yet the thought still can be associated and discovered with that personage even if it originates in someone else's thought altogether. Since Plato has less of an exclusive claim to this thought, it can move to Emerson. We are left with an image of sharing, an ideational and linguistic crossing between Plato and Emerson that establishes their relation. It is but a convention to say that this commonality has dissolved their boundaries. Emerson signals that convention with the conditional parataxis ("our two souls . . . do, *as it were,* run into one"), but their confluence has not actually occurred. He still respects the doubled nature of his condition, then. He is both bounded and moving beyond bounds. Sovereign and alone in his study, he still commonally coexists with the subject of his studies.

Even if it doesn't really occur, the imagining of this commonality's possibility is the only means by which the reader produces a world in which he can live. He *needs* that fictive world of commonality with the past: "A man is a bundle of relations, a knot of roots, whose flower and fruitage is the world. His faculties refer to natures out of him, and predict the world he is to inhabit, as the fins of the fish foreshow that water exists, or the wings of an eagle in the egg presuppose air. He cannot live without a world" ("History," 2:20). To "predict" and cultivate that possibility of an inhabitable world, the individual must read and look to the past to figure his singular experiences. That is, *figure* in the sense of "articulate" and "imagine," rather than categorically know (i.e., "figure out"). With that rhetorical imagining, he can write his own passages. Such cultivation is the only way to multiply the paths he may be free to take by unwriting a seemingly fated identity. "Broader and deeper we must write our annals—from an ethical reformation, from an influx of the ever new, every sanative conscience,—if we would trulier express our central and wide-related nature, instead of this old chronology of selfishness and pride to which we have too long lent our eyes" ("History," 2:23).

Yet, do we not risk losing the lessons of our reading, of uprooting the multiplied selves that we have cultivated, if we try to voice our experience? Narrative, we know, is inevitable, but it does produce reductive identities that set undesirable limits to our continuing emergence as subjects and circumscribe new relational possibilities within conventionally sympathetic modes. How do we come to write for our own future selves, our own reading? How do we continue to produce difference so as to make history and new commonalities, across time? Emerson supplies a clue about how to avoid the trap of simple narration. The annals of history only effectively produce an experience of commonality if they are written "broader and deeper" and do not repeat "the old chronology." Perhaps they are not to be written as prose. Remember that when we "attain and maintain that lofty sight where facts yield their secret sense," when the reading mind comes to find a commonality with what remains in the historical distance and then cultivates future selves from that discovery, "poetry and annals are *alike*" ("History," 2:6, emphasis added). The exemplars of Emersonian difference are poets. If readers are to author their own lessons in response to the texts and the ideas and secrets they find there, they must come into a form of poetic writing like those used by those they read. But what are they writing? What does Emerson mean by writing poetically if so much of experience depends on reading? How is poetry read before it is written? Can criticism be poetic, or is it hopelessly chronological?

To tease out the answers to these questions, we must appreciate how Emerson's ideal poet cannot be a *camerado* like Whitman. He spurns the company of others and seeks out a private retreat. His journey begins in the same way that the ideal reader's does. "Solitude takes off the pressure of present importunities that more catholic and humane relations may appear. The saint and poet seek privacy to ends the most public and universal: and it is the secret of culture, to interest the man more in his public, than in his private quality" ("Culture," 6:83). This withdrawal is not "the safeguard of mediocrity" (6:83) but is a means of avoiding the reproduction of one's identity and hackneyed conventions in one's art. "He who should inspire and lead his race must be defended from travelling with the souls of other men, from living, breathing, reading, and writing in the daily, time-worn yoke of their opinions" (6:83). Poets' public value demands their withdrawal into themselves, for the good of the race. One writes for the possibility of one's own future by withdrawing from others in one's social surroundings, by estranging one's self from the present. But that writing has consequences for the others who, as one must believe, will eventually read it, too. As he imagined it, poetry is a pedagogical tool that offers citizens instruction in how to realize an empowering and experiential (rather than cognitive or epistemological) difference from their present senses of self by remaining open to differences from elsewhere and from other times. Those lessons might be offered without recapitulating fateful identity structures via a polemical dictation of a social program.

For Emerson, poetry's especial pedagogical value is to teach readers how to become better listeners. "For poetry was all written before time was," he tells us, "and whenever we are so finely organized that we can penetrate into that region where the air is music, we hear those primal warblings, and attempt to write them down, but we lose even and anon a word, or a verse, and substitute something of our own, and thus miswrite the poem. The men of more delicate ear write down these cadences more faithfully, and these transcripts, though imperfect, become the songs of the nations" ("The Poet," 3:5–6). Sovereignty is not lost when poets listen for the music around them. In fact, the poet "is a sovereign, and stands on the centre" (3:5). But these writers' sovereignty is qualified: their "transcripts" of what they hear in their solitary meditations are always "imperfect." That imperfection indicates a faithful attitude that refuses to debase experience in a mimetic reproduction or a descriptive recording of it, yet the poet also refuses a subjective interpolation of events and phenomena that would merely render his verse a record of his own identity. He tries to make a sovereign song with universal possibilities. He can't help but sing a song of nation since his civic experience affects how he hears the world, but his poetry need not be just an anthem that identifies a people. To avoid such an identificatory song, he must minimize voicing his own personality. He must avoid producing a sovereign personal lyric with epic aspirations, a lyric easily absorbed into a nationalist enterprise that replaces free individuals' power to differentiate their selves with an imperial imposition of one sovereign body's identity. Instead, he must remain as faithful as possible to the subject of his song.

Rather than presupposing that ethics entails an actual response or a political enactment of justice in the name of a present identifiable sub-

ject, Emerson's view of poetry constructs literary culture as ethical because it models and cultivates a condition of responsiveness. At once
private (as a product of the poet's solitary withdrawal) and public (as a
text published and read), the poem offers an alternative *habitas*, a space
from the past and from an other, a where or a when that the reader might
inhabit in order to recondition her old habits while in the company of the
text's own singular difference. We listen to the text like the poet listens
to nature: we are sovereign, at the center of the experience, yet (if we
are good and faithful readers) we cannot overwrite it with our own personality or demand that it conform with or be sympathetic to our own
agendas. By reading poetry, we learn how to be by our selves—a distinct
condition from being by ourselves. Moving into the foreign space of the
text, and then letting the other ideas we find there secretly move in with
us, compels a self-reflexivity in which we see our identities differently so
that we have become beside, or by, our selves. As Emerson would have it,
we need not literally write back in order to be responsible to the text. If
we are *by* our selves, we are also our own authors. More precisely, we are
coauthored by the selves we experience in reading since the experience,
as "History" maps out, causes our selves to multiply.

However, authoring one's self, to be by one's self, is not an utterly
hopeful exercise. It first necessitates that one come to be beside one's
self. As Emerson knew, coming into contact with difference via a solitary
retreat is a risky business. Losing one's self is the only means of finding
one's self, differently. And that loss is never easy and is not without its
dangers. "It is a secret which every intellectual man quickly learns, that,
beyond the energy of his possessed and conscious intellect, he is capable
of a new energy (as of an intellect doubled on itself), by abandonment to
the nature of things; that, beside his privacy of power as an individual
man, there is a great public power, on which he can draw, by unlocking,
at all risks, his human door, and suffering the ethereal tides to roll and
circulate through him" ("The Poet," 3:15–16, emphasis added). This necessary risk is the ethical core of Emerson's solitary reading, and it holds
the greatest weight for our own political revaluation of the role of the
American scholar today. We no longer can afford to let the virtues of risk-
ing our selves remain a private secret locked up in our studies. Recall the
map of the trajectory experienced by the solitary reader in "History": he
privately communes with past actors and their public ideas to come back

with a secret, an idea that lends him a new appreciation and transformation of his still private sovereignty. The poet's and the critic's work, though, must make the solitary experience of self-authoring public again. We must risk writing about our private trysts with the ideas we discover in others' texts in order to make our solitude political. A new humanistic criticism must begin with an ethics of risk, a responsible sovereignty that assumes we, like poets, cannot claim to be the originators of our own agency. Instead, we come into our own because of our vulnerability to otherly ideas, a vulnerability that can only come by refusing to hold history and literature at a distance. Instead, we must give our selves over and allow it to pull us close and out of our selves.[20]

CONCLUSION: THE HUMANITIES AND RISKY READING TODAY

Emerson's studies of ten-year-old reports of, and more recent historical accounts about, British Emancipation drive him to make "the most painful comparisons." Ostensibly happy events actually beleaguer him, and he finds himself "oppressed by other thoughts."[21] Rather than being occupied with the praiseworthy images of British Parliament, there were

> other images that intruded on me. I could not see the great vision of the [British] patriots and senators who have adopted the slave's cause:—they turned their backs on me. No: I see other pictures— of mean men: I see very poor, very ill-clothed, very ignorant men, not surrounded by happy friends,—to be plain,—poor black men of obscure employment as mariners, cooks, or stewards, in ships, yet citizens of this our Commonwealth of Massachusetts,—freeborn as we,—whom the slave-laws of the States of South Carolina, Georgia, and Louisiana, have arrested in the vessels in which they visited those ports, and shut up in jails so long as the vessel remained in port, with the stringent addition, that if the shipmaster fails to pay the costs of this official arrest, and the board in jail, these citizens are to be sold for slaves, to pay the expense. This man, these men, I see, and no law to save them. (23–24)

Alone in his study, reading about British political heroes from a decade ago to research his address, Emerson is pitched into a crisis. He is subjected to a painful awareness of what's missing in his own day. It is worth mentioning that his speaking about the West Indian Emancipation is intellectually risky. At the outset of his remarks, he admits that "I might well hesitate, coming from other studies, and without the smallest claim to be a special laborer in this work of humanity" (7). But he risks more than claiming authority over a matter about which he is not credentialed. Rather, he risks his very claims to liberal selfhood, or the sovereignty of his own status as a speaker: "In this cause, no man's weakness is any prejudice; it has a thousand sons; if one man cannot speak, ten others can; and whether by wisdom of its friends, or by folly of the adversaries; by speech and by silence; by doing and by omitting to do, it goes forward. Therefore I will speak,—or, not I, but the might of liberty in my weakness" (7). Liberty—the property of commonality—speaks in this address, not Emerson. That is to say, the common strives to articulate itself by speaking *through* him. What we hear is the difference of humanity, those compelling and painful images that he describes as intruding on him, those undesired images that are not narrated in the celebratory accounts of others' historical deeds done. After introducing their presence more than midway through his talk, and expounding briefly on the injustice of American slavery, Emerson returns to the "rightful theme" and "the bright aspects of the occasion" of which he is, admittedly, no scholar.[22] Although it passes relatively quickly, the crisis-moment of Emerson's oration is important. It is the only time when he embodies his own ideal of the American Scholar in this address.

I am closing my solitary reading of Emerson, performed as it has been without much regard for other critics' opinions, with this final anecdote from our subject because my reading has been anything but isolated. In the time I have spent with Emerson, other images have intruded on me, not unlike those that haunt his writing and research, images of unlawful incarceration and detainment: Orange jumpsuits and satellite surveillance photos. Infrequently viewed pictures of dismembered limbs on desert sands. My imagining of individuals rounded up for deportation. Stories of soldiers court-martialed for publicly protesting the invasion of Iraq while in uniform. Images of men stripped naked and masked with canvas bags, smeared in their own feces or bruised from beatings. Women arrested and accused of prostitution and then subjected to being humiliatingly forced to undress for their captors' cameras. I am drawn to the irony that Emerson refers to the images of captured free black men unsettling him as *intrusions*, for, indeed, the intrusive images that surface as I read Emerson are related to the current rhetoric of protecting us against all forms of intrusion. As I muse on Emerson's career-long insistence that reading undoes what he terms individuals' "security," usually of an economic or class sort, I can't help but draw my own painful comparisons—obvious though they may seem—of what his ideas have to say to today's mandate of Homeland Security.

In "The Young American," Emerson remarks that "the wise and just man will always feel that he stands on his own feet; that he imparts strength to the state, not receives security from it" (1:241). To believe in such security is to be weak, and "nothing is so weak as an egotist" (1:241). The egotist, the liberalist, is the one whose own ontological and economic security is based on a faith in the sovereignty not only of her own subjectivity but of the state itself. Emerson's antistatism is not a dismissal of nationalism, of a vision for the nation. "One thing is plain for all men of common sense and common conscience," he writes shortly after his condemnation of security, "that here, here in America, is the home of man" (1:241). Before dismissing this nationalism and idea of home out of hand, though, let's take the sage advice that Emerson would offer decades later: "But let us not be the victims of words" ("Society and Solitude," 7:8). In 2007, *home* and *nation*—much like the terms that he sets out to resignify in 1870 (i.e., *society* and *solitude*)—are "deceptive names" ("Society and Solitude," 7:8). We need not fear Emerson's idea of national belonging or even national sovereignty. Indeed, the fact that recurrent visions of interdependence and cosmopolitanism can only be represented through a lexicon of some form of internationalism or transnationalism "show[s] just how inescapable the national reference is," as Étienne Balibar puts it.[23] Similarly, we need not fear the idea of individualism or the citizen-subject's sovereignty, her capacity to act. We also need not fear the idea that the individual and the land can provide a home. What we must be wary of is any effort to align sovereignty and homeland with security and a devaluation of risk.

Current legislative and political discourses of Homeland Security deploy a rhetoric of risk management that reveals just how traditionally conservative so-called liberal ethical premises really are if they set out to contain risk. The only kind of risks that are socially and culturally valued are those that pursue neoliberal or Third Way programs that advance and secure the interests of the few in the name of globalized capitalism and an imperialist war-state.[24] They emphasize consensus, a masquerade of pluralist commonality, and the actual squashing of difference by identifying markers of a preexistent democratic commonality in spite of national or other identificatory differences. Set categories through which we can identify others are provided for us as the only acceptable options. Polarizing and adversarial mentalities about alterity prevail in the recent Bush administration's rhetoric of "You're either with us, or against us." As the authors of the *National Strategy for Homeland Security* put it, processes of classing others "guarantee the sovereignty and independence of the United States, with our fundamental values and institutions intact."[25] The present global climate and transnational economic infrastructures have produced a "permanent condition" of risk and a constant exposure to external threats (2). The state's integrity depends on managing those risks, on identifying who sympathizes enough with the project of globally expanding democratic liberalism to count as allies.

The *National Strategy for Homeland Security* marks (but does not truly define) a distinction between "the twin concepts of national security and homeland security" (5). Its "homeland" project is a cultural, rather than political, form of risk management. In the present political moment, then, culture is used in an absolutist and uncritically sovereign fashion. It is a reactionary form of liberalism that bolsters a cultural exceptionalism congruent with a political and nationalist one. This "homeland" project invokes identifiable cultural others to call into existence a political national body that does not exist: a global United States. It is an imaginary nation of potentialities, consisting of an ever-changing and "almost infinite array of potential targets," both inside and outside national boundaries (vii).[26] "Difference" is imagined and rhetorically invoked, rather than experienced, so that it might be attributed to an other. If deemed an ally, the other is then absorbed as sympathetic with the United States' liberalist cultural agenda, which imperialistically promotes its economic interests and, in turn, safeguards the legitimacy of its political sovereignty. If deemed an adversary, the other's difference is deemed so incomprehensible that the other is excluded from the very order of humanity.

Subjectivated by such ideologies, and often falling victim to misunderstandings of the word *liberalism*, we might wonder, in an echo of the questions Emerson posed in "The Fugitive Slave Law": Who are the readers and thinkers of the first decade of the twenty-first century? Who are equipped to question the opinions girding antidemocratic rhetoric and policies? Emerson's ontological critique of liberalism supplies us with some tools to become better readers and thinkers. The curse of modernity and liberal democracy, one that affects even how we read, is an unexamined faith in the *discretionary,* a word etymologically at the root of how we link private subjects with the dispensation of property. A sense of self different from the proper, the discretionary, and the absolutely sovereign must be cultivated. As Emerson instructs us in his lessons about reading, our identities emerge from a cultural making that is never truly ours. Not only is culture shared, but it is driven, in a manner like—but different from—how we are driven as living beings, by instinct and forces of nature. In reading, we are driven in that process of cultivation by the secrets embedded in the texts we encounter. Our readerly approaches, then, must make better efforts to abnegate the absolute liberal sovereignty that renders textual artifacts discrete, distanced entities we use to bolster our own identities or to secure our own civic power.

What we do in the privacy of our studies—that is, how we read— enables us to live in a critical, and potentially political, relationship to our selves and our culture. The best readers among us are those who are affected by ideas, which are always strange to and originate outside our selves. Ideas and thought are the secret substance of potential commonalities. They are improper and belong to no one and to no age. Those who work in my field of literary studies already value close reading practices, allowing literary and other cultural texts to speak first. More generally, we must cultivate an appreciation of critical practices that also respect culture's lack of transparency and so let the texts murmur, not so articulately, as Emerson believes poetry does. Only then can close reading become like Emerson's valued creative reading. Critics must be given some room to risk murmuring back, awkwardly yet poetically working in the new language that they have come to share with the texts they study. After Emerson, I posit that this constitutes a first step for the humanities' promotion of a necessary state of risk and a culture of homeland insecurity, a refusal of static identification and a fateful statist consensus.

NOTES

1. Ralph Waldo Emerson, *The Collected Works of Ralph Waldo Emerson*, ed. Alfred R. Ferguson, Robert E. Spiller, et al., 8 vols. to date (Cambridge, Mass.: Harvard University Press, Belknap Press, 1971–2010), 1:104. Subsequent quotations from Emerson's writing are from this source and are cited parenthetically in text by volume and page numbers. Citations may include essay title if the essay from which a quotation is taken is not clear from the text.

2. On naturalistic empiricism (also called naturalistic humanism), see John Dewey, *Experience and Nature*, 2nd ed. (LaSalle, Ill.: Open Court, 1929).

3. See Edward W. Said, *Humanism and Democratic Criticism* (New York: Columbia University Press, 2004).

4. See, for example, Jean-Luc Nancy, "Literary Communism," in *The Inoperative Community*, trans. Peter Connor (Minneapolis: University of Minnesota Press, 1991), and *Being Singular Plural*, trans. Robert D. Richardson and Anne E. O'Byrne (Minneapolis: University of Minnesota Press, 2000); Michael Hardt and Antonio Negri, *Empire* (Cambridge, Mass.: Harvard University Press, 2001) and *Multitude: War and Democracy in the Age of Empire* (New York: Penguin, 2004); and Paolo Virno, *A Grammar of the Multitude*, trans. Isabella Bertoletti, James Cascaito, and Andrea Casson (New York: Semiotext(e), 2004).

5. "The Fugitive Slave Law," in *Emerson's Antislavery Writings*, ed. Len Gougeon and Joel Myerson (New Haven, Conn.: Yale University Press, 1995), 73, 80.

6. Although Emerson's writings on slavery invoke reading as a liberating practice leading to social justice, he amazingly makes little reference to the fact that some of the most powerful materials for producing such realizations are those same slave narratives that were foundational for antebellum abolitionist politics. Instead, he tends to laud either the writers of history or "the newsboy," the latter being the unlikely "humble priest of politics, philosophy, and religion" (ibid.). At the close of this essay, I discuss the effects on Emerson himself, as a reader and scholar, of such writing about the slavery debate.

7. "An Address Delivered in the Court-House in Concord, Massachusetts, on 1st August 1844, on the Anniversary of the Emancipation of the Negroes in the British West Indies," *Emerson's Antislavery Writings*, 30–31.

8. Walt Whitman, "Emerson's Books, (The Shadows of Them)," in *Specimen Days and Collect* (1883; New York: Dover, 1995), 320, Whitman's emphasis.

9. Walt Whitman, "Song of Myself," in *Leaves of Grass and Other Writings*, ed. Michael Moon (New York: Norton, 2002), lines 497–99.

10. Walt Whitman, "Starting from Paumanok," in *Leaves of Grass*, line 160.

11. D. H. Lawrence, *Studies in Classic American Literature* (1924; New York: Penguin, 1971), 174.

12. Ibid., 181.

13. Charles Taylor, "The Politics of Recognition" (1992), in *Multiculturalism: Examining the Politics of Recognition,* ed. Amy Gutmann (Princeton, N.J.: Princeton University Press, 1994), 66. For a representative sampling from the vast literature on multicultural identity politics, see Will Kymlicka, *Liberalism, Community, and Culture* (New York: Oxford University Press, 1989), 136–81; Kwame Anthony Appiah, "Liberalism, Individualism, Identity," *Critical Inquiry* 27, no. 2 (Winter 2001): 305–32, and *The Ethics of Identity* (Princeton, N.J.: Princeton University Press, 2004); and Amy Gutmann, *Identity in Democracy* (Princeton, N.J.: Princeton University Press, 2003).

14. Alexander García Düttmann and Judith Butler turn to Hegel to think recognition beyond a Whitmanic sympathizing or a Taylorian identity politics, and deserve more space than I can give them here. See Butler, *Undoing Gender* (New York: Routledge, 2004), 131–51; and García Düttmann, *Between Cultures: Tensions in the Struggle for Recognition,* trans. Kenneth B. Woodgate (New York: Verso, 2000), 181–201.

15. Walt Whitman, "A Song of Joys," in *Leaves of Grass,* lines 115, 120.

16. Gilles Deleuze, *Essays Critical and Clinical* (1993), trans. Daniel W. Smith and Michael A. Greco (Minneapolis: University of Minnesota Press, 1997), 4. Deleuze would disagree with my characterization of Whitman since he reads the poet as establishing relations originating outside the self. See "Whitman," in ibid., 56–60.

17. Samuel R. Delany, "Coming/Out," in *Shorter Views: Queer Thoughts and the Politics of the Paraliterary* (Hanover, N.H.: Wesleyan University Press, 1999), 88–89.

18. For an analysis of the relationship between affect, narration, and group solidarity, see Iris Marion Young, *Inclusion and Democracy* (New York: Oxford University Press, 2000), 52–120.

19. Ann Lauterbach, "A Clown, Some Colors, a Doll, Her Stories, a Song, a Moonlit Cove," in *On a Stair* (New York: Penguin, 1997), 35.

20. Stanley Cavell develops a similar idea of vulnerability out of Emerson's "moral perfectionism." See his *Philosophy the Day after Tomorrow* (Cambridge, Mass.: Harvard University Press, 2005).

21. "West Indian Emancipation," in *Emerson's Antislavery Writings,* 23.

22. "British East Indies," in *Emerson's Antislavery Writings,* 26.

23. Étienne Balibar, *We, the People of Europe? Reflections on Transnational Citizenship,* trans. James Swenson (Princeton, N.J.: Princeton University Press, 2004), 12. For strong critical challenges to much contemporary theory's cele-

bratory rhetoric of cosmopolitanism and postnationalism, see Samir Amin, *The Liberal Virus: Permanent War and the Americanization of the World,* trans. James H. Membrez (New York: Monthly Review Press, 2004); and Pheng Cheah, *Inhuman Conditions: On Cosmopolitanism and Human Rights* (Cambridge, Mass.: Harvard University Press, 2006).

24. As is evident in Anthony Giddens's explicit linking of his sociology of risk to Third Way politics, a view of risk as necessary for advancing the nation-state in the current stage of late modernity is key to a centrist liberalism—an individualism that seems to be reconciled with the differences of commonality and is imagined as more suitable for a globalized age than either socialist democracy or laissez-faire neoliberalism. See Anthony Giddens, *The Third Way: The Renewal of Social Democracy* (Cambridge, England: Polity Press, 1998). I also invite readers to explore the extensive literature from the specialty of reflexive (or risk) sociology.

25. Office of Homeland Security, *National Strategy for Homeland Security* (Washington, D.C.: Office of Homeland Security, July 2002), 5.

26. Slavoj Žižek describes the imaginary of a global United States in this way: "If we scratch the surface, we are all Americans." *Iraq: The Borrowed Kettle* (New York: Verso, 2004), 25.

SANDRA LAUGIER

TRANSLATED BY NEIL PISCHNER

7. Emerson, Skepticism, and Politics

For several decades, Stanley Cavell has been working to make Emerson's voice reheard in the core of American philosophy. This activity is not simply historical rehabilitation, nor is it a return to the source. What appears very clearly in a series of recent texts assembled in his collection *Emerson's Transcendental Etudes* is that Cavell also wants to make heard the present-day pertinence of Emerson's thinking, notably its political pertinence in the context of America today.

THE EMERSONIAN VOICE

Emerson's political ambivalence is a fact known by his readers; he seems to combine, for example, the call to self-reliance and obedience to nature and destiny, the affirmation of the universal spirit shared by all and the dismay caused by the weak quality of his contemporaries, the glorifica-tion and hopelessness of democracy and the people's power.[1]

This ambivalence belongs as well to Emerson's reception;[1] as a found-ing father of American philosophy, he is a sort of tutelary figure, at once an object of reverence and irony and an emancipatory figure.[2] It is per-haps in twentieth-century cinema that we find the most important traces of Emerson's moral influence, notably in two classics, Frank Capra's *It's a Wonderful Life* and Joseph L. Mankiewicz's *The Late George Apley*. The latter film evokes precisely the ambivalence of Emerson's figure; the family man designated by the title of the film lays claim to Emerson, sometimes because he incites submission to established customs and sometimes (notably at the end of the film) for rejecting conformism ("after all, Emerson is a radical!"). The genius of Mankiewcz's film is to show that it's all the same Emerson, the same voice that breathes hot and cold, good and bad.

Cavell describes well this specific difficulty in Emerson's tonality that sometimes gives his writings the allure of the rhetoric of a self-made man (the reading of which would make Emerson a precursor of liberal individualism), sometimes that progressive rhetoric, à la Dewey, that would make Emerson the first link in a neopragmatist recovery and conversational chain that would lead us today to Richard Rorty or even Robert Brandom and Jürgen Habermas. Cavell has given himself the task—notably in his texts "What Is the Emersonian Event?" and "What's the Use of Calling Emerson a Pragmatist?"—of clearly differentiating Emerson from these ideological trends that assimilate and trivialize him, turning him over to the service of ideas that he himself rejected. It is no longer a question, for Cavell, of making heard an unknown voice, but of making known a poorly known thinking, even to those who pretend to be Emerson's inheritors. Such an approach was already, in part, used in the 1990 work *Conditions Handsome and Unhandsome,* devoted to Emerson's moral perfectionism. Cavell noted there that America constantly seems to present us ridiculous and embarrassing versions of Emerson's formulas and principles of perfectionism, which gives the order to constantly look for a better version of oneself and (to make this possible) to trust in oneself:

> False or debased perfectionisms seem everywhere these days, from bestselling books with titles like *Love Yourself* to the television advertisement on behalf of Army recruitment with the slogan "Be all that you can be." Someone is apt to find these slogans difficult to tell from a remark from Emerson's in which he lists, among the "few great points," what he words as "courage to be what we are."[3]

But it is not because there exist debased versions of perfectionism (or democracy) that it is necessary to renounce it. On the contrary, an essential element of Cavell's political position is that the possibility of debasement forms a part of democracy, defining it. Hence the skeptical dimension of politics that Cavell constantly puts forth. His remarks, in *Conditions*

Handsome and Unhandsome, take on particular meaning today, "in a world of false democracy":

> Whatever the confusions in store for philosophical and moral think-
> ing, ought we to let the fact of debased or parodist versions of a pos-
> sibility deprive us of the good of the possibility? The inevitability of
> debased claims to Christianity, or to philosophy, or to democracy, are,
> so one might put it, not the defeat, not even the bane, of the existence
> of the genuine article, but part of its inescapable circumstance and
> motivation. So that the mission of Perfectionism generally, in a world
> of false (and false calls for) democracy, is the discovery of the possibil-
> ity of democracy, which to exist is recurrently to be (re)discovered.[4]

It is precisely today that Emerson becomes pertinent, in the possibility that he gives us to rediscover democracy, or to discover that its possibility must always be rediscovered, that it is never acquired. Such a discovery happens through the reappropriation of Emerson's veritable voice. And the only way to differentiate versions (debased or veritable) of perfectionism is not in the content (as in meaning) of what is said, but in the specific tone of Emerson. As Cavell says early on (this time regarding the difference between Pragmatism and Ludwig Wittgenstein): "It might be worth pointing out that these teachings are fundamental to American pragmatism; but then we must keep in mind how different their argu-ments sound, and admit that in philosophy it is the sound that makes all the difference."[5] This tone in Emerson (that Cavell in a previous text called "mood" and, later, "pitch") is not a variable element, which it would be only in the subjective impression that a particular person might derive from Emerson's words. For Cavell, the important thing in philosophy is the voice or tone. This question is equally at the heart of Emerson's phi-losophy under the form of philosophical speech, regarding our capacity to speak, to stand up and speak, for oneself or for others. We can think about this subject—insisted on by Cavell—of ordinary language, ac-cording to the fact that language is said and must be said in order to really be meant (herein lies the meaning of the title of his first text "Must We Mean What We Say?").[6] We need to understand that Cavell is at odds with Derrida in *A Pitch of Philosophy* beyond just a conflict over the in-terpretation of Austin. For Cavell, philosophy, far from giving priority to the living word, stifled it and wanted to eliminate the fact that language is always said by a living being, in a certain context, with a certain breath, a human respiration. Hence the importance of the theme of the voice in philosophy, the voice of the philosopher who claims to speak in the name—of whom? It all goes back to the problem of philosophical authority, that Emersonian theme, if it is indeed one: "I propose here to talk about philosophy in connection with something I call the voice, by which I mean to talk at once about the tone of philosophy and about the right to take that tone."[7]

The voice is precisely what is defined, at the start of "Self-Reliance," as the very demand to trust oneself, which Cavell calls the "arrogation of voice" that leads oneself to say "we," to speak in the name of the rest of humanity. This voice is the sign not so much of a certainty as of a difficulty: I claim to speak for another, but I can only base myself on myself. The voice is pure claim—another of Cavell's central concepts—and it is the vocal tone of this claim (which others have analyzed as whining) that makes approaching Emerson difficult and gives rise to the debased versions of his work already mentioned. Not that Emerson is an oral author (whatever that might mean), but all of his writing is worked through the voice, a voice that is at once personal and universal (in the sense, of which Cavell is fond, of Kant's "universal voice" that claims to go from the particular to the general, as in the beginning of "Self-Reliance"). This illegitimate demand, which asks that my subjective voice be a "we," is at the heart of the political thinking of Cavell and of Emerson: "Can it be seen that each of us is everyone and no one? Emerson famously takes the oscillation: 'I am God in nature; I am a weed by the wall' ("Circles"). Who beside myself could give me the authority to speak for us?"[8]

The first question for Cavell is the one of knowing how one can speak—who, apart from me, could give me the authority to speak for us? This is the question he had already asked in *Must We Mean What We Say?* where he examined the method of ordinary language philosophy, which consists in elucidating what *we* say, which led him in turn to J. L. Austin's defense. This question of the voice comes years before Cavell's discovery of it in Emerson, with its themes of the acceptance of speech, of the autobiographical, and the act of (dis)possessing by the self of one's speech as the only way, paradoxically, of accessing representativeness. (The theme of representativeness, we know, is an obsession with Emerson.) Cavell generalizes the autobiographical dimension of any speech act in the first person, in clearly Emersonian terms:

> The autobiographical dimension of philosophy is internal to the claim that philosophy speak for the human, for all; that is its necessary arrogance. The philosophical dimension of autobiography is that the human is representative, say, imitative, that each life is exemplary of all, a parable of each; that is humanity's commonness, which is internal to its endless denials of commonness.[9]

This philosophical exemplariness, with its skeptical dimension, is the first question regarding self-reliance, and it is a naturally moral question: to be an example is indeed to give a rule to follow, to oneself and to others. But it is not a rule in the sense of a maxim or a norm, which would tell us how to act, because the only example is me, and each life is exemplary of all lives. The enigma of representativeness is then the central enigma of politics. How can I relinquish my voice and consider that someone represents me and can speak for me?

We can refer to the analysis of Rousseau's theory of the community that Cavell proposes at the beginning of *The Claim of Reason:* Rousseau claims as a philosophical datum the fact that men (and he himself) can speak in the name of society and that society can speak in his name. It is this mutual intimacy (of the private and public interests) that defines the problem of society. The "epistemological" problem put forth by society is discovering with whom I am in community, "and to whom and to what I am in fact obedient."[10]

It seems that Cavell's discovery of Emerson, which took place some years after the publication of *The Claim of Reason,* responds to the problem raised here. Cavell remarks, in his first texts on Emerson, that he was for a long time deaf and indifferent toward Emerson. One is thus only the more struck by the Emersonian tone of these classic passages at the start of *The Claim of Reason:*

> But since the genuine social contract is not in effect (we could know this by knowing that we are born free, and are everywhere in chains) it follows that we are not exercising our general will; and since we are not in a state of nature it follows that we are exercising our will not to the general, but to the particular, to the unequal, to private benefit to privacy. We obey the logic of conspiracy. (26)

It is once again a question of skeptical discovery of a new mode of ignorance (of oneself). It is only in a skeptical version of self-knowledge that
we can understand what it means *to make use of myself in order to access
the society of this me.* The community is at once what gives me a political
voice and what might take it away from me, disappoint me, deceive me to
the point that I no longer want to speak for the community or let it speak
for me in my name. It is with such a case of deception—and because of
this, of optimism—that all of Emerson's work resonates, like an echo of
Rousseau.

The question of the voice is thus the political question, from Plato
to Rousseau to Emerson. We now understand better why Cavell, who devoted his first works to Wittgenstein and Austin, then took it upon himself to make Emerson's voice reheard in the field of philosophy, later inscribing Wittgenstein himself in the extension of the Emersonian voice.
The question of the political voice (or moral code) is one of language in
general:

> To speak for oneself politically is to speak for the others with whom
> you consent to association, and it is to consent to be spoken by them—
> not as a parent speaks for you, i.e. instead of you, but as someone in
> mutuality speaks for you, i.e. speaks your mind. Who these others are,
> for whom you speak and by whom you are spoken for, is not known a
> priori, though it is in practice generally treated as given.[11]

TRANSCENDENTALISM, PRAGMATISM, AND POLITICS

Democracy, for Emerson, is inseparable from self-reliance, that is to say,
from confidence—not as hollow self-conceit or a feeling of superiority (a
debased version of perfectionism), but as a refusal of conformity, of letting oneself be spoken for by others. This self-reliance is also the capacity
that each person has to judge what is good and to refuse a power that does
not respect its own principles (its own constitution). Self-reliance is thus
a political position, claiming the voice of the subject from conformism,
from uses that are accepted in a noncritical way, and from dead institutions, or those no longer representative or confiscated.

It is this theme that Cavell wants to take up again with Emerson
and that he proposes in order to constitute an alternative to the liberal
political thinking that is made emblematic, notably by the work of his

colleague at Harvard, John Rawls. For Cavell, and for Emerson, I must consent to my government, consider that it speaks in my name, to give it my voice. But how is such an agreement possible? When did I give it my consent? Self-reliance claims the right to take back one's voice from society by civil disobedience. My concern is what I think, not what others think; the principle of self-reliance is also one of democracy. Cavell proposes, along with Emerson, a form of radical individualism that is not a selfish claim of private concern; on the contrary, it is pubic and ordinary. Demanding the ordinary is a revolution that Emerson regards as the building of a new ordinary man, the man of democracy. It is here, according to Cavell, where we find the specifically Emersonian contribution to political thought.

Rorty's proposition, which consists in seeing in Emerson the precursor of a pragmatism whose tradition continues on into the twentieth century with liberalism, rests, for Cavell, on a lack of understanding of Emerson's specificity. The disagreement between Rorty and Cavell is thus concerned with the American figures of philosophy that they would like to promote. Of course, Cavell, Hilary Putnam, and Rorty approach one another in their wish to prompt the rediscovery of unjustly neglected American thinkers (Emerson, William James, John Dewey). But everything depends here on what one wants to do with this rediscovery. The current return to Pragmatism, although in keeping with a felicitous movement of reappropriation of the American philosophical past, circumvents Emerson's originality. One would have to take care—after having for a long time centered the history of American philosophy on the analytical tradition—to not repeat this mistake in a way that is just as mythological, centered around an overly encompassing Pragmatism, going from Emerson the proto-Pragmatist to Wittgenstein the post-Pragmatist, and even to current figures of American philosophy. For Cavell, reading Emerson means rediscovering his specificity, a certain approach to the ordinary and to democracy, which is insoluble in terms of the consensual thinking on democracy that has developed in America during the twentieth century.

But in order to realize this, it is necessary to hear Emerson's voice, the difference in tone in the treatment he proposes of themes now familiar in the writing of John Dewey. In "What's the Use of Calling Emerson a Pragmatist?" Cavell wants to differentiate Emerson from Dewey, and from Pragmatism in general, by the tone of his democratic aspiration.[12] The question is therefore knowing which Emerson we wish to inherit today: the precursor of Pragmatism, who would poetically formulate some principles to later be rationalized (as the call to commonality and practicality), or the radical thinker of individualism. Cavell wants to establish a caesura between Transcendentalism and Pragmatism, which is the only way of promoting a radical vision of democracy.

Cavell's position toward Pragmatism appears inevitably unjust, notably toward sincere defenders of democracy like Dewey or toward philosophers like James who claimed (certainly not without ambiguity) a part of the Emersonian legacy.[13] It is precisely in the democratic demand, however, that Cavell hears what is different in Emerson, even if we find more than an echo of Emerson in Dewey, who never ceased to refer to his debt regarding Emerson.[14] Dewey, like Emerson, demanded commonality, that the ordinary or everyday life be shared by all men, and both called for an ideal community. But in the Emersonian approach to commonality, there is nothing of a consensus or a rational agreement. A characteristic of Emerson's politics is his critical dimension, a perfectionist refusal of society such as it exists—a refusal to recognize it as belonging to oneself, as soon as one searches for a better me. Hence the notes of hatred for his contemporaries that sometimes sound in his work, which only justifies itself by a hatred of oneself: "Emersonian Perfectionism requires that we become ashamed in a particular way of ourselves, of our present stance, and the Emersonian Nietzsche requires, as a consecration of the next self, that we hate ourselves, as it were impersonally."[15]

This is the critical requirement with Emerson: a critique, first of all, of oneself, one that inscribes itself at the heart of the contemporary American debate on political radicalism and its legacy, a political question of individualism as a principle of the agreement to society.[16] For Emerson, "Words are deeds," as is trust in oneself.[17] But self-reliance only has strength or practical value if its aversion to conformism also addresses itself to oneself: "So we are to remember that an aversive address may be taken toward oneself as much as toward any institution. Not thus to address the self is to harbor conformity, and I think Emerson invites us to see this as a political choice."[18]

When Emerson notes about his contemporaries that "every word they say chagrins us" ("Self-Reliance," 2:32), his skeptical disappointment concerning everyday life and speech, as they were practiced in America in his time, seems hardly compatible with Pragmatism and the recurrent call to the thinking of the "common" man. There's a world of difference, in other words, between what is common (which is already here) and the ordinary, which is to be attained in perfectionism, in "the transformation of genius into practical power" ("Experience," 3:49).

This realistic transformation of genius into practicality seems likely to herald Pragmatism. For Emerson, however, practicality is about not manipulation but rather patience: "Patience and patience, we shall win at last. We must be very suspicious of the deceptions of the element of time" ("Experience," 3:48–49). This plea by Emerson in favor of endurance and waiting seems to be the negation of the primacy of practicality. However, things are not so simple, and what is in question here is more of a surpassing of the active/passive duality, the equivalent of surpassing the other traditional categories in the same essay, "Experience." (Passiveness is also an agent of change for Henry David Thoreau—for example, when he withdraws from his social environment.) Patience, too, is what leads to "the transformation of genius into practical power."

Neither can intelligence be conceived as being simply active. Cavell, citing Dewey—"[Pragmatism] is the formation of a faith in intelligence, as the one and indispensable belief necessary to moral and social life"[19]— compares Dewey's treatment of intelligence with what Emerson wrote in "Self-Reliance": "To believe your own thought . . . that is genius" (2:27). When Emerson evokes the genius in each person, he expresses the hope that man is *one* and that he can therefore become ordinary, attain his ordinariness, and such a hope has nothing to do with increase of knowledge or scientific progress. Attaining the ordinary and democracy by way of individual genius instead of by science and the reform of intelligence: there we find the alternative that separates Transcendentalism from Pragmatism.

We could also characterize this difference by turning to science, which rendered Pragmatism more presentable in the twentieth century and thus more easily assimilated by analytical philosophy than Transcendentalism. Cavell thinks that there is a certain conflict between the appeal to science and the appeal to ordinary language, which has been constant since the entrance of the latter into philosophy.[20] It is the specific difficulty in turning to ordinary language, and more generally in rediscovering what is *common* to us, that is forgotten in Pragmatism. We could then characterize the difference between Transcendentalism and Pragmatism as the difference between the appeal to the ordinary and the appeal to commonality—except that commonality, in Pragmatism, appears as given, while for Transcendentalism it is an object of skepticism:

> The philosophical appeal to the ordinary, the words we are given in common, is inherently taken in opposition to something about my words as they stand.... The appeal challenges our commonality in favor of a more genuine commonality (surely something that characterizes Dewey's philosophical mission) but in the name of no expertise, no standing adherence to logic or to science, to nothing beyond genius.[21]

Emerson, like Thoreau, begins with a situation of conformity and the inadequateness of language, which he describes as "silent melancholy" and Thoreau calls "quiet desperation." Dewey himself engages the problem of a generalized nonintelligence, and proclaims his faith in intellect and his wishes for education. There is a convergence here between Dewey and Emerson in the desire to break these barriers to the future. But there is also an important divergence that has to do with their connections to the Enlightenment and its scientific or moral paradigm of progress that we supposedly await:

> But the ways are as different as the accompanying ideas of the future; they amount to different ideas of thinking, or reason. I once characterized the difference between Dewey and Emerson by saying that Dewey wanted the Enlightenment to happen in America, whereas Emerson was in the later business of addressing the costs of the way it has happened.[22]

We can refer here to the critique carried out by Emerson in "Experience" of the theory of knowledge:[23] "It is very unhappy, but too late to be helped, the discovery we have made, that we exist. That discovery is called the Fall of Man. Ever afterwards, we suspect our instruments.... Once we lived in what we saw; now, the rapaciousness of this new power, which threatens to absorb all things, engages us" (3:43–44).

It is indeed in the connection to knowledge and skepticism that the difference between Pragmatism and Emerson inscribes itself. Pragmatism can only incorporate Emerson by denying skepticism, its dimension of mourning our loss of all links to the world. This point also has political significance. By erasing the skeptical dimension of self-reliance, one loses a dimension of democratic thought, and the idea—strictly Emersonian— that self-reliance is aversion to conformity and that commonality is only built from this aversion: "This is the latest in the sequence of repressions of Emerson's thought by the culture he helped to found, of what is distinctive in that thought."[24]

THE EDUCATION OF ADULTS

As James indeed saw, in his own way, the question is about choosing between Enlightenment and a post-Enlightenment project and knowing if Pragmatism's place is next to the Enlightenment or at its border, at the moment when it would be necessary to be able to surpass it in order to create a distinctive way of thinking, an autonomous one. This is exactly the meaning of self-reliance. If, as Thoreau remarked in *Walden,* men in the America of their time led lives of "quiet desperation," it is for having lost the capacity of speech to give a voice to their thoughts. One thinks of Emerson's famous declaration: "Man is timid and apologetic; he is no longer upright; he dares not say 'I think,' 'I am'" ("Self-Reliance," 2:38).

It is not enough to say or to think "I think, therefore I am," in going back to European thinking. It is necessary to *claim* it. Here as well, it is a question of tone. This gives self-reliance a political and moral position well beyond an affirmation of the Transcendental subject: the autonomy of the subject only holds if it is a voice. The concept of trust in oneself is then political: the right to withdraw one's voice from society is founded on the idea that I can govern myself (the concept of self-government that is at the base of the Declaration of Independence).[25] In all cases, it's about obeying one's constitution—a play on words of which Emerson was fond: "the only right is what is after my constitution, the only wrong what is against it" ("Self-Reliance," 2:30). The inner constitution, being physiological with the individual, is the principle of ordinary political life.[26] Thus, self-reliance has public stakes; my private voice is "the universal sense" precisely because it is ordinary ("Self-Reliance," 2:27). To make the private sphere public—in such a way that my private voice (which expresses constitution) be public, or that it take on a public tone—is indeed the problem of democracy and of the ordinary. How can my individual voice become communal, representative, and how can I, at times, relinquish it and let others speak in my name?

Self-reliance allows today, then, a shaking up of not only modern liberalism (à la Rawls, founded on a prior agreement that I would have made), but also communitarianism (à la MacIntyre, founded on the inevitable adhesion to a tradition), revealing in advance their common foundation: the idea that if I am here, I am necessarily in agreement (with my society or a tradition, which can speak for me); I have given assent. Emerson has already given a name to this common foundation: conformism. And this is what trust in oneself, taken then in the political sense of trust in one's constitution, must shake, that the scholar or the intellectual American (to come) must overcome, not in order to laboriously reach the Enlightenment but to surpass it: "We have listened too long to the courtly muses of Europe. The spirit of the American freeman is already suspected to be timid, imitative, tame.... Not so, brothers and friends,—please God, ours shall not be so. We will walk on our own feet; we will work with our own hands; we will speak our own minds" ("American Scholar," 1:69–70).

This surpassing, indeed, involves a form of radical individualism, which Emerson demands in "The American Scholar." But this individualism is not an apology of the self-made man, a paradigm of liberalism (one is reminded here of certain interpretations of Emerson, for instance, by George Kateb).[27] Liberal individualism, notably in its present-day interpretations (Rawls), claims moral neutrality. Emerson's individualism rejects neutrality, affirming itself in speech. Voice, because it is political, is what allows the individual to at once affirm its singularity and also its public nature. Individualism is not then a demand of private interest but rather of public interest.

It is first of all necessary to find one's voice. The political and social task of the education of others is first through education of oneself. At first glance, the Transcendental and Pragmatist tasks are rather similar: the education of man. Emerson indeed said of other men: "Every word they say chagrins us, and we know not where to begin to set them right" ("Self-Reliance," 2:32). It is precisely that: *we do not know* where to begin. Man's education is a problem, not a solution, and the position that consists in wanting to improve other men, to change them despite themselves, is the most immoral position that there is. The only veritable education is education regarding self-reliance. By affirming—in a famous passage in *The Claim of Reason*—that philosophy is "the education of grownups" (125), Cavell does not wish so much to extend to adults the "ordinary" idea of education, as he does to renew the concept of education. To admit that I need an education is to admit that I don't really know what I know, and in order to know this, I need a radical transformation. The idea of the education of grownups is indissociable from that of change, or even of metamorphosis or rebirth (to use an important concept with Emerson and Thoreau). It is such a transformation that is at work, according to Cavell, in the films that he studied in his book devoted to American comedy, *Pursuits of Happiness*, that also explains his entire interest in cinema, as if to bring into play a form of education for the characters and the spectators.[28]

By acknowledging that education does not cease after childhood—and that once grown up, we require our own education—one acknowledges that education is not only a question of knowledge but also concerns the "upbuilding" of a human being ("American Scholar," 1:65). To speak of the education of grownups is to make an exit from the theme of edification and moralism in order to enter a completely different zone, that of skepticism.

Emerson perceived well the moral nature of all teaching: to learn is to become able to take over, to be capable of carrying on (by himself). This solitude is inherent in all education—the problem is not in learning but in finding (or not) a voice in society. This is where we get the fantasies of radical exclusion and incomprehension that run through the writings of the second Wittgenstein and which, for Cavell, are inseparable from the idea of learning, of its skeptical dimension. This is also the origin of the theme—an obsessional one with Emerson—of isolation and the community (of isolation *in* the community). To wonder about education and normalcy is to suddenly ask oneself if what one has accepted thus far is a matter of course. It is necessary to learn to discover this by oneself. The question is then in managing by oneself, discovering it, and trusting sufficiently in oneself to do this. Trust in oneself and in one's own experience is thus indispensable in adult education:

> No conclusion is more foregone for me than that is human suffering, that is a continuation of a series, that is a painting, a sentence, a proof. I cannot decide what I take as a matter of course, any more that I can decide what interests me; I have to find out. What I took as a matter of

course (e.g. that that is a proof, that that is not serious painting) I may come to see differently (perhaps through further instruction or tips or experience). What I cannot now take as a matter of course I may come to; I may set it as my task. ("American Scholar," 1:65)

When it is no longer enough to say "that's how it is"—then I am forced to face up to my responsibilities, and I understand that all I consider as matter of course was wholly absorbed by me, conventional and conformist.

It is on this point that philosophy emerges as an educator of adults—at the moment when we understand that we are children, that we *don't know*. It is not so much a question—in this new definition of philosophy—of what is conventional, but rather of what is natural: "Underlying the tyranny of convention is the tyranny of nature."[29] Philosophy must reexamine a fact of nature: "that at an early point in life the normal body reaches its full strength and height" (125). Thus, philosophy must wonder about our necessity—a natural one—to be educated, to continue, in a way, to grow after the end of childhood:

Why do we take it that because we then must put away childish things, we must put away the prospect of growth and the memory of childhood? The anxiety in teaching, in serious communication, is that I myself require education. And for grownups this is not natural growth, but change. Conversion is a turning of our natural reactions; so it is symbolized as rebirth. (125)

The education of adults—in order for it to no longer be a question of natural growth—is then a change or mutation. Upon what grounds can such a change be based? Upon oneself, one's own constitution, and Cavell's reference is therefore no longer Wittgenstein, but Emerson. Self-reliance is an aversion to conformity, and it is therefore the calling into question of conventions—not as such, but because they are not thoughts by me, not *my* thoughts. Self-reliance is therefore at the base of adult education, which is a moral education since it is an education of oneself. It entails once again learning to ground oneself upon oneself and not upon others—and here we find what Cavell calls "Moral Perfectionism," which simultaneously defines self-reliance and self-education.

Hollywood comedy about remarriage, according to Cavell, stages this education of the adult. A particularly good example is the film *Bringing Up Baby* (Howard Hawks, 1943), analyzed by Cavell in *Pursuits of Happiness*, where the theme of education and the possibility of growing up after childhood is explicitly treated (for example, in the title itself). The French title of the film, *L'impossible monsieur Bébé* (The Impossible Mister Baby), in its absurdity also captures something of the content: the baby to be educated is apparently the leopard named Baby as well as the character played by Cary Grant, who has to deal with his body while going through a whole range of experiences (including being outcast from society, finding himself dressed in a negligee, and coming face-to-face with a ferocious leopard) alongside Susan (Katharine Hepburn). The result of this education is in the final moment of rediscovery when he acknowledges that he had never had so much fun in his life. He changed, not because he wanted to change or because someone else wanted him to change, but because he *let himself be changed* by this adventure. This bringing of perfectionism into play in his passive wish to change is a major discovery by Cavell concerning classical American cinema. Education of the adult would then be education of the self by the self, which inscribes Emerson in a perfectionist tradition that starts with Plato and continues with Wittgenstein and Michel Foucault,[30] rather than in the Pragmatic tradition that would call for us to actively seek out progress.

THE ORDINARY AND POLITICS

All of this has, for Cavell, political consequences that still go unnoticed. We know that the democratic influence of the philosophical appeal to the ordinary is an essential question for Emerson and Dewey. But for Cavell, the fact that Dewey jointly appeals to science gives a different tone to his appeal to the ordinary. Cavell supports this by citing the following passage of *Experience and Education* that is characteristic of Dewey: "Scientific method is the only authentic means at our command for getting at the significance of our everyday experiences of the world in which we live."[31] For Emerson, it is just the opposite (even if elsewhere he frequently expresses his admiration for the figure of the inventor);[32] access to the world is not given by science. This is the whole subject of his essay "Experience." One hardly sees how science could give us the elements of daily life such as he describes in "The American Scholar," evoking his attention to commonness: "What would we really know the meaning of? The meal in the firkin; the milk in the pan; the ballad in the street; the news of the boat; the glance of the eye; the form and the gait of the body;—show me the ultimate reason of these matters ... —and the world lies no longer a dull miscellany and lumber room, but has form and order" (1:67–68).

It is for this reason that the symptom of Pragmatism's ignorance of the ordinary is, for Cavell, its casualness regarding skepticism, or the idea that science constitutes a response to skepticism. Emerson's entire work is run through, at least after *Nature,* with the menace of skepticism. The refusal of skepticism is, conversely, a characteristic of Pragmatism: "In contrast, neither James nor Dewey seems to take the threat of skepticism seriously. . . . Pragmatism seems designed to refuse to take skepticism seriously, as it refuses—in Dewey's, if not always in James' case—to take metaphysical distinctions seriously."[33]

For Cavell, James's position is too cursory, and he notes that in his treatment of the "sick soul" James sees something in the concept of skepticism, but only as being part of a particular temperament and not as belonging to the human as such. Emerson's idea of the ordinary, on the contrary, only takes on meaning as an echo of the permanent and real risk of skepticism—of the loss or removal from the world, associated with a lack that renders speech, by definition, inadequate and ill-fated. It is this inadequacy of language that Emerson defines in "Self-Reliance" as being the conformism of his contemporaries, which leads, in "Experience," to the mourning of the initial experience of the world.

Emerson and Thoreau, through their attention to the ordinary, thus announce the philosophy of ordinary language—not because the ordinary, or "the low" ("Self-Reliance") would be a response to the problem of knowledge (which it would be in the cognitive problematic that Emerson wanted to surpass), but because the connection with the ordinary is another way of formulating the question of the relationship with the world, which is a question of mourning before it is a question of knowledge. Not that Emerson is not concerned with knowledge. But the beginning of knowledge is the separation of oneself from the world (as, Cavell said, the separation from the child in "Experience"), which is the only way to no longer see one's private interests as exclusive, the only way to begin again. This is the meaning of the play on words mourning/morning, as well as the idea of rebirth: "Emerson finds a work of what he understands as mourning to be the path to human objectivity with the world, to separating the world from ourselves, from our private interests of it."[34]

The call to the ordinary, the question of mourning, and the foundation of democracy are thus enunciated in Emerson in a singular manner, one that is insoluble in Pragmatism, especially in its connection to the common man and the idea of a metaphysics of commonality.[35] The appeal to the ordinary and commonality is in no way—for Emerson or Wittgenstein—a solution (even less a scientific solution) to the question of knowledge of the world. Commonness is never given. The low is always to be attained, in an inversion of the sublime. As a result, it is not sufficient to want to start from the ordinary, from the man in the street (a central theme in American cinema, such as with Capra) in order to attain it. Dewey's wish, in *Experience and Education,* to correct the child's speech through education contradicts the idea of the ordinary—such as Emerson saw it—as giving veritable attention to the speech of another or of oneself: "In Dewey's writing, the speech of others, whose ideas he wishes to correct, hardly appears. Before Emerson can say what is repellent in the thoughts or noises of the others, he has to discover or rediscover a language in which to say it" (219).

It is not a question, then, of philosophy correcting the legacy of European philosophy, nor of creating new categories, dualisms, and so forth. It is necessary to restore another meaning to these inherited words (such as "experience," "idea," "impression," "comprehension," "reason," "necessity," and "condition") to bring them back to the sphere of commonness—or, going back to Wittgenstein's expression of the metaphysics of the ground of the ordinary, to do something else in order to have a new language, since the words are inherited from Europe: "Emerson retains stretches of the vocabulary of philosophy but diverts it of its old claims to mastery."[36]

SELF-RELIANCE/SELF-KNOWLEDGE

To uncover for oneself a conversation deserving of this name, a context or tone that gives a real meaning to our words—such is the veritable finality of self-reliance. The democratic ideal becomes one of veritable conversation, where each person can find and make heard his or her voice.[37] This is what explains Cavell's interest in that particular type of community—

the couple—determined by a contract that gives standing to equal individuals, but where it remains to surmount the inequality of speech that is constitutive of this given equality, to invent a new language and to build a conversation. This is what makes the ideal couple—such as Cavell describes in *Pursuits of Happiness*—into a paradigm for society: the couples in Hollywood comedies of remarriage present their marriage as a place for making demands and for mutual education. The ideal of a veritable political conversation—another name for democracy—would be one of movement of speech where no one would be less significant, where each person could follow his thinking, his constitution.

Self-trust is thus not the umpteenth subjective foundation; it is reliance on our experience. But on what reliance is it founded? "The magnetism which all original action exerts is explained when we inquire the reason of self-trust. Who is the Trustee? What is the aboriginal Self on which a universal reliance may be grounded?" ("Self-Reliance," 2:37). There is not a self in whom to trust, or who is the initial foundation for self-reliance: "To talk of reliance, is a poor external way of speaking. Speak rather of that which relies, because it works and is" ("Self-Reliance," 2:40).

To speak about self-reliance is to refer to a reflexivity that is already too static in relation to what reliance really is (practicality). It is in displaying the practical (not cognitive or epistemological) dimension of trust in oneself that Emerson noted (in a characteristic about-face) that the expression "self-reliance" is poor and external, and that he proposes "that which relies." "Relies," being bizarrely used in the absolute, in a refusal of a thinking-over of the self, avoids the reflexivity belonging to definitions of the subject, of all illusion of a knowledge that would have the self look at itself in order to find something, a certainty or confidence. Self-reliance functions as pure practice, not as a subject or object of reliance. It is not any more active than passive, and its practicality ("it works and is") permits it to challenge the mythology of reflexivity and the mythology of agency. Self-reliance is not then trust in a given self, but simply in one's own experience.

Transcendentalism orders the self—contrary to skepticism, but also contrary to the theory of traditional knowledge—to trust in its experience. This apparently naive idea is at the center of Emerson's thinking because it states his conceptions of reliance and experience and radically calls into question the duality of activity and passivity—and this with the simple idea that practice is also a form of patience. To discover contact with the self is to discover the world through trust in experience. This entails (as in approaching film) the ability to trust in the experience of the object in order to find the right words for describing and expressing it. For Cavell, it is the viewing (repeated, and often collective or communal) of films that leads to trusting in one's own experience and acquiring, through this, an authority over it: "To subject these enterprises and their conjunction to our experiences of them is a conceptual as much as an experiential undertaking; it is our commitment to being guided by our experience but not dictated by it. I think of this as checking one's experience."[38] Beyond the labels of Transcendentalism and Pragmatism, it is indeed empiricism that is involved here: "I mean the rubric to capture the sense at the same time of consulting one's experience and of subjecting it to examination, and beyond these, of momentarily stopping, turning yourself away from whatever your preoccupation and turning your experience away from its expected, habitual track, to find itself, its own track" (12). It is on this point that the paradoxical yet crucial link between experience and trust is established. It is necessary to educate one's experience in order to trust in it: "The moral of this practice is to educate your experience sufficiently so that it is worthy of trust" (12).

We again note the ambiguity and the reversal of the Kantian legacy. It is necessary not to surpass experience by way of theory, but rather to run counter to what is—in traditional philosophy—the very movement of knowledge (which is also what leads to skepticism). It is somehow necessary to surpass theory by way of experience, to educate one's experience, and it is this movement that defines reliance in oneself (in one's experience), as well as the paradox of self-reliance: one cannot have experience (the education of experience) before having trust, and vice versa:

> The American inheritance of Kant is essential to making up Transcendentalism, and hence it goes into what makes Emerson Emerson and what makes Thoreau Thoreau. Encouraged by them, one learns that without this trust in one's experience, expressed as a willingness to find words for it, without thus taking an interest in it, one is without authority in one's own experience.[39]

This authority over one's own experience brings us closer to the idea—expressed and developed in *The Claim of Reason*—of acquiring a voice in the question of oneself. The Emersonian "know yourself" is not then yet another reformulation of self-knowledge, rather it is the first moment of the acceptance of the unknownness (we might say) of oneself, a prelude to trust in oneself. For Cavell, whether in *The Claim of Reason* or in the comedy of remarriage, this moment is indispensable in the acknowledgment of others and in my consent to society.

But how can this acceptance be made into a political principle? Skepticism, associated with self-reliance, teaches us the depth of our link with society, as well as the distancing of society, "so that it appears as an artifact."[40] The theory of social contract is educative in the strict sense previously defined. It allows me to have the experience of my attachment, of my agreement to society, in weighing the advantages therein: "It is hardly news to theorists of the social contract that in the overwhelming number of instances in which the actual questions of advantages has arisen, or will arise, I will, and ought to, decide against withdrawing consent" (25).

The question of my membership in society is like the question of the existence of the world, or of another person. In the same way, skepticism can appear to me as being devoid of meaning from the moment that daily life (or practice) takes me away from it. But this changes nothing of what Cavell calls "the truth of skepticism," of what this questioning can teach me. Whatever the motivation of the theorist of the contract—either to justify the idea that the moment has come for a dismantling of the artifact, or just the opposite, to forever exclude such a moment—the "significance of the writing lies in its imparting of political education."[41]

Self-knowledge then becomes a political question. The method of the social contract is the examination of myself—by calling into question my postulates—but the terms of this examination of the self are the terms that reveal to me that I am a member of the city. It is indeed a question of an education, not because it teaches something new, but because it teaches me the nature of my consent: "I learn that the finding and the forming of my knowledge of myself requires the finding and the forming of my knowledge of that membership (the depth of my own and the extent of those joined with me)."[42]

To know my membership would consist in surmounting the inherent skepticism at question in this membership and the grammatical impossibility, as it were, of this skepticism. If the fact of speaking in the name of others and accepting that others speak in my name is an integral part of political consent, then the mere withdrawal from the community (exile, internal or external) wouldn't amount, grammatically speaking, to the withdrawal of consent on which this community rests. On the contrary, the withdrawal of consent is part of the membership. It is exactly the problem of civil disobedience.

We encounter here the enunciation of the "I" and the "we," at once the foundation of knowledge and also of politics. But this enunciation, instead of being rationalist, as in many contemporary political theories, is skeptical: I no longer recognize society as my own; I separate myself from it. The "we" is no longer maintained together by our consent. Such a disagreement is not the dissolution of consent, but rather conflict over its content. And it is this internal conflict that defines democracy, as well as speech in democracy: if I cannot speak in the name of others, then I also do not speak in a private capacity; I am radically mute; I literally have nothing to say. Worse than being mute is being without a voice.

In this acceptance of speech, of self-expression and self-knowledge, politics defines the use of language. We are indeed—to use Emerson's phrasing—"victims of expression" ("Experience," 3:38): "Dissent is not the undoing of consent but a dispute about its content, a dispute within it over whether a present arrangement is faithful to it. The alternative to speaking for yourself politically is not speaking for yourself privately. The alternative is having nothing (political) to say."[43]

This is where we derive politics from the question of skepticism. My relationship with myself, for Cavell, is expressed by the statement "I don't know myself," and hence the necessity for an education through self-reliance. I, of course, do not know myself—this is the entire focus of Emerson's *Essays*. The question of self-knowledge has for its sole response (to which Cavell comes to in *The Claim of Reason*) Emersonian self-reliance: to want to know oneself is to refuse conformism. It is a practical response, not a theoretical one. The question is not knowing oneself as in being familiar with the world, but in wanting to say what one says in order to find the adequate expression of one's experience. The question of self-knowledge becomes the practical difficulty of having to hook thinking to the world, in particular to a social and political world, one of history. How does one come up with an adequate expression, with the possibility of closing the gap—that Kant and Emerson equally well described—between thinking and the world, between me and society? This is precisely the question of politics and agreement to society as it exists: "The sense of gap originates in an attempt, or a wish, to escape (to remain a 'stranger' to, 'alienated' from) those shared forms of life, to give up the responsibility of their maintenance."[44]

How does one resolve this question of responsibility in relation to something to which I want to be a stranger? This is where self-reliance intervenes, as a way of finding the right tone in this practical difficulty of entering into contact with the world (social and political), of finding one's voice in politics. Emerson's individualism thus precisely reverses liberal individualism, through its perfectionist dimension; it does not reclaim the individual nor the private sphere from the community, but instead wants to work toward making the individual and society, the private and public spheres, expressions of each other. Disagreement and making this demand form therefore a part of the democratic conversation, just as skepticism and mourning form part of our conversation with the world: "Whoso would be a man must be a nonconformist" ("Self-Reliance," 2:29).

This is what leads Cavell, in "What Is the Emersonian Event?" to reject the interpretation of Emerson's individualism that would lead to founding again the liberal order of society by grounding itself on self-reliance as a positive principle of activity. Cavell specifically attacks the reading of Kateb, who saw in self-reliance a radically individualistic principle, one at odds with society if it is considered in too wide a sense, in which the very idea of association disrupts reliance on oneself "when association moves out of a small circle of friends and includes a number of people, many of them strangers."[45] Cavell disputes the idea of a society that would thus be ideally reduced to a small circle of friends (see "Circles," 2:177–90)—a reduced community that would contrast with society. In order to understand all of the political dimensions of self-reliance, it would instead be necessary to imagine how trust moves from circle to circle, from me to others, to my close relations, and to my society, creating not rival communities or gatherings of local selfishness, conspiracies, and base actions, but what Cavell calls a "city of words" that gathers together an invisible community of equals—not partners, but rather strangers to each other.[46]

Cavell thus imagines that this community is that of Emerson's readers: "People keep telling me that there cannot be millions of people who actually understand Emerson. How do they know?" Which community? Not one of little elitist circles (a frequent misinterpretation of perfectionism)[47]—which easily leads to the reading of violent passages by Emerson such as those in "Self-Reliance" that he devotes to philanthropy ("Are they *my* poor? I tell thee, thou foolish philanthropist, that I grudge the dollar, the dime, the cent I give to such men as do not belong to me and to whom I do not belong" ["Self-Reliance," 2:30–31, Emerson's emphasis])—but rather a community of concentric circles whose occupants are without an ascribable number: "No reader of Emerson is a priori closer to him than any other, and no one is closer to him than a true reader (for them, for what he calls his poor, this writer declares that he shuns mother and father, sister and brother)."[48] This community of Emerson's readers (a discrete or even invisible group) can thus represent or express the democratic aspiration, as a movement of speech between equal strangers.

NOTES

1. See Sandra Laugier, ed., "Ralph Waldo Emerson: L'autorité du scepticisme," special issue, *Revue Française d'Etudes Américaines,* no. 91 (2002). My essay here continues this first study, notably developing the conclusion (126–28).

2. See the excellent introduction by editors F. Brunet and A. Wicke in *L'œuvre en prose d'Emerson* (Paris: Armand Colin, 2003).

3. Stanley Cavell, *Conditions Handsome and Unhandsome* (Chicago: University of Chicago Press, 1990), 16.

4. Ibid., 16–17.

5. Stanley Cavell, *Emerson's Transcendental Etudes* (Stanford, Calif.: Stanford University Press, 2003), 216.

6. Stanley Cavell, *Must We Mean What We Say?* (Cambridge: Cambridge University Press, 1969).

7. Stanley Cavell, *A Pitch of Philosophy* (Chicago: University of Chicago Press, 1994), 7.

8. Ibid., 9.

9. Ibid., 10–11.

10. Stanley Cavell, *The Claim of Reason* (New York: Oxford University Press, 1979), 25.

11. Ibid., 27.

12. Cavell, *Emerson's Transcendental Etudes,* 216.

13. I refer here—for yet a further nuanced view of the debate, and notably for the originality of James' position—to Mathias Girel's excellent studies. See Mathias Girel, "Héritages philosophiques d'Emerson I," in *L'œuvre en prose de R. W. Emerson,* ed. Brunet and Wicke. See also Vincent Colapietro, "The Question of Voice and the Limits of Pragmatism: Emerson, Dewey, and Cavell," *Metaphilosophy* 35, no. 1–2 (January 2004): 178.

14. See John Dewey, "Emerson—the Philosopher of Democracy," in *The Middle Works,* vol. 3 (Carbondale: Southern Illinois University Press, 1977).

15. Cavell, *Conditions Handsome and Unhandsome,* 16.

16. See Sacvan Bercovitch, *The Rites of Assent* (New York : Routledge, 1993).

17. Ralph Waldo Emerson, *Nature,* in *The Collected Works of Ralph Waldo Emerson,* ed. Alfred R. Ferguson, Robert E. Spiller, et al., 8 vols. to date (Cambridge: Harvard University Press, Belknap Press, 1971–2010), 1:7. Subsequent quotations from Emerson's writing are from this source and are cited parenthetically in text by volume and page numbers. Citations may include essay title if the essay from which a quotation is taken is not clear from the text.

18. Cavell, *Emerson's Transcendental Etudes,* 190.

19. John Dewey, "The Development of American Pragmatism" (1931), in *Philosophy and Civilization* (New York: Capricorn Books, 1963), 34–35.

20. See Cavell, *Must We Mean What We Say?* See also Sandra Laugier, *Du réel à l'ordinaire* (Paris: Vrin, 1999).

21. Cavell, *Emerson's Transcendental Etudes,* 218.

22. Ibid., 222.

23. See Laugier, *Ralph Waldo Emerson;* and Stanley Cavell, *This New Yet Unapproachable America* (Albuquerque: Living Batch Press, 1989).

24. Cavell, *Emerson's Transcendental Etudes,* 222.

25. On this point, see the remarkable analysis by Michel Imbert, "Self-Reliance ou l'infini en personne," in Brunet and Wicke, *L'œuvre en prose d'Emerson.*

26. On this point, see Cavell's essay "Emerson's Constitutional Amending," in *Emerson's Transcendental Etudes.*

27. George Kateb, *Emerson and Self-Reliance* (Thousand Oaks, Calif.: Sage Publications, 1995).

28. Stanley Cavell, *Pursuits of Happiness* (Cambridge, Mass.: Harvard University Press, 1981).

29. Cavell, *The Claim of Reason,* 122–23.

30. In the tradition of the "Exercices spirituels" ("Spiritual exercises") as defined by Pierre Hadot in *Exercices spirituals et philosophie antique* (Paris: Etudes augustiniennes, 1981); *Philosophy as a Way of Life* (Oxford, England: Blackwell,

1995); and *Qu'est-ce que la philosophie antique?* (Paris: Folio, Gallimard, 2000). See also A. I. Davidson, "Spiritual Exercises and Ancient Philosophy: An Introduction to Pierre Hadot," *Critical Inquiry* 16, no. 3 (1990): 475–82.

31. John Dewey, *Experience and Education,* in vol. 13 (1938–39) of *The Later Works* (Carbondale: Southern Illinois University Press, 1984), 59.

32. François Brunet, "Emerson et la figure de l'inventeur," in Laugier, "Ralph Waldo Emerson."

33. Cavell, *Emerson's Transcendental Etudes,* 221.

34. Ibid., 217.

35. Ibid., 213.

36. Ibid., 219.

37. For a more political approach to this project, see Sandra Laugier, *Faut-il encore écouter les intellectuels?* (Paris: Baynard, 2003). See also Sandra Laugier, *Une autre pensée politique américaine: La démocratie radicale d'Emerson à Cavell* (Paris: Michel Houdiard Editeur, 2004).

38. Cavell, *Pursuits of Happiness,* 10.

39. Ibid., 12.

40. Cavell, *The Claim of Reason,* 25.

41. Ibid., 125.

42. Ibid.

43. Ibid., 28.

44. Ibid., 109.

45. Kateb, quoted in Cavell, *Emerson's Transcendental Etudes,* 188.

46. Stanley Cavell, *Cities of Words: Pedagogical Letters on a Register of the Moral Life* (Cambridge, Mass.: Harvard University Press, Belknap Press, 2004).

47. See Cavell, *Conditions Handsome and Unhandsome.*

48. Cavell, *Emerson's Transcendental Etudes,* 189.

III.
RETHINKING PHILOSOPHY

GREGG LAMBERT

8. Emerson, or *Man Thinking*

> Now that we are here, we will put our own interpretation
> on things, and our own things for interpretation.
> —RALPH WALDO EMERSON

EMERSON AND CAVELL

In his recent meditation on the affinities between Nietzsche and Emerson—"hence their endless differences"—Stanley Cavell addresses what could be called the ethical attitude toward the moment of silence in each thinker. What Nietzsche and Emerson share in common, according to Cavell, is a certain aversion toward chatter that marks the habit of thinking in their respective cultures. This aversion can be directly related to the untimely character of each thinker; as Nietzsche writes in *The Gay Science*, "the extraordinary furtherer of man . . . has always found himself, and *had* to find himself, in contradiction to his today."[1] Of course, it is this spirit of aversion that also defines each philosopher's general stance toward their contemporaries (toward their countrymen, in particular), and especially toward the higher institutions of learning, the profession of scholars who occupy these institutions, and, most importantly, the same scholars who "breed" (using Nietzsche's term) the younger generation of scholars to become "students of Nature" (Emerson). It is this aversion, for example, that becomes the hallmark of each philosopher's path as a *free spirit, a wanderer,* or *a man about town,* in other words, as one who keeps a certain distance from such institutions.

But let me immediately underscore, following Cavell's argument, that both the untimely character that defines each thinker's attitude toward "his today" as well as Emerson's "chagrin" for the habit that passes for thinking in the professions of teaching and scholarship must be understood in terms of what each will define as the proper philosophical response to the event of silence, that is, to the essence of philosophy *(logos).*[2] As Cavell highlights, we can bear witness to this response in the opening line to the preface of what became the second volume of *Human, All Too Human:* "'One should speak only where one must not be silent. . . . Everything else is chatter' *(Geschwatz;* he also sarcastically calls it '*Literatur*')."[3] We can hear this silence as well in the following passage from Emerson's "Literary Ethics": "The scholar may, and does, lose himself in schools, in words, and become a pedant; but when he comprehends his duties, he above all men is a realist, and converses with things" (1:100). Here, pedantry and discourse (chatter) are set in opposition to realistic conversation, to communing directly with things. Two kinds of speech are distinguished and set apart: "words" (or rather, "mere words") and "learning" (or rather, "mere learning"—i.e., pedantry), as opposed to true conversation and a spirit of realism (a conversation with things and not words), which Emerson invokes as the moral duty of the scholar (what Cavell calls his invocation to "moral perfectionism"). Acceding to this duty requires discipline, however, which is precisely a certain disciplining of the mind to remain in silence before things—and this would necessarily entail an active silencing of words and of previous learning! Here, again, we come upon the connection between silence and aversion, or the untimely character of the free thinker, since in order to silence the endless chatter and the din of mere thinking that echo in the courts of knowledge today, one must first learn how to keep one's distance, to remain outside, which, topologically speaking, may be another way of understanding the future from which each thinker speaks.

As for Nietzsche, of course, he is more direct, less polite, in voicing his contempt for the thinkers and scholars of his day, especially for his German contemporaries. In *Thus Spoke Zarathustra,* in the section "Of Scholars," the figure of the outside is directly evoked, as Zarathustra says, "For this is the truth: I have left the house of scholars and slammed the door behind me."[4] How does Nietzsche describe scholars? He describes them with the attribute of "dust": as sitting in dusty rooms, "cracking knowledge like cracking nuts," as mills that grind golden corn in order to make white dust of it, as themselves being filled with so much dust that when you get hold of them "they involuntarily raise a dust like sacks of flour" (147). Thus, in addition to the parallel with the passage above by Emerson in which dust could also be composed of words and old sayings, there is also a reference to things that are outside in Nietzsche's commentary as well: to corn, the "golden joy of summer fields"; to the burning sun upon the steps outside. According to Zarathustra, it is precisely these *things* that scholars grind into dust and that fills them so that their bodies become like sacks of flour. And even when they do happen to venture outside, Zarathustra complains, they still prefer the shade rather than to stroll in the summer fields and the sunlight, and it is in the shade that they sit and become pure spectators who "stare at thoughts that others have thought" (147).

As a counterpoint to this habit of thinking, we find the proclamation that stands as the epigraph of this essay: "Now that we are here, we will put our own interpretation on things, and our own things for interpretation." In the final meditation that concludes *Philosophy the Day after Tomorrow*, "The World as Things," Cavell takes up the question of interpretation by comparing it to the philosophical activity of collecting, that is, to the concept of philosophical writing. In a certain sense, all philosophical activity can be understood as a kind of collecting, and philosophical systems are cabinets where philosophers put words and things. The manner in which things are placed together in each respective cabinet constitutes a world, which is equivalent to the philosophical vision, or "system of representation." Cavell ends his meditation on this activity with two questions followed by a statement: "Why do we put things together as we do? Why do we put ourselves together with just these things to make a world? To put things together differently, so that they quicken the heart, would demand their recollecting" (280).

At the same time, "[philosophy] leaves everything as it is."[5] Cavell observes that this statement can be interpreted to underscore a conservative spirit that is characteristic of the philosophical tradition, a spirit that is also famously criticized in the proclamation by Marx and Engels: "Our task is not to understand the world (i.e., to leave everything as it is), but to change it (i.e., to put things together differently, or to put things right)." However, Cavell immediately qualifies his interpretation of this statement by saying that "one is left with having to put this together with the radical destruction of the philosophical tradition that his writing undertakes."[6] Here, Cavell is underscoring a fundamental trait that unites the thinkers that he constantly refers to throughout his entire philosophical career, who constitute a kind of *gang of four* in Cavell's own philosophical cabinet: Emerson-Nietzsche-Heidegger-Wittgenstein. Each of these philosophers, in very different manners and using different means, sought to effect a radical destruction of the philosophical tradition they took up; in other words, it was precisely through their manner of putting things together differently that they sought to "leave everything as it is." The last phrase must be understood as the product of both the difference and repetition that these philosophies enact through their writings, and particularly, as Cavell has discerned, by the manner in which they write.

But what does silence—since I have introduced it as the subject of my essay—have to do with the occurrence of difference and repetition in these philosophies? In fact, everything! Silence is the goal of their philosophizing activity; it is the objective of their interpretations; it is the condition of their habit of putting things together differently. But here, we must not understand silence as a theme (a representation) that can be used to unite these philosophical systems around a central idea (an image), in such a way that it would be of any use to compare and contrast the way in which silence appears in their respective writings, in this or that passage by Emerson, Nietzsche, Heidegger, or Wittgenstein. Rather, silence must be understood to be without image, which to say that it is equal to an action that determines their philosophical activity, the act of thinking itself.

At the risk of contradicting myself and turning silence back into a theme for comparison and contrast, something that academic philosophers often mistake for actually "doing philosophy," I wish to cite a passage from a discarded draft of *Ecce Homo*, from the third section, "Why I Write Such Good Books":

> Silence is as much of an instinct as is garrulity with our dear philosophers. I am *brief*; my readers themselves must become long and comprehensive in order to bring up and together all that I have thought, and thought deep down.

On the other hand, there are prerequisites for "understanding" here, which very few can satisfy: One must be able to see a problem in its proper place—that is, in the context of the other problems that *belong with it;* and for this one must have at one's fingertips the topography of various nooks and the difficult areas of whole sciences and above all of philosophy.

Finally, I speak only of what I have lived through, not merely of what I have thought through: the opposition of thinking and life is lacking in my case. My "theory" grows from my "practice."[7]

In this passage we have a confirmation of Cavell's comparison between philosophical activity with collecting and the philosophical system as a kind of cabinet for placing things. In Nietzsche's case, however, the metaphor is reversed: due to the silence that defines Nietzsche's instinct for philosophizing, the incredible brevity that marks his style, it falls to his readers to become "long and comprehensive" enough to understand him and to already have cabinets that include the difficult areas of whole sciences and all of philosophy. This is defined in the quote above as one of the "prerequisites" for understanding a single word of his philosophy, the other prerequisite being that the opposition of theory and practice is completely lacking, and thus he only speaks of things that he has actually lived through and not merely thought through. This last can be seen as a repetition of the statement cited earlier: "One should speak only where one must not be silent." In all three senses silence is the condition of what Nietzsche earlier describes as "the most *abbreviated* language ever spoken by a philosopher," which is the source of the difficulty of his writings.[8] In each sense, silence is not offered as an image, but rather is equal to the act of thinking for which theory cannot be divorced from actual practice. In some sense, Nietzsche's sense of theory being equal to practice can also be found in the Emersonian maxims: "Thinking is the function. Living is the functionary" ("The American Scholar," 1:66).

It is crucial to observe that Nietzsche determines the place of this silence in direct relationship to the "reader" of his writings, who, as we already know, is the entire motivation for writing *Ecce Homo* and is not to be found among his German contemporaries, given the posthumous and "untimely" nature of his philosophy. In fact, it is Heidegger who will emerge a generation later to claim the position of being Nietzsche's only reader up to that moment, historically, and sets out in the four volumes that compose his work on Nietzsche's entire philosophical trajectory to demonstrate his ability "to elucidate the fundamental unity in which Nietzsche unfolds the guiding questions of Western thought and responds to it."[9] (Given how other readers of Nietzsche's philosophy during the same period were interpreting his works, we see this claim as somewhat heroic, albeit hopelessly abstruse.)

Nevertheless, this returns us to the thematic of philosophical education, to the institution of knowledge, and to the untimely nature of philosophy with which we began on the affinities between Nietzsche and Emerson around the subject I have defined as outside thought, which is an extremely abbreviated manner of addressing the function of silence from three distinct perspectives. Formally, the thematic of outside thought concerns the question of style, the manner of writing, or, as in the passage by Nietzsche cited earlier, it concerns what philosophers actually *do* with silence, in which there is no opposition between theory and practice. Topologically, the outside has to do with the position from which the philosophy speaks to us, with the "untimely" character of the philosopher's stance, even aversion, toward the present moment, one of being in "contradiction to his today." Although Nietzsche is the philosopher who is most associated with this position, it is no less present in the others, particularly in the case of Emerson whose aversion and "chagrin" before his contemporaries were noted in the beginning of this essay. As for Wittgenstein, Cavell makes note of the accusations made by his contemporaries that he has "destroyed everything of interest and importance," and his reply that if this were indeed true, "then whatever he has destroyed cannot have been of genuine interest—it was all a house of cards."[10] Of course, this taste for destruction could be extended to Heidegger, in a different manner, as well as his own aversion to the technological thinking of his day. Moreover, in each case, if a philosopher is aware that what he is actually doing under the banner of philosophy is destined to be misunderstood—another famous complaint of Nietzsche's—and would fall on deaf ears for the most part, then this silence becomes the condition of having to speak, given that all speaking is already made pointless by the same condition of silence. Cavell writes, "If we take this sense [of pointlessness as a characteristic threat or mood] against the background of Wittgenstein's picturing speech—talking—as the distinctive life form of humankind, then human existence, with its gift of language, chronically presents itself as a melancholy, disappointing business." Elsewhere he says: "Thinking as melancholy reproduction characterizes Hamlet."[11]

On a second level, the topological meaning of the outside has to do with the foundational myth of philosophy itself revealing the truth of things in the light of day. Of course, in some sense this metaphor (if it is indeed a metaphor) can be understood as very old, and deeply Platonic, and one only has to recall the topology of the outside and of things that are shown in the light of the sun (in their truth) from the allegory of the cave. However, what makes this figure particularly modern in the philosophies of Nietzsche—but in Emerson as well—is their emphasis on the future and the character of repetition that defines the outside topologically in each philosophy. Of course, the problem of repetition and of the future is clearly announced in Nietzsche's doctrine of Eternal Recurrence. In Emerson, we know, the problem of repetition occurs in the constant polemic against the cultural and intellectual habits of "mere thinking," against the buzz of words and the clouds of antiquated ideas from the Continent that cover over the discovery of distinctly new American nature. Again, as Cavell has argued, this has to do with silence and with ordinary language. Things are not revealed through representation (via Ideas, nor even clear and distinct perception), but rather may appear only in what Emerson defines as a "conversation with things" ("Literary Ethics," 1:106) that is said to take place outside words and knowledge, a conversation that takes place in the future, or on the bridge to the future, one whose main subject is that of silence itself. Thus, to solicit the line that Cavell cites from Nietzsche, the outside thought would be the hallmark of a man of "tomorrow, or the day after tomorrow."[12] Here, we can discern the transfiguration that Nietzsche has effected on the Platonic myth in the very image of the sun. In the Platonic system, the sun is a static symbol, a hypogram or metaphor. We must imagine it always to appear at its zenith and thus to remain as unchanging and eternal as an Idea without recurrence. In Nietzsche's system, however, the sun can only be understood to recur each day, specifically at dawn, and thus every sun appears as an image of its eternal recurrence. It is in this manner that we might understand the notion that is present in Nietzsche, and not in Plato, of a new sun and of a new dawn, that is, of a future. As Cavell asks: "To what end? Take *Morgen* in its sense of morning, as well as of tomorrow, and we may discern the idea of an after-, or over-, or super-morning"

(118). One can find Cavell's observation confirmed in the following passage by Emerson (again, from the address on "Literary Ethics"):

> Whilst I read the poets, I think that nothing new can be said about
> morning and evening. But when I see the daybreak, I am not reminded
> of these Homeric, or Shakespearian, or Miltonic, or Chaucerian pic-
> tures. No; but I feel perhaps the pain of an alien world; a world not yet
> subdued by the thought; or, I am cheered by the moist, warm, glitter-
> ing, budding, melodious hour, that takes down the narrow walls of
> my soul, and extends its life and pulsation to the very horizon. *That* is
> morning, to cease for a bright hour to be a prisoner of this sickly body,
> and to become as large as nature. (1:106, Emerson's emphasis)

Finally, morally, what I am calling "outside thought" (as a very abbreviated manner of talking about the function of silence in philosophy,
or, at least, in these philosophies) has to do with the scene of instruction and education, or rather, with the process of true learning, which
is the goal of all philosophical activity and is opposed, as we saw in the
cases of Nietzsche and Emerson, to mere knowledge and to how learning is instituted in schools. Again, it is important to note in the passage
cited earlier that Nietzsche determines silence in a pedagogical relation
to his reader, calling the proper reception of this silence a "prerequisite"
to understanding his philosophy. We recall that *Ecce Homo* is a book that
purports to "teach" how to understand Nietzsche and contains as its
curriculum the entire body of his writings from "Birth of Tragedy" to
Thus Spoke Zarathustra. The fact that a reader has replaced the student
in this pedagogical form only again evokes the untimely character of
Nietzsche's situation and the fact that there are no "students" living in
his own time. This is stated quite clearly in the second paragraph of the
preface: "I only need to speak with one of the 'educated' who come to the
upper Upper Engadine for the summer, and I am convinced that I do *not*
live."[13] We might also recall that Zarathustra was primarily defined as a
teacher; at least, this is what his ring of animals claimed—"you are the
teacher of the eternal recurrence, that is now *your* destiny!" And yet, corresponding to the function of silence, it is important to remind ourselves
that Zarathustra did not confirm this claim, but himself remained silent,
or rather, silently conversed with his own soul, so much that the serpent
and the eagle, Zarathustra's animals, stopped talking themselves and "re-

spected the great Stillness around him and withdrew discretely."[14] Here, it is the teacher who falls silent, or who converses silently with his own soul, while his students chatter on, until the students themselves perceive something in this silence itself that they *learn to respect,* which is a moral understanding of Zarathustra's silence that leads directly to action.

They respected the silence and they withdrew, echoing a moral lesson that Cavell draws from a similar pedagogical scene in Wittgenstein, when he writes: "What I think of as the moral of recurrent silence is to say at some point the pupil must go on—and want to go on—alone. Another way is to say that the teacher has to know both when, even how, to fall silent and when and how to break her silence."[15] Here, silence and speaking are not opposed to one another as two different states, just as opposition of theory and practice is said to be absent in Nietzsche's earlier statement, or the opposition of thinking and living in Emerson as well. One must presume one is already speaking in order to know when, even how, to fall silent; and, of course, silence can also be a form of speaking, as in the above example. Therefore, the distinction between discourse (chatter) and true conversation with things with which we began is only a secondary appearance of this more primary distinction between two manners of speaking and two forms of silence. The silencing of repetition in language (discourse) becomes a sign of knowing when, even how, to remain silent in order to converse directly with things, that is to say, the sign of difference in repetition, to say things differently. If there is a moral sense attached to this distinction, it is in the discernment of the value of saying anything at all. According to Cavell, who learns a great deal from Emerson in this regard, the primary moral lesson of a philosophical education concludes when this knowledge of silence becomes identical to the act of Man Thinking.

EMERSON AND DELEUZE

Having characterized the different meanings of silence (the formal, the topological, the moral) that belong to this tradition of philosophy that I have defined by the thematic of outside thought, I would now add another philosopher to this tradition. This thematic, as well as many of the characteristics described earlier, is also prevalent in the philosophy of Gilles Deleuze. In effect, I am adding one more member to Cavell's gang of four (Emerson-Nietzsche-Heidegger-Wittgenstein) by bringing Deleuze's philosophy of difference and repetition into conversation with Emerson. I have already addressed the affinities between Nietzsche and Emerson, and these are well known, but I would argue that the affinity between Emerson and Deleuze can most clearly be shown in one chapter from Deleuze's *Difference and Repetition*, "The Image of Thought."[16] Here Deleuze takes up in a systematic manner the problem of repetition in thinking, and I will employ the balance of my commentary on reading this argument in light of some affinities, and differences, with Emerson's figure of Man Thinking. Of course, any relationship between these two thinkers can only be indirect, which is to say, through Nietzsche, who functions as a bridge between these two philosophers. Nietzsche is the only one of this group who avows a direct encounter with Emerson, particularly during the period of his youth when Emerson's writings cheered him up even in the blackest periods. According to the chronological index given in *Ecce Homo*, the period of Nietzsche's youth, when he was most influenced by Emerson, was during the time of *Human, All Too Human: A Book for Free Spirits*. Cavell appears to confirm this, as most of his comparisons between Nietzsche and Emerson stem from this volume. And yet, this might be too nitpicky. If we were to regard this tradition of philosophy that is remarked by the characteristics of outside thought as a river, according to the most common metaphor, then Emerson would simply be determined as that point in the river that is farthest upstream. Just as it makes little sense to examine the water downstream to determine how many parts originate from a point closest to the source, or which parts enter the river from points farther down, it would make just as little sense to try and measure how much of Nietzsche's influence on the philosophy of Deleuze would contain a little Emerson in it as well. I will simply proceed with the answer "some," for the sense of this metaphor gives us to understand that all parts of the river must flow together at some point.

According to the common image of thought and speech, silence precedes words and lies at the condition of the thinking that comes to replenish it with words and representations. However, this must be understood as an inversion, a reverse-image or, properly speaking, a distortion of silence, since silence only comes at the end when all the words have been exhausted and silence emerges for the first time as the condition of saying something new. Technically speaking, there is a fundamental relation here between what we are describing and Heidegger's later meditations on poetry and sayings, but we should not be precipitous in drawing this parallel too strictly (or neatly) or in applying it to the image of silence in Emerson or Deleuze (or even Wittgenstein for that matter), which would run the risk of confusing these different images of silence altogether and losing the manner in which each thinker chooses to approach this problem and, consequently, of making no sense at all. As Deleuze chooses to pose this problem, how does one speak of an outside thought without already giving it an image? How does one imagine thought without image? Here, one can immediately see the recourse to the temporal reference to the future, to an image of thought that is beyond the present, as a manner of solving this problem.

But this introduces a new problem, the problem of repetition itself, or as Deleuze says, "In-Itself." If all speaking is repetition, in some sense, and is helpless to step outside this vicious circle of saying and the said, then how does one speak without an image, or rather, how does one truly begin? The answer is both simple and tortuous: one can say something new only by means of repetition itself, or rather, by a certain manner of repeating. As Deleuze writes in another context, "It is precisely because repetition has made us ill that only repetition can heal us." Therefore, in the very opening of his reflections on this problem, Deleuze comes to the conclusion that "there is no true beginning in philosophy, or rather that the true philosophical beginning, Difference, is in-itself already Repetition."[17]

> For if it is a question of rediscovering at the end what was there in the beginning, if it is a question of recognizing, or bringing to light or into the conceptual or the explicit, what was simply known implicitly without concepts—whatever the complexity of this process, whatever the differences in the procedures of this or that author,—the fact remains that all this is still too simple, and that this circle is truly not tortuous enough. The circle image would reveal instead that philosophy is truly powerless to begin, or authentically to repeat. (129)

Emerson makes a similar claim in the following passage concerning the circular web of nature, mind, and spirit:

> The first in time and the first in importance of the influences upon the mind is that of nature. Every day, the sun; and, after sunset, the night and her stars. Ever the winds blow; ever the grass grows. Every day,

men and women, conversing, beholding and beholden. The scholar must needs stand wistful and admiring before this great spectacle. He must settle its value in his mind. What is nature to him? There is never a beginning, there is never an end to the inexplicable continuity of this web of God, but always circular power returning into itself. Therein it resembles his own spirit, whose beginning, whose ending he can never find—so entire, so boundless. ("American Scholar," 1:54)

In his famous lecture on "The American Scholar," Emerson poses the question of thought without image in the figure of Man Thinking. In a very definite sense, this question runs parallel to the one posed by Deleuze: how to begin? How does one truly begin to think without already proposing a prephilosophical image of thought, or a common sense? According to Emerson's initial allegory of the state of society as Man divided into men, and men into things, the prephilosophical image of thought can be understood as all the manners in which men are reduced to the state of being thinking-things—the delegated intel-lectual or professor, the parrot of other men's words, the bookworm, the restorer of readings, the emendator, the bibliomaniacs of all de-grees are all prephilosophical images, or what Deleuze and Guattari would call "conceptual personae."[18] Moreover, as a faculty, thinking for Emerson cannot be possessed by any individual function or role; even the thinker-man does not represent Man Thinking. If we some-how managed to distill all the different images together once again as a whole, we could never achieve an original image of thought prior to its dissemination and distribution into various functions. "Unfortunately," Emerson writes, "this original unit, this fountain of power, has been so distributed to multitudes, has been so minutely subdivided and peddled out, that it is spilled into drops, and cannot be gathered" ("American Scholar," 1:53). For Emerson, as for Deleuze, the original faculty of Man Thinking cannot be captured by any model of recognition and cannot be submitted to any image that exists or is already reduced to a func-tion. This is because, particularly for Emerson, it is nature itself. Would nature in Emerson be what Deleuze defines as the very "Being of the Sensible,"[19] which functions as a sign and not as an object of recogni-tion? Here, I think, Emerson and Deleuze are very close, even though this closeness is not one of simple comparison or resemblance, since this would again invoke a model of recognition that both seem to renounce.

In order to test this proximity, therefore, we must ask how nature appears in Emerson, as a sign or as an object of common sense?

This leads us to ask in what way is the faculty of thinking common to Man? Here, "common" refers to an object that can also be grasped by the other faculties, an event that underlines the model of recognition; what is grasped by one sense is recognized by another, and then by the next, and so forth. As Deleuze defines this model, "Recognition may be defined by the harmonious exercise of all the faculties on the supposed same object: the same object may be seen, touched, remembered, imagined or conceived."[20] Here, I come back to the question of silence. Does the particular silence we have been speaking of already have an image that can be recognized by the other senses? As I said earlier, there are actually two silences. One is a silence that already functions as an object of common sense, a silence for which the word is simply lacking, or which would simply be replenished or interrupted by the next note. Is the other silence, the "being of the sensible," a sign? The principle that Deleuze gives for how common sense functions under the conditions of this sign is the following: "Common Sense is only there in order to limit the specific contribution of sensibility to the conditions of joint labor: it thereby enters into a discordant play, its organs become metaphysical" (140). According to Deleuze, it is precisely in this event that "sensibility is raised to the level of a transcendental exercise" (140).

It seems that I am hypothesizing that what Deleuze calls the "being of the sensible" is identical with Emerson's nature. This is merely a hypothesis and really doesn't do much work on its own; however, it may give us a hint with regard to the function of sensibility in both philosophies. What I am really interested in is what happens when sensibility is given a transcendental exercise. This statement bears an uncanny resonance with Emerson's description of thinking, and one only has to replace the word "sensibility" with the word "nature" in order to bring this resonance into tune. It is true that Emerson and Deleuze do make the same claim concerning the condition of thought: "the condition [of sensibility, of thought] must be a condition of real experience, and not of possible experience. It forms an intrinsic genesis and not an extrinsic conditioning."[21] Or, as Emerson exclaims, "'every object rightly seen, unlocks a new faculty of the soul'" (*Nature*, 1:23). This maxim forms the basis of Emerson's principle of self-trust, which can be translated as placing more confidence in one's own real experience than in the possible experience expressed by others.[22] "That which was unconscious truth, becomes, when interpreted and defined in an object, a part of the domain of knowledge,—a new weapon in the magazine of power" (*Nature*, 1:23). And yet, this self, or intellectual power, that the maxim refers to is defined by its infinitude and, most of all, by its impersonality: "When he has seen, that it is not his, nor any man's, but that it is the soul which made the world." ("Literary Ethics," 1:101). By the very fact that this impersonal soul is still "accessible to him" (the scholar, or the thinker) (1:101), this imparts the spirit of confidence that gives the sensibility belonging to real experience a transcendental expression of this impersonal power. Only in this manner and with this knowledge (that it is not his), Emerson writes, "He will then see, that he, as its minister, may rightfully hold all things subordinate and answerable to it" (1:101). It is this very self-same spirit of confidence that allows Emerson to declare, "Now that we are here, we will put our own interpretation on things, and, moreover, our own things for interpretation" (1:102).

These are brave words, of course, and one might wonder who has had the courage to act on them. (Certainly not the scholars of our day, for the most part, any more than this was true of Emerson's or Nietzsche's time either.) And yet, rather than understanding the kind of action this would require as a power to intervene directly into the state of things, either to transform them or bend them toward one's own purpose or will, Emerson again alludes to a certain state of silence and to the impersonal power of nature itself as the only agency of such action. Here, nature only appears as a last resource when all other resources are exhausted; it is thus presented as a moment of passive synthesis, in which one finds a limit of the sensible in what is sensed.

> When the artist has exhausted his materials, when the fancy no longer paints, when thoughts are no longer apprehended, and books are a weariness,—he always has the resource *to live*.... Does he lack the organ or medium to impart his truths? He can still fall back on this elemental force of living them. This is a total act. Thinking is a partial act. ("American Scholar," 1:61; Emerson's emphasis)

In this last description of what Emerson calls the "great soul" (1:61), we see another meaning of silence, which is that of action itself. If action lacks an image, having neither organ nor medium, this is because it has become equal to itself. Action is its own medium; in other words, it is its own expressed. Thus, there is a particular silence that belongs to all real action that cannot be expressed by another faculty. One needs no words to express its meaning, no concept to comprehend its sense, that is, outside the meaning that it gives itself by acting and by the sign of its action. This is what Deleuze calls an "event."

I can find no better example of this event, when "sensibility is raised to the level of a transcendental exercise," than in the act of learning, which Emerson constantly refers to as the true cause of all thinking. Is not the condition of true learning "real experience," which must have the form of "an intrinsic genesis and not an extrinsic conditioning"? Can one actually learn anything from the possible experience related by others? This might be one way of understanding why the problem of repetition is inherent to the condition of true knowledge; in the process of learning, there is an event that issues from an unconscious source that first causes us to think. This event becomes a sign through which sensibility is given a transcendental function, which enters into a "discordant accord" (Deleuze) with all possible experience heretofore—and precisely because one doesn't yet know what this sign might yet signify or what this event would mean. How does one come to learn what love is, for example, except by taking the sensible being of the beloved as the very sign of love and raising one's own experience to the level of a transcendental exercise in which there is no knowledge of love except what this sign expresses? This may account for the infinity and the impersonality of all the possible experiences of love recounted by the poets, all of which lack real experience, which is to say, the intensity that only belongs to the unconscious soul of the lover. Nevertheless, it is true that one's own experience still retains the qualities of infinity and impersonality, but the difference lies in the fact that henceforth one only has access, as Emerson says, to these qualities through the sign that one has, in part, *created*—unconsciously or not—in order to fathom these very qualities of the Eternal Idea. As Deleuze might say, it is precisely this sign that is empowered to make all the difference, including the possibility of imagining a world without love.

Of course, here I am referring to Deleuze's earlier study of Proust, *Proust and Signs,* in which "apprenticeship" (education, true learning) constitutes the goal of the philosophical activity that Deleuze discovers

in Proust's three volumes, and above all this concerns learning to distinguish between two types of signs: arbitrary or extrinsic signs, and real
and necessary signs. In "Conclusion to Part I: The Image of Thought,"
Deleuze cites Proust on this distinction, which then forms the basis of
his own philosophical education:

> "The truths that intelligence grasps directly in the light of day have
> something less profound, less *necessary* about them than those that
> life has communicated to us *in spite of ourselves* in an impression, a
> material impression because it has reached us through our senses, but
> whose spirit we can extract.... I would have to try to interpret the
> sensations as the signs of so many laws and ideas, by attempting to
> think, that is, to bring out of the darkness what I had felt, and convert
> it into a spiritual equivalent."[23]

It is from this passage that Deleuze derives his concept of apprenticeship.
Following Proust, Deleuze reverses the traditional philosophical metaphor of understanding: "The truths that intelligence grasps directly
in the light of day have something less profound." Rather, it is only from
"the dark regions" that are "elaborated with the effective forces that act
on thought" (95) that true signs first emerge, which is to say, from unconscious sources. At first, this would appear to depart from Emerson's
use of this same metaphor, except we must remember that for Emerson
the sun that first reveals things in the light of day is specifically the light of
a new day, which implies that it is a sun that has never appeared before and
could not have been expected. Here, Deleuze's use of the unconscious to
refer to these "dark regions" of experience from which real and necessary
signs first emerge is in strict adherence to Proust's own rhetoric of involuntary memory. It is because these signs are unexpected that they are
not recognized, and the first effect that they bring is one of shock, which is
identified with a force that causes us to think. These signs are not natural,
meaning that the natural intelligence is not up to understanding them,
which is why they must, in turn, be interpreted, deciphered, translated,
in short, created. Concerning this event, which stimulates learning how
to think, perhaps even for the first time, Deleuze writes:

> What forces us to think is the sign. The sign is an object of an encoun-
> ter, but it is precisely the contingency of the encounter that guarantees
> the necessity of what it leads us to think. The act of thinking does not

proceed from simple, natural possibility; on the contrary, it is the only
true creation. Creation is the act of genesis within thought itself. This
genesis implicates something that does violence to thought, which
wrests it from its natural stupor and its merely abstract possibilities.
To think is always to interpret—to explicate, to develop, to decipher,
to translate a sign. (97)

The resonances between this passage and the Emersonian description
of thinking, or of Man Thinking, are clear, if not uncanny. The creative actions of explicating, developing, deciphering, and translating
signs corresponds to Emerson's descriptions of the different faculties of
thinking in "The American Scholar," which Emerson calls the process
of "transmuting life into truth" (1:55); "a strange process too, this, by
which experience is converted into thought, as a mulberry leaf is converted into satin. The manufacture goes forward at all hours" (1:59). The
analogy of this process as "manufacture" very much recalls the passage
above by Proust concerning those truths that are made to be "necessary" because they are first imparted to us, even despite ourselves, from
our senses, and so whatever truth these events may bear for our spiritual
life must be extracted. What Proust defines as the process of extrac-
tion, and Deleuze simply as creation, Emerson determines as "transmuting," which is further defined as a process of "distillation" (1:55).
As he writes: "In proportion to the completeness of the distillation, so
will the purity and imperishableness of the product be. But none is quite
perfect" (1:55). In other words, "each age . . . must write its own books"
(1:56), or to translate this maxim back into Deleuze's language, "each
age must create its own signs."[24]

Finally, I want to return to the statement by Proust that life communicates to us, *even despite ourselves,* truths that are necessary because
they are imparted by our senses. The phrase "even despite ourselves" entails that these events and these encounters, which become the condition of learning, are involuntary, and are not comparable to events that
we might seek out with an active will. As Emerson writes in the essay
"Experience":

Life is a series of surprises, and would not be worth taking or keeping,
if it were not. God delights to isolate us every day, and hide from us the
past and the future. We would look about us, but with grand politeness

he draws down before us an impenetrable screen of purest sky, and another behind us of purest sky. "You will not remember," he seems to say, "and you will not expect." (3:39)

It is the involuntary nature of these events that accounts for what Deleuze calls the "force" that causes us to think and to transmute these sensible encounters into signs that will express the truth of these encounters. I think Cavell has also discerned this aspect of involuntary memory in his recent meditations on the comedy of divorce, where learning also is given a transcendental function, that is, the capacity to derive from real experience a sign with which one can begin to think philosophically about this experience itself. The very fact that this sign is said to be comic evokes the particular pathos that already inhabits the idea (or the concept) of love and marriage, the incredible pathos of repetition itself. If Cavell chooses the genre of comedy in order to distill and extract the signs of love, rather than jealousy, as was the case with Proust, then this might be owed to his Emersonian disposition for a kind of philosophical writing in which "affection cheer(s)."[25] However, about midway through the lectures that constitute *Emerson's Transcendental Etudes*, Cavell, I think, comes closest to broaching the Emersonian spirit of optimism and hope with Deleuze's dark regions of unconscious violence where the signs of nature first emerge, when he translates Emerson's notion of life with the Freudian term "instinct" *(Trieb)*. Thus, the earlier passage from "The American Scholar" that defines thinking as a process of "transmuting life into truth" can now be translated to read: thinking, the transfiguration of the instinct to live. (Here, we might recall the earlier statement: "Thinking is the function. Living is the functionary." Of course, there is also something very Nietzschean about these statements as well.) The term "instinct" hails from a more modern determination of life, as issuing from "our unconscious life," as something infinitely corruptible in its interest *(Triebfeder)*, as what Emerson himself referred to as his "lowly roof" under which thinking must act with partiality and justice. Here, I will cite a longer passage from Cavell's lecture in which he describes this new determined concept of life, which is much closer to Deleuze's own definition of life as "pure instinct," or elsewhere in his writings as a "Body without Organs":

But what is the corruptible life, this pretransfigurative existence of his [Emerson's] prose, unconscious of itself, unconscious to us? It is, on the line that I am taking, one in which Tuition is to find its Intuition, or in which Emerson's thinking finds its "material" (as psychoanalysis puts it). In the opening two paragraphs of "The American Scholar" it accepts its topics in hope, and understands hope as a sign, in particular of an "indestructible instinct," yet an instinct that thinking must realize as "something else." I suppose this to mean that thinking is replacing, by transfiguring, instinct (as Nietzsche and as Freud again will say). The opening reluctance and indefiniteness of Emerson's definition of his topic in "The American Scholar" [and we have established that Emerson's primary topic is Man Thinking] . . . suggests to me that his topics are everyday letters and words, as signs of our instincts; they are to become thought. Then thinking is a kind of reading.[26]

In commenting on this passage—I will not go into great detail on the resemblances here between Deleuze and Cavell's representation of thinking—I will only point out (1) that philosophy issues from an encounter with an "indestructible instinct" (life itself), in which its only response is the hope that thinking must realize "as 'something else'"; and (2) that "then thinking is a kind of reading" (in the creation and interpretation of signs of these encounters with life), and in this sense, it is nothing natural (see "The American Scholar," 1:52). Of course, these could be said to be intuitions that belong to Deleuze's philosophy as well, if ever such an ascription would provide these statements with more truth than they already have on their own. But they do not.

Nevertheless, if this passage by Cavell strikes us as being very Deleuzian, without having to prove or even bother to raise the question whether Cavell has ever actually read Deleuze (perhaps because he has read "the source," and I am not referring simply to Emerson here but rather to life itself), I could also refer to what I have always considered to be perhaps the most Emersonian passages of *Difference and Repetition*, where Deleuze also remarks on the transcendental character of learning:

"Learning" always takes in and through the unconscious, thereby establishing the bond of a profound complicity between nature and mind. . . . We never know in advance how someone will learn: by means of what loves someone becomes good at Latin, what encounters make them a philosopher, or in what dictionaries they learn to think.... There is no more a method of learning than there is a method for finding treasures, but a violent training, a culture or *paideïa* which effects the entire individual.[27]

Here in the image of learning we see the conditions of "a sensibility that is raised to the level of a transcendental exercise." The violence this event communicates to the faculties, in the form of a shock or of a "discordant accord," is precisely the feeling that belongs to the limits of a common sense that can no longer function in a regulatory fashion, in the form of an "extrinsic conditioning." The violence is inflicted on common sense, a silencing of its order of repetition, caused by its submission to the order of difference (i.e., "intrinsic genesis"). In this moment, as Deleuze describes it, "The limits of the faculties are encased one in the other in the broken shape of that which bears and transmits difference" (165).

Of course, one could easily resolve this event and its discordant aspect too precipitously by submitting its sign again to the condition of possible experience and making it signify something that was already possible or known beforehand. But this again takes on the form of extrinsic conditioning of the sensibility of nature in which the process of learning is stopped short and the sensibility is submitted to the straitjacket of representation and common sense. Perhaps it is the predominance of the form of extrinsic conditioning that violently supplants the nature of Man Thinking that can account for Emerson's aversion toward all the habits of thought promulgated by so-called institutions of learning and by books. Concerning the particular dangers of books, Emerson writes, "I had better never see a book than be warped by its attraction clean out of my own orbit, and made a satellite instead of a system" ("The American Scholar," 1:56). And yet, it is precisely because "the book, the college, the school of art, the institution of any kind" are "built upon" the extrinsic conditioning and disciplining of the sensibility that all men remain "obstructed, yet unborn" (ibid.). To be "unborn" is to remain truly inexperienced. By contrast, Emerson invokes the student of Nature: "to him, to this school-boy under bending dome of day, is suggested, that he and it [nature, or sensibility] proceed from one root.... And what is that Root? Is that not the soul of his soul?—A thought too bold—a dream too wild" (1:54–55).

NOTES

1. Stanley Cavell, *Philosophy the Day after Tomorrow* (Cambridge, Mass.: Harvard University Press, 2005), 117; Friedrich Nietzsche, cited ibid. (emphasis in original).

2. See "Self-Reliance," in Ralph Waldo Emerson, *The Collected Works of Ralph Waldo Emerson*, ed. Alfred R. Ferguson, Robert E. Spiller, et al., 8 vols. to date (Cambridge, Mass.: Harvard University Press, Belknap Press, 1971–2010), 2:32. Subsequent quotations from Emerson's writing are from this source and are cited parenthetically in text by volume and page numbers. Citations may include essay title if the essay from which a quotation is taken is not clear from the text.

3. Cited in Cavell, *Philosophy the Day after Tomorrow,* 116.

4. Friedrich Nietzsche, *Thus Spoke Zarathustra,* trans. R. J. Hollingdale (New York: Penguin, 1961), 147.

5. Ludwig Wittgenstein, cited in Cavell, *Philosophy the Day after Tomorrow,* 279.

6. Cavell, *Philosophy the Day after Tomorrow,* 279.

7. Friedrich Nietzsche, *Basic Writings,* ed. Walter Kaufmann (New York: Random House, 1990), 796 (emphasis in original).

8. Ibid.

9. Martin Heidegger, *Nietzsche,* 2 vols., trans. David Farrell Krell (San Francisco: HarperCollins, 1991), 1:4.

10. Cavell, *Philosophy the Day after Tomorrow,* 114.

11. Ibid., 115; Stanley Cavell, *Emerson's Transcendental Etudes* (Stanford, Calif.: Stanford University Press, 2003), 151.

12. Cavell, *Philosophy the Day after Tomorrow,* 117.

13. Friedrich Nietzsche, *Ecce Homo,* trans. Walter Kaufmann (New York: Random House, 1967), 217.

14. Nietzsche, *Thus Spoke Zarathustra,* 237–38.

15. Cavell, *Philosophy the Day after Tomorrow,* 114.

16. Gilles Deleuze, *Difference and Repetition,* trans. Paul Patton (New York: Columbia University Press, 1994), 129–67.

17. Ibid., 129.

18. Gilles Deleuze and Félix Guattari, *What Is Philosophy?,* trans. Hugh Tomlinson and Graham Burchell (New York: Columbia University Press, 1994), 70.

19. Deleuze, *Difference and Repetition,* 140.

20. Ibid., 133.

21. Ibid., 154.

22. Emerson repeats the phrase "self-trust" in (for instance) "The American Scholar," "Literary Ethics," "Self-Reliance," and "Experience."

23. Gilles Deleuze, *Proust and Signs,* trans. Richard Howard (Minneapolis: University of Minnesota Press, 2000), 95–96, emphasis in original.

24. Deleuze, *Difference and Repetition,* 97.

25. Cavell, *Philosophy the Day after Tomorrow,* 150.

26. Ibid.

27. Deleuze, *Difference and Repetition,* 165.

PAUL GRIMSTAD

9. Emerson's Adjacencies

Radical Empiricism in *Nature*

I am only an experimenter.

—RALPH WALDO EMERSON

SCRIPTURE/SENSATION

Ralph Waldo Emerson's last sermon before resigning his pulpit in the Second Unitarian Church of Boston (1832) took the form of a defense of his conviction "that Jesus did not intend to establish an institution for perpetual observance when he ate the passover with his disciples":

> Now observe the facts. Two of the evangelists (namely, Matthew and John) were of the twelve disciples and were present on that occasion. Neither of them drops the slightest intimation of any intention on the part of Jesus to set up anything permanent. John especially, the beloved disciple, who has recorded with minuteness the conversation and the transactions of that memorable evening, has quite omitted such a notice. Neither did it come from the knowledge of St. Mark, who relates the other facts. It is found in Luke alone, who was not present. . . . Still we must suppose that this expression—This do in remembrance of me—had come to the ear of Luke from some disciple present [while] I can readily imagine that [Jesus] was willing and desirous that when his disciples met, his memory should hallow their intercourse. . . . I cannot bring myself to believe that he looked beyond the living generation, beyond the abolition of the festival he was celebrating and the

scattering of the nation, and meant to impose a memorial feast upon the whole world [and thus the passover dinner was] never intended by Jesus to be the foundation of a perpetual institution.[1]

With this line of reasoning, Emerson tells the Boston congregation of his own "proposal to the brethren of the church to drop the use of the elements and the claim of authority in the administration of this ordinance, [suggesting instead] a mode in which a meeting for the same purpose might be held, free of objection" (19, 21). While the church brethren considered Emerson's proposal "with patience and candor," they finally "recommend[ed] unanimously an adherence to the present form," a decision that led Emerson formally to announce his resignation from the Second Unitarian Church: "As it is the prevailing opinion and feeling in our religious community that it is an indispensable part of the pastoral office to administer [the commemoration of the Lord's Supper in the rite of the Eucharist], I am about to resign into your hands that office which you have confided to me" (25–26).

Blind adherence to formal ritual was not the only thing Emerson abandoned in the years following his break with the Second Unitarian Church of Boston. The linear reasoning of the sermon all but vanishes from the strikingly disjunctive lectures and essays he begins to compose soon after his resignation. Yet while Emerson abandons, along with the duties of the pastoral office, any overtly systematic method of argumentation, his new style of expression does arise from the same schism that led him to leave the pulpit. If the slightly brazen detective work of the Eucharist sermon is a matter of sorting out the relation between, on the one hand, the revelatory authority of foundational rites and rituals and, on the other, a vigilant observation of "the facts," then Emerson's post-pulpit style could be said to arise from an ongoing preoccupation with the relation of Scripture to sensationalist empiricism.

In his *American Renaissance*, F. O. Matthiessen described the way the relation between Scripture and sensation led Emerson to the increasingly aphoristic style he adopted in the years following the Eucharist sermon:

> The want of continuity in Emerson's form was a natural product of . . . the confusing alternation of his experience. The reasons for the cleavage between his two lives, of the understanding and of the soul . . . could

start with the breakdown, after [Jonathan] Edwards, of the Puritan synthesis. Edwards had managed to reunite the two chief strains from the seventeenth century, its logic and its emotion, its hard grasp of fact and its deep capacity for mysticism, but after his death they split apart. The mysticism was caught up in Methodism and the evangelical movement, and was proportionately discredited in the cool eyes of the rationalists, who were Emerson's forerunners in the Unitarianism which he grew to find so inadequate.[2]

In his first major piece of writing following the break with the Second Unitarian Church—the short book *Nature* (1836)—Emerson experiments with what Matthiessen calls the "want of continuity" between reason and revelation. Specifically, in *Nature* Samuel Taylor Coleridge's Christianizing reformulations of Immanuel Kant's first Critique are set alongside the taxonomies of natural science, which Emerson viewed in the summer of 1833 in Georges Cuvier's cabinets of comparative anatomy. In essays and addresses like "The Uses of Natural History," "The Method of Nature," the Divinity School address, "Circles," and "Experience," the split between Scripture as the conduit for divine revelation and an empirical attention to sensuous materiality of the natural world becomes a catalyst for an increasingly disjunctive expression. It is this dynamic—by which an expression no longer beholden to any "perpetual institution" arises as an affirmation of the tension between Scripture and sensation—that will become the organizing principle for Emerson's literary experiments of the 1830s and 1840s.

If *Nature* is an attempt at thinking the adjacency of scriptural revelation and the empirical facts of the here and now, it is not, I will argue in the following pages, a matter of unifying them. It is not a transcendentalism of the sort we have conventionally come to associate with Emerson's thought and that has itself become something of a perpetual institution, reducing Emerson's writing to a programmatic doctrine. Rather, the experimentation of Emerson's immediately post-Unitarian writing is a matter of the way a "confusing alternation of experience" itself becomes the premise for an expression that would *resist* transcendental synthesis. At stake in this writing is the possibility of getting from the "alternation of experience" to a writing that would take account of such alternation without synthesizing it into a higher unity. It is such a thinking of the here and now that Emerson speaks of in rhetorical questions such as "Why should not we also enjoy an original relation to the universe?" (*Nature*, 1:7) and more cryptically, and with less whimsical assurance, "Where do we find ourselves?" ("Experience," 3:27).

RADICAL EMPIRICISM

If Emerson's thought and writing is not a matter of transcendental synthesis—that is, if it does not seek to sublate into a higher unity the "alternations" of experience—it would not then depend on the kind of identity that underlies, for example, Kant's pure intuitions and conceptual categories. That is, it would not depend on an a priori that would prescribe the conditions of possibility for experience in advance.[3] And if Emerson's new kind of expression arises from the way he is able to affirm jarring adjacencies like Scripture/sensation, it would at the same time operate outside the transcendental guarantees of both the rites and rituals of a divinely revealing Scripture and the necessity and universality of a pure a priori.[4]

While I do want to treat Emerson as a certain kind of empiricist, I do not here wish to set up a simple dyadic schema that would pit a posteriori knowledge, inductively derived from experience, against the a priori categories of transcendental idealism. Rather, taking my cue from the tension between reason and revelation in Emerson's farewell sermon, I want to show how adjacency itself begins to serve as an organizing principle for the strange new kind of writing found in *Nature*. In this way, then, Emerson's idiosyncratic empiricism would gesture toward what William James called "radical" empiricism. Here is how James defined this type of empiricism, in his 1904 essay "A World of Pure Experience":

> [If] rationalism tends to emphasize universals and to make wholes prior to parts in the order of logic as well as in that of being . . . empiricism, on the contrary, lays the explanatory stress upon the part, the element, the individual, and treats the whole as a collection, and the universal as an abstraction. My description of things, accordingly, starts with the parts and makes of the whole a being of the second order. It is essentially a mosaic philosophy, a philosophy of plural facts, like that of Hume and his descendents.[5]

But James goes on to tell us that his empiricism "differs from the Humean type of empiricism in one particular that makes [him] add the epithet 'radical.'" For James, "the relations that connect experiences must themselves be experienced relations, and any kind of relation experienced must be accounted as 'real' as anything else in the system" (43–44). James later defines this reality of relations as a "bare witness between some parts of the sum total of experience and others." Radical empiricism argues for the reality of this "withness" (47).

While the transcendental idealist will agree that the content of thought arises from experience, she parts company with the radical empiricist when he says that the *form* of thought—the rules of cognition itself—also arise from experience.[6] The idealist will reply that there must be *some* organizing principle—an ability to grasp categorical and hypothetical logical functions, for example—that would enable the subject to synthesize the sensory manifold, and that such organizing principles are necessary for there to be experience at all. This is precisely what Kant gives us in the first Critique: a set of faculties by which the subject is able schematically to organize sense data into intelligible representations. For Kant, space and time are the most intuitive of these (the faculty of sensibility), presided over by a table of a priori conceptual categories (the faculty of understanding) that organize the data furnished by the intuitions into representations arising as the making of judgments. These pure intuitions, and the schematism that forms from their working in tandem with categorical concepts, are not "prior" to experience (since they exist only as the *organization* of experience) but are nevertheless the a priori form through which the empirical content of experience becomes intelligible. According to the transcendental idealist, if such categorical concepts were not already in place the external world would be unintelligible.[7]

If radical empiricism argues that even such organizing principles are part of experience (and not the other way around), then this sort of empiricism amounts to an exact reversal of the Kantian transcendental critique. Radical empiricism finds its "faculties" within a transcendentally *empirical* field of pure experience, where the relations that connect the terms of experience are as real as the terms themselves. In *Difference and Repetition* (1968), Gilles Deleuze describes an overturning of Kant's transcendental idealism that is remarkably close to William James's. For Deleuze,

> a schema [of the Kantian sort] ... is conceived [*est pensé*] and put to
> work in relation to concepts understood in terms of logical possibility

[and] it does no more than convert logical possibility into transcendental possibility. It brings spatio-temporal relations into correspondence with the logical relations of the concept. [But] a concept alone is completely incapable of specifying or dividing itself; the agents of differenciation are the spatio-temporal dynamisms which act beneath it, like a hidden art [comme un art caché]. . . . Everything changes when the dynamisms are posited no longer as schemata [of the Kantian sort] but as dramas of Ideas [des drames d'Idées].[8]

What I want to focus on in Deleuze's linkage of the concept to "logical possibility" is the alignment of this relation with an a priori deduction that would move from universals to particulars (logical demonstration from general axiom to particular case), and, conversely, a "hidden art" that would be external to this operation. Such an art, operating outside conceptual representation, is what Bruce Baugh calls the way the "nonconceptual differences between one instance of the concept and another" are the basis for "multiplicity."[9] If Ideas, for Deleuze, are the basis for multiplicity, then they are far from timeless Platonic Forms, mentalist Lockean copies, Kantian regulatives, or Hegelian absolutes. They are rather something like the actualization of relations external to conceptual representation. Like James's pluralism, Deleuze's Ideas designate an externality of relations which are the condition of real, rather than possible, experience.[10]

Remembering Emerson's injunction that one should have an "original relation to the universe," and considering his later description of nature as a "work of ecstasy" ("The Method of Nature," 1:125, Emerson's emphasis), we might say that his writing marks a similar overturning of the Kantian critique in its power to produce "ecstasies" at the level of grammatical and logical relations.[11] Emerson's "ecstatic" expression makes legible the reality of relations in that his arguments are often made, to use another of James's characterizations, in mosaic-like collages rather than in the propositional chains that typically serve as the glue holding metaphysical systems together.[12] This extra-logical writing, this "ecstasy" of side-stepping discrete instantiations of the concept ("The Method of Nature," 1:129–32), occurs when words begin to function independently of the subject-predicate grooves of deductive reasoning (or what James describes as placing "wholes prior to parts in the order of logic"). To do philosophy in resonating blocks, rather than as an architectonic system held together by a lattice of syllogisms, is to move from the necessities of top-down deductions to a pluralism that would proceed from the bottom up—from the concrete particularity of the here and now to ever-evolving collections.

Before moving on to some close readings of *Nature*, I want to look briefly at an example of how Emerson's writing can be thought of as a radical empiricism of the sort described in James's and Deleuze's overturning of transcendental idealism. Following the disorienting provocation "Where do we find ourselves?" in Emerson's great essay "Experience," we are left to "find" an organizing principle for linking "stairs," "Ghost[s]," "opium," "water," or "factories" (and, to point further ahead in the essay, "prison[s] of glass," "quicksand," and fragments of "Labrador spar" [3:27–33]). Rather than presupposing a bond between the rules of logic and the rules of representation, these figures connect up in ways external to conceptual legislation. Thinking and writing in this way is radically empirical because it shows grammatical and logical relations to be as real as the terms they relate. In "Experience," empiricism is a matter of producing a writing at all times in the process of foregrounding what James called "withness," a process that will serve as the guiding compositional strategy for the essays and lectures Emerson began working out shortly after abandoning the rites and rituals of the pulpit.[13]

FROM IDEALISM TO MOSAIC PHILOSOPHY

The particular philosophical concerns of Kant's *Critique of Pure Reason* inform every page of Emerson's *Nature* (1836). While I take my cue from David Van Leer's claim that the specific arguments made in the "Idealism" chapter are "clearly Kantian," and that the "theory of 'noble doubt' rehearses" a version of Kant's idealism, I trace the effects of Emerson's borrowed terminology along a very different path. If Van Leer spends many pages showing how Emerson's writing is a "surprisingly precise" run through transcendental idealism, I want to show how Emerson's engagement with Kant foregrounds the way adjacencies work to unsettle a presumed universal and necessary bond between logical rules and the categories of the understanding.[14]

Emerson begins the "Idealism" section of *Nature* like this:

> A noble doubt perpetually suggests itself, whether this end [of conveying the meaning of every object of sense to man] be not the Final Cause of the Universe; and whether nature outwardly exists. It is a sufficient account of that Appearance we call the World, that God will teach a human mind, and so makes it the receiver of a certain number of congruent sensations, which we call sun and moon, man and woman, house and trade. In my utter impotence to test the authenticity of the report of my senses, to know whether the impressions they make on me correspond with outlying objects, what difference does it make, whether Orion is up there in heaven, or some god paints the image in the firmament of the soul? The relations of parts and the end of the whole remaining the same, what is the difference, whether land and sea interact, and worlds revolve and intermingle without number or end,—deep yawning under deep, and galaxy balancing galaxy, throughout absolute space, or, whether, without relations of time and space, the same appearances are inscribed in the constant faith of man? Whether nature enjoy a substantial existence without, or is only in the apocalypse of the mind, it is alike useful and alike venerable to me. (1:29)

In addition to the obvious allusion to idealism in the chapter's title, Kantian language echoes through the passage in a number of more or less encrypted ways.[15] But a divergent tendency arises as Emerson reasons not from necessities stemming from a priori premises (by which chains of propositions would hang together through rules internal to predication), but rather through a mosaic-like parataxis of adjacent figures: pupil, sun, moon, man, teaching, woman, house, impotence, intermingling, trade, Orion, paint, firmament, parts, wholes, land, sea, worlds, revolution, yawning, galaxy, inscription, apocalypse. While a certain Kantian narrative runs through this heap of figuration, there remains, as a kind of anamorphic effect in Emerson's prose, the charged adjacency of the figures themselves.

Read through this alternate network, we find that the lesson taught to the human mind (to paraphrase Emerson) is how to make the jump from universalism (whether the rites and rituals of a "perpetual institution," or of the a priori concept) to a radical empiricism sensitive to real relations in the here and now. This lesson does not teach the immutable laws of scriptural doctrine nor of how ideal categories "in" man ensure an eternal congruency between mind and world, but rather how having an "original relation" with Nature leads to new ways of thinking and writing. This "teaching" arises, in *Nature,* as the relation between one figure and another becomes, to use Barbara Packer's description, "charged terminals that the reader must take the risk of connecting."[16] If such "charged terminals" are, as I have been saying, directed against the memorializing rites and rituals that led Emerson to leave the pulpit (as well as against the deductions of the Critique), then here Emerson dramatizes this agon in an act of self-transformation by which an Emerson-in-the-making "teach[es]" an earlier churchman-Emerson how to make a "wholly new" kind of writing.

This experiment in literary self-transformation functions at the level of the physical mark in the passage, where a reality of relations is made explicit in the device of comma and dash (,—).[17] As a literal instantiation of adjacency, it becomes a kind of shorthand for Emerson's receptivity to the sensory manifold as an extra-logical plurality, and accordingly marks Emerson's own "pupil"-like "condition [as] a solution in hieroglyphic to those inquiries he would put" to "nature" (*Nature,* 1:7).

The comma-dash appears in the middle of a long sentence:

> The relations of parts and the end of the whole remaining the same, what is the difference, whether land and sea interact, and worlds revolve and intermingle without number or end,—deep yawning under deep, and galaxy balancing galaxy, throughout absolute space, or, whether, without relations of time and space, the same appearances are inscribed in the constant faith of man? (*Nature,* 1:29)

Before focusing specifically on how the mark functions in the passage, it might be helpful first to parse this elaborate sentence. It is one long rhetorical question in which different kinds of relations are compared, contrasted, and ultimately made real in the Jamesian sense. In the first section of the question Emerson takes as his premise the identity between relations at the level of the "par[t]" and the "end of the whole": that is, two ways of conceiving the same totality. "What is the difference," then, marks a turn toward a rhetorical question, a shift that opens onto two "whether[s]," each of which corresponds, in a kind of grammatical parallelism, to the previously mentioned modes of relation ("whole"/whether[a];

"par[t]"/whether[b]). Preserving the ideal harmony between part and whole, the first of these "whether[s]" ("whether land and sea interact, and worlds revolve and intermingle without number or end") radiates out into "absolute space" (whole), while the second burrows inward, toward something "inscribed in the constant faith of man" (individual; part). Again, the Kantian question about what it is that makes experience possible (loosely) determines the stakes of the passage, where the mind would be universally and necessarily pre-equipped to cognize worldly phenomena (but not noumenal things in themselves). Such a subject would contain within itself the conditions of possibility for experience in the intuitions of "time and space." But at "what is the difference," Emerson's language moves into territory not legislated over by the logical identity of the concept, and so a crack opens up within the very premises of transcendental idealism. The comma-dash appears, then, in the first of these "whether[s]," immediately following "what is the difference." Like a lever prying open the hermetic shell of the concept, the comma-dash interposes its unmediated typographic actuality, both to mark a disruption in the propositional chain and to actualize adjacency in putting two pieces of writing into connection without prescribing for them any explicitly subordinating grammatical relationship. From out of this charged terminal, then, spills an extravagant concatenation of figures, like so many free relations that had been hidden under identically recurring instances of the concept. Here, "land[s]" and "sea[s]" and "worlds" that "revolve" are sent into "deep[s] yawning under deep[s]," the whole chain finally flying out into the galactic parataxis of adjacent galaxies (Emerson's "galaxy"). In short: the passage enacts both the opening of an inconsistency in the concept's logical bond with experience as representation and makes legible the reality of relations in replacing subordinating syllogisms with mosaic-like adjacencies.

BECOMING EYEBALL

Rather than securing an eternal harmony between mind and world, the well-known announcement "I become a transparent eye-ball" (*Nature*, 1:10) marks a point in *Nature* where the materiality of writing is shown literally to arise from the robust sensuousness of the external world. The relation of Scripture to the extended physicality of nature brings us back to that "cleavage" Matthiessen identified as setting Emerson's experimental writing into motion, even if Matthiessen kept that "alternation of experience" secure within a programmatic transcendentalism. But seeing Scripture as the materiality of writing (rather than as timeless Law), and as existing on a continuum with the sensuous physicality of the natural world, would be closer to Warren Montag's description of Baruch Spinoza as

> the first philosopher explicitly to consider Scripture, that is, writing, as a part of nature in its materiality, as irreducible to anything outside itself . . . instead of speaking of its meaning, we ought to speak of the effects it produces. . . . [In this] parallelism of nature and Scripture . . . we see the abandonment of the theme, essential to any hermeneutic, of the interior and the exterior of Scripture. There is no reserve of meaning, no residue beyond its surface. Meaning and form coincide exactly in the graphic materiality apart from which Scripture has no existence. . . . Accordingly, there is nothing sacred in the *sententiae* of which Scripture is fashioned, no Logos filling an essential hollowness or animating dead letters. Scripture is [for Spinoza] "paper and ink," and "markings letters and words" thus writing is fundamentally corporeal, not only in its being but in its effects: writing can affect bodies . . . it is at this point that Spinoza's alliance with the ancient atomists takes on its full significance. Lucretius . . . describes not only speech as a subtle matter that produces the effects of meaning by impinging upon the auditory sense organ but writing itself as a disposition of material elements, letters, whose arrangement determines meaning.[18]

Spinoza's heretical ideas about the depthless materiality of Scripture can be linked to Emerson around the term *pantheism,* and perhaps also to empiricism,[19] insofar as Montag finds a Lucretian resonance in Spinoza's materialism.[20] But the specific connection between Spinoza's biblical criticism and the language of *Nature* should also be considered in light of the linguistic theory Emerson himself sketches in the fourth chapter of *Nature,* on "Language":

> Every word which is used to express a moral or intellectual fact, if traced to its root, is found to be borrowed from some material appearance. *Right* originally means *straight; wrong* means *twisted. Spirit* primarily means *wind; transgression,* the crossing of a *line; supercilious,* the *raising of the eye-brow.* (1:18, emphasis in original)

For Emerson, before it has acquired the baggage of "moral or intellectual facts," Scripture as writing is first an extension of the corporeality of nature. While such a view might be seen as a continuation of Locke's description of the relation between perceptions, ideas, and names, Emerson is not as mentalist as Locke.[21] The linguistic theory offered in *Nature* rather "trace[s] to [the] root" of a "material appearance" that could serve as the condition of real experience, rather than limiting experience either to primary qualities that through perception become ideas accessed through reflection (Locke), or the discursive cutouts of a priori concepts that underwrite a merely possible experience (Kant). The consequence of treating words as so many aftereffects of the "material appearance" of nature (and not, as Locke puts it, "*Signs of internal Conceptions*")[22] would both disrupt the idealist tracing of extended bodies from transcendental conditions of possibility and, following Montag's description of Spinoza's biblical criticism, begin to treat written marks as themselves "part of nature in its materiality."

With all of this in mind, let us consider the anecdote in which Emerson celebrates the wave of ecstacy he receives from "crossing a bare common, in snow puddles, at twilight": "Standing on the bare ground,— my head bathed by the blithe air, and uplifted into infinite space,—all mean egotism vanishes. I become a transparent eyeball."[23] Much of the exegetical industry that has led to the perpetual institution of transcendentalism has had something to say about this scene in the bare commons, often describing it as a (perhaps somewhat weirder) version of the idealism I discussed earlier. Here, I want to focus on how the passage shows words to exist on a continuum with the materiality of nature, and in doing so renders the adjacency of "scripture" (markings; letters) and "sensation" (the intoxicating sensuousness of the "bare common[s]") as a catalyst for the production of the experimental figure "eyeball." The process Emerson describes as "becom[ing] a transparent eyeball," is both a making fluid of the relations between words, letters, and phonemes and the making of writing into a process existing on a continuum with—and so quite literally expressing—the sensuous materiality of nature.[24]

Following from the way the linguistic theory in *Nature* posits a continuum between the materiality of nature and the materiality of words, Emerson's anecdote of the bare commons converts the vowels of "air" into the remade shapes "b-[a]-t-h-e" and "b-l-[i]-t-h-e." Continuing this process, following the "i" becoming "blithe" and the "a" becoming "bathe," the "i" sets off on its own course, forming the staccato concatenation: "upl*i*fted *i*nto *i*nfin*i*te." When "all m**e**an **e**got*i*sm van*i*shes," these same short "i"s are put into connection with two long "e"s, amplifying the phonetic transformation first heard in "blithe," toward the long "i" of "**I** become a transparent eyeball." The word "eyeball" then begins to come into focus from the way the "air" of the commons again releases its middle letter into the chain "bl(*i*)the" → "upl(*i*)fted (*i*)nto (*i*)nf(*i*)n(*i*)te" → "all m(*ea*)n (*e*)got(*i*)sm van(*i*)shes" → "*I*" (a transmission that can also be heard in transp(*air*)ency). Through this phonetic and alphabetic plasticity, "*I*" shifts to "*eye*," the double *e* a variant of the earlier "blith(*e*)/bath(*e*)" frame, the *y* a forked pictograph of the fissuring of relations external to the ready-made conditions of conceptual representation. The second half of the word then arises as the splicing of the "(*b*)lithe/(*b*)athe" frame with the "all" of "(*all*) mean egotism." With two instances of the comma-dash as relations placeholders, we arrive at the construction **I(e)**,—[**b-**],—[-**all**].

In this way, Emerson "become[s]" the light-sensitive substrate onto which the material appearance of nature imprints itself, giving rise to a writing as fluid as the flux of sensations in the bare commons. To "become a transparent eyeball" is both to move from I(e),—[b-],—[-all] to "eyeball" and to set in motion the experimental linguistic "transparen[cy]" that arises from a receptivity to the here and now as multiplicity external to conceptual representation. While this is played out as a radical empiricism in which relations are external to and as real as their terms, it is again also a matter of affirming the adjacency of Scripture (linguistic materiality) and sensation (the impressions of the bare common[s]).

Lest this series of close readings seem merely ludic exercises in playing around with letters, I would remind the reader that the argument here began with the claim that Emerson treated the adjacency of a revelatory Scripture and an observation of "the facts" as a jumping-off point for a series of literary experiments. The affirmation of such adjacencies anticipates the open-ended pluralism William James called radical empiricism, which posits the externality and reality of relations. The close readings presented here explore this link between adjacency and the reality of relations. From the Scripture/sensation value differential to the literal withness of the comma-dash, to the process Emerson calls "becom[ing] a transparent eyeball," I have tried to show how the swirl of relations that escape idealist conditions of possibility are put to use in Emerson's refusal of priors, both theological and metaphysical. To have an "original relation to the universe" would be not only to recognize that relations themselves are real and experienceable in the here and now, but to read in such a way so as not to reduce Emerson's injunctions to the fossilized sound bites of transcendentalism and rather begin to see them as the expression of an empirical field of pure experience.

NOTES

The epigraph comes from the 1844 essay "Circles," in Ralph Waldo Emerson, *The Collected Works of Ralph Waldo Emerson,* ed. Alfred R. Ferguson, Robert E. Spiller, et al., 8 vols. to date (Cambridge, Mass.: Harvard University Press, Belknap Press, 1971–2010), 2:188: "But lest I should mislead any when I have my own head, and obey my whims, let me remind the reader that I am only an experimenter. Do not set the least value on what I do, or the least discredit on what I do not, as if I pretended to settle anything as true or false. I unsettle all things. No facts are to me sacred; none are profane; I simply experiment, an endless seeker, with no Past at my back. Yet this incessant movement and progression, which all things partake, could never become sensible to us, but by contrast to some principle of fixture or stability in the soul." Here is an example of one of the more persistently recurring adjacencies in Emerson's writing: the constancy of a fixed principle set side-by-side with "incessant movement." Subsequent quotations from Emerson's writing are from this source and are cited parenthetically in text by volume and page numbers. Citations may include essay title if the essay from which a quotation is taken is not clear from the text.

1. Ralph Waldo Emerson, *Emerson's Poetry and Prose,* ed. Joel Porte and Saundra Morris (New York: Norton, 2001), 18.

2. F. O. Matthiessen, *The American Renaissance: Art and Expression in the Age of Emerson and Whitman* (London: Oxford University Press, 1941), 56. After Matthiessen, much of the scholarship on Emerson stresses the importance of this disjunctive "cleavage" on the formation of his style. Stephen Whicher describes the split in Emerson's thinking as his "two distinct personalities: the believer, who sees through to the mystical perfection of things, and the detached observer, Mr. Emerson of Concord, who gives their due to the facts" (Stephen

Whicher, *Freedom and Fate: An Inner Life of Emerson* [New York: A. S. Barnes, 1953], 32). Barbara Packer describes the Unitarianism of Emerson's Concord milieu as a "religion that wished to remain grounded in biblical revelation and, at the same time, loyal to an empiricism hostile to violations of natural law" (quoted in Sacvan Bercovich, *The Cambridge History of American Literature*, vol. 2, *Prose Writing, 1820–1865* [Cambridge: Cambridge University Press, 1995], 337). David Robinson also characterizes the specifically Unitarian dimension of the split between "reason and revelation": "Emerson's eventual departure from [the theological] tradition was due in part to his rejection of the idea that reasoning about nature had to be supplemented by belief in miracles as revealed in Scriptures" (David Robinson, "Emerson's Natural Theology and the Paris Naturalists," *Journal of the History of Ideas* 41, no. 1 [1980]: 73). Elizabeth Dant has described Emerson's conflicted intellectual temperament as a simultaneous "ease and familiarity with the revealed lore of neo-Platonism [and an] admiration for the open-ended method of Bacon and Montaigne" (Elizabeth Dant, "Composing the World," *Nineteenth-Century Literature* 44, no. 1 [1989]: 29), explicitly contrasting Plato's eternal Forms with the making of experimental inductions from experience.

3. By *a priori* I mean both the way the intuitions of space and time and the conceptual categories of the understanding outlined in Kant's first Critique are independent of experience, and the dependence of these faculties on a propositional logic that would move from general rules to specific empirical judgments (subsuming particulars under universals).

4. Stanley Cavell links Emerson's and Nietzsche's experimentalism around the term *affirmation:* "what Emerson calls 'the Sacred affirmative' [is] the thing Nietzsche calls 'the sacred Yes,' the heart of new creation" (Stanley Cavell, *Emerson's Transcendental Etudes* [Stanford, Calif.: Stanford University, 2003], 16). What I am describing as Emerson's affirmation of the adjacency between Scripture and sensation can also be heard in the Nietzschean maxim that calls for the "essential priority of the spontaneous, aggressive, expansive, form-giving forces that give new interpretations and directions" (Friedrich Nietzsche, *On the Genealogy of Morality,* ed. Keith Ansell-Pearson [Cambridge: Cambridge University Press, 1994], 79). Thus when, in *Twilight of the Idols,* Nietzsche says that Emerson is "enlightened, adventurous, multifarious, and ... above all happy and ... cheerful *[heiter]*" he seems to want to link this "cheerfulness" *[Heiterkeit]* to the making of "new interpretations and directions" (Friedrich Nietzsche, *Twilight of the Idols/The Anti-Christ,* trans. R. J. Hollingdale [New York: Penguin, 1990], 86). On the "cheerful" in Emerson, it is significant that he referred to himself, in a 1841 journal entry, as "a professor of the Joyous Science." See *The Journals and Miscellaneous Notebooks of Ralph Waldo Emerson,* ed. William H. Gillman

et al., 16 vols. (Cambridge, Mass.: Harvard University Press, Belknap Press, 1960–82), 8:8. Without getting into a detailed discussion as to whether Nietzsche borrowed Emerson's phrase for his *Die Fröhliche Wissenschaft* (see Richard Poirier, *Poetry and Pragmatism* [Cambridge, Mass.: Harvard University Press, 1992], 155–57, for a consideration of this issue), this linkage of the "adventurous," the "cheerful" and the "multifarious" is a fitting description of the experimental literary strategy Emerson adopts shortly after leaving the ministry.

5. William James, *Essays in Radical Empiricism* (Lincoln: University of Nebraska Press, 1996), 43.

6. Having never entirely shaken the shock of Hume's skepticism, Kant indeed refers to himself as an "empirical realist" (in addition to being a transcendental idealist). He writes: "All outer perception yields immediate proof of something real in space, or rather is the real itself. In this sense empirical realism is beyond question; that is, there corresponds to our outer intuitions something real in space" (Immanuel Kant, *Critique of Pure Reason,* trans. Norman Kemp Smith [London: Palgrave, 2003], A375).

7. Kant articulated the distinction like this: "But even though all our cognition starts *with* experience, that does not mean that all of it arises *from* experience. For it might well be that even our experiential cognition is composite, consisting of what we receive through impressions and what our own cognitive power supplies from itself (sense impressions serving merely as the occasion)" (ibid., A1/B1, my emphasis). Martin Jay has recently described this aspect of the First Critique as Kant's attempt to "ferret out the part of cognition that does not arise entirely from experience (understood in the sense of external stimuli alone) [which constitutes] perhaps his greatest philosophical innovation: the transcendental method" (Martin Jay, *Songs of Experience: Modern American and European Variations on a Universal Theme* [Berkeley: University of California Press, 2005], 72).

8. Gilles Deleuze, *Difference and Repetition,* trans. Paul Patton (New York: Columbia University Press, 1994), 218. Bruce Baugh describes Deleuze's "dramas of Ideas" as a kind of radical empiricism: "Against Kant, Deleuze [like James] argue[s] that the empirical is not what the concept determines would be in a representation if it occurred . . . but actuality itself, real existence, as opposed to the possibility of existence indicated by the concept. . . . If in its simplest form, the empirical is the reason for the non-conceptual differences between one instance of a representation and another, then it is the basis of multiplicity, of an external and non-conceptual relation between instances [of] the concept [and this is because] the actuality of an instance is not included within the concept, the relation between actualities is not internal and conceptual, or dialectical, but external and contingent . . . where relations are external and irre-

ducible to their terms" (Bruce Baugh, "Deleuze and Empiricism," *Journal of the British Society for Phenomenology* 24 [1993]: 17–18). On pluralism as a thinking of relations as being "external to their terms," Deleuze, in his 1953 monograph on David Hume, writes: "Relations are external to their terms. When [William] James calls himself a pluralist, he does not say, in principle, anything else" (Gilles Deleuze, *Empiricism and Subjectivity,* trans. Constantin Boundas [New York: Columbia University Press, 1991], 98–99). In a later essay on Walt Whitman, Deleuze writes: "When Whitman speaks in his own manner and in his own style, it turns out that a kind of whole must be constructed, a whole that is all the more paradoxical in that it only comes after the fragments and leaves them intact, making no attempt to totalize them. This complex idea depends on a principle dear to English philosophy, to which the Americans would give a new meaning and new developments: *relations are external to their terms.* Relations will consequently be posited as something that can and must be instituted or invented. Parts are fragments that cannot be totalized, but we can at least invent nonpreexisting relations between them.... Relations are not internal to a Whole; rather, the Whole is derived from the external relations of a given moment, and varies with them" (Gilles Deleuze, *Essays Critical and Clinical,* trans. Daniel W. Smith and Michael A. Greco [Minneapolis: University of Minnesota Press, 1997], 58, emphasis in original).

9. Bruce Baugh, "Deleuze and Empiricism," 19–20.

10. For a detailed analysis of the peculiar way in which Deleuze inherits the Kantian sense of Idea (as a regulative "as if" of Reason), see Daniel Smith, "Deleuze, Hegel, and the Post-Kantian Tradition," *Philosophy Today* 44 (2000), and my review of Peter Hallward's *Out of This World,* in *Radical Philosophy* 142 (March/April 2007).

11. Emerson, *Emerson's Poetry and Prose,* 81–93. For more on the affinity between Emerson's "original relation to the universe" and William James's radical empiricism, see Joan Richardson, *A Natural History of Pragmatism: The Fact of Feeling from Jonathan Edwards to Gertrude Stein* (Cambridge: Cambridge University Press, 2007).

12. Barbara Packer describes the a-logical effects of Emerson's style: "By the time Emerson published his first series of *Essays,* his style had achieved the distinctive form from which it never subsequently varied. A series of short, declarative sentences, whose logical relationship to one another is left deliberately unarticulated" (quoted in Bercovitch, *The Cambridge History of American Literature,* 2:388). James himself identified his own "mosaic philosophy" as being external to deductive logic: "One way of stating the empiricist contention is to say that the 'a-logical' enters into philosophy on an equal footing with the 'logical'" (William James, *Writings 1902–1910* [New York: Library of America, 1987], 1034n1).

13. We ought, at this point, to remember Emerson's jarring change of mood toward the end of his essay "Experience" when he writes: "But far be from me the despair which prejudges the law by a paltry empiricism" (3:48). This prejudging empiricism is "paltry" not, as Stanley Cavell reminds us, because of "its reliance on experience, but rather because of its paltry idea of experience" (Cavell, *Emerson's Transcendental Etudes*, 124). Here, I am identifying Emerson's non-"paltry" idea of experience as a "radical empiricism" in which the externality and reality of relations serves as the basis for pluralism.

14. Van Leer, *Emerson's Epistemology*, 26. According to René Wellek, "Emerson owned a copy of the 1838 translation of the *Critique of Pure Reason* . . . and the copy still preserved in his library at Concord shows pencil markings" (Rene Wellek, *Confrontations: Studies in the Relation between Germany, England, and the United States during the Nineteenth Century* [Princeton, N.J.: Princeton University Press, 1965], 188), but he then concludes that Emerson's recourse to Kantian terminology was primarily a result of various second-hand encounters: Drummond's *Academical Questions* in 1820, Dugald Stewart's *Dissertation* in 1823, Madame de Staël's account of German culture and philosophy, *De l'Allemagne,* Victor Cousin's *Cour de Philosophie* in 1828, and most of all, James Marsh's introduction to Coleridge's *Aids to Reflection* (1829). David Van Leer corroborates this, writing that "although Emerson knew German, there is no evidence of his having read Kant in the original. A more likely source are the second-hand accounts in various books and periodicals" (David Van Leer, *Emerson's Epistemology: The Argument of the Essays* [Cambridge: Cambridge University Press, 1986], 3). While Van Leer wants to show Emerson's Kantian idealism as "one more Transcendentalist revolt against corpse-cold liberal Christianity and the empiricist associationism that underwrote it" (21), I want to instead focus on how the turn from Unitarianism generates a move into a more "radical" empiricism.

15. Van Leer identifies in the passage not only Kantian language but a whole catalog of allusions to seventeenth- and eighteenth-century science and metaphysics: "Emerson accurately lays out . . . various possible [philosophical] positions, identifying each by characteristic terminology. He glances at empiricism in general, through Hume's 'impressions,' and summarizes Berkeley's idealist notion of a reality 'imprinted' in the senses by Spirit. . . . German philosophy is represented by its subjectivization of 'the relations of time and space,' and Fichtean absolute idealism, recalled in the vision of the world as a mere posit 'inscribed in the constant faith of man.' And the stable world view against which both idealisms react is clearly Newtonian as the reference to 'absolute space' indicates" (*Emerson's Epistemology*, 28).

16. Describing Emerson's style of expression in his first essay collection, Barbara Packer writes that the "ambiguities, lacunae, paradoxes, and under-

statements with which Emerson is so generous turn the sentences of his essays into charged terminals that the reader must take the risk of connecting; the latter's reward is a certain electric tingle" (Barbara Packer, *Emerson's Fall: A New Interpretation of the Major Essays* [New York: Continuum, 1982], 6).

17. While "the combination of dash and comma is actually quite common in mid-19th century prose" (Nina Baym, e-mail to author, November 7, 2005)—Thoreau's *Walden* and Stowe's *Uncle Tom's Cabin* come immediately to mind as works where this punctuation is used to the point of abuse—my argument here is that Emerson puts this device to work in a very specific way in *Nature*, such that it affirms and produces adjacency. The comma-dash appears at crucial moments in Emerson's oeuvre. In "The Method of Nature" it plays a role in Emerson's striking definition of nature as an "ecstatic" process: "Nature can only be conceived as existing . . . to a universe of ends, and not to one,—a work of *ecstasy*" (1:125, Emerson's emphasis). In "Experience," it explicitly marks the traumatic contingency that is the occasion for the essay; Emerson's characterization of the death of his son as his "hav[ing] lost a beautiful estate,—no more" (3:29). In my reading of the punctuation in *Nature*, I am looking at the original 1836 typographic setting. Another version of *Nature* was set in 1849, in which the comma-dash is used in a slightly different way.

18. Warren Montag, *Bodies, Masses, Power: Spinoza and His Contemporaries* (London: Verso, 1999), 19–20.

19. In his introduction to a recent edition of Spinoza's *Tractatus Theologico-Politicus,* Jonathan Israel calls Spinoza's Bible criticism an "austere empiricism" in which an "empirical conception of text criticism and experimental science are . . . wholly inseparable. [Spinoza's] particular brand of empiricism, important though it is to the structure of his thought, in no way detracts from the fact that his metaphysical premises rooted in one-substance doctrine, result from conflating extension (body) and mind (soul) in such a way as to lead him—quite unlike the members of the Royal Society, or followers of Boyle, Locke or Newton—to reduce all reality including the entirety of human experience, and the world of tradition, spirit and belief no less than the physical world, to the level of the purely empirical" (Baruch Spinoza, *Theological-Political Treatise,* ed. Jonathan Israel, trans. Michael Silverthorn and Jonathan Israel [Cambridge: Cambridge University Press, 2007], xv).

20. Montag refers to Lucretius's likening of atomic elements and letteral elements *(elementa)*. See Lucretius, *De rerum natura,* trans. W. H. D. Rouse (Cambridge, England: Loeb Classical Library, 1924), 1.196–97; 1.823–25; 1.912–14; 2.1013–18.

21. See John Locke, *An Essay concerning Human Understanding,* ed. Peter Nidditch (Oxford: Oxford University Press, 1975), 420–28. Indeed, Matthiessen

hears a Lockean resonance in Emerson's theory of language: "In such a view Emerson is following Locke and the succession of eighteenth century rhetoricians who for the most part simply echoed the brief section on 'Words' in the *Essay concerning Human Understanding*" (Matthiessen, *American Renaissance*, 32–33).

22. Locke, *Essay concerning Human Understanding*, 402.

23. Emerson, "Nature," in *Emerson's Poetry and Prose*, 13.

24. Van Leer writes of the passage that "the problem is not primarily tonal . . . we recoil not merely because no one ever was a transparent eyeball or because 'eye*ball*' is a silly word. Worse than unreal or embarrassing, the image is intellectually incoherent [but] the apparent incoherence of the image is not a miscalculation but an intentional dramatization of the kinds of tensions felt throughout the chapter" (*Emerson's Epistemology*, 22). While Van Leer's "recoiling" from the passage is a good example of how Emerson's experimental writing has the power to shock and unsettle, I agree with him that the passage is an "intentional dramatization of . . . tensions" in *Nature*, a dramatization that does not occur around the word "eyeball," but around "becoming." In a late piece called "Literature and Life," Deleuze describes the relation between writing and "becoming" like this: "To write is certainly not to impose a form on the matter of lived experience. Literature rather moves in the direction of the ill-formed or the incomplete. . . . Writing is a question of becoming, always incomplete, always in the midst of being formed [*toujours en train de se faire*]. . . . It is a process, that is, a passage of Life that traverses both the livable and the lived. Writing is inseparable from becoming" (*Essays Critical and Clinical*, 1). For a detailed discussion of how William James and Deleuze share this emphasis of an empiricism of that which is *en train de se faire*, see David Lapoujade's *William James: Pragmatisme et l'empirisme* (Paris: PUF, 1997), and "From Transcendental Empiricism to Worker Nomadism: William James," *Pli* 9 (2000).

10. "The Eye Is the First Circle"

Emerson's "Romanticism," Cavell's Skepticism, Luhmann's Modernity

If Emerson's "representativeness," his universalizing, is not to go unexamined, neither should his habitually condemned "individualism." If he is to be taken as an instance of "humanism" . . . then he is at the same time to be taken as some form of anti-humanist, working "against ourselves," against what we understand as human (under)standing.

—STANLEY CAVELL
"Emerson's Constitutional Amending: Reading 'Fate'"

Reality is what one does not perceive when one perceives it.

—NIKLAS LUHMANN
"The Cognitive Program of Constructivism and
a Reality That Remains Unknown"

I want to begin with an apparently simple set of questions, one that will, I trust, seem less simple—and more rhetorical, no doubt—by the end of this essay: Do we know how to read Emerson? How do we remain true to the essential strangeness, the unrepentantly eccentric and heretical quality of his writing, as it insists on itself at every moment (at least up to the end of the period capped with the essays that make up *The Conduct of Life*)?[1] That seemingly straightforward question has been complicated considerably—and, I hope, permanently—by philosopher Stanley Cavell's large and ambitious body of work on Emerson. As Cavell has argued for three decades, bypassing this fundamental question has

271

almost always eventuated in assessments ranging from negative to dismissive of Emerson's thinking, his ethics, his politics, or all three. I want to suggest, however, that we are only now beginning (thanks in no small part to Cavell's efforts) to understand just how difficult, how rigorous, and how *systematic* Emerson's writing and thinking really is. This is not to discount, of course, the invaluable efforts of scholars and critics over the years such as Stephen Whicher, Barbara Packer, Maurice Gonnaud, David Van Leer, Eric Cheyfitz, Lee Rust Brown, and many others who have attempted to grasp something like the systematic complexity of Emerson's work. It is rather to suggest that those efforts are only the beginning of a massive effort of rereading Emerson, the scale and proportions of which are only now, I think, coming fully into view.

As Cavell has pointed out, "Along with the gesture of denying philosophy to Emerson goes another, almost as common . . . namely that of describing Emerson's prose as a kind of mist or fog, as if it is generally quite palpable what it is that Emerson is obscurely reaching for words to say and generally quite patent that the ones he finds are more or less arbitrary and conventional . . . as though he cannot mean anew in every word he says."[2] For Cavell, as is well known, the power of the Emersonian project begins the rigor of its confrontation with the inescapability and consequences of philosophical skepticism: the fact, as Cavell puts it, "that the world exists as it were for its own reasons" (79). Emerson both acknowledges—"bears" or "suffers" will be a better term, eventually—and resists what Cavell calls the most famous "settlement" with the problem of skepticism in the philosophical tradition, namely, Kant's in *The Critique of Pure Reason*. As Cavell summarizes it,

> The dissatisfaction with such a settlement as Kant's is relatively easy to state. To settle with skepticism . . . to assure us that we do know the existence of the world, or rather, that what we understand as knowledge is *of* the world, the price Kant asks us to pay is to cede any claim to know the thing in itself, to grant that human knowledge is not of things as they are in themselves. You don't—do you?—have to be a romantic to feel sometimes about that settlement: Thanks for nothing.[3]

The irony of the Kantian settlement with skepticism—and it is an irony that will in no small part structure what Cavell characterizes as nothing less than Emerson's reinvention of philosophy—is that if "reason proves its power to itself, over itself" by discovering the difference between the mere appearances of which it can have knowledge and the *Ding an sich* of which it cannot (62), then the triumph of philosophy is also, at the same time, its failure (a final failure, as it turns out), because knowledge secures itself only by losing the world, leaving us locked (to borrow Emerson's phrase in "Experience") in "a prison of glass" ("Experience, 3:31). As Emerson puts it in a famous passage from "Experience" that Cavell returns to time and again, "I take this evanescence and lubricity of all objects, which lets them slip through our fingers then when we clutch hardest, to be the most unhandsome part of our condition" (3:29).

What this demands from philosophy, then, is a double gesture in the recognition that thinking must henceforward proceed differently. First, Emerson comes to understand—as Cavell brilliantly and even movingly demonstrates—that "philosophy has to do with the perplexed capacity to mourn the passing of the world."[4] In "Experience," that mourning is figured in some of the most shocking and vertiginous lines in all of American literature, where, reflecting on the grief attending the death of his son two years earlier, Emerson writes, "I cannot get it nearer to me . . . it does not touch me." Emerson grieves, Cavell suggests, not so much over the death of his son, but over the loss of the world, with which even the experience of grief cannot bring him into closer contact: "I grieve that grief can teach me nothing." "Grief too," Emerson writes, "will make us idealists" (3:29). Second, if the demand for foundational concepts, abstract synthesis, and unity of judgments only drives the world away from us in the very act of trying to grasp and apprehend it, then thinking must be reconceived as what Cavell calls "clutching's opposite."[5] Philosophy, to put it telegraphically, must *get out of hand*, which is exactly what happens in Emerson's reinvention of philosophy as antiphilosophy—hence the demanding wildness of Emerson's writing, which will lead the attentive reader, more than once, to ask, "Is he serious?"

Emerson thus inaugurates a rethinking of thinking that will eventually lead, as Cavell points out, to Heidegger's assertion that "thinking is a handicraft," but a handicraft carried out in respect of "the derivation of the word thinking from a root for thanking . . . as giving thanks for the gift of thinking."[6] (And eventually—as Cavell does *not* point out—it will lead to Derrida's analysis not only of the gift, but also his critique of Heidegger's humanism in relation to the question of species difference in the essay "*Geschlecht* II: Heidegger's Hand.")[7] There, Derrida deconstructs the purity of the distinction between giving and taking that Heidegger's humanism takes (we might even say, holds) for granted—a deconstruction that one might well argue is writ large in Emerson's essay "Fate," where he insists, "See how fate slides into freedom, and freedom into fate, observe how far the roots of every creature run, or find, if you can, a point where there is no thread of connection" (6:20). Thinking with Emerson, then, becomes not active apprehension (prehensile grasping of the world by our concepts, as it were), but rather an act of *reception*, a reception in which passivity—because it consists of a capacity to be affected by the world in manifold ways that exponentially outnumber the choked bottleneck of thought as philosophy has traditionally conceived it—becomes, paradoxically, a maximally *active* passivity, a process everywhere testified to in Emerson's work from beginning to end, from the "transparent eyeball" passage in *Nature* to the seemingly paradoxical assertion in "Self-Reliance" that "self-reliance is God-reliance," to his assertion in "Experience" that "All I know is reception; I am and I have: but I do not get, and when I fancied I had gotten anything, I found I did not. . . . When I receive a new gift, I do not macerate my body to make the account square, for, if I should die, I could not make the account square. The benefit overran the merit the first day" (3:48).

But as crucial as Cavell's work has been for enabling an entirely new and deeply compelling understanding of Emerson and his relationship to Continental philosophy, I want to suggest that a more rigorous and historically compelling understanding of Emerson's work is available to us if we reframe Cavell's account itself within a more comprehensive view of Emerson's Romanticism as a response to the condition of *modernity* and its epistemological and ethical fallout—a phenomenon marked in Cavell's reading by the broad brushstroke of "skepticism." In this connection, it is surprising, as Paul Jay has pointed out, that Emerson's work as a response specifically to modernity has not received more attention, as debates have instead been preoccupied with arguments in the 1980s and 1990s over whether Emerson is best understood as a transcendentalist or a pragmatist or, more recently, with the political status of Emerson's work—but with "political" understood, it turns out, in a quite ideologically specific way.[8] And even in more recent studies where the context of modernity *does* seem to be cultivated for understanding Emerson's work (for example, in Jay Grossman's *Reconstituting the American Renaissance*, which revisits Emerson in the context of a specifically American version of "the long eighteenth century"), the conjugation remains hampered by a certain American exceptionalism, replete with a very familiar set of assumptions about politics—how it is related to questions of ethics and agency, how individuals are related to social institutions, and so on—that has been endemic to American studies and its core theoretical and methodological commitments (as numerous commentators have noted) almost since the inception of American studies itself.[9]

Those assumptions and commitments, I would argue, are constituted by and reproduce a quite ideologically specific form of liberal humanism. But as one of its critics, Donald Pease, has recently pointed out, "What Emerson referred to as 'my genius [when it] calls me' achieved effects that were independent of the processes of identification, interpellation, and internalization associated with liberal institutions," and it thus "also undermined liberalism's conception of the possessive individual as its subject."[10] To put it bluntly, the liberal humanist assumptions taken for granted in most American studies critiques of Emerson are not just tangentially but *directly* under attack in Emerson's work. And so it should come as no surprise that we find the more or less automatic assumption in American studies work on Emerson that to abandon those very ideas about politics, agency, and so on is to be (more or less by default) politically conservative or regressive (which is, after all, the way ideology works through institutions like academia to reproduce itself). And though I cannot pursue the argument in any detail here, I would suggest—particularly in the current geopolitical moment, which can only be called, I think, a moment of crisis for liberal democracy and its ideology and institutions—that we would be better off taking seriously Emerson's interrogation of liberalism's assumptions about subjectivity, agency, and politics, even if those queries end (as they often do in Emerson) in anything but a sanguine view of our situation. We should take them seriously for the very same reasons that have generated such an upsurge in interest in figures such as Giorgio Agamben and Carl Schmitt. Indeed, what Chantal Mouffe writes about Schmitt could well serve as a paraphrase of Cavell's reading of Emerson's late essay "Fate" and its implications for politics: "The political cannot be restricted to a certain type of institution, or envisioned as constituting a specific sphere or level of society. It must be conceived as a dimension that is inherent to every human society and that determines our very ontological condition."[11]

We may now return with a somewhat different set of coordinates, and a different sense of their implications, to the question of modernity, whose chief philosophical challenge, as Jay points out, is the well-known process of "secularization." It is this challenge to which Romanticism, so the story goes, constitutes a finally flawed and even fanciful response, one whose contours we have already glimpsed in the fundamentally ironic structure of the Kantian transcendentalism and its settlement with skepticism. For Habermas, in *The Philosophical Discourse of Modernity,* secularization means that thought "can and will no longer borrow the criteria by which it takes its orientation from models supplied by another epoch; it has to create its normativity out of itself"; for Foucault—and here we return to Kant once more—it is that thought must put its "own reason to use, without subjecting itself to any authority."[12] If the upside of the philosophical situation of modernity is, as Jay puts it, that "the present represents an exit or a way out of subordination to traditional sources and modes of authority,"[13] then the downside, already traced in Kantian transcendentalism, is that the ungrounding of reason invites the various forms of idealism that have been attributed to Romanticism in the all-too-familiar narratives of secularization, where Mind, Spirit, Imagination, or the equivalent comes to take the place of self-generated knowledge and its authority previously reserved for God.

Now we might imagine any number of responses to this as a more or less standard characterization of Emerson's work. To begin with, one might well argue that such a position too rapidly assimilates Emerson's later work—particularly the second series of essays and *The Conduct of Life*—to the principles articulated in the early essay *Nature.* Cavell, for example, argues that the Emerson of *Nature* and its adjacent early essays is not just superficially different but *fundamentally* different from the later work. As Cavell puts it,

> I am at present among those who find *Nature,* granted the wonder-ful passages in it, not yet to constitute the Emersonian philosophical voice, but to be the place from which, in the several following years, that voice departs, in "The American Scholar, "The Divinity School Address," and "Self-Reliance." I would characterize the difference by

saying that in *Nature* Emerson is taking the issue of skepticism as solvable or controllable where thereafter he takes its unsolvability to be the heart of his thinking.[14]

It is precisely this "unsolvabability" that generates what Richard Rorty would characterize as an increasingly—and increasingly demanding—*antirepresentationalist* mode of philosophical practice in Emerson. As Rorty explains it, the problem with philosophical representationalism is the assumption that "'making true' and 'representing' are reciprocal relations," as if "the nonlinguistic item which makes *S* true is the one represented by *S*."[15] For philosophical idealism, that "item" will be something in the changeless character of the subject; for realism, it will be something in the nature of the object that "has a context of its own, a context which is privileged by virtue of being the object's rather than the inquirer's" (96). In either case, what representationalism fails to see is that "'determinacy' is not what is in question—that neither does thought determine reality nor, in the sense intended by the realist, does reality determine thought. More precisely, it is no truer that 'atoms are what they are because we use [the word] "atom" as we do' than 'we use "atom" as we do because atoms are as they are.' *Both* of these claims, the antirepresentationalist says, are entirely empty" (5). Both positions, as Cavell might say, find themselves unduly, even preeningly, "handsome"—hence the strange, insistent movement of Emerson's prose, which takes for granted, as it were, Rorty's contention that "words take their meaning from other words rather than by virtue of their representative character" and their "transparency to the real,"[16] that "'grasping the thing itself' is not something that precedes contextualization."[17]

For these reasons, as Rorty has quite lucidly explained, leveling the charge of "relativism" at antirepresentationalism is an empty gesture. "Relativism certainly is self-refuting," he writes, "but there is a difference between saying that every community is as good as every other and saying that we have to work out from the networks [where] we are." The idea, he continues, that every tradition or belief or idea or community "is as rational or as moral as every other could be held only by a god.... Such a being would have escaped from history and conversation into contemplation and metanarrative. To accuse postmodernism of relativism is to try to put a metanarrative in the postmodernist's mouth."[18] It is precisely this kind of embeddedness, of course, that is everywhere under intense scrutiny in essays of Emerson's such as "Fate." The problem for critics of antirepresentationalism (to stay with Rorty's terms)—and it is the same problem that keeps them from being able to read Emerson, I would argue—is that they are only able to understand "contingency" as "relativism" or "idealism" and not (to move now *beyond* Rorty's terms, toward systems theory) as *complexity*.

And so—to return now to Cavell—to take the unsolvability of skepticism to heart is not just, at the same stroke, to abandon the representationalist philosophical project; it is also to change our view of the relationship of thinking and language. What Kant confronted as "merely" a problem of thought, Emerson will grapple with under the additional rigors of writing and language—of philosophy as a writing practice—so that the "stipulations or terms under which we can say anything at all to one another" will themselves be subjected to endless—and endlessly unfinalized—scrutiny.[19] As Cavell puts it:

> [In Emerson] I find the *Critique of Pure Reason* turned upon itself: notions of limitation and of condition are as determining in the essay "Fate" as they are in Kant, but it is as if these terms are themselves subjected to transcendental deduction, as if not just twelve categories but any and every word in our language stands under the necessity of deduction, or say derivation.... Emerson is commonly felt to play fast and loose with something like contradiction in his writing; but I am speaking of a sense in which contradiction, the countering of diction, is the genesis of his writing of philosophy. (113)

What this means is that when we come upon such apparently full-bore idealist statements in Emerson as the following, from the essay "Fate"—"Intellect annuls fate. So far as a man thinks, he is free"—"this apparently genteel thought," Cavell writes, "now turns out to mean that ... our antagonism to fate, to which we are fated, and in which our freedom resides, is as a struggle with the language we emit, of our character with itself."[20]

One striking example of this new philosophical practice that Cavell finds in Emerson—this time in relation not to Kant but to Descartes—occurs in "Self-Reliance" when Emerson writes, "Man is timid and apologetic; he is no longer upright; he dares not say 'I think,' 'I am,' but quotes some saint or sage." If the central feature of the Cartesian subject is, as Cavell writes, the "discovery that my existence requires, hence permits, proof (you might say authentication) . . . requires that if I am to exist I must name my existence, acknowledge it," then the real rigor of Emerson's confrontation with these "terms" is that it "goes the whole way with Descartes insight." It insists on the proof of selfhood—including its proof in and through the "terms" of thinking—without providing a fixed, a priori subject on which such a proof could rely and of which it could be, as it were, the representation—"as if there were nothing to rely on," Cavell writes, "but reliance itself."[21] The "beauty" of Emerson's answer to Descartes," Cavell writes,

> lies in its weakness (you may say in its emptiness)—indeed, in two weaknesses. First, it does not prejudge what the I or self or mind or soul may turn out to be, but only specifies a condition that whatever it is must meet. Second, the proof only works in the moment of its giving, for what I prove is the existence only of a creature who *can* enact its existence, as exemplified in actually giving the proof, not one who at all times does in fact enact it. (87)

The "self" of Emersonian "self-reliance," then, is "not a state of being but a moment of change, say of becoming—a transience of being, a being of transience" (89).

In Cavell—and this marks quite precisely his difference with Rorty—the paradoxical self-reference of the "proof" of the Emersonian self is crucial to what we might think of as its generative incompleteness. This movement of the Emersonian self—in which the self might be said to be alive only to the extent that it *is* moving—is crucial to what Cavell sees as the political import of Emerson's work, what he calls its "democratic" or "moral" "perfectionism." As Cavell describes it, "I do not read Emerson as saying . . . that there is one unattained/attainable self we repetitively never arrive at, but rather that 'having' 'a' self is a process of moving to, and from, nexts. . . . That the self is always attained, as well as *to be* attained, creates the problem in Emerson's concept of self-reliance . . . that unless you manage the reliance of the attained on the unattained/attainable (that is, unless you side that way), you are left in precisely the negation of the position he calls for, left in conformity."[22] In its "onwardness," the Emersonian self must constantly surpass the selves it has already become, but not to attain an ideal, fixed selfhood. And yet, "since the task for each is his or her own self-transformation," Cavell sensibly observes, "the representativeness implied in that life may seem not to establish a recognition of others in different positions, so as to be disqualified as a moral position altogether." Emerson's remarkable twist on this problem, however, is that his writing "works out the conditions for my recognizing my difference from others as a function of my recognizing my difference from myself";[23] after all, strictly speaking, only you can transform you, and only I can transform me. So "Emerson's turn is to make my partiality itself"—what I am here calling (somewhat at a tangent to Cavell, as will become clear) my "contingency"—"the sign and incentive of my siding with the next or future self, which means siding against my attained perfection (or conformity), sidings that require the recognition of an other—the acknowledgment of a relationship—in which this sign is manifest."[24]

Emersonian perfectionism may thus be conceived as a kind of ongoing act of radical negative capability that provides the foundation (though that is eventually not the word we would want, of course) for democratic relations with others, with those other selves I have not yet been but who also—and this is the engine of Emerson's constant polemical project—need to surpass *themselves,* in an ongoing process of democracy conceived as otherness always yet to be achieved, or *if* already achieved, only achieved in the present by the other and not by me. As difficult as it is to see, Cavell is right that this idea of perfectionism is "projected in contrast to the idea of 'one's own nature'";[25] and all of Emerson's talk—and a considerable amount of talk it is—of "self-recovery" both early and late in his work (see, for example, "Nature," 1:39; "Experience," 3:46) directs us to not an originary, fixed self-substance but toward a *power* and a *process:* not toward the past, but rather toward the future, or rather toward futurity itself, conceived as a horizon, where, paradoxically, the only "self" to "recover" is a self that one has not yet been, for the self *only* exists in its becoming. Indeed from this vantage, we might read "recovery" very differently as a "re-covering," as burying and covering over once more the past self, that casualty of what Cavell calls Emerson's "onwardness."

It is in the context and the services of these future selves and against what Emerson calls "conformity" that we are to understand the political involvement of the Emersonian self in the sense insisted on at the end of "Experience," where Emerson writes that "the true romance which the world exists to realize, will be the transformation of genius into practical power" (3:49). As Cavell writes, when Emerson's critics read the line "self-reliance is the aversion of conformity," they "take this to mean roughly that he is disgusted with society and wants no more to do with it."[26] But if we understand the Emersonian self as movement toward futurity and not a being, then instead of *conversion* to a truth we already know and to a being we already are, *aversion* means "that his writing and his society incessantly recoil from, or turn away from one another; but since this is incessant, the picture is at the same time of each incessantly turning *toward* the other"[27]—a process that is dramatized perhaps nowhere more forcefully than in late essays and addresses like "Fate" and "The Fugitive Slave Law," where Emerson insists time and again on turning away from society and its institutions, toward the domain of justice and ethics, only to turn back to the realization of freedom not in transcendence but in "practical power" ("Experience," 3:49).

On the one hand, Emerson asserts in "The Fugitive Slave Law," "No forms, neither Constitutions nor laws nor covenants nor churches nor bibles, are of any use in themselves; The devil nestles comfortably into them all. There is no help but in the head and heart and hamstrings of a man."[28] On the other hand, as Emerson writes in "Fate," "A man must thank his defects, and stand in some terror of his talents. A transcendent talent draws so largely on his forces, as to lame him; a defect pays him revenues on the other side" (6:19), and he reminds us that his "power is hooped in by a necessity, which, by many experiments, he touches on every side, until he learns its arc" (6:11). A corollary of this "aversive" movement of the Emersonian self is that the world—and we already know this from the Kantian anatomy of skepticism—always already "vanishes from me," as Cavell puts it, becomes a *horizon* that we can only approach but never reach, one that is in a radical sense dependent upon the terms we use: not to apprehend it, but rather to *receive,* or as Cavell says, "acknowledge" it, just as I am impelled toward the other by my "partiality" toward myself, my contingency.

Here, I think, we can begin to get a sense of the usefulness of Niklas Luhmann's work for helping us to read the full letter of Emerson's thinking. First of all, Luhmann's theorization of these questions is more analytically rigorous than Cavell's, which remains largely at the level of a philosophical thematics characterized by what one might call—at least from a Luhmannian point of view—an excessive "literariness." That would be of less moment were it not for the fact identified by Cavell himself: that "literariness" has typically been used as a kind of code for dismissing Emerson's rigor and philosophical seriousness. Second—and this is all the clearer in light of Rorty—Cavell's reading of Emerson under the master rubric of skepticism remains tied, one might argue, to the representationalism he would otherwise seem to disown, because skepticism holds onto the desire for a representational adequation between concepts and objects even as it knows that desire to be unappeasable (how else are we to understand Cavell's insistence on taking seriously the "mourning" of the loss of the world—and not of the child Waldo, as Sharon Cameron insists in her classic essay "Representing Grief"—in Emerson's "Experience"?).

Third, and most important of all, Luhmann puts acute pressure on the relentlessly paradoxical and confounding dynamics of observation that are so central, and so increasingly vexing, in Emerson's work— dynamics that are usually thematized in criticism of Romanticism under the rubric of "imagination," and more specifically in Emerson's work, in his well-known theatrics with the trope of vision (as in the famous "transparent eyeball" passage in the opening pages of *Nature,* "I am nothing. I see all" [1:10]). In fact, if we believe Maurice Gonnaud, it is Emerson's movement away from such solutions to the paradoxes of observation in the early 1840s that has made his later work in lectures and essays such as "The Method of Nature" and "Nomimalist and Realist" all the more vexing for his critics. After 1840, Gonnaud writes, "If the Romantic was dead, the optimist had survived him and was ready to make a virtue of necessity"—specifically, I will argue in a moment, a necessity called *contingency.*[29] "Although he continued to call himself an idealist," Gonnaud continues, "he had ceased to be one in Kant's sense or even in Coleridge's. The universe gradually comes to resemble that 'old Two-Face, creator-creature, mind-matter, right-wrong' which he was to evoke in 'Nominalist and Realist'" (301; see "Nominalist and Realist," 3:144).

Emerson's insistence on the contingency, not transcendence, of observation—what Gonnaud calls his effort to "fling out a new bridge— less ethereal, less harmonious perhaps, but tougher—between the One and the Many," purchased by taking it upon himself "to be the champion of the acknowledged facts, honored in their richness and diversity,"[30] led to Emerson being even less understood than he had prior to 1840. Remarking on "The Method of Nature," Gonnaud writes that "his listeners confessed to understanding very little of it; the word 'ecstasy' recurs like a leitmotif, applied now to Nature and now to human beings and thus compounding the confusion" (301), not just for Emerson's contemporaries but even for later critics such as Stephen Whicher, who finds that such work "incorporates two irreconcilable perspectives and suffers from a profound incoherence" (302). What I want to suggest, however—and we will need Luhmann's work to fully explain why—is that it is precisely at these moments that we find Emerson at his most rigorous, systematically extrapolating in his later work the paradoxical dynamics and consequences of observation that were, as both Gonnaud and Cavell rightly observe in their different ways, certainly central to the Emersonian corpus from the beginning but were papered over by the more conventional idealism and Romanticism we find in essays such as *Nature*. And while Gonnaud regrets in the post-1840 Emerson "the author's centrifugal disposition of mind, which keeps him from transforming the profoundly contradictory impulses within him into dialectical movement" (302), Luhmann's work on observation will help to make it clear why Emerson's relentless explorations of these problems cannot and should not resolve themselves into a dialectic. Here again, it is not incoherence or vagueness of thought we find, I would suggest, but rather the rigor of what we might call Emerson's undoing of Romanticism.

Of the Emerson critics I have read, the one who has come closest to realizing this fact about Emerson's work is Lee Rust Brown in his wonderful book *The Emerson Museum*. As he observes about Emerson's contention in "Compensation" that "the value of the universe contrives to throw itself into every point," such moments "have been cited by readers who attack or applaud Emerson as a cheerful mystic who vaguely sees everything in everything."[31] What we have here instead, he suggests, is a bit more complicated process in which Coleridgean "multaeity in unity" is subordinated to the workings of the observers, where "the sense found in natural objects is precisely the viewer's own original *means* for seeing them. . . . By virtue of these means, vision rises to a place of authority over objects, to a kind of perspectival remove sufficient to reveal relations within the whole scope of things" (71–72). And yet such an observer is not transcendent in the usual idealist sense—indeed in any sense. Instead, on display here is the more complicated dynamic of Emersonian "transparency"—that ability to perceive the "unity" of the "multaeity"— that "is the one fatal condition of moving on intellectually; it is the way we pay for all worthwhile adjustments of attention." That is the only way we achieve what Emerson calls "new prospects"—in Brown's words, "at once the new object and the prospect of its future conversion into transparency" (47). Far from being transcendent, then, "we see one object only at the cost of another" (46), and "transparency, far from signifying a passive state or continuity or unity, testifies to the way the eye manufactures its own discontinuous intervals" (45–46).

At this juncture, Luhmann's work can give us a more precise and fully articulated sense of Emerson's pressure on the problem of observation, in part because observation in Luhmann is *disarticulated* from vision per se, and in part because systems theory takes the additional step of assimilating the problem of observation to that problem to that *other* central topos of Romanticism invoked by Brown—multaeity in unity— which must now be rewritten in systems theory's terms as the problem of *complexity* and how it is handled in system/environment relationships. It is this convergence—the paradoxical dynamics of observation and the related problem of complexity, how observation both reduces *and* produces complexity—that Emerson's writing insists on more and more rigorously as his career unfolds, rendering it in his mature work literally *unavoidable*—as in, for example, one of his more brazen assertions, in "Circles," that "I am a God in nature; I am a weed by the wall" (2:182). Such a statement—and there are many of them in Emerson—insists on the radical *identity* of what, in the philosophical tradition, are opposites: namely, on the one hand, the absolute, all-constitutive subject of knowledge familiar to us from various forms of philosophical idealism (the "god" that gets secularized as "imagination" in Romanticism), and, on the other hand, what Kant called the "pathological" contingency of the object world and the empirical. Luhmann can help us to see how in such apparently outlandish and fanciful paradoxes Emerson precisely registers the epistemological fallout of the very modernity to which his Romanticism is responding—not as a mystification or "imaginative" solution but as a kind of relentless anatomy. And here we may locate another advan-

tage of Luhmann's work over Cavell's: that it links these philosophical
and epistemological complexities to the historical conditions of their
emergence. Only by following this tack can we understand the rigor and
systematicity, rather than the incoherence or "fogginess," of the paradox
at the core of Emerson's work: his constant movement between asserting, on the one hand, that "thought dissolves the material universe" and,
on the other, that "if in the least particular, one could derange the order
of nature,—who would accept the gift of life? ("Fate," 6:15, 6:26).

Emerson insists, in other words, on the radical contingency and, at
the same time, the radical authority of self-referential observation, whose
positive existential valence gets figured in the "whim" of "Self-Reliance,"
while its more vexing effects are registered in the isolation and vertigo
of the opening of "Experience" and, finally, in the paradoxical fatedness
to freedom of *The Conduct of Life*. Such paradoxes are, from Luhmann's
point of view, masked in the theological tradition that Emerson inherits and famously rejects early in his career as a minister. In fact, were
we to follow Luhmann's suggestion, the closest thing we could find to
Emerson's work in the theological tradition would not be Quakerism or
Unitarianism but the line of medieval theology that works its way from
Saint Augustine through John Scotus Eriugena to the fifteenth-century
theologian Nicolaus Cusanus. "No traditional epistemology," Luhmann
writes, "could dare to go this far—obviously because the position from
which it would have had to deal with distinctness was occupied by theology."[32] But with the secularization of these questions in Romanticism's
philosophy of the subject—itself, Luhmann argues, a product of the
unavoidable movement from hierarchical to functionally differentiated
society under modernity, in which the Church no longer has a centering
role—they begin to become ever more unavoidable. "With the retreat
of the religious world order," Luhmann writes, the "question of how the
world can observe itself" becomes more pressing and vexing, and it is
typically answered in Romanticism and its forerunner, German idealist philosophy, by such makeshift terms as "Spirit," "Idea" and so on.[33]
"Inspired by the idea of God as observer," Luhmann writes,

> Theology began to observe this observer, even though it was forced to
> concede that an observer who creates and sustains the world by vir-
> tue of his observation excludes nothing and hence cannot assume an
> observable form. By externalizing this paradox and by incorporating

the notion of observing the unobservable into the idea of God, one
sought to shield the conventional notion of the world as *universitas
rerum* from infection by logical paradoxes. (92)

The problem with this "solution," of course—as Harro Muller among
others has pointed out—is that in an increasingly "acentrically conceived
society" (the society of modernity) "it is difficult to preserve the notion
of an Archimedean point from which and towards which both world and
society might be understood.... It is also prohibited from assuming a
strictly privileged extramundane observer's perspective. Such a perspective would place collective singulars such as God, Spirit, History, Man,
Nature, the subject, the individual or intersubjectivity at the center of a
foundational discourse." But these foundational discourses—whether of
an ontological, natural, or anthropological nature—"are predominantly a
matter of self-attributions or self-simplifications that are functionally in
need of explanation."[34] And this is where we need Luhmann.

We need, in other words (to use Luhmann's shorthand), to replace
"what" questions with "how" questions.[35] Here, the fundamental postu-
late of systems theory—its replacement of the familiar *ontological* dichoto-
mies of humanism (culture/nature, mind/body, spirit/matter, reason/
feeling, and so on) with the *functional* distinction system/environment—
is indispensable in allowing us to better understand how systems respond
to modernity's central challenge of "functional differentiation" (what
other critical vocabularies would call its "specialization" or, more moralis-
tically or nostalgically, its "fragmentation"). As Muller summarizes it,

> Perspectives are multiplied within functionally differentiated mod-
> ern society without one's being able to adopt any privileged central
> perspective or assign a hierarchically superior leading position to any
> one partial system.... No partial system may represent the whole
> and become active in a representative manner; no partial system may
> replace another as its functional equivalent. It is precisely functional
> differentiation, with its internal increase in control in individual par-
> tial systems, which increases "disorder" and risk.[36]

—a dynamic that eventually results in what has been variously characterized as the opaque (post)modern condition of "hypercomplexity."

For Luhmann, both psychic and social systems—and I won't be able
to take up here his extraordinarily interesting and original exploration of

the differences and relations between them[37]—respond to this complexity by means of autopoiesis and self-referential closure as a means of self-preservation. Such systems find themselves by definition in an environment that is always already more complex than they are, and all systems attempt to adapt to this complexity by filtering it in terms of their own, self-referential codes. The point of the system is to reproduce itself, but no system can deal with everything, or even many things, all at once. The legal system, for example, responds to changes in its environment in terms of—and only in terms of—the distinction legal/illegal. In litigation, decisions are not based—and it is a good thing too—on whether you are black or white, male or female, whether you went to school at Oxford or Cambridge, and so on.

Two subsidiary points need to be accented here. First, in responding to environmental complexity in terms of their own self-referential codes, subsystems build up their own internal complexity (one might think here of the various subspecialties of the legal system, say, or the specialization of disciplines in the education system); in doing so, systems become ever more finely grained in their selectivity, and thus—in increasing the web-like density of their filters, as it were—they buy *time* in relation to overwhelming environmental complexity. As Luhmann puts it in *Social Systems,* "Systems lack the 'requisite variety' (Ashby's term) that would enable them to react to every state of the environment.... There is, in other words, no point-for-point correspondence between system and environment.... The system's inferiority in complexity [compared to that of the environment] must be counter-balanced by strategies of selection."[38] Emerson's way of putting this, in "Nominalist and Realist," is that "the world is full. As the ancient said, the world is a *plenum* or solid; and if we saw all things that really surround us, we should be imprisoned and unable to move" (3:142). But if the self-reference of the system's code reduces the flow of environmental complexity into the system, it also increases the system's "irritability" and thus, in a very real sense, its *dependence* on the environment.

Here—and this is crucial to understanding the "engine," if you like, of what Cavell calls Emersonian "transience," "onwardness," and "abandonment"—the term "complexity" should be understood not as an aggregation of substance (a big pile of lots of things), nor only, and better, as an abstract set of *relations*, but more importantly as a set of *temporalized* relations that have the character of the Derridean or Deleuzean "event." Systems use self-reference not just to build up their own internal complexity but also to stabilize themselves in the temporal flow of events and to render events meaningful for the system. As Luhmann explains, "We need a concept of meaning ... as the simultaneous presentation ... of actuality and possibility."[39] "The totality of the references presented by any meaningfully intended object offers more to hand than can in fact be actualized at any moment. Thus the form of meaning"—the copresentation of the difference between the actual and possible—"through its referential structure, *forces* the next step, to *selection*."[40] But that selection, of course, immediately begins to deteriorate in usefulness under the pressure of the temporal flow of events, the "specious present," which then forces *another* selection, and so on and so forth.[41] Or as Luhmann puts it, "One could say that meaning equips an actual experience or action with redundant possibilities"—namely, what *was* selected (the actual) and what could have been (the possible)—and this is crucial for any system's ability to respond to environmental complexity by building up its own complexity via the form of meaning, through which the system uses time even as it is subjected to its pressure. "The genesis and reproduction of meaning presupposes an infrastructure in reality that constantly changes its states," Luhmann writes. "Meaning then extracts differences (which only as differences have meaning) from this substructure to enable a difference-oriented processing of information. On all meaning, therefore, are imposed a temporalized complexity and the compulsion to a constant shifting of actuality, without meaning itself vibrating in tune with that substructure."[42]

Read against this background, the rigor of moments such as this one in Emerson's "The Method of Nature" becomes, I believe, more apparent:

> The method of nature: who could ever analyze it? That rushing stream will not stop to be observed. We can never surprise nature in a corner; never find the end of a thread.... The wholeness we admire in the order of the world, is the result of infinite distribution.... Its permanence is a perpetual inchoation. Every natural fact is an emanation, and that from which it emanates is an emanation also, and from every emanation is a new emanation. If anything could stand still, it would be crushed and dissipated by the torrent it resisted, and if it were a

mind, would be crazed; as insane persons are those who hold fast to one thought, and do not flow with the course of nature. (1:124)

Subordinating the problem of self-referential observation to the larger problem of complexity helps clarify why it is misguided at best to charge systems theory in general and the theory of autopoiesis in particular with asserting a kind of solipsistic relationship between the system and its environment. What such a characterization misses is the seemingly paradoxical fact that the autopoietic closure of a system—whether social or psychic—is precisely what *connects* it to its environment. As Luhmann explains it, "The concept of a self-referentially closed system does not contradict the system's *openness to the environment*. Instead, in the self-referential mode of operation, closure is a form of broadening possible environmental contacts; closure increases, by constituting elements more capable of being determined, the complexity of the environment that is possible for the system."[43] And this is why, as Luhmann puts it,

> Autopoiesis and complexity are conceptual coordinates.... Dependency and independence, in a simple causal sense, are therefore not invariant magnitudes in that more of one would imply less of the other. Rather, they vary according to a system's given level of complexity. In systems that are successful in evolutionary terms, more independence typically amounts to a greater dependency on the environment.... But all of this can happen only on the basis of the system's operative closure.[44]

Or as Luhmann will put it in one of his more Zen-like moments, "Only complexity can reduce complexity."[45]

All of this leads to a paradoxical situation that is central to Luhmann's work, and central to understanding his reworking of problems inherited from both Hegel and Husserl—problems that bear directly on our reading of Emerson: what links the system to the world, what literally makes the world available to the system, is also what hides the world from the system, what makes it unavailable. Given our discussion a moment ago of the problem of "representing the unrepresentable," this should ring a bell (namely, the Romantic sublime), but this is a different bell, as it turns out. To understand just *how* different, we need to remember, first, that all systems interface with their environments in terms of, and only in terms of, their own constitutive distinctions and self-referential codes, then the "environment" is not an ontological category but a functional one. That is to say, it is not an "outside" to the system that is given *as such*—it is not, in other words, either "nature" or "society" in the traditional sense—but is rather always the outside *of* a specific inside. Or as Luhmann deftly explains it, the environment is different for every system, because any system excludes only itself from its environment.[46] "With this turn," Luhmann writes, "the distinction between self-reference and hetero-reference is relocated within the observed observing system" or, to put it another way, "the distinction between self- and hetero-reference is nothing other than the re-entry of the distinction system/environment into the system itself."[47]

This means, however, that there is a paradoxical identity between the two sides of the system's constitutive distinction, because the "re-entered" distinction between both sides (system and environment) is itself a product of only *one* side (the system). In the legal system, for example, the distinction between the two sides legal/illegal is instantiated by only one side of the distinction, the legal. But no system can acknowledge this paradoxical identity of difference—which is also in another sense simply the contingency—of its own constitutive distinction and at the same time *use* that distinction to carry out its operations. It must remain "blind" to the very paradox of the distinction that links it to its environment. It can use the two-sided distinction to carry out its operations, but it must remain blind to the underlying *form* of the distinction that secures the paradoxical identity of both "opposite" sides.

That does not mean that this "blind spot" cannot be observed from the vantage of *another* observer, *another* system using another code—it can, and that is what we are doing right now—but any *second-order* observation will itself be based on its *own* blind spot, the paradoxical identity of both sides of *its* constitutive distinction, and so on. First-order observations that deploy distinctions as differences simply do what they do. Second-order observations can observe the unity of those differences and the contingency of the code of the first-order observer, but only by in turn doing what they do, thus reproducing a blindness that is (formally) the same but (contingently) not the same as the observed first-order system. This is what Emerson is insisting on, I think—again in "Nominalist and Realist"—when he writes:

Nature will not be Buddhist: she resents generalizing, and insults the philosopher in every moment with a million of fresh particulars. It is all idle talking: as much as a man is a whole, so is he also a part; and it were partial not to see it. What you say in your pompous distribution only distributes you into your class and section. You have not got rid of parts by denying them, but are the more partial. You are one thing, but nature is *one thing and the other thing*, in the same moment. (3:139)

Such a passage may be quite precisely unpacked, I think, against the background of Luhmann's fruitful reworking of the Hegelian problematic: not the "identity of identity and non-identity," as in Hegel, but rather as the "*non*-identity" (or *difference*) of identity and non-identity—a *difference* that inheres in the contingency of self-referential distinction itself ("you are one thing") or, in another sense, in the difference between first- and second-order observation ("you have not got rid of parts by denying them, but are the more partial"). And this is, of course, a *productive* difference; from the vantage of the problem of complexity, it has no choice but to be.[48]

This is what Emerson is reaching for in "Nominalist and Realist," I think, when he writes that "excluded attributes burst in on us with the more brightness, that they have been excluded. 'Your turn now, my turn next,' is the rule of the game. The universality being hindered in its primary form, comes in the secondary form of *all sides:* the points come in succession to the meridian, and by the speed of rotation, a new whole is formed" (3:142, Emerson's emphasis). This might sound, at first blush, Hegelian, but the key difference—contra the invocation of dialectic by Gonnaud—is Emerson's strident insistence on the primacy and paradoxical contingency of the observer, an insistence that reaches its peak in *Essays: Second Series*. As Luhmann explains the relationship between observation and what Emerson calls the "horizon,"

> The source of a distinction's guaranteeing reality lies in its own operative unity. It is, however, precisely as this unity that the distinction cannot be observed—except by means of another distinction which then assumes the function of a guarantor of reality. Another way of expressing this is to say the operation emerges simultaneously with the world which as a result remains cognitively unapproachable to the operation.
>
> The conclusion to be drawn from this is that the connection with

the reality of the external world is established by the blind spot of the cognitive operation. Reality is what one does not perceive when one perceives it.[49]

Or as he puts it in somewhat different terms, the world is now conceived "along the lines of a Husserlian metaphor, as an unreachable horizon that retreats further with each operation, without ever holding out the prospect of an outside."[50] This is the way Emerson's essay "Circles" begins: "The eye is the first circle; the horizon which it forms is the second; and throughout nature this primary figure is repeated *without end*. . . . Our life is an apprenticeship to the truth, that around every circle another can be drawn; that there is no end in nature, but every end is a beginning" (2:179, emphasis added).

The question, then—and this is directly related, of course, to the problems raised by the topos of the Romantic Sublime—is, in Luhmann's words, "how to observe how the world observes itself, how a marked space emerges [via a constitutive distinction] from the unmarked space, how something becomes invisible when something else becomes visible." Any observation "renders the world invisible" in relation to its constitutive distinction, and that invisibility must itself remain invisible to the observation that employs *that* distinction—which in turn can only be disclosed by *another* observation that will also necessarily be doubly blind in the same way.[51] Here is Emerson again, from "Circles":

> There is no outside, no enclosing wall, no circumference to us. The man finishes his story,—how good! how final! how it puts a new face on all things! He fills the sky. Lo! on the other side rises also a man and draws a circle around the circle we had just pronounced the outline of the sphere. Then already is our first speaker, not man, but only a first speaker. His only redress is forthwith to draw a circle outside of his antagonist. And so men do by themselves. (2:181)

"In this twofold sense," as Luhmann puts it, "the notion of a final unity—of an 'ultimate reality' that cannot assume a form because it has no other side—is displaced into the unobservable. . . . If the concept of the world is retained to indicate reality in its entirety, then it is that which—to a second-order observer—remains invisible in the movements of observation (his own and those of others)."[52]

We can now return in this light to a rather different understanding of the significance of the Kantian settlement with skepticism, reframed in terms of the signal importance of the formal dynamics of observation. As Luhmann puts it succinctly, if we ask "what new insights the concept of observation (first- and second-order observation) has to offer," the answer is "it traces the problem of unity back to the ultimate form of paradox."[53] In a way, Luhmann writes,

> All this can be handled with the de-reification of the concept of the world introduced already by Kant. World is no longer a totality of things, a *universitas rerum,* but rather the final, and therewith unobservable, condition of possibility of observations, that is, of every sort of use of distinctions. To formulate this another way, the world must be invisibilized so that observations become possible. For every observation requires a "blind spot," or more precisely: it can only indicate one side of the distinction being used, employing it as a starting point for subsequent observations, but not the distinction itself as a unity and above all not the "unmarked space," precisely the world from which every distinction, as soon as it is marked as a distinction, must be delimited.[54]

Even more striking, perhaps, are the *consequences* of this fact, as they are described by Luhmann and recorded with rather bracing astringency in essays like Emerson's "Experience." Luhmann continues,

> This invisibilization of the nevertheless doubtlessly given and presupposed world had dramatic consequences for Kant, Fichte, and above all for the Romantics. Its leads to an overburdening of the individual with expectations regarding the production of meaning and therewith to the collapse of the communication weighed down with such expectations. The individual endowed with reflection now received the title "subject." But the higher and more complex the expectations that subjects direct toward themselves and their others, the greater is the probability of a failure of their communications.[55]

It is precisely this overburdening, I think, that is rather remarkably on display in Emerson's essay "Experience," where he writes, "We must hold hard to this poverty, however scandalous, and by more vigorous self-recoveries, after the sallies of action, possess our axis more firmly. The life of truth is cold, and so far mournful; but it is not the slave of tears, contritions, and perturbations." It is a truth, we are told, "that all the muses and love and religion hate," and they "will find a way to punish the chemist, who publishes in the parlor the secrets of the laboratory" (3:46), not the least of which is the quintessentially Emersonian announcement that "it is very unhappy, but too late to be helped, the discovery we have made, that we exist" (3:43). Such is what Luhmann calls "the toxic quality" of second-order observation,[56] and it is on display not just in Emerson's middle and late phase (in *Essays: Second Series* and *The Conduct of Life*), but even in earlier works as well, such as "The American Scholar," where he writes, "We are lined with eyes. We see with our feet. The time is infected with Hamlet's unhappiness,—'Sicklied o'er with the pale cast of thought.' Is it so bad then? Sight is the last thing to be pitied. Would we be blind?" (1:66–67).

Here too, we may locate the signal advantage of the ability of systems theory to combine epistemological and historical frames in ways that are especially useful for sorting out the relationship between Emerson's thinking and his terminology—ways that would open up a rather different understanding of the relationship between Emerson's thinking and writing from what we have already seen in Cavell. What I have been arguing is that a term such as "self-recovery" in the passage just cited should not be understood, despite itself, as recovery of a primordial, preexistent self, but rather as recovery of the onwardness of the self's movement, through which and only in which—as we have already seen in Cavell's analysis of the "proof" of the self in "Self-Reliance"—the self actually exists at all. As Emerson puts it in "Circles," "The way of life is wonderful: it is by abandonment" (2:190). Or more flatly still, from "Experience," "Life is a series of surprises, and would not be worth taking or keeping, if it were not" (3:39).

"Self-recovery," then, is, paradoxically, oriented not toward some originary state but toward *futurity*, toward not being but *becoming*. As Emerson writes in "Circles," "Valor consists in the power of self-recovery, so that a man cannot have his flank turned, cannot be outgeneralled, but put him where you will, he stands. *This can only be by his preferring truth to his past apprehension of truth*" (2:177, emphasis added). Paradoxically, as I have been arguing, the only way for the Emersonian self to "stand" is to *not* stand, to not stand still, but to move in "abandonment" beyond the self of "apprehension" that one was only a second ago. The only way to "stand," then, is to "*under*-stand," to "stand down," if you like. And the achievement of the self is now to be seen not as an active willing that paralyzes itself in spite of (but also from this vantage because of) itself, but rather as a maximally (and paradoxically) active *passivity*, whose activity derives from the fact that it can be affected by the world in manifold ways that far outnumber what is available to the self through the narrow bottleneck of thought as philosophy has traditionally conceived it. As Emerson puts it in "Experience": "All I know is reception" (3:48).

This same misdirection could be said of a whole host of terms in Emerson (Intuition, Reason, Law, Spirit, Being, just to name a few) that have encouraged readers for years to understand Emerson's work as a quaintly failed metaphysics. What systems theory enables us to do, however, is to map the residual versus emergent dimensions of Emerson's work (to use Raymond Williams's well-known terms) in ways not reducible to his terminology alone (as Eduardo Cadava has done quite subtly, I think, with Emerson's relationship to the discourse of race), for which we have to attend to the systematicity—and not just the lexicon— of his thought.[57] Once we do so, we find, as Harro Muller puts it, that "self-descriptions must themselves be temporalized.... Assumptions of substance or of metahistoric essences, metahistorical anthropologies, metahistorically grounded notions of experience, and so on are all forms of thought that are no longer reconcilable with functional differentiation. From Luhmann's perspective, this is all part of an *old-European* heritage that . . . can at best be correlated with the still existing stratificatory elements in modern society."[58] Which is simply to explain, in so many words, why "Experience"—even as it also uses the term "self-recovery"—is a far more interesting text than *Nature*.

And far more interesting, too, not least of all because it confronts in a number of emotional and philosophical registers another consequence noted by Luhmann: that "the forcing of subjectivity as the single answer to the problem of world makes intersubjectivity difficult, indeed, if one is conceptually rigorous, actually impossible."[59] As I have suggested elsewhere, it is precisely on the basis of the disclosure of that impossibility that the possibility of democracy is founded—but only, as Cavell would put it, by being "unfounded" or left "foundering."[60] But rather than pursue that argument further here, I will simply end with the very last lines of Emerson's essay "Nominalist and Realist," which enigmatically, beautifully, maddeningly gathers together some of the threads I have been tracing, only to throw them to the winds. Emerson writes,

> Is it that every man believes every other to be an incurable partialist, and himself an universalist? I talked yesterday with a pair of philosophers: I endeavored to show my good men that I liked everything by turns, and nothing long; that I loved the centre, but doated on the superficies; that I loved man, if men seemed to me mice and rats . . . that I was glad of men of every gift and nobility, but would not live in their arms. Could they but once understand, that I loved to know that they existed, and heartily wished them Godspeed, yet, out of my poverty of life and thought, had no word or welcome for them when they came to see me, and could well consent to their living in Oregon, for any claim I felt on them, it would be a great satisfaction. (3:145)

NOTES

Epigraphs are taken from Stanley Cavell, "Emerson's Constitutional Amending: Reading 'Fate,'" in *Philosophical Passages: Wittgenstein, Emerson, Austin, Derrida* (Cambridge, Mass.: Blackwell, 1995), 36; and Niklas Luhmann, "The Cognitive Program of Constructivism and a Reality that Remains Unknown," in *Selforganization: Portrait of a Scientific Revolution,* ed. Wolfgang Krohn et al. (Dordrecht: Kluwer Academic Publishers, 1990), 76.

1. Emerson delivered much of the contents of the book as lectures from 1851 to 1853, though the book itself did not appear until 1860. See Barbara Packer's "Historical Introduction" to *The Conduct of Life,* l, lxii, in vol. 6 of *The Collected Works of Ralph Waldo Emerson,* ed. Alfred R. Ferguson, Robert E. Spiller, et al., 8 vols. to date (Cambridge, Mass.: Harvard University Press, Belknap Press, 1971–2010). Subsequent quotations from Emerson's writing are from this source and are cited parenthetically in text by volume and page numbers. Citations may include essay title if the essay from which a quotation is taken is not clear from the text.

2. Stanley Cavell, "Finding as Founding: Taking Steps in Emerson's 'Experience,'" in *Emerson's Transcendental Etudes,* ed. David Justin Hodge (Stanford, Calif.: Stanford University Press, 2003), 111.

3. Cavell, "Emerson, Coleridge, Kant," in *Emerson's Transcendental Etudes,* 63.

4. Cavell, "Finding as Founding," 115.

5. Ibid., 117.

6. Cavell, "Aversive Thinking: Emersonian Representations in Heidegger and Nietzsche," in *Emerson's Transcendental Etudes,* 147.

7. See my discussion of this cluster of texts in *Animal Rites: American Culture, the Discourse of Species, and Posthumanist Theory* (Chicago: University of Chicago Press, 2003), 63–64.

8. Paul Jay, *Contingency Blues: The Search for Foundations in American Criticism* (Madison: University of Wisconsin Press, 1997), 21.

9. Jay Grossman, *Reconstituting the American Renaissance: Emerson, Whitman, and the Politics of Representation* (Durham, N.C.: Duke University Press, 2003). One should no doubt applaud Grossman's "opposition to the standard model derived from Matthiessen in which the abundance of the Renaissance springs, Athena-like, out of the head of an Emerson-Zeus," which he attempts to move beyond by "looking backward to the nation's founding for a renewed understanding of the intersections between the political and the literary" (hence the pun—"representation"—that anchors the volume) (6–7). The problem is that in "specifying the discursive contexts out of which the period known as the Renaissance emerges," Grossman's study does not go far enough in this direction. By simply attacking the periodizing break between the eighteenth and nineteenth centuries that has been taken for granted in American studies, and insisting instead that "debates over representation that catalyzed the Revolution . . . continued to swirl at the time of Constitution" (4), forming the key discursive context in which the writings of Emerson and Whitman "resonate anew with echoes that have their origins in facets of the Constitutional settlement" (15), Grossman simply extends, rather than rethinks, exceptionalism. What is crucial here is not the chronological terrain reaching backward to the Revolution but rather the *ideological and methodological* commitment to liberal humanism and to liberal democracy that accompanies it. For if it is true, as Grossman rightly points out, that "representing" and "constituting" inescapably depend upon the "originary relations between the political and the literary" (6), and that "finding a beginning within this history opens out a pattern of potentially infinite regress" (7), then the exceptionalist decision that frames Grossman's book can only be justified on pragmatic or ideological grounds (especially in light of his salutary critique of work that takes for granted the unproblematic distinction between the "literary" and the "empirical" [18]). That is to say, it can only be understood in terms of a strategic decision to limit the full implications of these questions within a prior commitment to the context of liberal democracy itself and its core assumptions about what politics and agency are (a fact made even more evident, ironically enough, by reading Grossman's study alongside the

book that is key to its framing and formation, Brian Seitz's *The Trace of Political Representation* [Albany: SUNY Press, 1995]). But Emerson, I am suggesting, respected no such limit and thus took those questions—and their implications for politics, agency, and much else—more seriously than Grossman understands. To put it another way, if Emerson is antidemocratic in places, it is in the services of a more fundamental commitment to being anti-*ideological.*

10. Donald E. Pease, "'Experience,' Antislavery, and the Crisis of Emersonianism," reprinted as chapter 5 of this book.

11. Chantal Mouffe, *The Return of the Political* (London: Verson, 1993), 3.

12. Habermas quoted in Jay, *Contingency Blues,* 26; Foucault quoted in ibid., 29.

13. Jay, *Contingency Blues,* 28.

14. Cavell, "Finding as Founding," 111–12.

15. Richard Rorty, *Objectivity, Relativism, and Truth: Philosophical Papers* (Cambridge: Cambridge University Press, 1991), 4.

16. Richard Rorty, *Philosophy and the Mirror of Nature* (Princeton, N.J.: Princeton University Press, 1979), 368.

17. Rorty, *Objectivity, Relativism, and Truth,* 100.

18. Ibid., 202.

19. Cavell, "Finding as Founding," 113.

20. Cavell, "Emerson, Coleridge, Kant," 72.

21. Cavell, "Being Odd, Getting Even (Descartes, Emerson, Poe)," in *Transcendental Etudes,* 84, 87. Cavell reminds us that most readers will "remember or assume the cogito always to be expressed in words that translate as 'I think, *therefore* I am.' But in Descartes's Second Meditation, where I suppose it is most often actually encountered, the insight is expressed: '*I am, I exist,* is necessarily true every time that I pronounce or conceive it in my mind.' Emerson's emphasis on the *saying* of 'I' is precisely faithful to this expression of Descartes's insight" (85).

22. Cavell, "Introduction: Staying the Course," in *Conditions Handsome and Unhandsome: The Constitution of Emersonian Perfectionism* (Chicago: University of Chicago Press, 1990), 12.

23. Cavell, "Aversive Thinking," 160.

24. Cavell, "Introduction: Staying the Course," 31.

25. Cavell, "Aversive Thinking," 160.

26. Cavell, "Hope against Hope," in *Emerson's Transcendental Etudes,* 181.

27. "Emerson's Constitutional Amending," in Cavell, *Emerson's Transcendental Etudes,* 193.

28. Emerson, "The Fugitive Slave Law," in *Emerson's Antislavery Writings,* ed. Len Gougeon and Joel Myerson (New Haven, Conn.: Yale University Press, 1995), 83.

29. Maurice Gonnaud, *An Uneasy Solitude: Individual and Society in the Work of Ralph Waldo Emerson,* trans. Lawrence Rosenwald (Princeton, N.J.: Princeton University Press, 1987), 299.

30. Ibid., 299.

31. See "Composition," 2:60. Lee Rust Brown, *The Emerson Museum: Practical Romanticism and the Pursuit of the Whole* (Cambridge, Mass.: Harvard University Press, 1997), 73.

32. Niklas Luhmann, "Cognition as Construction," trans. Hans-Georg Moeller, Appendix B in Hans-Georg Moeller, *Luhmann Explained: From Souls to Systems* (Chicago: Open Court Press, 2006), 250. As Luhmann summarizes the point that if "God is beyond all distinctions, even beyond the distinction between distinctness and indistinctness" (250), then the problem becomes how can that which is transcendent insofar as it transcends distinctions be observed to be compatible with Christian dogma ("identifiable as a person and as the trinity," and so on) (251). "One had, in God, to save the possibilities of observation and thus on the one hand to be careful not to ascribe to God the impossibility of self-observation, and, on the other hand, to avoid to come close to the devil who was the boldest observer of God....The escape route came fatally close to the assumption that God needed creation and the damnation of the devil in order to be able to observe himself, and it led to writings that Nicolaus believed unprepared minds with their weak eyes had better not read" (251).

33. Niklas Luhmann, *Art as a Social System,* trans. Eva M. Knodt (Stanford, Calif.: Stanford University Press, 2000), 90.

34. Harro Muller, "Luhmann's Systems Theory as a Theory of Modernity," *New German Critique* 61 (Winter 1994): 40.

35. Luhmann, *Art as a Social System,* 89.

36. Muller, "Luhmann's Systems Theory as a Theory of Modernity," 45.

37. But see, for a full discussion, my essays "Lose the Building: Systems Theory, Architecture, and Diller + Scofidio's *Blur,*" *Postmodern Culture* 16, no. 3 (2006), http://muse.jhu.edu/login?uri=/journals/pmc/v016/16.3wolfe.html, and "Meaning as Event-Machine, or Systems Theory and 'The Reconstruction of Deconstruction,'" in *Emergence and Embodiment: New Essays on Second-Order Systems Theory,* ed. Bruce Clarke and Mark N. B. Hansen (Durham, N.C.: Duke University Press, 2009).

38. Niklas Luhmann, *Social Systems,* trans. John Bednarz Jr. with Dirk Baecker, foreword by Eva M. Knodt (Stanford, Calif.: Stanford University Press, 1995), 25.

39. "The Paradoxy of Observing Systems," *Cultural Critique* 31 (Fall 1995): 41–42.

40. Luhmann, *Social Systems,* 60.

41. Here, we encounter systems theory's version of what Derrida calls the dynamic force of *différance* as "temporization" and "spacing," a process that "is possible only if each so-called present element . . . is related to something other than itself, thereby keeping within itself the mark of the past element" while at the same time being "vitiated by the mark of its relation to the future element," thus "constituting what is called the present by means of this very relation to what it is not." Derrida, *"Différance,"* in *Between the Blinds: A Derrida Reader,* trans. Alan Bass et al., ed. Peggy Kamuf (New York: Columbia University Press, 1991), 65–66.

42. Luhmann, *Social Systems,* 63.

43. Ibid., 31.

44. Luhmann, *Art as a Social System,* 158.

45. Luhmann, *Social Systems,* 26.

46. Ibid., 17.

47. Luhmann, "A Redescription of 'Romantic Art,'" *MLN* 111, no. 3 (1996): 508, 511.

48. See my *Critical Environments: Postmodern Theory and the Pragmatics of the "Outside"* (Minneapolis: University of Minnesota Press, 1998), 67–68.

49. Niklas Luhmann, "The Cognitive Program of Constructivism and a Reality that Remains Unknown," in *Selforganization: Portrait of a Scientific Revolution,* ed. Wolfgang Krohn et al. (Dordrecht, Germany: Kluwer Academic Publishers, 1990), 76.

50. Luhmann, *Art as a Social System,* 92.

51. Ibid., 91.

52. Ibid.

53. Ibid., 96.

54. Luhmann, "A Redescription of 'Romantic Art,'" 517.

55. Ibid.

56. Luhmann, *Art as a Social System,* 95.

57. See Eduardo Cadava's *Emerson and the Climates of History* (Stanford, Calif.: Stanford University Press, 1997), especially chapter 1.

58. Muller, "Luhmann's Systems Theory as a Theory of Modernity," 47.

59. Luhmann, "A Redescription of 'Romantic Art,'" 516.

60. Specifically, in the conclusion to my *Critical Environments.*

Afterword

With the essays collected here ringing in my ears—so many of the words music to my ears—I say at once that I feel myself in a world new to me of Emerson reception, before all one in response to which I feel no defensiveness over my ways of showing admiration of the Emersonian text. It is a privilege to accept the invitation to venture some celebratory thoughts accompanying what I trust will be the fruitful voyage of the present volume by allowing the ringing to bring to life for me a few remarks of Emerson's that I do not recall having ever stopped over before. There is no question here, as the phrase goes, of doing justice to what is here. I can at best, or at most, simply note certain causes of pleasure and instruction it has afforded me.

Take a few sentences from the opening paragraph of Emerson's "Fate" that I spent some time with a few years ago: In response to his remembering having discovered a coincidence of public texts "on the Spirit of the Times," Emerson writes: "To me, however, the question of the times resolved itself into a practical question of the conduct of life. How shall I live? We are incompetent to solve the times."[1] What struck me that earlier time, impressed that the title "Fate" was given to an essay essentially about freedom, was the repetition of the idea of solving and resolving, which succeeding paragraphs take forward. I associated this emphasis with the repeated "Resolutions" in the constitutional language of Henry Clay's 1850 compromise bill rationalizing issues of slavery. This led to understanding Emerson's point at the beginning of his "Fate" to be saying, roughly: instead of speculating to no end about questions of some metaphysical spirit of the times, let us do something in the moment to correct the all-too-human actual spirit of the times in which a law is to be further strengthened to protect the vice of slavery.

But this time I hear, in addition, one more tone to the question "How shall I live?," relating the question to the emphasis in "Fate" on thinking as painful ("[taking] sides with the Deity who secures universal benefit by his pain" [6:26]), repeated at the end of the essay "Experience" in the phrase "patience and patience" (3:48–49), relating as it were understanding to withstanding, bearing up under knowing, discovering the power in passiveness, permitting change; and relating the question at the same time to the stress in "Experience" on thinking as "mournful" (3:46), as a process of mourning (something a number of contributors to the present volume touch upon), a task Freud portrays, in contrast to melancholia, as one of separation from the world (in order to know it as it is at any time), something Thoreau can be understood to have written in his inexhaustible *Walden,* with its mo(u)rnings and dawnings and perpetual anticipations, to consider and to have considered.

I can hardly apologize for letting Thoreau inspire or reassure a strain in Emerson, since I take it as unarguable that Thoreau and Nietzsche are Emerson's two great readers, or writers who use Emerson most radically, in the nineteenth century at the least. There is something called an Emerson revival in progress in recent decades, but nothing, I gather, to be called a Thoreau revival. There are obvious reasons for this lack, but they do not satisfy me. The suffering in Emerson's writing, produced by and producing his sallies of ecstasy, can never, I believe, be overestimated. Seen so, the question "How shall I live?" is no longer merely a matter of finding which way to live (whether for time or for eternity, for poverty or for riches, for necessity or for transience, whether to "accept the place the divine Providence has found for you" or the place your townsmen require of you ["Self-Reliance," 2:28]) but beyond this, as a basis for this, a matter of determining how it is you can go on with life knowing what you know (that America, like the self, is undiscovered, perhaps undiscoverable; that I can no more save it alone than I could save Waldo; that it is debased by slavery and mastery; that it persists in failing to track daily, specific, promptings of desire and instead accepts the general offer of despair, Emerson's "secret melancholy" ["New England Reformers,"

3:158], Thoreau's "quiet desperation," rendering itself incapable of transfiguring these into the exercise of mourning). Whether Martin Heidegger's call for "onward thinking" and Ludwig Wittgenstein's repeated question whether we know how to go on (which I have taken as an allegory for going on with a word in unforeseen contexts, which at any time becomes a question whether we shall go on with words at all or find a cause for speech) should be brought into play here, I leave open. I might add that Wittgenstein's recurrent appeal to reasons coming to an end, to having to say something like "This is simply what I do," should never be heard as an utterance of satisfaction, complacency, or conformity, but as an expression of discovery.

I should mention that my insistence on claiming Emerson for philosophy concentrates my claim for his modernity, his contemporaneousness. (It is what allows me to include Emerson's among the texts that are for me not alone objects of interpretation but means of interpretation.) Emerson allows the genteel array of familiar philosophical terms to pervade his discourse in order to bring them to the experience of, the ongoing discovering of, America, "these bleak rocks" ("Experience," 3:46), transfiguring each in the absence of an established tradition and pedagogy of philosophy. Glance at how it happens in the closing paragraph of "Experience": it opens with the observation, or confession, "I know that the world I converse with in the city and in the farms, is not the world I *think*" (3:48, Emerson's emphasis). I have noted in the past that this declaration of the knowledge that we (speaking for, conversing with, mankind) do not live solely in the world of knowledge (of information or assertion, of objects and the laws of objects) invokes implicitly Kant's summary of his monumental labors by declaring that we live in two worlds, or see ourselves from two standpoints, which moreover conflict, perhaps as freedom and law conflict. Moreover, as the paragraph proceeds, Emerson explicitly cites a classical or textbook opposition to Kant, an opposition he calls "a paltry empiricism" (3:48), further specifying this invocation of the British Empiricists in using their familiar term for the origin or gate from which or through which human experience is derived, the term *impression*. But Emerson invokes this term in a way that challenges it, I would say modernizes it.

It seems to be true from the beginning of philosophy that a philosopher's demand of an inheritance from a former generation or a former era requires an aggressive acceptance and rejection, a refashioning for a new time, of what is inherited, as when Aristotle takes over Plato's Forms of ideas or Ideas of forms and, simply dismissing the idea of a separate changeless realm, reconceives Form as an inherent component, along with Matter, in things. Aristotle's consequent idea of potentiality or possibility, a couple of millennia later evidently prompts Heidegger's idea that the way characteristics of a human existence (he calls them *existentiale*) identify that existence is not as predicates identify a thing over time but as possibilities set paths or tasks during time, following the Romantics' idea that the mark of the human being is to become what it is, a phrase modified explicitly in Emerson (in "Considerations by the Way," 6:129–48). (If I ask a reader to note the phrase "the Way," linking it with Thoreau's "walking" and Emerson's "lasting," I do not know whether I am being helpful or insufferably obvious. Fortunately for me, or not, I regard obtrusive obviousness as an inescapable risk in one of the modes of philosophy that attracts me most.) "Experience" ends by transfiguring this thought of becoming as "the transformation of genius into practical power" (3:49)—in which we hear a late quite literal variation of Emerson's guiding duality of form and power, in which form is contrasted not, as in Aristotle, with inactive matter but with something like its opposite. In reaching Wittgenstein's *Investigations,* in which forms—what more recent philosophy has called universals—are altogether disempowered, "Don't say: 'There *must* be something in common between objects named by the same word,' but *look and see* whether there is anything common to all."[2] The differentiation among things is a matter of what Wittgenstein idiosyncratically but with unsettling insight calls "grammar," which, while playing the role of the a priori in our knowledge, is not known a priori but is endlessly open to philosophical investigation.

In the sentence preceding the last of "Experience," Emerson notes that the things that mostly make up our daily lives "make no impression" (3:49), as if we live each passing day mostly in a vacancy of ourselves. I once suggested a comparison of the explicit claim of Emerson's early "The American Scholar," that we (in America) are not yet thinking, with Heidegger's explicit claim in *What Is Called Thinking?* that we are still not thinking. To suppose that Emerson's claim confines itself to an empirical claim about an absence of philosophical cultivation in the new world ("'tis new to thee," as Prospero observes), rather than taking that patent fact, universally observed, as an incitement to pick up an unprecedented opportunity to engage the transcendental task of finding a new thinking, is a familiar degradation attached to a certain praise of Emerson. In the present case I might epitomize the urgency of "Experience" by considering that where Heidegger has said, and repeats, "Most thought-provoking in our thought-provoking time is that we are still not thinking,"[3] Emerson had in effect urged, "Most impressive about our impressive space is that we are not yet impressed."

I suppose I would not light-heartedly epitomize Emerson this way without the example of Heidegger, but I think it is the case at the same time that I might well not have been so seriously interested by Heidegger without the sense that its call for thinking can produce philosophy that looks like Emerson's writing. A decisive difference from my point of view is that in Emerson the terms that need rethinking are not only those establishing undisguised philosophy, but every term in our language, passing us by every day. (This is the Wittgensteinian strain in him, I mean from the period leading to and from *Philosophical Investigations*.) One may suppose that Heidegger's perception and discussion of speech as "chatter" provides theory enough for understanding Emerson's remarking, for example, "Every word they say chagrins us" ("Self-Reliance," 2:32). Surely Heidegger's and Emerson's paths cross here, especially in the shared perception that the necessary departure from this condition will require a change of, let's say, character, struggling with ourselves. But for me the spectacle of Emerson's prose, written in awareness that every word can, and does, betray him, that each harbors chagrin among its possibilities—and where are there others?—exhibits the struggle in a way I would not forget or forgo. It is an enactment of a sense that the language that discovers the world is that which veils or covers it. The theory of the inhabited world is the perpetual revision of the incessant expression of the world.

One step prompts another in parting. I just spoke of what Emerson's prose exhibits, and I recognize in the ringing I acknowledged at the outset the provoking thought that Emerson does not mention the concept of manifest destiny where you might well expect him to. I do not propose an explanation for this, but I note the depth of irony (where laughing sounds like sobbing) in the thought that since, as Emerson also puts the matter, the concept of character refers always (so far as I recall instances) at once to ourselves (as it were) and to our writing, however it is we impress ourselves upon a world. So the struggle with language is a struggle, an occupation, with ourselves. Then the idea that character is fate, or call it destiny, now becomes the idea that our character, with every breath or word, manifests and obscures itself, as our nation does.

That I have over the years published something like a book's worth about Emerson, yet never written a book about him, registers the circumstance that I seem always surprised by what prompts me to a further response to a moment of his writing, together with the fact that, once started, I find it hard, or arbitrary, to stop. Here I stop where I might have begun, with the thought that if I have played some role in prompting the further hearing for Emerson represented by the present collection of texts, I would feel free to clap my hands in infantine joy.

NOTES

1. See Ralph Waldo Emerson, *The Collected Works of Ralph Waldo Emerson,* ed. Alfred R. Ferguson, Robert E. Spiller, et al., 8 vols. to date (Cambridge, Mass.: Harvard University Press, Belknap Press, 1971–2010), 6:1. Subsequent quotations from Emerson's writing are from this source and are cited parenthetically in text by volume and page numbers. Citations may include essay title if the essay from which a quotation is taken is not clear from the text.

2. Wittgenstein, *Philosophical Investigations,* trans. G. E. M. Anscombe, 3rd ed. (Oxford: Blackwell, 2001), §66, p. 27; emphases in original.

3. Heidegger, *What Is Called Thinking?* trans. J. Glenn Gray (New York: Harper and Row, 1968), 6.

Contributors

BRANKA ARSIĆ is associate professor of American literature at the University at Albany, State University of New York. She is author of *On Leaving, a Reading in Emerson* and *Passive Constitutions or 7½ Times Bartleby.*

EDUARDO CADAVA teaches in the Department of English at Princeton University. He is author of *Words of Light: Theses on the Photography of History* and *Emerson and the Climates of History* and coeditor of *Who Comes after the Subject?, Cities without Citizens,* and a special issue of *South Atlantic Quarterly,* "And Justice for All? The Claims of Human Rights."

SHARON CAMERON is William R. Kenan Jr. Professor of English at Johns Hopkins University. Among her publications are *Impersonality: Seven Essays, Thinking in Henry James,* and *Writing Nature: Henry Thoreau's "Journal."*

STANLEY CAVELL is the Walter M. Cabot Professor Emeritus of Aesthetics and the General Theory of Value at Harvard University. His books include *Philosophy the Day after Tomorrow, Emerson's Transcendental Etudes, Pursuits of Happiness: The Hollywood Comedy of Remarriage, The Claim of Reason: Wittgenstein, Skepticism, Morality, and Tragedy,* and *The Senses of Walden.*

RUSSELL B. GOODMAN, Regents Professor of Philosophy at the University of New Mexico, is author of *American Philosophy and the Romantic Tradition* and *Wittgenstein and William James*. His writing on Emerson has appeared in *Journal of the History of Ideas, ESQ: A Journal of the American Renaissance, The Oxford Handbook of American Philosophy,* and edited volumes on Neoplatonism, nature in American thought, and the philosophy of religion. He is editor of *Contending with Stanley Cavell, Pragmatism: Critical Concepts in Philosophy,* and *Pragmatism: A Contemporary Reader.*

PAUL GRIMSTAD is assistant professor of English at Yale University. His current project is on experience and experimental writing in Emerson, Poe, Melville, and Henry and William James. His writing has been published in *Radical Philosophy, Parallax,* and *Journal of Modern Literature.*

ERIC KEENAGHAN is associate professor of English at the University at Albany, State University of New York. He is author of *Queering Cold War Poetry: Ethics of Vulnerability in Cuba and the United States.* His essays on ethics and modern poetry have been published in journals such as *Contemporary Literature, Journal of Modern Literature, modernism/modernity,* and *Translation Studies.*

GREGG LAMBERT is Dean's Professor of the Humanities and founding director of the Humanities Center at Syracuse University. His most recent books are *On the (New) Baroque* (a revised and expanded edition of *Return of the Baroque in Modern Culture*) and *Who's Afraid of Deleuze and Guattari?*

SANDRA LAUGIER is professor of philosophy at Université Paris Panthéon-Sorbonne and a former member of the Institut Universitaire de France. She has written books and articles on philosophy of language, American philosophy, and moral philosophy, including *Du reel à l'ordinaire* and *Une autre pensée politique américaine: La démocratie radicale, de R. W. Emerson à S. Cavell.* She has translated several books by Stanley Cavell and a volume of Emerson's essays into French.

DONALD E. PEASE is the Avalon Foundation Chair of the Humanities at Dartmouth College. He is author of *The New American Exceptionalism* (Minnesota, 2009), *Theodor Seuss Geisel,* and *Visionary Compacts: American Renaissance Writing in Cultural Context,* as well as the editor of eight volumes, including *The American Renaissance Reconsidered, Revisionist Interventions into the American Canon, Postnational Narratives,* and *Futures of American Studies.*

CARY WOLFE is Bruce and Elizabeth Dunlevie Professor of English at Rice University. His books and edited collections include *The Limits of American Literary Ideology in Pound and Emerson; Critical Environments: Postmodern Theory and the Pragmatics of the "Outside"* (Minnesota, 1998); *Zoontologies: The Question of the Animal* (Minnesota, 2003); *What Is Posthumanism?* (Minnesota, 2009); and *Animal Rites: American Culture, the Discourse of Species, and Posthumanist Theory.* He is founding editor of the Posthumanities book series published by the University of Minnesota Press.

Index